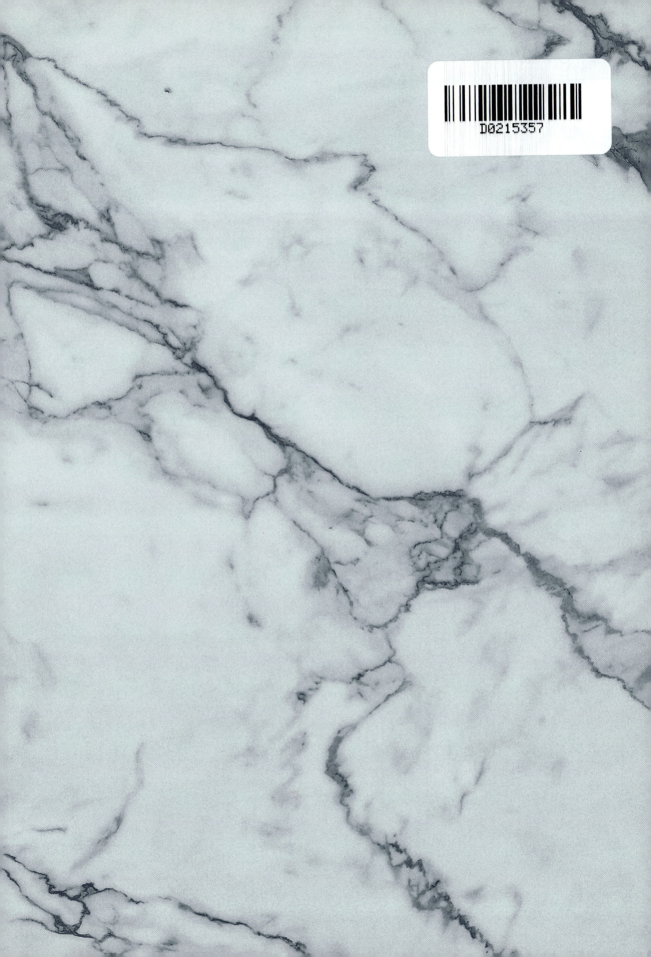

LUXURY
AND
MODERNISM

LUXURY AND MODERNISM

ARCHITECTURE AND THE OBJECT IN GERMANY 1900–1933

ROBIN SCHULDENFREI

PRINCETON UNIVERSITY PRESS

PRINCETON AND OXFORD

FOR HENRY AND THEO

CONTENTS

LUXURY IN MODERNISM

In 1930, as part of the Bauhaus's book series, Walter Gropius published *Bauhausbauten Dessau* (Bauhaus buildings Dessau), which described the recent architectural work of the Bauhaus, including a thorough description of the school building, his own director's house, and the other masters' houses, accompanied by photographs fully documenting the buildings and their interiors. One detail, albeit small, is telling: the published version of Lucia Moholy's photograph of Gropius's bathroom has been retouched—the marble veining from the double-basin sink has been erased to make it appear as if it were made of porcelain, suggesting an industrial product rather than a luxury object (fig. I.1).[1] Indeed—and in striking contrast—the less lavish bathrooms in the masters' houses have porcelain single-basin sinks of standard manufacture. Gropius's marble sink is a curious element in a bathroom otherwise representative of the pared-down, industrial ideals of modern architecture: a band of horizontal windows lets in abundant light, and an unornamented, unframed mirror is affixed directly to the wall, while a naked light bulb extended on a metal arm, exposed radiator, glass shelves, and the other bathroom hardware all seem to celebrate the products of industry. The richly veined marble sink, a seeming anomaly, makes for a more visually welcoming and warmer room, softening the potentially more jarring elements such as the bare light bulb. But the published photograph makes the room appear more modern, more industrial, and less luxurious than it was in reality. This, perhaps, is the essence of the intersection of modernism and luxury—the ideal of industrial production as a new visual trope of modern life, undercut, upon deeper investigation, by materially and psychologically lavish interiors used to promote a way of living and an enviable (but often hidden) opulence in a new register. In order to demonstrate its pervasiveness in, and centrality to, the development of modern architecture and objects in Germany in the period 1900–1930, this study considers the luxury of modernism in its many manifestations—technological, material, spatial, social, economic, philosophical, psychological, and intellectual.

Modernism in design and architecture encompassed social and material goals, in addition to aesthetic ones—a new concern for the welfare of the masses as well as a sustained focus on the development of standard types and improved mass production, with the desired end centered on the proliferation of well-designed buildings and industrially produced goods. Following Christopher Wilk, this study understands the term "modernism" as describing not a style but a loose collection of ideas,

Figure I.1. *Below*: Walter Gropius, director's house, bathroom, Dessau, 1926. Photograph by Lucia Moholy.
Opposite: Same bathroom as published in *Bauhausbauten Dessau* (Munich: A. Langen, 1930). Photograph
by Lucia Moholy, retouched.

abb. 122 wohnungen der bauhausmeister
badezimmer im einzelhaus gropius
die wände sind mit kristallglasscheiben belegt

including an espousal of the new, a rejection of history and tradition, a utopian desire to create a better world, a belief in the potential of the machine and industrial technology, a rejection of applied ornament and decoration, an embrace of abstraction, and a belief in the unity of all of the arts.[2] Because design reform in early twentieth-century Germany was predominantly led by architects, ideas related to modern objects were most often described using the same terms employed in the field of architecture. Gropius, Ludwig Mies van der Rohe, and other modern architects variously used the terms "modern movement," "modern architecture," or "new building" (*Neues Bauen*) to describe their ideas and work, but the terminology did not remain fixed over time.[3]

Design of furniture, objects, and decorative details has always been in the purview of architects. In the beginning of the twentieth century, architects (several of whom began their careers as artists, such as Peter Behrens and Henry van de Velde) renewed their focus on the status of the object in society as an essential component of architectural and cultural discourse. They particularly turned from preponderantly composing individual designs for customers who commissioned specific work to the design of objects for customers unknown to them. On this new terrain arose the discourse of modernism, but also an important disconnect between this discourse and existing design and production structures. This book examines the emergence of modern luxury objects and elite architectural commissions, with their attendant utopian implications and democratic ideals. It argues that all too often these designs were out of the reach of the very people they purported to serve. Discussions surrounding modernism have often focused on the idea of "good design" for the masses, a position that was promoted by a select group of architects, designers, artists, cultural theorists, and industrialists. These protagonists, it will be argued, revealed their own elitist attitudes through both their discussions and the luxury objects they designed and analyzed. The ostensible subject of period debates was the masses and the middle-class consumers with newly acquired purchasing power and leisure time to frequent exhibitions and department stores. However, the generators of—and audience for—this discourse was instead essentially an intellectual elite represented by forward-thinking architects and designers, sociologists, cultural critics, and economists. Modernism's consumer base was made up of the upper class. Criticism of the elitism and luxury of the modern movement was present in its day. Czech critic Karel Teige's 1932 excoriation is worth quoting at length:

> At present, construction practice and commercial architecture are a public service only to the extent that they serve the "modern builder"—that is, the ruling class. We may read in one book statements such as "the real creator of modern architecture is not the architect, but the modern customer," but discover a more honest confession and a more exact definition of what a "modern builder" really represents in another, such as W. C. Behrendt's *Der Sieg des neuen Baustils* [*The Victory of the New Building Style*, 1927], where the same customer is exhorted to accept the "new style" because in his daily practice as businessman, factory owner, or banker, he represents the most modern human type—a type that manages a modern enterprise, drives a luxury automobile, travels by air or in a railroad sleeping coach, and daily receives his stock market quotations by teletype. And yet, the ideal of this most modern man "human type" is more likely than not a house or apartment resembling historical replicas of the Petit Trianon, the

Belvedere, Venice, or Nuremberg: of course, once the taste of such a modern builder has become really "modernized," it then becomes acceptable to build in place of the Trianon Le Corbusier's Villa Garches or Villa Poissy, or Loos's Villa in Prague, or Mallet-Stevens's Villa in Paris, while Mies van der Rohe builds as the pinnacle of modernist snobbism and the ostentation of a millionaire's lifestyle a villa for the factory owner T[ugendhat] in B[rno]. All these houses with all their technical luxury and radical design devices, with all their formal originality, are really nothing other than new versions of opulent baroque palaces, that is, seats of the new financial aristocracy. A machine for living? No, a machine for representation and splendor.[4]

The exclusive nature of the modern movement in architecture has mainly been downplayed in favor of the populist positions established by the protagonists themselves, as well as the early historians of the movement, continuing, with some exceptions, to the present. The seeming disconnect between modernism's goals and its realities will be closely examined for a richer, more nuanced reading of modern architecture and its objects. Luxury embodies modernism's critical shortcomings but was also employed toward constructive ends; both parts of this dialectic will be considered. *Luxury and Modernism* explores the seemingly familiar territory of Wilhelmine and Weimar German architecture and design to argue that the under-recognized presence, and indeed theme, of luxury in modernism was not only a critical shortcoming but also a productive creative practice among German modernists. Instead of being simply a contradiction of modernism's leftist leanings, luxury was, at times, also a useful statement of its wider ambitions. By repurposing the notion of luxury away from being solely a taint, a more nuanced understanding of the depth, complexity, and challenges of modernism as it was practiced, sold, and consumed comes to the fore.

In order to examine the tension between the rhetoric of the modern design movement and the architecture and objects it produced, *Luxury and Modernism* engages multiple perspectives on this period. One group to be considered is made up of the architects, designers, intellectuals, theorists, and sociologists of the period who framed the terms of the debate—an elite, who theorized production through the lens of economic and social thought. The second group consists of the consumers themselves, a varied set to be considered in tandem with the interiors they inhabited, the objects they acquired, and the means by which they were enticed to consume them. By examining the shifting social relations of this period in terms of class, status, and viewpoint, this study draws a fuller picture of the accessibility—and inaccessibility—of modernism in its time.

New complexities and realities surrounding the promotion and consumption of modernism are brought to light by looking closely at how modern buildings and objects were designed, manufactured, and sold. In addition to built exemplars, modernism's protagonists articulated the movement's aspirations through a multitude of media—print, public lectures, plans and drawings, graphic design, advertising, film, and photography. This source material, often promotional or aspirational in nature, is contextualized against actual practices and production methods to highlight the inconsistencies between the rhetoric of modernism and the production of material objects and architecture. Price structures, materials, and the types of objects designed demonstrate that luxury was a pervasive element in modernism. In addition to theoretical texts that offer critical insight into the elitism of period design, more widely circulated sources, such as general trade periodicals, popular books on dwelling, magazines, and fiction further show how luxury was represented in modernism's new forms. These printed sources, accompanied by carefully composed photographs, created wider consumer desire for modern architecture and objects. Thus, *Luxury and Modernism* studies both the makers and the consumers of modern objects and architecture in order to look closely at the mechanisms through which these two groups interacted. The positive—and negative—critical reception of modern design across varying social strata provides a more nuanced view of the audience for modernism. Taking these strains of inquiry and the period's written and material evidence together, this study looks at the ways in which the modern object's position in society was articulated and contested, promoted and consumed.

While this mode of investigation—positioning luxury as both an argument and as material evidence—has broad implications for a wider understanding of modern objects and architecture produced across Europe, in the United States, and in certain instances globally, the focus here is on currents in Germany in the period 1900 to 1933, from modernism's early stirrings until the year that the National Socialists shut down the Bauhaus in Berlin. In order to explore the varying but consistently central place of luxury in both the discourse and the objects of modernism, *Luxury and Modernism* reinvestigates some of the most influential objects, movements, groups, and protagonists of the period. It demonstrates that in promoting modern buildings and their interiors and in the display and selling of modern goods, luxury played an important role—at times blatant, in other instances, more nuanced.

LOCATING LUXURY IN MODERN ARCHITECTURE: DEFINING THE MODES OF INQUIRY

The beginning strains of the modern architectural movement in Germany, and across Europe, coalesced against a backdrop of earlier design movements. In the nineteenth century, the English arts and crafts movement, inspired by John Ruskin's theories and the myriad written and practical efforts by William Morris, had reintroduced the workshop methods of the medieval period with its craftsmen who labored over hand tools rather than machines. Around the turn of the century, artists of the Vienna Secession, founded in 1898, and the Wiener Werkstätte, founded in 1903, reestablished crafts workshops to train artisans to create furniture, household items, textiles, and clothes. In Germany, the Mathildenhöhe artistic community in Darmstadt, in which Peter Behrens was a chief protagonist, had been formed in 1899 under the patronage of Ernst Ludwig, Grand Duke of Hesse. The artists of the Mathildenhöhe, like their counterparts elsewhere, were devotees of the nascent art nouveau movement, known as *Jugendstil* in German, which placed a new emphasis on the design of handmade goods—a practice intended to counter the inferior factory output of the period with high-quality products. Jugendstil architectural commissions typically represented the work of a single architect who took responsibility for the entirety of a house's design and its contents, creating a total work of art, or *Gesamtkunstwerk*. Jugendstil objects tended to be luxury items because they were commissioned as single works in negotiation with an individual architect or craftsman; their acquisition indicated a certain level of social status and taste on the part of a usually wealthy client. However, a paradigm shift occurred when these same types of objects began to be easily acquired, as a result of factory production and distribution to department stores. In the turn from the single, crafted object to one that was ready-made, a broader public came to be consumers of Jugendstil; the acquisition of a few signal examples could give middle-class homes an air of the exclusivity and "artistry" that the style connoted.[5] Although modernism sought to distance itself from Jugendstil, as well as earlier eclectically historicist interiors, as exemplified by Bernhard Dernburg in his Berlin study, it shared much in common with both predecessors ideologically, if not stylistically, including architects' desire to design both the architecture and the furniture and objects within it, creating, in effect, a total work of art (fig. I.2). Even though modern products were intended to be the result of the mass production of a perfected object-type, they were often costly singular objects produced in workshops, akin to Jugendstil objects.[6] Sleek modern objects, with their patina of the new and the innovative, obtained the allure that had once been the domain of Jugendstil. What had been the downfall of Jugendstil—namely, mass production and wide distribution that watered down the quality of its construction, its uniqueness, and its desirability—was seized by modernism as a strength and an end goal. However, despite their simplified appearance, modern products, such as a Mies cantilever chair, were often just as costly to produce and acquire as their earlier, handmade counterparts.

Industrial production and modernization had affected the design community in Germany in unprecedented ways. The German Werkbund was founded in 1907 by Hermann Muthesius with the goal of uniting art, craft, and industry to improve the quality of goods manufactured in Germany. This swift-growing group, originally composed of twelve artists and twelve industrialists, wanted to reconcile art and craft with industry and trade and to improve the overall design of mass-produced goods. The members of the Werkbund, designers and businessmen, were interested in standardized, well-designed objects that were free of superfluous ornament and represented "good form." They were especially interested in inserting designers into the industrial process of goods production. Ongoing debates, at the Werkbund and among the protagonists of modernism's other circles, revolved around craftsmanship,

Figure I.2. Dr. Bernhard Dernburg in his study, Berlin, 1912. Photograph by Waldemar Titzenthaler.

quality, and design reform; the plight of the worker in a rapidly industrializing society; and the changing role of the designer. These questions influenced the development of modern architecture and its objects.

For Werkbund members and others, standardized "type-objects" and modern buildings alike were to forge a new direction in design. In objects, standardization was to replace the singularity and lavishness of Jugendstil. Buildings were to embody a stripped-down modern form, an aesthetic that took inspiration from new sources, such as industrial architecture. As early as 1902, Hermann Muthesius, one of the Werkbund's founders, summed up many of the objectives that came to be associated with the modern movement:

> If we wish to seek a new style—the style of our time—its characteristic features are to be found much more in those modern creations that truly serve our newly established needs and that have absolutely no relation to the old formalities of architecture: in our railway terminals and exhibition buildings, in very large meeting halls, and further, in the general tectonic realm, in our large bridges, steamships, railway cars, bicycles, and the like. It is precisely here that we see embodied truly modern ideas and new principles of design that demand our attention. Here we notice a rigorous, one might say scientific objectivity, an abstention from all superficial forms of decoration, a design strictly following the purpose that the work should serve. … They must embody an expressive modern form; they must mirror the sensibility of our time, just as the richly acanthus-laden cannon barrel did the seventeenth century or the carved and gilded sedan chair the eighteenth century.[7]

The recipient of these modern ideas and principles of design was to be society as a whole, rather than the upper echelon, as had generally been the case in earlier times, up to and including Jugendstil commissions. From Muthesius to the radical functionalist architect Hannes Meyer, there was a call for rationality in design; the recipient was to be the masses, or at least the middle classes, as opposed to the very wealthy. As Muthesius noted, "Today, no movement that seeks to be a reform movement can direct itself only to the production of luxury art; its goal, rather, must be to pursue an art suited to middle-class society, which defines the general character of our modern social condition."[8] This emphasis on the lower end of the social spectrum—the middle classes (in this case, by Muthesius) and the workers (for example, by Hannes Meyer)—as the ideal recipients for the new style and objects of modern architecture is well documented. However, all too often it has been taken at face value. A different trajectory can be charted when the production of the period—its objects, interiors, buildings—is measured against the actual economic situation and the cultural desires of early twentieth-century consumers.

In some cases, luxury in modernism was simply a continuation of certain traditions already prevalent in society and architectural culture alike. Despite the austerity often proposed by modernism's rhetoric, in reality architects were frequently loath to design in the absolutes required by the ideals of standardization and functionalism. The design of modern homes and interiors encompassed many holdover bourgeois traditions and habits, such as the inclusion of reception rooms, ladies' parlors, or separate bedrooms for husband and wife, that died only slowly. These domestic features were propagated by architect-protagonists who often came from

9

upper-middle- and upper-class backgrounds, such as Gropius, or, conversely, designers such as Mies van der Rohe, who came from an artisan background but who aspired to membership in the upper echelons of society. The masses were envisioned as the recipients of "new living" (*Neues Wohnen*)—a catchall phrase that described the new modes of living in a modern manner, including dwelling with new kinds of objects, new materials, and an overall modern aesthetic.

Yet this study shows that the consumers of modern design objects, and the dwellers who elected to live in modern architecture, ultimately constituted an elite. While modernism was never truly able to reach the masses in the form of either ideas or objects, similarly, the intellectual elite could not become truly proletarian.[9] A privileged mode of thinking prevailed, a top-down system that began with architects and their showcase homes and was meant to descend to the masses. But in the period under discussion, 1900–1933, most modern buildings and objects remained beyond the economic grasp of the masses, and even most of the middle class. By and large, these groups also rejected them on grounds of taste. Thus this study addresses broader questions surrounding period class structures, class-based determinations of taste, and ingrained modes and habits of living, to reveal that modernism—perhaps admirably in its desire for remaking society—made few concessions to existing taste. This exposes a fairly condescending attitude prevalent in modernism that impeded its widespread acceptance on many different levels in this period. It remained out of reach of its intended audience both economically and ideologically.

The role played by industry and developing technology in Germany in this period is examined to elucidate the unexpected ways in which these two entities did not ease, but rather contributed to, modern architecture and objects remaining in the realm of luxury. As architects and designers sought to assert themselves in the marketplace, they viewed the various newly booming industries as the ideal aesthetic and practical partners for their endeavors. Peter Behrens and the Allgemeine Elektricitäts-Gesellschaft (commonly known by its initials, the AEG was Germany's main electric company), Gropius and the Bauhaus, the Werkbund and its member-led initiatives, and the technically advanced villas of Mies van der Rohe provide the material evidence for complicating the role of industry and technology vis-à-vis luxurious modern architectural developments. Yet the legacy of *Kunstgewerbe*—the applied arts, taught by master craftsmen in arts and crafts schools specifically set up for fine design and handwork—also affected the design of goods. New objects, especially those for export, were to be well designed and well made in order to overcome Germany's previous reputation for inexpensive, badly designed products. It will be shown that despite the ideology of the period, industry never entirely embraced architects' new modern designs in an effective way, nor did consumer demand significantly spur mass production, which would have resulted in higher volumes of modern goods being produced at more affordable prices.

Another key area in which luxury and luxurious modern living was especially present was in media representations. Modernism in this period was popularized through a thriving print culture that produced an extensive array of well-illustrated books and periodicals showcasing modern dwellings, again mainly inhabited by the affluent. Inexpensive, mass-produced books on modern architecture and interiors sold briskly in this period, aided by advances in publishing technology that lowered production costs.[10] Books on new architecture often pictured modern villas with a luxury automobile parked outside, while intimating a life of repose depicted by chaise longues in the living room and sunbeds on open roof gardens. Popular magazines, in particular, used lavish photographic spreads to portray the lives of the famous and the affluent, who often lived in luxurious modern dwellings. Films, too, pictured opulence and the ease of living in new modern interiors, sometimes crassly contrasting this way of life against the meager existence of the poor masses. For example, the film *Neues Wohnen* (New dwelling) of 1926 details the well-appointed interior of Walter Gropius's house, capturing the maid at work hanging up fur coats and demonstrating new types of appliances in the kitchen. Another film, Hans Richter's *Die Neue Wohnung* (The new apartment, 1930), portrays happy, rich families and their exuberantly healthy children living in open, modern homes and playing on roof terraces, purposefully juxtaposing them against the poor and the middle classes of the city, shut up in dark interiors. After opening the film with light and airy examples of modern architecture and its components of flexible room dividers and walls of windows, Richter stages two women shown in full-length fur coats opening their dangling purses, while in the next frame a fashionably dressed man and woman drink champagne; the text between the two shots reads: "for all who have the necessary money."[11] The film is unsparing in its depiction of the affluent as modern architecture's principal inhabitants, but it expresses the hope that in the future the masses will be able to attain the same quality of life. These are just a few examples of the many ways in which modernism, in effect, was sold via a purposeful association with the wealthy and their lifestyle.

Lavish, large-scale exhibitions introducing the public to new, modern design provided yet another context in which modern architecture was presented as luxurious. These popular events drew large numbers of visitors and were covered extensively in the press. They were often organized as two simultaneous exhibitions,

Figure I.3. *Below*: Ludwig Mies van der Rohe, apartment block at the Weissenhof Housing Settlement, Stuttgart, 1927. Mercedes-Benz advertisement, photograph c. 1928. *Opposite*: Ludwig Hilberseimer, house at the Weissenhof Housing Settlement, Stuttgart, 1927.

deploying two modes of display—a large-scale exhibition hall featuring modern products organized by materials, object- or machine-type, or manufacturer—and stand-alone, fully furnished show houses, through which visitors could walk and admire the contents.[12] For example, in 1927, the Werkbund organized *The Dwelling* (*Die Wohnung*), a major exhibition of modern objects and architecture in Stuttgart, which attracted teeming crowds of interested visitors. Between July 23 and October 30, more than half a million people visited the two-part exhibition. It was composed of an exhibit of technological appliances and modern furniture in Stuttgart's city center, coordinated by Lilly Reich, and a full-scale housing development, known as the Weissenhof Housing Settlement (*Weissenhofsiedlung*), organized by Mies van der Rohe. Located on a hillside above Stuttgart, it featured new modern plans, building techniques, and ways of dwelling. Mies coordinated the project, developing the overall site plan, selecting an international group of architects for the buildings, overseeing their completion, as well as designing a large apartment building himself, at its apex. These dwellings, which showcased modern furniture and products, were meant to represent low-cost housing prototypes for workers, but in fact they were expensive to build and were eventually sold to members of Stuttgart's upper middle class, after the exhibition closed. With the exception of Mies's large, multi-unit building, Peter Behrens's smaller-sized apartment building, Mart Stam and J.J.P. Oud's modest sets of row houses, and Gropius's low-cost panel house, the other display houses were spacious double houses designed for two families (Le Corbusier, Josef Frank) or big, modern villas designed for a single family (Le Corbusier, Hans Poelzig, Bruno Taut, Max Taut, Ludwig Hilberseimer, Victor Bourgeois, Hans Scharoun, Richard Döcker, Adolf G. Schneck, and Adolf Rading). Other period exhibitions, unsparing in their lavish displays, proved key to introducing modern ideas and objects to the public. In 1931, for the *German Building Exhibition*, Mies van der Rohe and Lilly Reich presented exhibition houses that showcased modernism at its most

sumptuous. Similarly, the Bauhaus's ensemble of masters' houses in Dessau, which displayed the products of the school in an appropriate domestic context, functioned as an informal exhibition of Bauhaus objects and ideology. Display cases in the Bauhaus building, as well as the school's presence at the annual Leipzig Trade Fair, were important venues for exhibiting objects. And in gold lettering on its plate glass window, the AEG electricity firm specifically identified its Berlin store as an "exhibition" space (*Ausstellung*) for AEG goods, a luxurious setting designed by Peter Behrens that elicited consumer desire for electrical appliances.

Modern architecture and its interiors served as an aspiration rather than an attainable reality for most of its audience. Even when large-scale housing developments were built, the waiting list was often prohibitively long, with demand far outstripping supply. Modernism was especially linked to the *image* of an elite, played out in photographs such as the dapper, top-hatted Mies greeting the king and queen of Spain and escorting them through his German Pavilion in Barcelona. A similar image is projected through the iconic photograph of a well-dressed woman with a Mercedes-Benz parked in front of Mies's apartment house at the Weissenhof Housing Settlement in Stuttgart (a second, similar photograph used Le Corbusier's houses as the backdrop) (fig. I.3). Well-dressed customers filled the brand-new film palaces, glitzy cafés, and nightclubs of the metropolis, enjoying the otherwise rarely accessible experience of modern design. Elegant modern buildings and luxurious interiors were more mirage than reality, viewable and accessible for a limited period (the duration of a film or the time it took to consume a coffee), yet essentially out of the reach of the masses and the middle class alike. These spaces connected expensive opulence to modernism in the public's mind and whetted consumer desire for modern design, which was further heightened by limited access to it. The underacknowledged reality is that modern architecture prior to World War II had a less direct impact on actual dwelling than it otherwise might have, had it been within the economic reach of a greater number of its interested followers. It thus failed to reach a large mass audience, a significant segment of which, in any case, also remained unconvinced by its visual appeal.

Whether by association with an elite social group, the use of sumptuous materials or costly new technology, or showcased as exclusive in print, film, or lavish exhibitions, modernism and luxury remained inseparable in this period. Over the course of this study, more subtle ways that the two were interconnected are explored in depth.

CRITICAL DISCOURSE AND LUXURY

"Luxury" as a term had already emerged with new frequency throughout Western thought in the mid- to late nineteenth century. While recent scholarship on luxury in today's context tends to consider the rise of the luxury brand and the marketing of expensive goods, luxury as an earlier subject was closely tied to the larger spheres of law, morality, production, and political economy.[13] German seventeenth- and eighteenth-century literature on the topic generally focused on luxury in terms of articles of fashion and other rarified goods, and on their taxation. In the late nineteenth and early twentieth centuries, discussions about luxury began to take on more social and cultural imperatives, as evidenced by numerous studies on the economic consequences of luxury and its impact in relation to issues of class.[14] In the popular press and in academic circles alike, the concept—and problem—of luxury was a much-discussed topic; for example, from 1900 to 1914 more than thirty articles and several books on luxury were published in Germany.[15] Historians, architects, and architectural critics gave added nuance to discussions of luxury in the early twentieth century. These writers identified specific issues at the intersection of architecture and luxury—such as the observation that the visual simplicity of modern architecture and the production of modern furniture was much more costly than expected, turning them into luxuries. Over and over again, period critics noted, to their dismay, that modern objects remained beyond the reach of their intended consumers. A concern over the impact of luxury was shared by a wide range of period thinkers who considered it within the context of their fields of study. Karl Marx wrote on the topic of luxury in terms of production and capital. In his explanation of the transformation of surplus-value into capital in *Das Kapital*, Marx noted: "[A] nation can change articles of luxury either into means of production or means of subsistence, and vice versa."[16] In a capitalist system, Marx argued, luxury goods were "absolutely necessary for a mode of production which creates wealth for the non-producer and which therefore must provide that wealth in forms which permit its acquisition only by those who enjoy."[17] Others tracked luxury's significance in culture at large—for example, in books and articles by early economists and sociologists, such as Werner Sombart, Georg Simmel, and Thorstein Veblen. These figures were read widely, and their texts, as well as lectures, offered important, nuanced formulations on topics that informed luxury's relationship to modernism, such as the functioning of capitalism and the money economy, the bourgeoisie, entrepreneurship, industry, conspicuous consumption, and pecuniary emulation.

In 1913, economist and sociologist Werner Sombart published his important book *Luxury and Capitalism*, which presented one of the most definitive perspectives for examining luxury in this period. Sombart defined luxury as "any expenditure in excess of the necessary," with the necessary evaluated both subjectively against an ethical or aesthetic value, and objectively, measured in either "man's physiological needs or in what may be called his cultural wants." Sombart then defined two aspects of luxury, quantitative (which he characterized as synonymous with prodigality, such as "the keeping of a hundred servants when one would do") and qualitative (the use of superior quality goods). From the concept of qualitative luxury he derived the concept of "luxury goods," or "refined goods," in which refinement was any treatment of a product—either to the material or to the outward form—over and above that which was needed to make it ordinarily useful.[18] It is this category into which a Peter Behrens electric kettle for the AEG or a silver Bauhaus tea service would certainly fit. Furthermore, Sombart articulated two ways in which goods could be sold, either by the more extensive sale of mass products or by the limited sale of high-priced goods.[19] Modern objects were designed with the intention of fitting the former category, but were more often the product of the second.

Sombart established the link between luxury and capitalism, which he read through structures of consumption, a trio that is critical to the present study. Crucially, Sombart concluded that "the most appreciated factor in luxury was its effectiveness in creating new markets."[20] He argued that the organization of industrial production was influenced to a great extent by an increase in the consumption of luxury goods and that the increase in this type of consumption opened the door to capitalism.[21] Sombart elaborated further, arguing that the consumption of luxury goods spurred the expansion of capitalism because the luxury industry was more adaptable to capitalistic organization, which, in turn, meant the production of more goods. For luxury goods, "the man with capital" had an advantage in obtaining the valuable raw materials needed and simultaneously benefited from the savings in industrial production processes; thus the luxury industry, according to Sombart, was in a "far better position than handicraft to maintain itself under adverse fluctuations and to profit by favorable market conditions."[22] Industrial organization at the AEG resulted in the manufacture of successful products in great quantities. This was also the aspiration for Bauhaus products and Mies-designed furniture, neither of which were made in significant quantity in the period. Rather, as will be shown, these products and furniture remained expensive objects produced in small workshops, made in limited batches out of materials that were expensive to obtain. They were much more akin to handicraft than modern products of industry, as their designers intended and their appearance suggests. Sombart's investigation into the relationship between the bourgeois capitalist and the status of technology in culture, as it relates back to capitalism, is useful for considering modern architecture and its objects, particularly the technically advanced aspects of new design. In numerous texts—*The Bourgeoisie*, *Luxury and Capitalism*, and elsewhere—Sombart identified modern culture's new insatiable appetite for luxury—which can be exemplified by many different types of objects, including new technical ones. More broadly, Sombart tracked a change through time in access to luxury—from the aristocracy to the bourgeoisie, who, thanks to the engine of capitalism itself, could accumulate enough wealth to purchase luxury objects.

Artists, architects, and designers also considered a diverse set of issues related to luxury in modern design. In 1902, designer and Werkbund protagonist Hermann Obrist considered the question of "Luxury Art or People's Art," Alexander Elster weighed in on "Useful and Harmful Luxury" in 1910, the Werkbund's journal discussed "Luxury Tax" in 1918, and early modern architectural historian Adolf Behne reflected on "Luxury or Comfort" in 1928—to cite just a few topics of articles that related to luxury in the first third of the twentieth century.[23] In *Die neue Wohnung: Die Frau als Schöpferin* (The new apartment: The woman as creator, 1924), modern architect Bruno Taut explicitly states that the examples he is discussing are luxury spaces, illustrating the most elite typologies of modern, new dwellings.[24] The instances that Taut cites are characterized by "a simplicity that is bound with the most refined luxury"—though not in the sense of the accumulation of museum-worthy objects, but rather in "the most clear and pure presentation of the elements."[25] Luxury as represented by designs bearing a highly refined simplicity is a trope that this study returns to often. Taut suggests that these designs be used as the standard-bearers from which other, less luxurious, spaces can be generated. These "clear and pure" elements, Taut argues, allowed for a relationship between forms and space and for a subjective experience by the inhabitants—rather than one dictated by room designation and contents, as in earlier models. This will find echoes in the discussion of individual autonomy in modern spaces by Mies in chapters 5 and 6.

Frank glimpses into the realities of the high costs associated with modern architecture and design objects illuminate instances of luxury throughout this study. In 1927, Bruno Taut published *Ein Wohnhaus* (A residential house), a book that examines his own house. He notes that from the perspective of the lowest standard of living, given the high costs of construction, much can appear superfluous in the modern house. For example, he cites the expensive rubber floors, the slab roof over the balcony with its sheet glass, and the glass walls of his stairwell. Taut admits:

> Whether these things are luxury would be answered simply through the ques-tion of what use they serve. If this question is answered affirmatively [i.e., that they are luxuries], then the concept of luxury shifts in another direction [from where it has traditionally been located], one that in this house is in principle avoided: it is that individual pieces leap out through their overaccentuated mate-rial worth, through a costliness, which stands in contrast to the modesty and simplicity of the house as a whole. In this direction there are some "derailments," which are especially large when in an otherwise simple dwelling such a piece of furniture, carpet, light or the like only displays an affected costliness.[26]

In this discourse, Taut is moving away from a discussion of luxury as refinement or as an abstract element, to the real costs associated with modern architecture and its objects. Here, luxury can be signified through unnecessary design elements, costly materials, and the expense and ostentatious display of individual objects.

Luxury can be defined in yet another way—not through materials, expensiveness, or refined aesthetics, but those objects understood to be in the realm of the super-fluous, the unnecessary. Adolf G. Schneck, an architect, interior designer, and furniture designer, now largely forgotten but well-known in the period (he designed two of the single-family houses and an interior in the Mies apartment building at the Weissenhof Housing Settlement) wrote widely on modern furniture, objects, and materials. In his 1928 essay "About Type-Furniture," he called for standardized furniture to be limited to essential items, because "more than 90 percent of the consumers today cannot buy more furniture than they absolutely need in their apart-ment." Given consumers' economic limitations, Schneck argued, "They should not buy more. Less furniture, therefore less ballast. One has up to now made the attempt to standardize furniture that is not strictly necessary. The piece of furniture that is not absolutely necessary is a luxury object. The luxury object that has been made into a standard type is called kitsch."[27] Under this rigorous formula, items of furniture are labeled luxury objects to the extent that they are expendable. When these objects have been mass-produced and are thus inexpensive, they are then reduced further, to "kitsch."

Other designers questioned the rampant consumption spurred on by industry, including the desire for the latest technical products, as they reflected social posi-tioning. Architect Mart Stam, writing in 1928, lambasted the Werkbund's Weissenhof exhibition houses as luxurious, while also condemning the ostentatious purchasing patterns of certain consumers—whom he terms "parvenus," the period term for nouveau riche:

> The creation of a minimal dwelling [*Minimalwohnung*] is an exercise that would have also been of great significance for the Werkbund exhibition in Stuttgart. That is to say, it would have been necessary that one for once demonstrate how much in apartments is superfluous. Industry is very guilty here. Driven by com-petition, it lets one novelty follow another, without there ever having been any need for any of these "inventions." It is understood that we celebrate the progress of technology. But whoever holds every technical refinement in his apartment to

be indispensable makes the impression of a parvenu. And to where do all the inventions lead us in the end? Is the circle of consumers really so large? Who are these consumers? A very great percentage cannot afford these things; they remain luxuries.[28]

Linking subjects with objects, Stam suggests that succumbing to novel products of inferior taste, especially technical gadgets, can be equated to the poor social posturing of a parvenu—a person without an assured social position. Stam is also drawing attention to a problem in modern exhibitions, such as that put on by the Werkbund in Stuttgart, which strove to answer the housing crisis with dwelling and furniture solutions for the masses. But in the end, this period observer notes, they remained luxuries, out of the reach of the majority of consumers. Over and over again, economic considerations and a nuanced view of period social standing—aspirational or actual—will be instrumental for understanding modern architecture and its luxury objects.

This thread was also taken up by architectural critic Werner Gräff, who, in his book *Zweckmässiges Wohnen für jedes Einkommen* (Functional living for every income, 1931), lamented that mass-produced furniture was still not as inexpensive or as widely available as it ought to be, compounded by the transportation costs and potential adjustments needed once it was installed in the home.[29] Moreover, objects that serve a "need for luxury" (*Luxusbedürfnis*), he argues, ought to be a lower household priority. Taking a slightly different line of argumentation than Stam with regard to the price and status of technological objects, Gräff asks, "Doesn't one find a grandfather clock in many otherwise entirely modest dwellings, while the purchaser, for example, holds a vacuum cleaner at half the price to be an unattainable luxury?"[30] This points to the ways in which different subjects categorized objects as "luxury" in this period. Gräff, an advocate for the modern movement, considered a grandfather clock to be a luxury item, while, in turn, the everyday consumer he describes viewed a modern appliance such as a vacuum cleaner to be an unnecessary or unattainable luxury. Technological household objects as luxury is a subject that is discussed more fully in chapter 1, in the context of Peter Behrens's work for the AEG.

The most trenchant period critique of modern architecture as luxury and its use in social positioning came from Czech architectural critic Karel Teige in 1932. In the foreword to his book *The Minimum Dwelling*, Teige railed against the villas recently built by Mies in Brno, Le Corbusier in Garches and Poissy, Adolf Loos in Prague, and Robert Mallet-Stevens in Paris: "All of these houses with all their technical luxury and radical design devices, with all their formal originality, are really nothing other than new versions of opulent baroque palaces, that is, seats of the new financial aristocracy. A machine for living? No, a machine for representation and splendor." He condemns contemporary society, "with its mask of opulence and high culture," and indicts the work of Gropius, Mies, Wright, Le Corbusier, and Loos, charging that "it has become the habit of contemporary architectural journals to call this kind of architecture, this so-called *Baukunst* ("building art"), and this technical sumptuousness 'our housing culture.' If that were true, and if we designate as culture only that which is accessible to the rich, then the slogan of the 'minimum dwelling' is indeed a *crie de guerre* against bourgeois culture and against bourgeois architectural ideology."[31] From a Marxist socialist standpoint common to the period, Teige sought improvements in access to adequate housing for the poor, unemployed, and under-employed, criticizing modern architects for not addressing this central problem in practice and for failing to live up to their own purported goals for architecture. He laments the contemporary reality that "modern architecture has compromised its admirable principles and turned its lofty ideals into kitsch. Instead of holding fast to the principles of economy and functionality and to the promise that one day it will be able to solve the housing problem in the spirit of these principles and on a social scale, architecture has chosen to pander to the rich with a new version of luxury, a luxury of calculated simplicity for their new palaces."[32]

Arguing from varying artistic, theoretical, and political standpoints for differ-ing—specialist and nonspecialist—audiences, these critics and designers give a sense of the range of conflicting concerns surrounding luxury, consumption, and patterns of social behavior. For some architectural critics, luxury was present in everyday objects—because they were not affordable to one group, they fostered consumer desire. For others, luxury was more of a theoretical construct, one that described a relational divergence between objects, for example, differentiating "convenience" or "comfort" from "necessity." Social variances, too, resulted in consumers labeling very different categories of objects as out-of-reach "luxury." And luxury could be repre-sented in a purely economic manner, in which objects and buildings, by dint of their expensive materials, refined construction, or steep price tag, bespoke luxury. Rather than settling on one definition or conception of luxury, this study examines the myriad ways in which modern architecture and design represented luxury—contextualized in the period's own terms and stated goals, and in less obvious, nuanced ways.

Modern architects themselves were vocal in their claims for redressing perceived dwelling needs, but often less articulate about whose needs were ultimately being addressed. Caught in the middle, between visions of modernism and social forma-tions, modern architecture and its objects were asked to function on many levels, both practical and symbolic. Elite origins, contexts, and discourses would ultimately stymie modernism's democratic desires and built outcomes in this period. In light of users, this study of modern architecture and design illuminates the sometimes ambivalent and contradictory articulation of modernism's goals and its countervailing claims and theories. It shows that, in many ways, modernism's objects and spaces were driven by economic, social, and class formulations as much as by design ideals. If architects and cultural theorists had engaged more firmly with the realities of these formations, it suggests, many of the outcomes of this period might have been different or more far-reaching.

THE MODERN FICTIONAL SUBJECT AND MATERIALIST QUALITIES OF MODERNISM UNDER CAPITALISM

In metropolises across Europe in the first half of the twentieth century, many urban areas were undergoing significant and rapid architectural transformation, while in other sections, especially for the housing of the poor and working poor, the status quo prevailed or worsened. Dwelling conditions took on particular significance in Berlin, where urban transitions were taking place at breakneck speed as industri-alization continued apace. Workers in search of employment flocked from the countryside and from smaller towns to the metropolis in great numbers; their presence was felt in the bustling streets and in Berlin's overcrowded apartment buildings known as "rental barracks," run-down buildings that served as visible reminders that the city could not meet dwelling needs. While this exuberant urban atmosphere was charted with remarkable clarity and evocativeness in film, photography, and painting, in architecture the need to house the masses took on a pragmatic urgency and spawned much new thinking on how to contend with physical needs that were not being adequately met. The change to the material fabric of the city, often stretched to the breaking point in attempting to support its most vulnerable new citizens, was significant. At the same time, vast new fortunes were being made—not only by factory owners and those directly connected to industry, but also by an affluent managerial class and successful creative class (those involved in the film industry and in publishing, for example) that began to emerge at this time. These new groups desired to be housed in dwellings representative of their status and wealth. The urban upheaval also caused much social change, instability, and uncertainty among the differing, jostling social classes. Material possessions, especially, expressed their owners' present status or their social aspirations. How class differences played out in culturally complex Berlin interiors can perhaps best be seen in Weimar novels, which vividly illustrated the economic, social, and cultural nuances of the period. Even more vibrantly than the continuity and change amply charted in period journalism, descriptive fictional portrayals of Berlin offer a view into the social and cultural life of the various classes. Fiction especially illustrates the multivalent relationships between subjects and interiors, people and the objects with which they surrounded themselves during this time. Not only can meaning be read in the settings that urban dwellers across the social spectrum constructed for themselves, but period fiction sheds light on how these figures themselves understood and projected this meaning outward.

Goodbye to Berlin, the account by the British writer Christopher Isherwood written in 1929–33 based on his stay in Berlin, provides compelling period social portraits interlinked with the material substance of dwellers' interiors.[33] Isherwood was well positioned to capture the era in this manner—as a member of the British elite, he had a keen awareness of social norms and was well trained to sniff out parvenu behavior. Throughout the novel, Isherwood pairs his protagonists with detailed descriptions of their larger architectural contexts, as well as the contents of their specific interiors. The value judgments placed on the fictional characters are directly linked to the cultural and social meaning of the architecture and objects of their surroundings. Isherwood opens his chronicle with a telling architectural description, while simultaneously opining on the deterioration of the middle class. Especially key here is his connection of object status to social status: "From my window, the deep solemn massive street. Cellar-shops where the lamps burn all day, under the shadow of top-heavy balconied facades, dirty plaster frontages embossed with scroll-work and heraldic devices. The whole district is like this: street leading into street of houses like shabby monumental safes crammed with the tarnished valuables and second-hand furniture of a bankrupt middle class." Isherwood's alter-ego rents a single room in an apartment of an upper-middle-class woman who has been forced by economic necessity to take in lodgers. He describes the space at length: "The tall tiled stove, gorgeously colored, like an altar. The washstand like a Gothic shrine. The cupboard also is Gothic, with carved cathedral windows: Bismarck faces the King of Prussia in stained glass. My best chair would do for a bishop's throne. In the corner, three sham medieval halberds (from a theatrical touring company?) are fastened together to form a hat stand. … Everything in the room is like that: unnecessarily solid, abnormally heavy and dangerously sharp. Here, at the writing-table, I am confronted by a phalanx of metal objects—a pair of candlesticks shaped like entwined serpents, an ashtray from which emerges the head of a crocodile, a paper-knife copied from a Florentine dagger, a brass dolphin holding on the end of its tail a small broken clock. … Every morning Fraulein Schroeder arranges them very carefully in certain unvarying positions: there they stand, like an uncompromising statement of her views on Capital and Society, Religion and Sex."[34]

Here the interiors and objects, with particular reference to their varying materials and forms, are seen as standing for the interior life—the thoughts and points of view—of the proprietress. Because of the landlady's reduced financial circumstances, a common situation given the economic upheavals of the 1920s, she has elected to use the objects and the upkeep of her interior as an essential means through which to maintain her class standing. The materiality of these objects stand as bulwarks against the waves of change that have taken place for her personally and in Berlin more widely. The literal and figurative weight of the heavy materials carried meaning that was legible in the period. Even real interiors, such as those photographed by Waldemar Titzenthaler in the same years, show rooms filled with these types of objects—furniture in an eclectic mix of historicist styles, often elaborately carved, an array of busts and sculpture, and a myriad of other small decorative items (see fig. I.2).[35] The choice of materials and objects had deep significance, both for the inhabitants themselves and in terms of what they wanted to outwardly express. Period denizens, when visiting friends, acquaintances, or on business, were accustomed to reading others' interiors; but even more commonly, they would have the opportunity to do so by studying newspapers and magazines, which frequently featured photographs of inhabitants in their homes, the affluent and the destitute alike.

Another of Isherwood's protagonists, chronicled in *The Last of Mr. Norris* (1935), is Mr. Norris himself, who operates a dubious import-export business trading in antiques and clocks. A first visit to his apartment reveals little about him, in keeping with his mysterious airs: "Everything was in good taste, the furniture, the carpet, the color scheme. But the room was curiously without character. It was like a room on the stage or in the window of a high-class furnishing store; elegant, expensive, discreet. I had expected Mr. Norris's background to be altogether more exotic; something Chinese would have suited him, with golden and scarlet dragons."[36] The narrator is able to see through the artifice of these two characters. Both are using possessions to create the appearance of stability—the landlady hangs on to the last physical vestiges of her formerly affluent life in hopes of keeping her position in society, while the material possessions of Mr. Norris are intended to express complete normalcy where none exists. Both use their interiors to indicate something different from the truth of their circumstances, underscoring the way in which interiors and domestic situations registered on social and cultural levels in this uncertain period. It was an era of heightened visuality, and viewers came to develop keen observational skills; like Isherwood's alter ego, they could ascertain the difference between genuine and sham. Unlike other eras in which imitation was the vogue, such as in the case of the false perspectives and imitation patterns printed on nineteenth-century wallpapers, in this period, attention was paid to—and placed upon—genuine quality and materials.

Isherwood describes modern architecture as well. In contrast to the apartments inhabited by his friends and acquaintances in the city center, his affluent private pupils—to whom his protagonist gives English lessons as a means of supporting himself in Berlin—lived in single-family villas in the leafy outskirts of the city, characterized by Isherwood as "a millionaire's slum." He reveals both the bourgeois character of the private, modern villa and the staid—rather than avant-garde—lives contained within:

> Fraulein Hippi Bernstein, my first pupil, lives in the Grünewald, in a house built almost entirely of glass. Most of the richest Berlin families inhabit the Grünewald. It is difficult to understand why. Their villas, in all known styles of expensive ugliness, ranging from the eccentric-rococo folly to the cubist flat-roofed steel-and-glass box are crowded together in this dank, dreary pinewood. Few of them can afford large gardens, for the ground is fabulously dear. … The hall of the Bernsteins' house has metal-studded doors and a steamer clock fastened to the wall with bolt-heads. There are modernist lamps, designed to look like pressure-gauges, thermometers and switchboard dials. But the furniture doesn't match the house and its fittings. The place is like a power-station which engineers have tried to make comfortable with chairs and tables from an old-fashioned, highly respectable boarding-house. On the austere metal walls, hang highly varnished nineteenth-century landscapes in massive gold frames. Herr Bernstein probably ordered the villa from a popular avant-garde architect in a moment of recklessness, was horrified at the result and tried to cover it up as much as possible with the family belongings.[37]

The tutor is greeted by a footman and then plied with fruit and other treats, the result of his pupil's summoning the maid repeatedly via an in-house telephone in a ploy to avoid her English lessons. Throughout the story, the inhabitants of this modern house exhibit ostentatious, thoroughly bourgeois behavior, which Isherwood exploits to great effect. The interior was similar to Mies's Lange and Esters commissions, in which the families incorporated their older furnishings in Mies's modern house (see chapter 5). Situations in which the family was loath to give up their material possessions—whether family heirlooms or traditional upper-class furnishings—presented an aesthetic quandary and highlighted a difficulty in domesticating the modern. The result was that Isherwood's fictional house and the Lange and Esters houses had a very different type of interior from the visual coherence of Mies's Tugendhat House interior, where his clients allowed him to design nearly all of the furniture. Perhaps, as Isherwood suggests, retaining family heirlooms was a means of taming the house. Isherwood's protagonists, despite their modern home—perhaps more accurately described as a "modernistic" house—made no pretensions about living an avant-garde life, but rather tried to eke out a cozy, bourgeois existence despite their modern surroundings.

The Weimar novelist Irmgard Keun conjures a similar image of the affluent families living in the same areas of the city as Isherwood's Bernsteins in her 1932 novel, *The Artificial Silk Girl*.[38] Keun's "Onyx" family is simply referred to by the source of their fortune, which sustains them generation after generation. This is a noteworthy convergence, given Mies's well-known use of onyx in the years just prior to the novel's publication, but also a reminder of the degree to which natural resources, in addition to new industries, generated fortunes in this period. Young Doris, the sharp-eyed protagonist, describes the family and their behavior: "And so I was taking care of obnoxious kids of a high-society family, the incognito children of a former general's daughter. Tilli [Doris's friend] had arranged it—she used to watch the onyx kids. They live at the river bend and they are knowingly insolent, like grownups. The husband has onyx and stocks and white hair that stands straight up, finding itself attractive. And he's tall and stately looking. The wife is young and lazy and understands nothing. ... So there comes the White Onyx and says 'Mademoiselle.' And makes eyes at me and I was ready."[39]

The reader follows the fate of plucky Doris who arrives in Berlin alone with little more than a stolen fur coat and aspirations for a glamorous acting career. Seeking her fame, Doris is prepared to trade herself for material goods. Her ups and downs in fortune are directly mirrored by her material possessions and the domestic interiors she inhabits. Even the book's title refers to the social importance of distinctions in materials—affluent women in this period wore pure silk, while the poorer protagonist of the novel, Doris, wears artificial silk in imitation and emulation of the members of the class that could afford the original material rather than its ersatz. As Doris moves from apartment to apartment, each setting and its attendant objects, although sketched quickly, speak volumes about its inhabitants. About the apartment of a new lover, an older married man named Alexander, she writes, "[It] is so elegant, the chauffeur is so elegant, everything is fabulous. I stroll through the apartment. And there's dark red wallpaper, so incredibly elegant, and oak furniture and walnut. ... And easy chairs with ashtrays attached to them like wrist watches—that's the kind of apartment it is."[40] On the other hand, her next male benefactor, who works in advertising (and is thus part of the modern, booming economy), has a very different apartment: "Everything is very modern. Not this heavy oak you find at the industrialists'. ... With cork flooring, three rooms and a bath, a rubber-tree plant, and a divan, so wide, with a silk cover and fine steel dentist office lamps."[41] Working-class Doris understands this apartment less well and takes him shopping for carpeting to replace the linoleum in the parlor.[42] Throughout, Keun conjures interiors that directly relate to the social standing of the book's characters, who span many different classes while demonstrating the instability of class designations.[43]

Modern domestic objects and interiors required a conceptual understanding of the modern movement to be appreciated. Indeed, as both the journalism and the fictional accounts from this period indicate, the products of modernism were not inexpensive to procure, were not within the financial reach of everyone, and certainly were not consumed by the masses. The advertising man's modern apartment described by Doris featured a marble entrance hall, a mirrored elevator, and electricity, which was relatively exceptional considering that 81 percent of the inhabitants in Berlin's working-class areas lived without electricity at this time.[44] Thus, even if the materials (cork, steel, and linoleum) in the modern apartment *appeared* more utilitarian than those of the conventional industrialist's interior (oak, heavy furniture, and deep red wallpaper), they ultimately represented both modern, cutting-edge design and its patron's elite social standing and taste. Though their decorative schemes and possessions illuminate highly distinct *Weltanschauungen* (world views), the two interiors should be understood as equally luxurious, with the modern apartment perhaps the more elite of the two. Although these two examples of Weimar interiors come from fictional descriptions, real-life corollaries are abundant. For example, the study in the Berlin home of Dr. Bernhard Dernburg (see fig. I.2) can be compared to the modern dining room of theater director Erwin Piscator, designed by Marcel Breuer (fig. I.4).

Isherwood and Keun's fictional descriptions of the bourgeois families' houses—as well as their locations—were based on modern architecture being produced on the west side of the city from the 1910s to the early 1930s. Convenient to Berlin's many lakes and forest preserves, these areas were the domain of an affluent class who built large houses for their families there. Modern architects such as Mies, Gropius, Ludwig Hilberseimer, and others, were commissioned to build in districts such as Grünewald, Zehlendorf, and Wannsee.[45] (The architects themselves, however, tended to live in apartment houses in central Berlin.[46]) From these leafy enclaves, the head of the household could easily commute to the city center by private car or commuter rail, traveling from the modern, new stations designed by Hermann Muthesius and other well-known architects. The bourgeoisie that modern architects predominantly served was made up of industrial producers, businessmen, doctors, and creative intellectuals. For example, Mies's client base was overwhelmingly represented by successful industrialists—manufacturers or those in businesses related to modern industries—to whom technical innovation, the use of new materials, and modern conceptions of space appealed. They would have also been aware of the luxury and status that modern architecture conveyed. Mies's costly nickel- or chromium-plated

Figure I.4. Marcel Breuer, renovated interior of the Erwin Piscator Apartment, dining room, Berlin, 1927.

columns, expensive wooden veneers, and hand-wrought furnishings exude the materialist qualities of modernism under capitalism's affluence.

CLASS-INFLECTED OBJECTS AND INTERIORS
IN THE WEIMAR REPUBLIC

At all socioeconomic levels in this period, shifting class designations and aspirations were concretized by citizens' projection of self and social standing via their domestic interiors and contents. With modernism in architecture came a new emphasis on making well-designed domestic goods accessible to a wider spectrum of the consuming public and on articulating a nuanced relationship between dwellings, dwellers, and objects. Goods and the spaces into which they were inserted were understood as social, cultural, even moral, indicators of the values of inhabitants. The acquisition of a modern object, such as a Peter Behrens–designed AEG fan displayed proudly on a side table, would have resonated beyond its technical comfort, to signal its owner's taste, knowledge, and access to expensive goods. Photography in this period provides further insight into which classes were inclined toward certain types of interiors, revealing that modernism was most readily embraced by the upper middle and upper classes.[47] Within this affluent segment of the population, a wide variety of interior decorative schemes were popular, including replications of historic styles, art deco, and the modernism promulgated by modern architects.[48] As with objects designed in previous periods, modern goods became social markers, and those markers were tied to specific class distinctions.

However, the uneasy sense of class designations throughout this period was exacerbated by several serious financial crises in the 1920s that changed the economic and social standing of many. In Germany, the bourgeoisie (*Bürgertum*) represented a class delineated by a specific lifestyle and set of values.[49] Scholars have divided the *Bürgertum* into two categories, defined by occupation: the *Wirtschaftsbürgertum* was made up of merchants, manufacturers, bankers, owners of capital, entrepreneurs, and their top management, while the *Bildungsbürgertum* was more highly educated and composed of physicians, lawyers, secondary school teachers, professors, higher civil servants, engineers, and other qualified experts forming an upper middle class.[50] In addition, middle-class or white-collar workers could be broken into three groups: the *Grossbürgertum*, an upper-middle-class group made up of commercial and industrial magnates; the *Kleinbürgertum*, a more solidly middle-class group with aspirations upwards; and the *Mittelstand*, the lower middle class made up of white-collar workers (called *Angestellten* in German), small-business owners, and petty bureaucrats. On the very lowest rung of the social ladder was the *Arbeiter* class, Germany's blue-collar workers. In differing instances, each of these groups was targeted by modern designers with varied results. Some in the more affluent classes clung to tradition, while others consumed modern goods and architecture—although bourgeois constraints of propriety and habit often kept them from embracing the modern totality envisioned by architects. For those with the least capital, modern objects remained out of reach—conceptually as well as economically.

Modern interiors and their objects were particularly attractive to members of the *Bildungsbürgertum* whose professions were in fields such as science, medicine, and physical health, or wholly new areas, such as advertising. These affluent, professional, and creative groups illustrate the wider range of modern consumers. Buyers were drawn to modern goods for their link to the artistic realm, embracing them as a symbol of their own forward-thinking ideas and their interests in modernism, but they were also a highly legible expression of affluence. Among those opting for modern interiors were clients who were prominent in creative fields such as film or theater, exemplified by Breuer's interior for theater director Erwin Piscator (see fig. I.4). Art historians and those in the art world, such as Curt Glaser, the director of Berlin's famous art library, the Kunstbibliothek, also tended toward contemporary interiors. Working women, particularly those breaking gender barriers, commissioned modern interiors, such as the renowned gymnastics studio for Hilde Levi designed by Breuer, and the modern homes of notable female doctors, such as Dr. Edith Vohwinkel and Dr. Marie Valentiner. Certain well-to-do Jewish families were inclined toward modern interiors as well. A good example is the apartment designed by Breuer for Paul Boroschek, a stockbroker, who was also a newspaper publisher and an influential member of the Berlin Jewish community (fig. I.5).[51]

What was defined as "new," as in *Neues Bauen* (new building) or *sachlich* (objective, or functional), was often based on the terms that architects laid out, as opposed to an architectural response to changes driven by the broader society. This is important for how modernism was conceptualized and "sold" as a movement, and for understanding by what means this movement undertook to transform, or modernize, society. At a minimum, it calls into question modern architecture's supposed close relationship to the workers and its protagonists' desire to address the needs of the masses. While a wide range of social critics and theorists can be seen to be tracing larger cultural and social change, in each case to be examined here, it is the architects

Figure I.5. Breuer, renovated interior of the Boroschek Apartment, dining room, Berlin, 1930.

and designers who carefully articulated the "problems" of modern life and created their "solutions." For the most part, during this thirty-year episode, they did so through a top-down, elite-driven process, in which luxury and modernism were closely, and often inextricably, linked to each other.

THE FOCUSED STUDIES

At the core of *Luxury and Modernism* are modern architecture's most significant protagonists working in Germany in this period—Peter Behrens, Walter Gropius, Ludwig Mies van der Rohe, Marcel Breuer, Ludwig Hilberseimer, and Hannes Meyer—and institutions with which they were associated—the AEG, the Werkbund, and the Bauhaus. To these major figures and entities, critics and period theorists, such as Adolf Behne, Walter Benjamin, and Ernst Bloch, as well as many smaller groups, lesser-known figures, and institutions, provide added nuance that shows luxury's deep and broad reach in modernism. The chapters repeatedly return to modern architecture's major enduring themes and topics of debate—including taste, display, consumption, materiality, industry, technology, production, and reproduction—to investigate in sustained fashion how the period's concerns were directly connected to—or representations of—luxury. Other, less tangible, but equally important ideas, such as capitalism, objectivity, subjectivity, aura, and interiority are investigated for their relationship to luxury.

Chapter 1, on the tenure of Peter Behrens at the AEG, opens up discussions of technology as a distinct form of conspicuous consumption, arguing that high-end electrical products conveyed information about the social status and taste of their owners on multiple levels, beyond the cost of the objects themselves (which, in any case, remained high and out of the reach of the masses). It further examines patterns of consumption by giving sustained attention to the Behrens-designed AEG stores, contextualizing them in light of other small- and large-scale commercial architecture and urban form more generally.

Chapter 2 builds on these ideas through its examination of Werkbund-sponsored display windows, arguing that they functioned as both modern architectural objects and as variable conduits, spatial and social, between an outside urban context and an interior world of goods. Continuing to investigate capitalism's intricate role in—and its effects on—modern architecture and design, chapter 3 focuses on the Bauhaus's 1923 Haus am Horn to recontextualize modernism's eagerness to collaborate with industry. The Haus am Horn, as an early display of many of the theories and visual tropes of modern architecture, represents a multitude of modernism's desires and economic stumbling blocks—built as it was at the height of German hyperinflation and economic calamity. The Bauhaus further allows, in chapter 4, for an examination of the issues surrounding the production and reproduction of modern objects. This chapter illuminates a divide between Gropius's aspirations for the role the school could play in modern industry and the real, prohibitive costs of Bauhaus products. By looking at fabrication methods, materials, display, and issues of class, this chapter provides a closer look at the ideals of modernism against its material and social reality.

These previous chapters shed light on how objects and interiors resonated socially, as part of capitalist society, and in relation to urban spheres. Chapter 5 returns again to this study's initial forays into the luxury of technology and materiality, as discussed in the work of Peter Behrens, in order to focus on the expensive modern materials and extravagant natural resources found in Mies van der Rohe's architecture in the closing years of the Weimar Republic. In charting his lush materiality and his show-casing of technology, Mies's interiors are read as luxury; but as his domestic commissions show, they were also reassuringly bourgeois and traditional in many respects. Striking materials resulted in a multiplicity of new expressions, new spaces, and new modes of interaction. The distinct meaning in Mies's privileging of materials, this chapter argues, is that through the rich materiality of his architecture he created a way to forge renewed connections between people and their surroundings. The final chapter continues this exploration of Mies's architecture and interiors to discuss the period's new conceptualizations of what it meant to dwell. It argues that in his domestic commissions, in settings that were carved out from the city and from society at large, promising autonomy to their privileged inhabitants, Mies created spaces of luxurious interiority.

Bringing together the discourses of modernism with primary objects and their makers enables a rereading of modern architecture and design through the lens of period constructs and constraints, consumption and culture. By reevaluating the overall social and cultural milieu from which they emerged, the subtle complexities of the modern movement's origins and development in these years is brought to the fore. Simultaneously highlighting the continuation of deeply ingrained traditions and habits of an elite while focusing on the aspirations of the modern movement's protagonists and the realities and limitations—social, economic, cultural—that they faced, what emerges is a richly layered understanding of an intensely productive period in which so much innovative design materialized, not always consistent with the aims it proclaimed. This close examination of early-twentieth-century architectural culture as positioned at the intersection of modernism and luxury offers new ways of critically understanding the paths by which modern design paved the way in this period to our present, with implications extending far beyond design alone.

CONSUMPTION

It is tempting to view Peter Behrens's 1907–14 tenure at the Allgemeine Elektricitäts-Gesellschaft (AEG) as the paradigmatic example of modern architecture's involvement with industry. The logo-emblazoned turbine factory, completed in 1909, is often described as the high point of his activities, which ranged from redesigning the AEG logo and advertising materials to the design of objects and buildings. For potential consumers of modern design, however, Behrens's work at the AEG should be considered in the context of the sumptuous showrooms he designed in Berlin for the firm in 1910 and 1911 (fig. 1.1).

The AEG's hiring of Behrens could not have been foretold given the trajectory of his career to that point. Originally trained as a painter, he had additionally worked as an illustrator and bookbinder in Munich. It was then that he received his first major opportunity to design on a larger scale. In 1899, the Grand Duke of Hesse invited him to join the newly founded Darmstadt Artists' Colony, where experiments in the period's prevailing Jugendstil were carried out by its artist members. Given the chance to design his own house and all of its contents, he was able to develop his prodigious, wide-ranging talents. He went on to direct the School of Arts and Crafts in Düsseldorf, from 1903 to 1907, and then moved to Berlin to begin work for the AEG, whose founder and general manager was Emil Rathenau. He was not hired as a direct employee, but instead served as an artistic consultant. In the same year, 1907, he helped to form the German Werkbund, a group of designers, industrialists, and politicians dedicated to improving the quality of German manufactured goods. The AEG afforded a crucial early chance to test the many ideals of Werkbund members regarding the merging of art and design with modern industrial practices, one of which was the recommendation that companies employ artists to improve their goods (figs. 1.2, 1.3, 1.4).

Behrens's role in the promotion of modernism, however, runs deeper than the design of important factories or well-known teakettles: to be examined here are his contributions to the creation of *Kauflust*, or "desire to purchase," for modern products of industry as singularly manifested in AEG shops.[1] And also key is the situating of technology, especially electricity, as luxury, in relation to these products and stores.

The ground-level facade of Behrens's first store, opened in the fall of 1910 at number 4 Königgrätzer Strasse, was sheathed almost entirely in glass. An immense floor-to-ceiling pane formed the display window, flanked to the right by a pair of glazed entrance doors with an enormous, three-paneled clerestory light above. Set in from the building's flat plaster surface, this ensemble of windows was held by a severely beveled "frame"—an enormous, hammered sheet-copper border, edged with beading (see fig. 1.1, esp. the right side).[2] Allowed to oxidize to a powdery green, this burnished frame would have contrasted with the highly polished AEG wares on display. Half-height marble panels placed at the back of the window acted as a screen, creating an interstitial display space between the street and the store's main space, enticing pedestrians into the partly visible interior beyond it. Simultaneously, the marble panels created a serene realm for the customers within by shielding them from the commotion of the busy thoroughfare outside. Full-length silk curtains hung from the ceiling behind the window, emphasizing the great height of the space and forming a proscenium, which heightened the drama of the products on display.[3] Across the top of the window, modern, sans-serif gold lettering identified the company by its full name and the subset of electrical products "for household and workshop" on "display" (*Ausstellung für Haushalt und Werkstatt*).[4] To the right of the window, the entrance door featured the famous hexagonal logo with the company's initials, which were also painted on the three panes of its oversized light.[5] The logo on the door is the only eye-level indicator of the store's identity; all other text, placed high up on the glass panes, directed the viewer's attention to the entirety of the store's facade. This assemblage of text, floor-to-ceiling drapes, and plate glass especially emphasized the soaring height of the space, and yet, along with the frame, confined and encapsulated it, directing attention toward the gleaming goods on display.

Inside, smart leather club chairs set in mirror-glass niches were interspersed between shiny metal and glass vitrines and side tables (fig. 1.5). The upper white walls, topped by exaggerated dentils over the niches, added an element of reserved classicism to the opulent modernism of the interior. On the ceiling, bare bulbs simply set in shiny metal sockets emphasized the store's intent—an interior designed to sell modern products, but also to celebrate industry and technology.

For the second store, which opened in the spring of 1911 at 117 Potsdamer Strasse, Behrens again employed a combination of traditional and sumptuous modern materials (fig. 1.6). A vocabulary of even more stripped-down forms and a greater

Figure 1.1. Peter Behrens, AEG store, 4 Königgrätzer Strasse, Berlin, 1910.

emphasis on flat surfaces distinguished this store. Framed by monolithic, lightly veined, white marble slabs on three sides, the storefront was a simple portal beckoning in the affluent consumer. Chiseled on the marble like a Roman epitaph, the company name and a list of its most important products was inscribed in clear, elegant typography. Each of these marble slabs was surmounted by a faintly projecting cornice of green marble resting on a richly veined plinth of the same material. The door and the window frames were painted green, resulting in a unified, tasteful ensemble.[6] Deeply set in the store's marble proscenium was a tall, narrow entrance door crowned by a beveled clerestory window and a large plate glass display window. At the very bottom of the window, on low white plinths and shelving, Behrens placed an array of small, shiny AEG products; they twinkled like jewels, dwarfed by the majesty of this white marble proscenium. This green-and-white scheme with its rectilinear use of flat marble also stylistically connected this store with commissions

Figure 1.2. Behrens, AEG teakettles, 1909.

Figure 1.3 Behrens, AEG fan, 1914.

Figure 1.4 Behrens, AEG arc lamp, 1908. Advertisement, 1912.

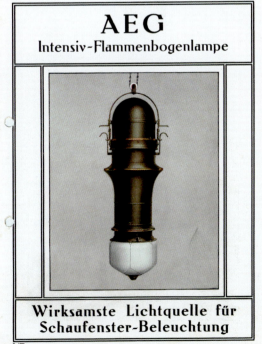

Behrens executed just prior to it, namely, the early Christian–style AEG pavilion for the German Shipbuilding Exhibition in Berlin (1908), the early Florentine Renaissance–style pavilion designed for the *Northwest German Art Exhibition* in Oldenburg (1905), and a crematorium in Hagen (1905–8). The latter two buildings both show the influence of San Miniato in Florence, and they both feature a round, beveled clerestory window, in addition to similarities in materials and color. Working in a pared-down, modern idiom, Behrens nevertheless connected his buildings, and the products he designed for the AEG, to the representative grandeur and elegance of previous stylistic periods.

Inside the store, Behrens deployed architectural elements and rich materials to evoke a luxurious world into which AEG goods were to be placed. Immediately upon entering, visitors encountered a rich, generously sized brown leather sofa set into a niche of geometrically paneled cabinetry in dark wood (fig. 1.7). A built-in, horizontal vitrine extended the length of the salesroom; installed at eye level, its parade of objects would have immediately caught the attention of potential buyers entering the store. Above the vitrine, punctuated only by a large AEG wall clock, dark green, patterned wallpaper ran to the ceiling.[7] As in Behrens's first store, classical elements are utilized in conjunction with restrained modernism. Here the dentils are more diminutive, ringing the square coffers, each of which features a single light bulb set into a bare metal holder. In both stores, then, recognizable, tasteful classical forms and materials (coffers, dentils, plinths, marble) were carefully combined with the materials and elements of industry (glass, metal, light bulbs, electricity).

Thus the visual vocabulary of these two select, high-visibility shops—with their ample plate glass, and spare, repetitive elements—represented key visual and material aspects of modernism. But they went further than merely visually and materially

Figure 1.5. Behrens, AEG store, main showroom, 4 Königgrätzer Strasse, Berlin, 1910.

Figure 1.6. *Opposite*: Behrens, AEG store, 117 Potsdamer Strasse, Berlin, 1911.

representing modernism's ideals. Indeed, as early as 1911, observers commented on the stores' overall *sachlich*, or spare, qualities and on their eliciting a sense of consumer desire. In selling modern technology, the AEG enlisted visual design and modern architecture in the endeavor of commodification. The carefully conceived stores were among the places where the company did so, representing an early and select method by which industry displayed and sold modernism to the public.

Exhibited in Behrens's modern stores, AEG products were staged to spur consumption by invoking a luxurious—and for most, elusive—world enhanced by modern technology and electricity (see fig. 1.5). For many modernists, and for companies that subscribed to modernism, creating consumer desire became a crucial goal of widening the audience for its machine mass-produced objects. The company could have elected to produce its objects more cheaply. Instead, the AEG did not market its electrical goods as advanced technology or rationalized, functional products. Rather, the firm displayed and sold its goods as alluring, even lavish, domestic objects. This has larger implications for a new understanding of the way that modern objects and architecture were conceptualized and sold in the period. In the words of Peter Jessen, a prominent German Werkbund member writing in 1912, Behrens's entire body of work at the AEG represented "a single spirit of true modernity."[8] Behrens's oeuvre has long been viewed in this unifying capacity. Examining the stores and the goods on display brings some much-needed complexity back into the picture, for they functioned as a crucial intermediary between the elite world of modern design with its theory, practitioners, materials, and alignment with industry and actual consumers. A key characteristic of the AEG's consumers is that they came very largely from affluent circles. As forerunners to the broader public that modernism aspired to transform, these buyers had to be convinced to consume

modern products. Evoking a sumptuous world, the stores showcased the products and conjured the luxurious modern environments for which they were intended. They were aimed at the affluent consumers that the AEG sought to woo, and window-shoppers at large.

THE CIRCUIT OF LUXURY: ELECTRICITY AND ITS CONSUMERS

At the end of the nineteenth century, electricity itself was a privileged, urban phenomenon, which had long been linked to luxury in the public eye because it had been used to illuminate important, preeminent shopping and public streets of cities. The cleaning of the street's arc lamps on Unter den Linden in Berlin, the great public boulevard, was a public spectacle.[9] In Germany, from its earliest availability, electricity had been generally confined to public locations, especially spaces of commerce and entertainment: lighting elegant cafés, restaurants, and hotels; big department stores; and small luxury shops. The evening illumination would be described by Ernst Bloch as late as 1928, who marveled at "the overly lavish lighting of which you have heard so much, the new cafés, the theaters, Berlin as the leading edge."[10] Citizens out at night generally would have enjoyed electrical illumination, but the vast majority would have retired to nonelectrified homes. Electricity was linked to places of evening entertainment in particular. Theaters and private clubs, for example, acquired it early on. Initially, these establishments purchased AEG generators and produced their own electricity privately in their basements. Often they banded together so that a single basement generator worked to supply a few locales as well as the neighboring streetlights. As local power stations were established, entire neighborhoods were eventually connected to the electric grid. The AEG's manifold business model allowed for a profit from the sale of generators for the self-production of electricity, as well as a large array of energy-consuming machines and appliances. Income brought in by the sale of electricity from its subsidiary company, the Berlin Electricity Works (Berliner Elektricitäts-Werke) also buoyed the company's profits. This was the context in which the AEG opened its stores in 1910–11.

Before consumers could even cross the thresholds of these stores, they had to either have electricity at home or at least be contemplating its acquisition. In the AEG's formulation, good-looking designs sold in centrally located stores that were easily accessible to individual consumers, rather than aimed at industrial tradesmen, would spur first the sales of electrical appliances and also, crucially, raise electricity consumption once they were brought home. Different pricing structures were in effect for different uses: electricity used for appliances was more expensive than that which provided lighting, necessitating the installation of two meters in the home, one for hardwired lighting and the other for appliances, which also explains the AEG's emphasis on appliances rather than lamps. It was important to the company that the electrical products it produced were highly desirable; thus, in this period, its electrical household appliances should be viewed as luxury objects. Businesses and workshops running electrical machines were given deep discounts and rebates for high volume, while domestic consumers paid a much higher rate. Electricity *was* expensive—in 1904, the charge was 40 pfennig per kilowatt-hour.[11] This was about the hourly wage for a day worker at the Wertheim department store in Berlin.[12] The

Figure 1.7. Behrens, AEG store, main showroom, 117 Potsdamer Strasse, Berlin, 1911.

AEG sought to put kilowatt-hours into perspective for consumers, and its examples are insightful: a single kilowatt-hour could provide the energy to electrically light three thousand cigars, or supply thirty trips up four floors in an elevator, or bring nine liters of water to boil.[13] A hair dryer used about 250 watts, and curling tongs consumed about 60 watts.[14] In this period, the AEG's profit was derived not only from the sale of the objects themselves but from their potential energy consumption, which was provided by the Berlin Electricity Works, which was held privately by the AEG from 1887 until it was taken over by the city of Berlin in 1915. The installation fees also posed an entrance barrier; in 1906, the household connection fee and installation of an electricity meter was between 25 and 100 marks for 1 to 5 kilowatts.[15] Additionally, to connect the house from the street customers paid 6 marks per meter of cable, after the first two (free) meters.[16] They also had to rent the electricity meter, which cost up to 5 marks per year.[17] Furthermore, there was an annual fee for the first ten years, based on the number and type of hardwired lighting; each small incandescent lamp required a 2-mark fee, while the larger sizes were 4 marks each.[18]

The AEG's products, although industrially produced, were not inexpensive to acquire. For example, the teakettles were priced by size, ranging from 18 to 26 marks ($95.40–$138 today); a kitchen motor cost 200 marks ($1,060); and a vacuum cleaner—brought out in 1913 and tellingly named the "Dandy"—cost 300 marks ($1,590).[19] A cigarette lighter for one's automobile seems like a bargain at 8 marks, but a car was still an extraordinary luxury in 1907 Germany. In contrast, a pair of men's good shoes cost 12 to 15 marks. Through industrial fabrication techniques, prices had fallen for some products; an arc lamp that would have cost 350 marks in the 1880s was priced at 60 marks by 1909.[20]

Given that electric objects produced by the AEG were expensive, as was the installation and consumption of electricity itself, the question of who had electricity in Berlin in this period is pertinent. Household connections grew steadily but only at about a rate of 100 to 150 per month so that about eighteen thousand houses were connected by September 1911, at a time when the city had a population of more than 2 million. Appallingly overcrowded and squalid conditions characterized the majority of Berlin dwellings, with families often lacking separate rooms for sleeping and eating. Amenities such as private bathrooms within these apartments were rare; instead, multiple units shared common facilities off of the stairhall. Therefore,

Figure 1.8. Illuminated ceiling from "The Electrical Lighting of Our Living Spaces," *Mitteilungen der Berliner Elektricitäts-Werke*, 1911.

it is not surprising that Berlin lagged behind other industrialized cities in terms of electricity connections: in 1910, 3.5 percent of Berlin apartment houses were connected to the electricity grid, but that rose to only 6.6 percent by 1918.[21] In comparison to other American and European cities, universal electricity came to Berlin late; for example, by 1927 only 50 percent of the apartments in Berlin had electricity, compared with 96 percent of the apartments in Chicago and 99 percent in Zurich according to a 1928 report by the Berlin municipal electricity works.[22]

At the 1908 annual meeting of the German electric companies, the board of directors voiced growing apprehension about the cost of electricity, and in particular, the high cost of electrical appliances and their repair, a key departure from the group's usual concerns, which tended to focus on technical issues such as inner workings of turbines. They acknowledged that it was not enough to simply call for the price of electricity to drop but that, for example, the price of purchasing or even renting an electric stove was so expensive that even if electricity were free, it would still be beyond the reach of the average consumer, especially in comparison with a gas stove.[23] It was also reported that the electricity to heat a single room cost up to 360 marks per month, while gas heat was only about 30 marks.[24]

Simultaneous with the opening of the stores, the AEG began strongly advocating the domestic—as opposed to commercial—use of electricity, with numerous didactic articles in its magazine with titles such as "Electricity in the Household" and "The Electrical Lighting of Our Living Spaces."[25] Telling, however, are the contexts in which electric goods are depicted in domestic settings: they are shown in homes with luxurious interiors (fig. 1.8). A 1911 article titled "The Modern, Electrically Configured Residential Building" noted that farsighted homeowners—either in building anew or renovating older houses—were connecting to the electric grid and declared, "Electricity in the house is no luxury, as many think; it has much more rightly become a requirement of modern living."[26] Moreover, the article informs readers that the featured household enjoys an early electric washing machine and wringer in the basement and an electrically rechargeable automobile, all decidedly luxurious examples, while images depict an elegant woman with a fur muff and a man in a top hat being led by a uniformed maid down a marble-lined hallway (fig. 1.9). In a similar vein, an advertisement for the AEG hair dryer, for instance, features a manservant blow-drying a poodle and a pampered child using it on her bear (fig. 1.10). In another, a woman is drying photographic plates, then still a pastime of the affluent. Well-to-do children are also portrayed playing with fully operational child-size cooking stoves, electric trains, and a dangerous-looking toy that consisted of an electrically heated steam engine attached to a dynamo (fig. 1.11).[27] The dynamo could light two to three miniature AEG street lamps, while the belt pulley attached to the engine worked little power tools, including a tiny band saw and a grindstone. The firm also offered an electric kaleidoscope for sale (fig. 1.12).

To evoke consumer desire for its technical objects and to create occasions for spending money on not-yet-essential products, the AEG aggressively marketed its objects as presents. Peter Behrens later recalled that a top executive at the company, Paul Jordan, once declared that the company's motors "must look like a birthday present."[28] One AEG electric iron came prepackaged in an imitation gold-hammered gift box with a purple ribbon (fig. 1.13).[29] Christmas was an important season for marketing the goods, which was done through elaborate Christmas windows and articles highlighting objects that would be appropriate as gifts. In one article, the AEG posited the objects in both appealing and functional terms, as "delicate" and "alluring" as well as "exceptionally practical," and on the ensuing pages lyrical words described the gift potential of travel irons, hair dryers, electric perfume atomizers, and even an electric "face and body massager."[30] Labeling these as "magnificent *modern* Christmas presents," the firm asserted that technological objects could be as luxurious as other types of gifts.[31] The AEG electric heater by Behrens, which featured hammered and decorated surfaces, goes one step further perhaps, in that it takes the outer appearance of a Carolingian reliquary, an elaborate housing that offered up electrically generated heat rather than precious relics. Electricity, then, was a luxurious amenity, and electricity-consuming objects were marketed to—and used by—the most affluent strata of society in this period. Behrens's stores were designed to serve as a space of exhibition and acquisition of AEG electrical goods, especially domestic objects.

Figure 1.9. "The Modern, Electrically Configured Residential Building," *Mitteilungen der Berliner Elektricitäts-Werke*, 1911. Image of affluent inhabitants accompanying the article.

Figure 1.10. Advertisement, AEG electric hair dryer, 1911.

Figure 1.11. AEG electric engine, 1911.

Figure 1.12. AEG electric kaleidoscope, 1911. Cover of the catalog and price list.

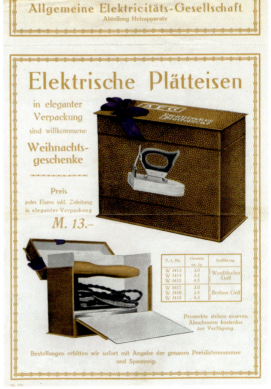

Figure 1.13. Advertisement, AEG electric iron, 1912.

THE AEG STORES: SUMPTUOUS MODERN INDUSTRY

Now nearly forgotten, the two stores designed by Peter Behrens in the center of Berlin represented the AEG in highly visible ways. They were intentionally situated to present modern technology and design to a growing, consuming public, drawing them to the AEG's electricity-consuming kettles and fans through the elegant modernism of the stores themselves (see figs. 1.2, 1.3). The famous industrial buildings designed by the architect were located in working-class, industrial areas of the city, such as Wedding and Moabit, and well beyond its limits, in places such as Hennigsdorf, where the teakettles were produced. These factories, also representative of the AEG's industrial modernism, would have been known mainly to those who worked or lived in those areas, to businessmen and tradesmen who visited these sites, and to readers of architectural publications, where Behrens's work was prominently featured. To note this is not to undermine the importance of Behrens's iconic AEG Turbine Factory and his other pathbreaking modern buildings celebrated by architects in his period, which continues to the present day. Rather, the aim here is to recognize the ways in which the Behrens-designed stores played a crucial role in making the modern products of industry alluring by situating them in the luxurious context of the AEG stores.

With the stores, the AEG made the decision to sell electrical objects directly to the public in spaces it could control: refined and elegant, they were aligned aesthetically and materially with key qualities of what would coalesce in the modern architectural movement, and yet they were carefully domesticated. At its own stores, the company was able to feature its goods in a suitable space and undercut the profit margin to be garnered by other retail outlets, while simultaneously eradicating the need for middlemen (although AEG goods were still sold elsewhere during this period).[32] Prior to their construction, the AEG had maintained a basement exhibition space in its administration building for commercial resellers. The new stores contrasted markedly with this previous site—they were glistening modern emporiums, laden with the best-designed products. Representing a change in focus from turbine buyers to winning over an expanded base of domestic consumers, the opening of

Figure 1.14. Mercedes showroom, Königgrätzer Strasse, Berlin, 1906.

Zander & Labisch, Phot., Berlin.

Die Automobile des „Mercedes-Palast" im Nernstlicht.

these stores and the way they presented goods signaled a major shift in the larger agenda of the company and the shaping of its image to the public.

The stores could have been built on the ground floor of any of the many buildings that the AEG owned in prominent locations around Berlin, including in the centrally located main administration building. However the sites for the stores—Königgrätzer Strasse and Potsdamer Strasse—were selected very carefully, on well-known, major thoroughfares in the well-to-do shopping districts of the period. The two streets both featured a mixture of stores, hotels, sumptuous single-family townhouses (many from the 1870s and 1880s), and apartment buildings.[33] Königgrätzer Strasse was a particularly fashionable shopping street in the center of Berlin, extending both north and south from Potsdamer Platz. Lined with major hotels and elegant restaurants, the other well-appointed stores on the street—including retailers of luxury furs, Steinway pianos, and Mercedes cars—indicate the general level of affluence of its patrons and the context into which the AEG inserted its first shop (fig. 1.14).[34]

The first Behrens-designed AEG store, 4 Königgrätzer Strasse, was carved out of the ground floor of an existing neo-Renaissance residence (fig. 1.15). Behrens

Figure 1.15. Schlüter and Berger, residential house, 4 Königgrätzer Strasse, Berlin, 1876–77, photograph c. 1880.

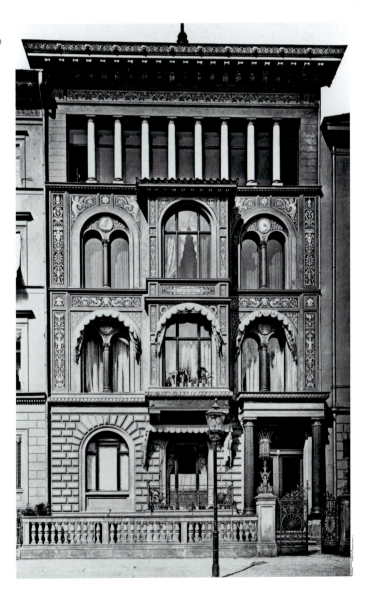

sheared off the facade of rusticated stone that had adorned the ground floor, replacing it with a flat plaster storefront (fig. 1.16). Published photographs of the store were cropped to show just the new plate glass front, obscuring the rest of the building and presenting the store as if it were part of a wholly modern building (see fig. 1.1).

In the display portion of the window, a circumscribed range of goods was initially grouped by type on the floor and raised up on black fabric-covered plinths (see fig. 1.1). Of the electric heaters, fans, and kettles on display, Behrens's designs are neither exclusively nor especially prominently displayed, but rather simply lined up in the front while non-Behrens designs are singled out on their own plinths (this was also the case for the wares displayed inside the store). This seems to suggest that while Behrens's improvements to AEG designs were important to the company's new selling strategies, the redesign of individual goods was not its only focus. Existing

Figure 1.16. Behrens, AEG store, 4 Königgrätzer Strasse, Berlin, 1910, photograph 1911.

product lines and goods not designed by Behrens were also prominently displayed. What was new for the firm was this luxurious architectural context—the Behrens-designed AEG shop—into which gleaming electrical goods were placed. These products were displayed by means of a variety of methods (plinth, vitrine, shelves, and tabletop), enhanced by Behrens's opulent interior architecture and furnishings, and new graphical elements, all of which contributed to an innovative, integrated commercial strategy for the AEG.

Shortly after opening, the store window was updated with elegant, modern metal and glass shelving for the display of wares (fig. 1.17). Two years later, in 1912, an electrically illuminated sign made up of tiny light bulbs forming the hexagonal company logo was added to the facade; placed perpendicular to the building, it would have been highly visible to pedestrians walking down the street (fig. 1.18). The AEG touted the importance of "good taste" in lighting, citing its own store as particularly indicative of "artistic design" in *Lichtreklame* (advertising lighting).[35] The lighting installed within the window itself was praised by a period architectural critic in the journal *Deutsche Bauhütte* as bringing about the effect of a "distinguished, gentle gleam" in the appliances on display.[36] This window was similarly lauded in the Werkbund's *Yearbook* for "enthralling viewers in the street" through its illumination and "innervating" marble walls, and subsequently drawing them inside to its comfortably furnished interiors.[37]

One entered the store via a small foyer that provided an intimate prelude to the main interior (fig. 1.19). It was a light-filled space dominated by a magnificent veined marble fireplace that featured decorative grillwork covering an electric heating element. Above it a mirror reflected the wares shelved on the walls of the showroom, setting the stage, through a set of curtains, for the interior's opulence.

Entering the main space, customers immediately encountered built-in glass and polished bronze vitrines that formed niches for a row of three leather club chairs

Figure 1.17. Behrens, AEG store window, 4 Königgrätzer Strasse, Berlin, 1910.

and the mounted wall mirrors interspersed between vitrines (see fig. 1.5). Three of the vitrines had carefully arranged electrical goods in them, while a fourth featured opaque glass with a list of the available goods and prices. The niches were continued in the wall structure above, with each span capped by a row of dentils. Single light bulbs in metal fixtures formed an outer ring along the ceiling. Along the back and left side, wall-length vitrines lined the room, each filled with objects in rows, arranged according to type and size. Two sales counters contained larger electrical appliances, and still larger machines were placed directly on the floor.

A door at the far end of the main showroom led to a series of back rooms, less ostentatious in nature than the outer showroom, yet still modern and *sachlich* in their straightforward simplicity (fig. 1.20). Here goods were laid out in rows, placed atop unadorned white cabinets, rather than in glistening metal and glass vitrines. Similarly, the heavy leather club chairs of the main salesroom were eschewed in favor of simple wooden chairs, an early response to the period's call for *Typen-Möbel*, or "type furniture." Behrens carried his framing device from the facade window into the depth of the interior by creating a series of half-walls with a similar beveled profile. This section of the store featured electric tools, heaters, and small motors on which attachments could be mounted to create a variety of kitchen appliances, such as meat grinders and juicers, among other less alluring, more utilitarian AEG goods.

Behrens designed a second store for the AEG at 117 Potsdamer Strasse, which opened in the spring of 1911 (see figs. 1.6, 1.7).[38] It was again a refurbishment of the ground floor of an existing building and likewise featured the modern flat expanse of an unarticulated facade (here in marble) and a large, floor-to-ceiling plate glass window. The AEG's name was on every exterior surface: incised on the white marble architrave across the top of the storefront, as a logo on the entrance door, in painted lettering underneath the display window, and on the marble slabs flanking each

Figure 1.18. Behrens, AEG sign in electric lights, 4 Königgrätzer Strasse, Berlin, 1910, sign added 1912.

Figure 1.19. Behrens, AEG store, entrance vestibule, 4 Königgrätzer Strasse, Berlin, 1910.

side, which also listed the objects sold within. Strikingly modern in 1911, this store was commended along with its companion, for having the same "bold conception and clarity" (*Grosszügigkeit und Klarheit*) as Behrens's factory buildings.[39] The modern nature of the AEG ensemble is most apparent when compared with the two adjacent storefronts—the door to the left is in an earlier, ornate style, and the signage above it is in an out-of-date Jugendstil typeface, while the store window to the right is packed with goods—both in marked contrast with the simple elegance of Behrens's design (see fig. 1.6).

THE ALLURE OF *SACHLICHKEIT*

The stores represent a clear break from the AEG's strategy of exhibiting goods in its "permanent showroom," a centralized space reserved for industrial tradesmen to view its factories' output. Maintained from 1886 onward, the permanent showroom was a series of crowded, unimaginative spaces filled with technical objects produced by the AEG, such as gauges and industrial motors, which overshadowed the fewer domestic goods that were on display. Usually located in the basement of its main administration building, the AEG relocated it several times over the history of the company, along with its administrative offices. Staffed by trained employees, the company intended the exhibition space to alleviate the need for trade buyers to visit several factories to view different categories of products by exhibiting and demonstrating the company's entire range of offerings in one place.[40] The AEG had sold domestic goods such as teakettles and cigar lighters very early on; for example, these objects were on display at an 1889 exhibition at the Lehrter Bahnhof, and earlier, when the company was still called the Deutsche Edison-Gesellschaft, it offered various small appliances for sale. In 1892, the AEG began producing electric irons,

Figure 1.20. Behrens, AEG store, back showrooms, 4 Königgrätzer Strasse, Berlin, 1910, photograph 1911.

and by 1896, its product catalog cited eighty appliances, including several irons (one of brass and one marketed as a nickel-plated "household" version), as well as electric curling tongs, water kettles, filter coffee machines, hot plates, and plate warmers.[41] The first AEG hair dryer appeared in 1899.[42]

Just prior to the completion of his first store, Behrens designed a new permanent exhibition space located in the AEG's Ackerstrasse appliance factory (figs. 1.21, 1.22). Motors, machines, gauges, and other electrical objects were placed in display cases, hung from the ceiling and mounted on the walls along with carefully lettered labels; precisely—even decoratively—arranged and set out in clearly delineated sections by object type. This informative space functioned differently from the stores—the latest goods were displayed as both whole objects and as single parts, because many industrial buyers purchased only switches, for instance, from the AEG. In this way, the company sought to differentiate between sales spaces intended for those in the trade versus domestic consumers, in settings that performed different didactic functions. Thus the goods available in the new Behrens-designed stores represent less the selling of new products themselves, but the selling of AEG goods directly to an entirely new audience in a strikingly modern architectural context.

The AEG could have built a single, major store, akin to the popular department stores of the period, but instead multiple sites on a more intimate and manageable scale were conceived. The Behrens design of the goods, the store facade and interior architecture, the locations on a major elite shopping hub, and the display techniques all served to lead away from the positing of electrical goods as "technical" objects of industry and to present them as luxury domestic objects. Period observers lauded Behrens's efforts; for example, one critic in 1913 wrote, "Out of storerooms that obscured vision and stockyards indifferent to their stacked up wares [Behrens] created rhythmically divided spaces that released each object from its mass-produced nature and permitted it to be seen in its individual singularity and quality."[43] The stores were both salesrooms and places of exhibition, semi-domestic spaces intended to orient consumers to electro-technical goods and imagine their place in their own homes—from the electric cigar lighter to the hot water heater.[44] According to period critic Fritz Hoeber, the AEG specifically sought to achieve more direct contact with the wider public, and Hoeber saw the turn to retail and the individual consumer as part of a larger cultural policy shift at the firm, one in which "elegantly formed" manufactured objects would be sold in Behrens's modern "exquisite, architectonic showrooms."[45]

The stores exemplified specific concepts from modern architecture, such as that of *Sachlichkeit* (straightforwardness, objectivity), that in turn helped sell goods. *Sachlichkeit* as a positive term occurs frequently in period writing about Behrens's work for the AEG.[46] Critics praised both his buildings and other work for the firm as displaying "good, clear *Sachlichkeit*."[47] Another commended Behrens's stores' "clean, calm *Sachlichkeit*," and, after describing the spareness of the few carefully selected, geometrically arranged objects placed on shiny, reflective surfaces, the reviewer advanced the opinion that the designer sought to "create a mood of taut energy."[48] Architectural critic Fritz Meyer-Schönbrunn, writing in 1912, pointed out that Behrens applied the same design approach to all of his display-related architecture, which became a means of publicity for the AEG: "With the same *Sachlichkeit* Behrens reformed every organ of modern advertising through his tasteful, effective

Figure 1.21. Behrens, design of the permanent exhibition, AEG Appliance Factory, Ackerstrasse, Berlin, 1910.

Figure 1.22. Behrens, design of the permanent exhibition, AEG Appliance Factory.

methods, which from year to year became more important: the exhibition buildings, the store window designs, and the stores."[49]

More than its peers, Emil Rathenau's AEG represented the powerful and widely influential interaction of investment capital, industrial enterprise, and—most important here—highly organized marketing.[50] If consumer desire was initially stimulated through the high visibility of the products through plate glass windows on two major city thoroughfares, the display windows working in conjunction with the stores' facades and interiors gave an enticing and luxurious context to these objects.[51] Luxury was directly referenced by the AEG with regard to its electric objects, which it described as "elegant" and "alluring" and as "enveloping themselves in an atmosphere of luxury."[52] Critics, too, praised the small appliances as pleasing through their "elegant, edgy vitality."[53] Period writers cited the decisive economic advantage of the stores as raising the *Kauflust*, literally "buying desire," of consumers.[54] Within this context, the stores were key to the AEG's divesting itself of its "factory" aura and its efforts to generate consumer desire for electrical objects.

Economist and sociologist Werner Sombart, in his important 1913 book *Luxury and Capitalism*, characterized luxury as "any expenditure in excess of the necessary" with the "necessary" evaluated both *subjectively* against an ethical or aesthetic value, and *objectively*, measured in "man's physiological needs or in what may be called his cultural wants."[55] The AEG products were luxury objects in both senses outlined by Sombart—evoking aesthetic and cultural desire. Sombart argued that luxury contributed in significant ways to the development of modern capitalism and that the exchange value of commodities was determined by two factors: the rapidity of turnover via the extensive sale of mass products or the more limited sale of high-priced goods.[56] With its factory capacity and technology, and its reserves of capital, the AEG could have selected either route, but chose the latter. Also significant here is Sombart's determination that "the most appreciated factor in luxury was its effectiveness in creating new markets" which the AEG achieved—creating a modernism that was simultaneously bold and cautious, and constituted its consumers by singularly merging industry with luxury to create consumer desire for its products.[57]

Through modernism a world of subtle commerce prevailed within the AEG stores, one that was very different from the synesthesia tactics practiced by the enormous department stores a block away. The prominence of the materials of modern architecture—flat planes of glass, opaque glass wall surfaces, metal-edging and a bare bulb-studded ceiling—combined with the reassurance of traditionally lavish materials of veined marble, leather, and silk resulted in store interiors in which "modernism" was insistently luxurious. Modern architecture, too, acted as a bridge for the *physical* and *conceptual* transition made by the AEG's products themselves in this period: from products of industry to luxury consumer goods.

PRESAGING THE AEG STRATEGY: BEHRENS'S ELITE
SURROUNDINGS FOR MASS-PRODUCED PRODUCTS

An important precedent for the AEG stores in Berlin was the store Behrens designed for Josef Klein in Hagen three years earlier, a luxurious setting similarly intended for the sale of a modern, factory-made product—in this case linoleum and wallpaper (fig. 1.23).[58] This early modern store combined massive expanses of exterior floor-to-ceiling plate glass with a series of interior partitions on which sample wares were mounted. This highly visible display technique, aided by an equally transparent side entrance foyer, allowed the maximum exposure of the goods from the street. In both Berlin and Hagen, nighttime illumination rendered the windows effective at all times. Here, electric lights illuminated the entire space handsomely, beckoning customers by means of large, bright lights at the entranceway, a line of simple hanging lights just inside the windows, and a grid of bulbs in the coffers of the ceiling. Behrens designed a large portal with Greek patterning motifs for the building's residents and to the right, a smaller, less monumental entrance door for the store. Period critic Fritz Hoeber noted the unusual arrangement in which the plate glass window bent around and continued the length of the entranceway, resulting in the "entire interior of the store being given over for sale to the public."[59] The obfuscation of the store's entrance in favor of this expanse of windows underscores Behrens's nuanced understanding of the importance of display in selling modern goods. And this remarkable opening up of the interior illustrates one way in which his stores should be read as an early and important exemplification of the larger ideas of the modern movement in architecture.

The architecture of Behrens's windows, especially their straightforward, virtually continuous layout, situates them in a broader movement taking place in window display generally, and the Werkbund's ideals more specifically—in which clarity, simplicity, rhythm, and patterning took precedence. A newly developing goal was that of presenting goods—especially modern objects—simply and in a highly legible way, so that the *sachlich* qualities of the wares could be admired. This was in opposition to the plenitude and the cacophony of objects as they were normally displayed in store windows, and against the kitschy narratives, so familiar in the windows of large department stores. Rather than creating the usual shallow display area, which only afforded the presentation of selected goods in an artificially delineated subspace, here Behrens's window opened up the entire interior world of the store to the outside. Karl Ernst Osthaus, in his crucial article "Das Schaufenster" (The display window)

Figure 1.23. Behrens, Josef Klein wallpaper and linoleum store, Hagen, 1905-7.

for the Werkbund's 1913 *Yearbook*, highlights Behrens's device of using the transparency and framelessness of the street-facade windows to collapse the space in such a way that from the perspective of the viewer, all of the goods between the window and the store's rear wall appeared as if they were affixed to—and framed by—the back wall.[60] This is a key early example of modern architecture's emerging emphasis on openness and transparency and presages Weimar-era attention to surface and flattening that would become so important in art, architecture, and modern display techniques.[61]

Inside, the relatively small floor plan was counteracted by the soaring height of the store, an effect that was enhanced by the grid of light bulbs in the ceiling that carried the eye upward. The open space and height allowed for the installation of wallpaper and linoleum in large swaths, with the half-walls placed in the middle of the store, preventing the creation of a warrenlike effect while still allowing many samples to be displayed simultaneously and in substantial quantities. This solution was particularly effective for the large-sized motif repetitions of the Wiener Werkstätte designs, but also, generally, allowed prospective customers to see the overall patterning effects of a given design, rather than having to imagine how the repeat of the pattern would appear.[62]

The nature of the commission—a store for linoleum and wallpaper—is significant. Invented in 1860 and made from solidified linseed oil, linoleum was popular with modern designers who viewed it as a less expensive and more hygienic substitute for wood, marble, or other flooring. Wallpaper, too, was promoted by modern architects as a hygienic covering as well as a simple intervention in the modernizing of a home.[63] Here is an important precursor to the AEG stores, in which alluring modern architecture was a mediating factor between an industrial product and consumers; this opulent point of sale helped to move linoleum away from its manufactured origins toward its intended domestic end, without covering up its modern associations.

In addition to the Josef Klein store, Behrens was engaged in several projects for the linoleum company Anker-Marke between 1905 and 1910.[64] He designed his first pavilion for Anker-Marke in the summer of 1905, for the *Northwest German Art Exhibition* (*Nordwestdeutsche Kunstausstellung*) in Oldenburg, followed by a pavilion for the *Third German Arts and Crafts Exhibition* (*Dritte Deutsche Kunstgewerbeausstellung*) in Dresden, in the summer of 1906. The spare, predominantly white pavilion interior at the *Northwest German Art Exhibition* featured a fitted display table with raw materials and semifinished product samples, behind which were full-sized rolls of finished linoleum, effectively laying out the stages of production while disassociating the products from the industrial process itself, inserting them in a modern architectural context instead. At the 1910 world's fair in Brussels, Behrens designed a third linoleum display for Anker, this time in the German section of the fair. He also created several linoleum patterns for Anker-Marke: a saccharine one featuring rabbits, birds, and gazelle in foliage, and three others consisting of much more *sachlich* designs—two with squares and circles in contrasting colors, and the one with repeating triangles in shades of gray.[65] In addition to Behrens, other well-known modern architects and designers, including Henry van de Velde, Josef Hoffmann, and Richard Riemerschmid, were invited by Anker-Marke to design patterns. Behrens also designed the logo and all of the office stationery for Anker-Marke in 1905–6.[66]

Begun two years prior to the commencement of his tenure at the AEG, Behrens's work for Anker-Marke was similar in scope—if not in scale—to that for the AEG. Behrens created Anker-Marke's corporate identity through the design of its trademark, several products, and, most important, through modern, well-designed structures for exhibiting its products; these provided significant exposure for the firm's commercial buyers and general consumers alike. A similar project for the AEG was Behrens's octagonal pavilion at the 1908 *Berlin Shipbuilding Exhibition* (*Schiffbauausstellung*) about which one period reviewer designated Behrens's role not as one strengthening the image of the technical prowess of the company, but as a "bringer of culture" (*Kulturbringer*) via the pavilion.[67] In all of the commissions, Behrens employed an overall design aesthetic in which the products on display were integrated with their enclosing spaces in a visually alluring manner, by means of such modern tropes as large expanses of glass, ample flat surfaces, the employment of new materials, and careful lighting.

By creating attractive displays and a corporate identity for Anker-Marke, a company that, like the AEG, sought to expand its consumer base from industrial buyers to domestic customers, he set a precedent. Behrens, at this point in his career well-known for his work at the artists' colony in Darmstadt and as a professor at the Düsseldorf Art Academy, was transitioning to his pivotal role as a mediator between industry and the buying public via modern architecture and design. The decision by the AEG to hire Behrens has long been seen as pathbreaking, but through his work for Josef Klein in Hagen and for Anker-Marke, he brought to the company significant experience in the design of industrial products, the creation of corporate identity, and exhibition design and display. Thus his tenure at the AEG might be viewed as remarkable more for the scale and speed of implementation (the many large buildings, showrooms, graphic and product designs in the relatively short period of 1907–14), and, chiefly, for the new associations he was able to forge, via consumer desire and modernism, between industrial objects and luxury.

Furthermore, the stores and pavilions that Behrens designed for the AEG and Anker-Marke provided a crucial context for the objects—the teapot promised both the luxury of tabletop hot water in an exquisite form and the modernism implied by owning a well-functioning electrical appliance; similarly the "good taste" indicated by a Behrens or Henry van de Velde linoleum design was combined with the modern ease of maintaining the linoleum itself. Anker-Marke and the AEG are just two examples from this period in which industrial producers sought to create consumer desire for their products through redesign rather than technical change. The real innovation taking place was in their pared-down modern displays and in the very act of making those goods desirable for consumers, which was mediated by the modern architectural movement, its materials, and its ideologies.

SMALL SHOP VERSUS LARGE DEPARTMENT STORE: THE AEG STORES IN THEIR SOCIO-URBAN CONTEXT

The AEG stores were strikingly modern; when compared with other Berlin stores they can be seen as austere gems that instantly conveyed the coveted, luxurious nature of the goods sold within. Certainly the two stores were a divergence from other period small-scale shops, even those by fellow early modern architects, such as Henry van de Velde's fussy and overwrought Jugendstil-style showroom for arts and crafts objects on the nearby Leipziger Strasse (fig. 1.24). The limited number of goods on display at any one moment, and the overall clarity of Behrens's stores and their windows also set them apart from the average small store in 1910; a more typical example is a purveyor of blouses and skirts at 37 Rosenthaler Strasse in which the windows are filled from floor to ceiling, and even the wall space surrounding the windows is hung with shirts (fig. 1.25). This is the type of store window that the Werkbund sought to reform in precisely the same period.

Behrens's stores were akin to the earlier high-end specialty stores in shopping arcades, or *Passagen*. One such example is the 1907–9 Friedrichstrasse arcade, a modern structure of reinforced concrete that featured electric lighting throughout and large plate glass display windows along its interior street.[68] This arcade boasted more than one hundred elegant small specialty stores aimed at affluent shoppers and featured goods such as oriental carpets. Like boutiques or the luxury stores of the arcades, the locale of the AEG stores indicated that they were welcoming only the class of consumers who could potentially buy their goods. While window-shoppers were invited to envy the electrical objects through the plate glass windows, the marble slabs prevented a direct view into the store itself, which remained a space of privilege.

The AEG could have reached the mass-consuming public by contracting to sell its products in Berlin's major department stores, but it is precisely this environment that the company was reacting against.[69] The physical massiveness of the department stores was remarkable, with new stores and ever larger expansions executed in this period (fig. 1.26). Their impressive facades ran the length of Berlin's oversized city blocks, and their main interior spaces were equally expansive, presenting a wide range of goods to all classes of buyers, and, importantly, browsers.

Visual exclusivity, then, was a key aspect of the allure of the AEG's presentation. At the department stores a virtually unlimited, dizzying array of goods was available in a wide range of prices, enticing in consumers of varying means; vast assortments of products can be seen in nearly every image of any department of the major stores of this period, for example, in Wertheim's lighting department (fig. 1.27). In contrast, the AEG stores offered a more circumscribed number of styles, sizes, and materials at prices that could not have had as high a turnover rate, nor as many customers crossing their thresholds. Early on, a central component of modernism was demonstrated—the offering of a limited selection of accepted types with the architect's role as arbiter of taste. Taste was not left to the whims and vagaries of the buying public; it was implied, or rather it was assured by stepping through the well-appointed threshold of an AEG store and examining its sparse vitrines.

The department stores, on the other hand, welcomed many and catered to a full spectrum of tastes. Paul Göhre, in his 1907 book *Das Warenhaus* (The department store) noted that the core goods types were essentially the same between stores, but the quality and selection differed, as did the makeup of the departments.[70] At this time, a general association existed between specific department stores and the income and social standing of their clientele. Göhre outlined these social divisions between the stores, and his investigation led him to conclude that Wertheim shoppers were from more upper-class social groups, while Tietz garnered the "good middle class," and Jandorf attracted the "better workers."[71] Significantly, these were only broad class markers, and Göhre was careful to point out that the more affluent shoppers

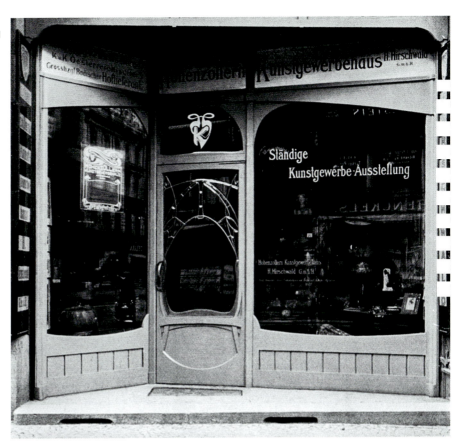

Figure 1.24. Henry van de Velde, Hohenzollern Applied Arts store and showroom, Berlin, 1904.

Figure 1.25. Blouse and skirt store, 37 Rosenthaler Strasse, photograph 1910.

Figure 1.26. Alfred Messel, Wertheim department store, interior, Berlin, 1896–1906, photograph, 1903–4.

Figure 1.27. Lighting department, Wertheim department store, Berlin 1904.

were also to be found at Jandorf's and that "simple workers" sometimes shopped at Wertheim's.[72] The three strata of shoppers for each store was echoed by Leo Colze, writing a year later in 1908, who considered Wertheim's a "luxury department store" (*Luxuswarenhaus*) for the circle of Berliners with the most purchasing power (*kaufkräftigsten*), with Tietz, again, for the *Mittelstand* and Jandorf for the workers.[73] But he pointed out that even the *kleiner Mann*, or petit bourgeois man on the street, sought to buy so-called luxury goods for which he had practically no need, a situation that Colze identified as a key source of income for the "modern department store organism."[74]

The large department stores sought to bring the prices of goods down to the point at which many people could afford to shop there; the result of smaller profit margins was counteracted by higher sales volumes (and more foot traffic). Tietz advertised this strategy to its customers as "greater turnover—smaller profits" (*grosser Umsatz—kleiner Nutzen*). Similarly, the prices for simple goods at Wertheim's were considerably lower than elsewhere, certainly aimed at luring the masses through the doors and hoping to entice them to purchase additional goods, which were compatible with prices at other stores.[75]

Thus, the department stores were instrumental in luring in the previously disenfranchised *kleiner Mann*—to acquire items he did not need and could scarcely afford, according to the period's reformers, a critique that coalesced in the Werkbund's campaign for well-designed, high-quality goods. However, because perceived "luxury articles" could be fairly inexpensively and universally obtained owing to the industrialized process of their manufacture, a predicament emerged for the AEG. It had to find a way to make its mass-produced objects desirable enough to compete with other similarly manufactured goods, and refined enough to warrant their expense over non-AEG or equally functioning nonelectric products.

BEHRENS'S AEG OBJECTS: REAPPRAISING THE DESIGN PROCESS

While the stores set the context for the objects, decisions surrounding the design or redesign of the products themselves represent another crucial shift in focus for the AEG and Behrens's role therein. During his tenure from 1907 to 1914, he redesigned certain AEG products, such as the fans and teakettles, but not others that the company aggressively promoted during the same years (see figs. 1.2, 1.3).[76] Entering the AEG stores, the customer would have been presented with a collection of goods designed by Behrens, but an equal or greater number of other objects not designed by anyone of note, such as the electric cigar lighters, hair dryers, toasters, irons, vacuum cleaners, and the motorized toys for children, including the electrically revolving kaleidoscope. These non-Behrens designs were featured prominently in the AEG's windows and in print advertisements, on shelves adjacent to Behrens designs (see fig. 1.17).[77] The distinction appears to be that the AEG had Behrens redesign objects that would have been on display in the public areas of the home, predominantly the dining and living rooms, such as the electric teakettles, fans, clocks, and humidifiers, as well as electric space heaters and fireplaces. The fans, clocks, and especially the kettles—appropriate for a dining room sideboard or a living room tea niche, an amenity that was very popular in this period—were all luxury electrical goods that visually signaled wealth in addition to providing modern comfort for the proprietors of the house. Electrical objects that were not likely to be on view or that were intended to ease the burden of the domestic help, such as irons, the early AEG vacuums, or electric stoves, were not designed by Behrens.

The AEG's managers made decisions regarding goods for redesign with respect to financial impact. In 1906, the year before Behrens joined the AEG, the company sold 2,727 appliances, including 2,097 fans but only 90 coffee grinders and roasters.[78] As one of his initial tasks, Behrens would work on the redesign of the briskly selling fan (which was also an object that would have been prominently displayed in the home or office and stood to benefit from an improved external design). Behrens understood that each new redesign meant a large financial investment on the part of the company, as well as a long design process working closely with its engineers, as architectural critic Fritz Hoeber was at pains to point out as early as 1913.[79] The investment paid off for the AEG, as Behrens's designs did impact resulting sales. There is ample evidence that the company was able to reap the rewards of the initial outlay for his work. The redesign of the arc lamps cost 200,000 marks, but the company was able to recoup that money and make a profit within a year, for example.[80]

In design and architecture circles in the period, Behrens's name became inextricably associated with the AEG, and his employment there was taken to symbolize the company's foresight in employing a designer to improve the aesthetic qualities of its industrial products. It was a concept very much part of the nascent Werkbund's and other architects' ideas at that time. And yet, outside of these select, artistic circles, in which his work for the AEG was greatly celebrated, Behrens's name was seldom advertised or linked to the products; his role was mainly behind the scenes. Not only were his designs not singled out in AEG store displays, but scarcely any print or publicity materials featured his name.[81] Instead, the company merely characterized the Behrens objects in its new store as "revealing the personal style of a notable artist."[82] The AEG put its faith in the tangible, visible improvements that Behrens could offer to its architecture, products, and advertising materials. Using Behrens's objects became a means of selling more goods to a consuming public: the firm was unconcerned with his growing status as a design luminary.

The AEG was very clear about the role that Behrens played vis-à-vis the redesign of its products and that his task was to visually improve existing objects by recasting their housings.[83] The famous Behrens teakettles retained the same technical design as previous models, which, notably, were kept in production, even after the new models entered the market; older models were even displayed in its stores alongside the new ones (see figs. 1.1, 1.6). Moreover, Behrens did not celebrate the industrial qualities or functions of the modern, electric kettles but instead visually distanced these electrical appliances from their mass-produced origins and brought them closer to luxury goods. He did so by referencing the earlier arts and crafts movement's visual vocabulary of handcraftsmanship, visible in the versions with machine-hammered surfaces that mimicked the appearance of hand-hammering. This is also true of the caned handles and the nickel plating, which resembled silver. The teakettles, then, although simple and elegant in design, were not undecorated and not without ornament. Behrens himself acknowledged the perceived need for more lavish versions in terms of the quality and finish of the goods, noting: "In addition to the standard models, however, there is in many cases a demand for a slightly more luxurious version using better materials (such as tombac), on which a degree of ornamentation is more justified."[84] In the kettles, he combines simple geometric forms in the body with a judicious use of materials and ornament—evidenced in the delicate finial at the top of the kettle, the weave of its handle's caning, the care with which the seemingly simple joint that links the caned handle to the metal body is designed, and in the highly polished or hammered finish of its surfaces (see fig. 1.2). He made them much more visually enticing and salable, elevating them from the average teakettles available on the market. In the glass and metal vitrines of the AEG stores, these electric kettles were nearly always displayed in serial fashion and grouped by shape, a gentle reference to their mass production (see fig. 1.5). Simultaneously, they conjured modernism and classicism, bespoke everyday rituals and an elite.

And yet, they never became as ubiquitous as could have been foreseen, given their aesthetics, usefulness, and the scale at which the AEG was capable of producing them. For example, at the Werkbund's 1927 exhibition *Die Wohnung*, the AEG had its own display stand of products in the main exhibition hall, but its goods were conspicuously absent in images of the actual apartments and houses in the development built outside Stuttgart. While electrical stoves and hot water heaters were showcased in these modern dwellings, electric kettles are noticeably absent; instead traditional water kettles can be seen placed on the stoves themselves, such as in the kitchen of Gropius's house (fig. 1.28).

At the AEG, Behrens did not produce more technically modern or functionally advanced objects—the company employed many engineers for that task. Rather, he translated these electrical goods for a select consuming audience by sensitively applying the *language* of modernism; this made them enticing and desirable and yet not so visually extreme as to estrange the AEG's upper-bourgeois customers. The AEG promoted them as such; for example, in 1908 the company touted his redesigned arc lamp as having "modern clothing" and highlighted the fact that the lamp had a "new aesthetic role" to play (see fig. 1.4).[85] Simultaneously, the firm was at pains not to alienate consumers with this new modernity; in the same article, the lamp's green was judged "friendlier" and the bronze edging promoted as "lively," and hence the lamp was now more appropriate for domestic settings.[86] His role at the AEG was well understood in his day. An architectural critic writing in 1911 noted that an essential and primary activity of Behrens was in the shaping of the material form—or *Gestalt*—of these technical objects, resulting in the emergence of good-looking types, an idea very much in currency during the period.[87]

Behrens maintained a carefully articulated position with respect to the design of industrial goods, in which he advocated for aesthetic success through restraint. He called for the products of his age to be constructed cleanly and do justice to the materials used, not to strive for the creation of an "egregiously new form" but rather to draw from the "good taste" of one's own time.[88] He renounced mass-produced trinkets that failed to serve any clear purpose, as well as purely functional objects, in favor of products that exhibited a formal simplicity and a harmony of relations between their required elements; he also called for mass-produced goods to acknowledge their status as one exemplar among many rather than for each object to seek a "pretentious subjectivity" for itself.[89] This modern restraint was key, and in the same vein, the AEG described its goods as demonstrating their purpose without "grandiosity."[90] An essential problem was that the machine-made goods had to compete with both real luxury objects, that is, handmade goods of expensive materials, and the impostor luxury goods produced cheaply by machine. Behrens and the AEG, working in concert, produced a third variant: luxurious modernism. They presented a collection of machine-made goods that were modern, tasteful, well designed, and profitable, yet they remained elite objects—shown in a luxurious context, costly to acquire, and destined for an exceptional domestic space.

———

In a time of shifting and uncertain class identity, the acquisition and use of the AEG's electrical objects can be seen as fulfilling not only perceived technological, but also social and cultural, ambitions and desires. Beyond the simple level of comfort

Figure 1.28. Walter Gropius, house number 16, kitchen, Weissenhof Housing Settlement, Stuttgart, 1927. Electric stove with water kettle.

that the presence of electricity in the home brought an owner, because it and its power-consuming objects were so expensive to acquire, it also conspicuously signaled wealth, as images of electrified homes underscore. While electricity can be tied directly to luxury in this way, it is also part of a practice of consumption, not only at the moment of the purchase of a Behrens teakettle, but in the simple presence of electricity as an indicator of consumption *yet to occur*. This was also a period of ersatz luxury—of readily available department store products such as artificial silk and cheaply ornamented objects in imitation of finely crafted ones, an outcome of the technical revolution that had arrived in Germany later than in other countries, such as England. But electricity signaled true luxury: it remained expensive in the early part of the twentieth century, and it was not possible to simulate its presence. With its factory capacity and technological expertise, as well as its reserves of capital, the AEG could have elected to mass-produce and widely distribute its domestic electrical products but chose the latter route instead—a limited selection of higher-priced wares sold in its own stores. Thus, for the AEG, the marketing of luxurious, electricity-consuming objects went hand in hand with the promotion of electricity itself. A sophisticated marketing strategy emerged, one that involved the role Behrens played in encouraging the consumption of these technological, modern products, and the related selective access to technology. The architecture of the AEG stores, the objects themselves, and the wider meaning of electricity in this period all contributed to a shift in the valuation of AEG products—separate from their intrinsic, technical value as individual objects—to that of luxury goods.

The history of electricity has long been linked to the idea of democracy and affixed to an image of a grid facilitating an inevitable spread of current, although this was more of a visual metaphor than a reality. Period authors celebrated Berlin as "Electropolis" but the illuminated, bustling city was to be found in the excitement of nearby Potsdamer Platz, not in the private quarters of the domestic realm.[91] The presence of the AEG stores in Berlin and the wares they introduced should not be interpreted as part of the everyday for the masses.

Behrens's tenure at the AEG was seen in the period as a paradigmatic example of the successful merger of "art" with "technology" or "art" with "industry," a formulation that has been problematized by Frederic Schwartz, who suggests, among other nuanced readings of period theory and culture, a move to "form" and "economy."[92] Under these terms, the AEG stores become key, as they provide a mode—as well as enact a space—by which the public could be reached. In any case, it is more germane to speak of the "technology" or "industry" the AEG offered as being in the service of an elite, of luxury, of consumption. It was this production of consumer desire, of *Kauflust*, for the objects of industrial production, that was an intangible yet crucial aspect of the AEG stores' functioning. With the help of Behrens, through its own outlets the AEG was able to control all aspects related to the consumption of its goods—design, quality, advertising, and the total environment in which the sale was to take place.

Nor should the hiring of Behrens for this purpose be read cynically as purely motivated by profit; on the contrary, the firm, like the Werkbund, sought to use capitalist industry to reform taste, form, even capitalism itself, as Schwartz has argued. Within this context, Behrens's AEG stores represent a mode of selling that can be seen as a critical response to the ways in which modern capitalism was viewed as operating generally—in an out-of-control manner—at sites such as the large department stores a short distance away. While both the small AEG stores and the nearby large department stores were conceived as final outlets for equally commercial concerns, the AEG stores can be characterized as promoting a modernism of restrained, elegant luxury, via its intimate spaces that offered a proscribed range of goods. This solution, the courting of a privileged set of shoppers, however, can be seen as problematic in that it forced the company to retreat to an earlier, selective mode of selling, as opposed to the more democratic department store that attracted a mass audience.

Ideas inextricably linked with modernism, especially those that were vibrant at the peak of 1920s Weimar, can be identified in their nascent iterations here—not only in the stores' *sachlich* qualities and the use of gleaming modern materials, especially glass, but the selling of goods via modern techniques of display. Much of the display in evidence here predates ideas about "surface" that have been identified with the Weimar era, albeit—as self-consciously elitist—without the later appeal to mass culture.[93] While the canonical story of modernism has been told as one of enabling positive social transformations, the reality of modern design was that it was often elite and out of reach of the very people it purportedly desired to serve. In many ways, "modern" goods were not so different from already available products, but rather, they took on a new appearance—the patina of modernism—or were sold in new contexts, or represented seemingly new ways of living. The AEG's products were not alone in this respect.

This does not undermine Behrens's role in the history and development of modernism, particularly ideas associated with modern architecture. The AEG's model of selling fewer, but carefully designed objects, rather than a seemingly infinite permutation of goods (which was often the case for mass-produced items in the nineteenth and early twentieth centuries) was key to the developing rhetoric and practice of modern architecture. This was recognized in Behrens's day. Modern architecture became the framework from which to sell the products of modernism itself. Behrens's stores played a crucial role by cultivating a modern allure—they were visible to all, but not accessible to all. The AEG sought to market modern design to those who could afford it by creating an atmosphere of carefully pared-down exclusivity and cultivating consumer desire for its products. This was an early version of what was to come in German modernism, to be replayed in visually innovative work by Mies van der Rohe and in the products of the Bauhaus, using the same basic operations—an aura of luxury affixed to modernism in order to create a market.

OBJECTIVITY

The store designed in 1927 for Leibniz Keks, a firm selling prepackaged baked goods and cookies, on Berlin's busy Kurfürstendamm shopping street, presents many of the aspects that the German Werkbund and Germany's modern archi-tects had already spent the better part of a decade championing: that is, a modern, spare storefront, a truthful display of its compositional materials, surmounted by straightforward, highly legible lettering of the brand name, "Leibniz Keks" ("Keks" are a packaged cookie) (figs. 2.1, 2.2). Seemingly devoid of ornament, the facade's flat planes of cladding express the natural beauty of the luxurious stone, especially its richly striated veining. While the double doors form the entrance to the main building, shoppers entered the store via the recessed doorway to the left. This allowed the full visual force of an unbroken facade and large glass display window to beckon potential consumers, in line with Werkbund recommenda-tions. The display window itself, a single expanse of glass, presents the goods on offer in a rational, objective way, while providing an alluring view into the modern interior beyond the display. With its backlit signage enabling a legibility that could be seen at a great distance, the storefront functioned as well at night as during the day, standing out against the cacophony of the major metropolis that Berlin had become by 1927. The modern movement's protagonists celebrated an ideal of rational, unornamented, stripped-down, objective—or *sachlich*—objects and interiors, which eventually coalesced in a movement in Germany that was sometimes termed *Neue Sachlichkeit*.[1] Here luxury was entwined with objectivity, both intellectually and materially: for example, in the pared down, straightfor-ward modernism consisting of a rigorous geometry and flat planes—luxury as elegant attrition. Luxury is also inherent in the sumptuous materiality expressed in the rich veins of the exterior stone and dark wood of the interior. And luxury is evinced in the tasteful restraint of the number and type of goods on display, further accentuated by the rational layout of the objects in the window and inside the store.

This chapter focuses on period ideas surrounding objectivity in design and architecture as they intersect with the Werkbund display window and the related concerns the Werkbund sought to highlight and pragmatically address through it. It looks to the burgeoning disorder of the urban visual realm, mainly 1910s and 1920s Berlin, and highlights one instance—the role of the display window (*Schaufenster*)—in which the Werkbund seemingly succeeded in organizing,

Figure 2.1. Adolf Falke, Leibniz Keks store, Berlin, 1927.

Figure 2.2. Falke, Leibniz Keks store, main showroom.

streamlining, modernizing, and improving that visual realm. From its initial involvement, focused mainly on issues surrounding the design and layout of the window itself following World War I, the Werkbund and modern architects (as well as newly professionalized window designers) began to move outward in their sphere of influence, to the role of the display window in relation to the entire building, to the signage (day and night), and to the street. From Hermann Muthesius's maxim of "sofa cushion to city planning," a related corollary can be proposed in this instance—from the "mass-produced cookie to the streetscape"—that allows us to see a particularly successful example of Werkbund intervention.

Broadly, the Werkbund represented an alliance of prominent architects, designers, businessmen, and government figures who promoted modern architecture and new forms of modern living.[2] In setting out to improve the quality of German design and the country's economy, Werkbund members sponsored a many-pronged set of large-scale—and small-scale—initiatives, which manifested themselves as publications, ambitious exhibitions, built architectural exemplars, and other programming, including, to be the focus here, reform of the display window. The core aspects of the group's reform initiatives can be clustered into three main areas of attention. First, activities centered on the Werkbund's desire to make modern and sustained improvements to dwelling standards, best exemplified by the 1927 large-scale exhibition, *The Dwelling*, a two-part endeavor composed of the Weissenhof Housing Settlement, a model community of full-scale modern houses built outside the city center and an accompanying exhibition in downtown Stuttgart that showcased technical equipment, appliances, furnishings, and other accoutrements of modern living (figs. 2.3, 2.4).[3] Posters advertising the exhibition illustrated the new types of modern objects, interiors, and architecture that the Werkbund supported, while other posters polemically struck through—with a vibrant red "X"—the historicist object-filled

Figure 2.3. German Werkbund, *The Dwelling* (*Die Wohnung*) exhibition, Weissenhof Housing Settlement, master plan by Ludwig Mies van der Rohe, Stuttgart, 1927. Aerial view.

interiors that the group opposed (fig. 2.5).[4] A second broad set of Werkbund initiatives was aimed at elevating the taste of the buying public and concomitantly improving the quality of German products by involving artists in design processes, especially their direct employment by industry, as exemplified by Peter Behrens's tenure at the AEG. A third aspect was the Werkbund's prodigious theoretical output, as Frederic Schwartz's landmark examination of the group has shown, which set the terms and aspirational goals for German design in the period.[5] Key to the group's activities was its focus on—and articulation of—the nuanced relationships between consumer, producer, and designer, and their interaction with the marketplace. The Werkbund focused on the role of advertising in shaping the market, new modes of display, and the rise of brand names, copyright, and trademarks, as well as other methods by which mass-produced goods might be sold.[6] These deliberations, and the intellectual climate of the Werkbund more generally, represented a further kind of luxury: that of an elite discourse aimed at—but elevated above—the common consumer.

Werkbund members' concerns—never monolithic but rather understood and articulated in varying and nuanced ways by different participants—were galvanized over a shared belief in the tenets of modern design, an interest in the modern means of fabrication and the quality of mass-produced output, in the elevation of consumer taste, and in the selling of German goods. As a group, it committed itself to raising the design standards of products for domestic consumption, as well as expanding the international market for German goods. Related to this goal was the promotion of a greater reliance on the machine and a desire to improve the visual design and material quality of German mass-produced goods. Werkbund leaders, especially Hermann Muthesius, sought to remediate the production of so-called cheap and nasty (*billig und schlecht*) machine-made articles of furniture and household objects (fig. 2.6). They vehemently rejected surrogate materials and "sham solutions"— defined as decoration or ornament thoughtlessly and superficially applied, often in abundance.[7] These cheap, but popular, products were derided and labeled "kitsch."

Figure 2.4. *Below and opposite:* German Werkbund, *The Dwelling* (*Die Wohnung*) exhibition, main hall, exhibition design by Lilly Reich, Stuttgart, 1927.

Figure 2.5. *Above and opposite*: Willi Baumeister, posters for *The Dwelling* (*Die Wohnung*) exhibition, 1927.

The group championed straightforward, honest forms and materials, ideals that had already been articulated by nineteenth- and early-twentieth-century reform programs, beginning with the arts and crafts movement led by William Morris in England, and continued by its adherents in America, as well as by the original and early proponents of the art nouveau and Jugendstil movements.

These ideals, if not forms, were given renewed attention in conjunction with Werkbund concerns over the effects of mass production. The Werkbund did not produce any objects itself but rather acted as an arbiter of taste, seeking to popularize products it viewed as tasteful, well-designed, and of good quality. For example, with the general public in mind, the group assembled a catalog, *Das deutsche Warenbuch* (The German book of products), which presented 248 pages of tasteful, quality household goods available on the market, ranging from ceramics and tableware, to pots and pans and other cookware, to lighting and small appliances, accompanied by information on the producing firms and shops where the items could be purchased (fig. 2.7).[8] Like other design reform movements before it, the desire to develop "good taste" among the buying public was a crucial component of the group's work, and it also was connected to the Werkbund's efforts in improving the quality of objects and relationships between designers and manufacturers. In 1921, the Haus Werkbund was completed by the group; it provided a showroom for goods evidencing the notions of quality and taste that the Werkbund promulgated (designed by Werkbund members and non-members alike), as well as a place from which to offer practical help to manufacturers interested in educating consumer taste.[9] However, like so

Figure 2.6. Mass-produced kitchen containers, example of prevailing German kitsch, early twentieth century.

Figure 2.7. German Werkbund, page from *Das deutsche Warenbuch*, 1915.

many of the group's initiatives, the Haus Werkbund proved more involved with the concept of luxury, tending to display expensive objects rather than products within the reach of the average German consumer.[10]

A problem for the period, and for the Werkbund very specifically, was the question of what it might mean to transfer older notions of worth, in terms of making or materials, into the sphere of machine-made goods. The Werkbund was concerned with promoting quality, well-designed products—a domain that had heretofore been represented by handmade objects in expensive materials. The group's associates were trying to retain what "quality" signified, while changing the means of production from handmade to machine-made. But quality goods tended to remain luxury goods, either because the price could not be lowered sufficiently, because machine production was often not feasible, or because the discourse as well as the aesthetics of the object itself meant that the consuming masses were uninspired to buy. This was an ongoing issue in the modern period.

It is within this purview that the group took a concentrated look at storefronts and especially the reform of the urban display window, the *Schaufenster*. The well-designed, rationally ordered *Schaufenster* could combat the status quo of "cheap and nasty" on multiple levels—as product, as visual object, and as architecture. For potential consumers, the group sought to use display as the means of developing an elevated, cultivated understanding of "taste" and "quality." Beginning in the same year as the Werkbund's founding, 1907, this chapter charts a long arc of growing attention to the subject of the display window, and its related architecture and urbanism, culminating around 1914, when Germany abruptly entered World War I, and then later, after the country stabilized and began to thrive again in the 1920s. The Werkbund's attention to the display window was much more efficacious than its other initiatives—despite much effort and expense, developments in architecture could hardly keep pace with actual need, and modern dwellings remained priced beyond the reach of many of the consumers it sought to relieve from substandard accommodations. While the Werkbund's large exhibitions, such as *The Dwelling* in Stuttgart—composed of a full-scale, furnished housing development and a related exhibition hall showcasing modern domestic products—did introduce many potential consumers to ideas, conveniences, materials, and aesthetics of modernism, and despite massive building programs undertaken by major cities such as Frankfurt and Berlin, only relatively few people experienced these truly modern environments prior to the post–World War II period. In an important contradistinction, I will argue, the display window—whether the street-length sequence of windows of the department stores or the carefully composed single shop window—introduced chance passersby and resolute shoppers alike to a Werkbund-mediated modernity. Following World War I, a boom period took place in the mid- to late 1920s, and window design burgeoned not only through ever more elaborate ensembles of windows and contents but, concurrently, through the codification of related theories and practices of design, many of them put forth by Werkbund members.

This crucial, sustained attention to window reform was discussed and took shape in a myriad of ways—windows were seen as architectural elements and as technical infrastructure relating to the physical layout of display windows in relation to buildings' facades; window reform related to the professionalization of window design as a career; and window reform was theorized in the pages of the Werkbund's journals (its own yearbook, the *Jahrbuch*, and later, *Die Form*) and in other print outlets, all to be examined here. Through education and display, the Werkbund sought to bridge the obvious (and less obvious) divides between objects and subjects, or producers and consumers, between exteriors and interiors, between surface facade and products enclosed in displays, all via objectivity and in ultimate pursuit of the elevation of German quality and taste. Via the *Schaufenster* the Werkbund attempted to further influence taste by training members of the emerging professional field of shop window design and independent small-business owners, who would then execute Werkbund ideas via the windows themselves. And with the direct interaction with pedestrians that the display window offered, ideals championed by modern architects and Werkbund members could be introduced to a mass audience via a store's architecture, with its window as a central focal point. While not everyone could engage in a progressive lifestyle ensconced in a modern dwelling, as architects envisioned, another route to participation in modernity was on offer: the visual realm presented by the Werkbund-endorsed shop window and perhaps even the acquisition of these modern products, many of which were affordable.

A prime example is the Leibniz Keks storefront with which this chapter began (see fig. 2.1). Bahlsen of Hanover, the parent company of the Leibniz product line, had been an early and eager participant in Werkbund initiatives. The firm's owner was a member of the Werkbund, and the company participated in the Werkbund's exhibitions, through pavilions and stands displaying Bahlsen products. In Bahlsen, the Werkbund and its supporters could point to a company that was an example of the successful result of art and industry working together for aesthetic and commercial ends—as exemplified by its modern buildings (permanent and temporary), display windows, graphics, and packaging design. Thus Bahlsen's Leibniz Keks—as marketed objects and in its point-of-sale outlets—embodied the triumph of the Werkbund and modern architecture's ideals. Bahlsen's products were sold in modern architectural settings, accessible to all comers in a way that a modern villa or even smaller apartments in newly built, large-scale modern apartment blocks, where demand outstripped supply, were not. Display window design also embodied the group's desire to improve the visual realm, especially the urban street. The product for which these qualities were on exhibit further represents what modernism had to offer at this juncture: namely, a line of long-life, mass-produced, standardized dry goods of uniform high quality at a price that the masses could universally afford. Their freshness had been extended through the use of modern packaging,

Figure 2.8. Peter Behrens, design for Leibniz Keks packaging for the Cologne Werkbund exhibition, 1914.

the TET-package, which protected and sealed the products from moisture. A further patina of modernism was achieved through the commissioning of designers such as Peter Behrens for the graphic design of the packaging (fig. 2.8).[11] Although the product itself was inexpensively produced and purchased, the nexus of protagonists and the larger debates taking place in Germany related to its marketing and display were tellingly sophisticated and involved the elite circle that the Werkbund represented. It is important to note that the products that demonstrated the Werkbund's ideals, and the goods that the group directly championed, rarely—in and of themselves—constituted luxury, per se. While some Werkbund-supported wares indeed represented expensive products (such as the electric AEG teakettles designed by Peter Behrens), many were common products, such as packaged foodstuffs and linoleum.

The display window initiative and its supporters were both elite. Top down, the advice was meant to trickle from producers to consumers, from architects constituting an avant-garde to street-level window-shoppers, from arbiters of taste who sought to transform the development of culture in Germany (as exemplified by Werkbund founding member Karl Ernst Osthaus with his many museum displays, cultural initiatives, and commissioned buildings), along with the many critics who theorized these changes in an ever-expanding publication and journalistic realm, to the average citizen. The metaphor of a filter is perhaps appropriate here: the Werkbund's goal was to act as a sieve for already existing wares and to allow through its mesh the tasteful designs of appropriate quality to end users, while discarding mass production's dregs. Quality and taste, with regard to the *Schaufenster*, was represented in *sachlich* displays—which were ordered, repetitive—rather than what the common people actually found compelling: namely, novelty, mountainous abundance, and narrative scenes, including mechanized movement. Objectivity thus represented luxury, in terms of its products and initiatives alike. In reforming the display window, the Werkbund instrumentalized modern architecture—its discourse and ideals, its aesthetics, its tools, and its materiality—in pursuit of a number of its reform goals, including those surrounding ideas of "taste," "culture," and "objectivity." However, despite its efforts, the Werkbund remained an elite organization that proved, by and large, unable to impose its agenda of good taste on the masses. The group engaged in an intellectual discourse that remained elevated, it championed high modernist design principles that were often alienating to the common person on the street, and its display techniques celebrated objectivity and rationality rather than relating to simplistic consumer desire. These factors, I argue, constitute luxury.

DISPLAY WINDOW DESIGN AND MODERN ARCHITECTURE

The role of the display window from around 1907 presents an alluring precursor for modern architecture; the *Schaufenster* could be modernized ahead of the larger metropolis. An accelerated pace of change was occurring in all major cities of this period, and in Berlin particularly. Albeit transitioning swiftly, architecture, especially domestic buildings, still moved more slowly—a result of a complex circulation of capital and stakeholders—whereas the display window could be quickly brought to bear on the ideas that modern architecture also sought to convey. Besides swiftly erected, short-term exhibition structures, buildings involving commerce, especially factories and department stores, represented the most rapid manifestations of modern

Figure 2.9. *Top and bottom*: Alfred Messel,
Wertheim department store, Berlin, 1896–
1904, photographs 1920.

architecture. The urban streetscape had been changed by the boom in department store and other commercial building that occurred between 1890 and 1910. As one period observer noted in 1909, "Our modern display windows are no longer small, lost in large architecturally neutral surfaces. They often take up the entire lower section of the facade, usurping for our eyes every architectonic function of the structure and having themselves a vivid structural meaning in the sense of the appearance of the architectonic organism."[12] The preponderance of glazing on large-scale department stores, and the visual role it played in the urban landscape, embodied an early instance of what was to become a key feature of modernism in architecture.

A good example is the Wertheim flagship department store (built in three phases, 1896–1904) on Leipziger Strasse in Berlin by architect Alfred Messel—its deeply carved stone facade and heavy stone columns appeared less modern than its display windows, rationally framed in brass (fig. 2.9).[13] Despite its heavy facade, Messel's building was celebrated by architects and architectural critics in the period for its modernism, particularly for its use of encased iron, which allowed for large open spans in the interior (see fig. 1.26). Even with the historicist detailing that most of the commercial buildings presented, the structural use of iron (and later steel or concrete) made large windows possible, so that the buildings looked modern. Importantly, even in older buildings, changes to the facade, especially the insertion of new display windows, connected these edifices to the quickly changing, general urban situation and made modernism visible to street-level pedestrians. This was the case, for example, in Hermann Muthesius's 1913 renovation of the fashion house Kersten & Tuteur (fig. 2.10). These innovations by architects would lead to a very changed streetscape by the 1920s. In its most idealized form, the Weimar display window was an optimized and fully integrated part of a building—drawing urban denizens to modern architecture, creating street-level vistas representative of the modern city, and connecting *sachlich* displays of objects to a larger modern architectural context. This modernism is exemplified by Erich Mendelsohn's Berlin store for C. A. Herpich Sons and his many other large department stores across Germany, with their rational use of glass and stone, clean lines, large display windows, and composed nighttime illumination (fig. 2.11).[14] The *Schaufenster* of this period went beyond representing a straightforward tool of capitalism and commerce—it did more than merely illustrate the goods to be found inside. Rather, via elaborate

Figure 2.10. Hermann Muthesius, renovation of the Modehaus Kersten & Tuteur, Berlin, 1886, renovation 1913.

Figure 2.11. Erich Mendelsohn, Herpich Sons department store, Berlin, 1924–28.

displays, these windows met the viewing needs of passersby in order to awaken "consumer desire" (*Kauflust*) and entice consumption. The display window can also be understood as a crucial communicator of modern ideals and modern architecture in this period.

The Werkbund display window, as object, was able to present many of the ideas associated with modern architecture, modernism, and modernity. It was in one sense a very concrete object, often articulating, via the display of its contents, an interest in repetition, in the machine, or at least the aesthetic of machine precision and mass production, *Sachlichkeit*, and a spareness of form, line, and color (figs. 2.12, 2.13). Moreover, in this period, through the display window and related theorizations, objects could be repositioned in the literal and figurative architecture of the marketplace. In a metropolis replete with wondrous arrays of consumable goods, it also evoked desire, one that reinforced class and economic divisions in terms of access to

Figure 2.12. Werkbund-approved window for Bahlsen, 1913. From the Werkbund's *Yearbook*, 1913.

Figure 2.13. Julius Klinger, design of a Werkbund-approved window for luggage purveyor Albert Rosenhain, 1913. From the Werkbund's *Yearbook*, 1913.

these goods. Despite its exacting modernism, even the *sachlich* display window conjured a fictive world, one that was at once literally within arm's reach and yet tantalizingly unavailable to the many who could only consume the goods visually, not in actuality. While some windows featured products available to all, such as Bahlsen's packaged butter cookies, others, such as Albert Rosenhain—a "specialty store for fine leather and luxury goods"—displayed leather trunks and suitcases that would have only been available to those with leisure time and the economic means to travel.

Through the store window, Werkbund theories of display—not one but many conflicted ideological spheres—could be tested.[15] Moreover, the disparate groups the Werkbund wanted to reach—producers, practicing designers, and consumers—could be brought together. The window, with its display of objects, was a site for consumption—visual or actual, but also for instruction, for temptation, and for the enforcement of exclusion. It was, in short, a highly complex and elite object. The self-contained Weimar display window functioned as both a modern architectural object and as a variable conduit, spatial and social, between the outside urban context and an interior world of goods. While the Werkbund tended toward lofty and often generalized reform goals, its intervention into store window design objectively aimed to exert some control over this capitalist space for its ideals. Werkbund protagonists treated the useful space of the window in the same manner as they would a designed architectural object—objects for sale were displayed but also self-consciously exhibited as a spatial ensemble. Additionally, the group engaged in related endeavors, which extended, for example, to advising on the placement of glass display windows vis-à-vis the viewer and the street, the construction of window display stands, and evening illumination (to be discussed below).

Contending with the new proliferation of mass-produced goods for sale, the Werkbund sought to contain the visual chaos by reconfiguring the way that objects were displayed and sold, favoring *sachlich* presentations and factorylike piles of goods—*Stapelfenster*—as part of an ongoing effort to reform the visual culture of everyday life (fig. 2.14). The overfilled, indiscriminate window—often with differing types of wares competing with one another, what one author of a guide to window

Figure 2.14. Henry van de Velde, design of a Werkbund-approved window for Tropon protein supplement. From the Werkbund's *Yearbook*, 1913.

design termed a "chamber of horrors" (*Schreckenskammer*)—was to be transformed, under Werkbund guidance, into an orderly representation of goods (fig. 2.15).[16] Another critic, in a 1916 guide, described with disdain the problem of "Eiffel towers from pocket handkerchiefs, wheels and wreaths from silk fabrics and shoes, airships from metal spoons," in which the viewer was thus not able to see the goods but rather the elaborately formed fantasy object.[17] The Werkbund sought to command legibility for goods via their display and to bring the windows into rational order, a precision not unlike that found on the factory floor, a place Werkbund members had already turned to for inspiration in their architectural work.

The years leading up to World War I represented the period in which the Werkbund formulations on display window design were at their zenith; in the postwar period and through the late 1920s, the fruits of their labor took hold and were exponentially expanded upon, owing to the wider growth of the city as well as the window design profession itself. More generally, the newly theorized window was projected to accomplish, in its ubiquity (in a capitalist society), a larger restructuring of objects by bringing the chaos, overabundance, and prevailing disorder of store windows into rational organization. Ultimately, the window evolved from an architectonic element to an integrated architectural form, one that, in its street-level pervasiveness—and through a rational reordering of the display of objects—the Werkbund hoped might accomplish a broader reordering of society.

THE WERKBUND DISPLAY WINDOW: DISCOURSE AND OBJECT

Very early on, the Werkbund sought to extend its influence beyond raising the design standards of German products, to actively influence buyers by whetting consumer desire through the device of the store window, among other means. Just prior to World War I, the Werkbund launched a lively discussion of the topic in its publications, especially in the 1913 edition of its *Yearbook*, which devoted that year's entire issue to the topic of stores, with articles focusing on a wide variety of subjects relating to windows, including advice on modes of display and techniques in which sales could be enhanced by the window design. These and other key articles

Figure 2.15. "Chamber of horrors" ("Die Schreckenskammer"), 1926. Published in a window design manual as an example of bad window design. From Hans Bode, *Ein Schaufensterbilderbuch* (Hanover: S. Hein, 1926).

underlined Werkbund members' aspirations surrounding the display window and their belief in its wider cultural impact. For example, key Werkbund leader Karl Ernst Osthaus, in his article "Das Schaufenster" ("The Display Window"), wrote compellingly of the need for a "culture of objective display windows" and the requirements to achieve that goal.[18] Osthaus did not just make an appeal for rationality but advised utilizing modern means to make the displays enticing; he praised one architect's use of covered, indirect lighting, for giving the resulting store windows "mystical charm."[19] The articles published by the Werkbund were accompanied by many pages of photographs of ideal store window displays (see figs. 2.12, 2.13, 2.14). The stores featured by the Werkbund were not unified by their sale of modern wares (indeed, many were selling traditional or luxury goods) but rather by their straightforward displays.

Werkbund protagonists made large claims for the importance of the store window, arguing that it was integral to the entire architectural effect and key to giving the store its own character.[20] The Werkbund's members were opposed to the narrative—often sentimental—displays frequently staged by the architecturally massive, multiwindowed, block-length department stores. They also emphasized the importance of the relationship of display windows to the architectural whole. Balance and the primacy of a cohesive architecture were key concerns, and the Werkbund warned of the danger of allowing the display window to envelop or take over the building, especially a risk with department stores. One Werkbund associate, in a 1913 article on "The Department Store" ("Das Warenhaus"), cautioned, "It is audacious to make the display window the main motive of the entire architectural program, and in giving glass the character of a monumental building material, one must proceed

Figure 2.16. Ludwig Mies van der Rohe, Adam department store project, Berlin, 1928–29, photomontage.

with the greatest of care."[21] In this early acknowledgment, the display window and its materiality already signaled a potential bold new direction and emphasis in building. Ludwig Mies van der Rohe's architecture of the post–World War I period, and that of his colleagues, was influenced by the changes that had taken place in urban Berlin of the 1910s, namely, the availability of larger panes of plate glass and the increasing visual prominence of display windows. This is evident in Mies's two Friedrichstrasse skyscraper proposals as well as his Adam department store scheme, which were entirely composed of glass facades in the form of curtain walls with interior structural supports (fig. 2.16). Instead of allowing the glass or the display window to *dominate* the architecture, which the Werkbund had cautioned against, seemingly the glass *became* the architecture itself—and it did so in a modern, striking manner. As Mies wrote to the Adam firm's owners, "You need layered floor levels with clear, uncluttered spaces. Furthermore, you need much light."[22] In his design for the Adam department store, the upper-story windows were proposed in matte glass, while the transparent ground-level windows allowed for highly visible displays that would have been useful for selling. Rather than dominating the facade, the display windows were recessed from it. They did not act as the main motive of the building and were integrated into—and did not compete with—the architectural whole, which satisfied Werkbund demands.

Overall, the Werkbund generally favored small architect-designed stores, and their publications often featured exemplars such as architect August Endell's Salamander shoe stores or Hans Heller's designs for Anker linoleum showrooms (figs. 2.17, 2.18).[23] In the 1913 *Yearbook*, architect and Werkbund member August Endell weighed in on the setting up and organization of small shops.[24] He argued

Figure 2.17. August Endell, Salamander shoe stores, Friedrichstrasse store (*left*) and Tauentzienstrasse store (*right*), Berlin, c. 1911. From the Werkbund's *Yearbook*, 1913.

that in order to "directly whet consumer desire," a store needed to utilize all of the means available to it—company signage, illuminated advertising, and most of all, the *Schaufenster*.[25] To be effective, he advised, these elements must be visible not only at close range but also from across the street and at a greater distance. Easy recognition of the seller's name was also key. Endell further stipulated that the display window should be tastefully arranged and that the wares on display, in their form and type, should induce the buyer into the shop. But from the moment a buyer crossed the threshold, Endell believed the course of the sale to be arbitrary. He abdicated sales responsibility on the part of the architect and ceded it to the store's proprietor. Once in the store, it was the sales arm that should organize how the goods were offered to the shopper, the methods by which they were laid out for the buyer's inspection, how they were tested or tried on, and subsequently bought.[26] This is not an insignificant point—Endell tasked the architect only with enticing buyers into the store, not with the layout or the components of the interior (even though he frequently designed the interior as well as the exterior in his own commissioned work). He cites the design of the facade and also the window and its display as essential elements of architecture and within the architect's purview.

Prominently featured in Werkbund publications and in architectural journals alike, Endell's store windows of the early 1910s had a decisive impact on modern window design. His Salamander stores—there were at least five in Berlin by 1913—were widely known and admired by architects in the period, and photographs of them were frequently reproduced in publications on modern architecture.[27] Despite employing stained glass, curvilinear lines, and traditional signage featuring

Figure 2.18. Hans Heller, Anker linoleum store, Hamburg, 1913. From the Werkbund's *Yearbook*, 1913.

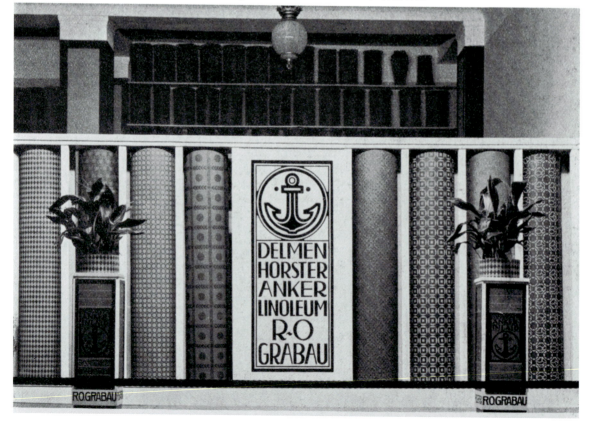

typography of the earlier, still lingering, art nouveau movement, the Salamander stores on Friedrichstrasse and Tauentzienstrasse in Berlin were early demonstrations of the essential components of an architecture concerned with modern display (see fig. 2.17). The three principal panes of plate glass of the Friedrichstrasse window read almost as one pane because they are brought together by two very thin vertical mullions, and the open expanse of the display window's interior is left uninterrupted by interior columns or supports. Like an open plan, the result is a completely flexible space that allows for the free play of the display window's interior. Emblazoned with a glowing, stained glass Salamander logo in the top, central pane, and illuminated by diffuse overhead lighting, this window ensemble would have particularly beckoned on dark Berlin winter afternoons, and its trademark would have been fully legible at night. In the window, the displays were *sachlich* and judiciously organized: individual shoes (never pairs) were placed jauntily but rationally on the window's base, a rhythm that was alternated at regular intervals by elevating one shoe on a simple, draped plinth. In the very front, set on the tilted window base, five identical nameplates identified the brand name "Salamander," while octagonal plates featuring the Salamander name and announcing the single, standardized price for its shoes were hung on the window's back wall. The uniformly set prices of 12.50 marks for regular models and 16.50 marks for luxury models reflected not only the economics of the shoes' mass production, as opposed to costlier handmade shoes, but also the modern concept of a fixed price, rather than the still-common practice of bargaining.[28] Although still cloaked in some of the aesthetic trappings of Jugendstil, Endell's windows should be read for their early influence on the period; celebrated by the Werkbund, they were pivotal in their openness, their expansiveness, their flexibility for display, and in their direct communication with viewers on the street. In many ways, the strikingly modern Leibniz Keks store, designed by Adolf Falke more than fifteen years later, adheres to these early ideas suggested by Endell and championed by the Werkbund (see fig. 2.1).

THE *LADENSTRASSE* AT THE WERKBUND EXHIBITION IN COLOGNE

The Werkbund's reform of the architecture of the display window and the window's essential role in educating the public, changing taste, and as a space of potential consumption came to an apex at the group's 1914 exhibition in Cologne. Until then, the Werkbund's exercises related to the *Schaufenster* had been largely confined to their publications and programming. But at the group's major exhibition in Cologne they sought to coalesce and present their ideas in built form. The Cologne exhibition was a large, fairground-type site comprising free-standing exhibition buildings, each filled with displays organized by theme, place, or maker, as well as a theater, halls, several demonstration homes, a model office and factory, smaller pavilions, and multiple sites for refreshment (fig. 2.19).[29] The Werkbund commissioned buildings from both established architects, such as Henry van de Velde, as well as younger, emerging modern architects, such as Walter Gropius. Furthermore, it exemplified in visual, built form the Werkbund's ideas of good taste, *Sachlichkeit*, and efforts at German design reform. As Despina Stratigakos, Mark Jarzombek, and other historians have shown, Werkbund formulations featured a design elite (reformers themselves and the firms that demonstrated the kind of change that the group championed, such as the AEG) that was set in opposition to a dilettantish "other" that still needed to be reformed.[30] The large-scale exhibition in Cologne was one way in which the Werkbund attempted to publicize its ideas.

In order to focus the public's and other shop owners' attention on the appropriate layout of display windows, a demonstration row, or "street of shops" (*Ladenstrasse*), designed by Oswin Hempel, was constructed along a main axis of the exhibition grounds.[31] The "street" contained forty-eight small shops in total, arranged in two facing rows of twelve stores, with each group of twelve linked under an arcade (fig. 2.20). Plans for the *Ladenstrasse* had already been formulated two years earlier, in 1912, at the annual Werkbund meeting held in Vienna, where the show's contours, if not its specifics, had been drawn up. Each large-scale display window along the *Ladenstrasse* was to model the best arrangements by window artists, with each demonstrating the optimal mode of selling a given type of ware.[32] The group's specific intentions for these display windows mirrored the Werkbund's generalized call for artists to collaborate with businessmen and for an integrated, coordinated

Deutsche Werkbund-Ausstellung Cöln 1914.

Figure 2.19. *Top*: Postcard of the German Werkbund exhibition, Cologne, 1914. *Bottom*: Exhibition plan. The *Ladenstrasse* is labeled number 13.

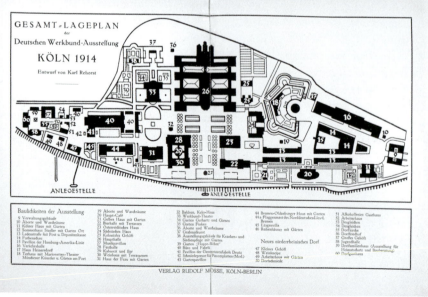

visual effect. As Werkbund member Carl Rehorst specified, "For the constantly changing product displays in the windows to be made in good taste, the permanent participation of artists will be required. Furthermore, all of the various fields should represent collaboration with artists, which the insightful businessman of today already utilizes, including the various kinds of printed trade materials, packaging, and especially advertising."[33]

Werkbund leader Karl Ernst Osthaus, in a letter to architect Oswin Hempel, called for the street to demonstrate a rhythmic connection between the architecture and its ornamentation, and for the elements of the display window, the firm's signage, and the lighting to be brought together in the facade.[34] Moreover, the Cologne *Ladenstrasse* was intended to showcase high-quality German products, reflecting a key Werkbund concern that the group champion national wares with an eye to the international export market. As Osthaus stated in the letter, the wares should be "where possible" German, and he suggested purveyors of tea, coffee, and men's

Figure 2.20. Oswin Hempel, design of the *Ladenstrasse*, German Werkbund exhibition, Cologne, 1914. *Detail*: Stacked goods in the display window.

fashions. However, quality took precedence over products' origins, and he noted that it was more important that what was on display be "good," even if it was English, or in the case of women's fashion, French.[35] Osthaus enjoined that the street should not be "boring," but full of fantasy, "spreading the magic that we might have felt as children in our capital cities just before Christmas," and concluded definitively, "otherwise it is just not worth anything."[36]

No single photograph appears to have been taken (or has survived) of the individual windows and shops, a result of Germany's surprise entry into World War I before the Werkbund had the chance to fully document the exhibition. However, the Werkbund exhibition's official catalog lists the medley of stores on the "street": a cigar store; a textile and interior design store; a shipping and travel agency; a chocolatier; an additional chocolate (and jam) shop; a hair stylist supply company; a pipe shop; a fabric store and haberdashery; a purveyor of cologne and perfume; a shop selling accessories and furs for women; a store for photography, projection, and cinema; and a coffee supplier.[37] The organizers, however, had difficulties in finding representative wares and backers for the *Ladenstrasse*.

In reference to the *Ladenstrasse*, the official catalog emphasized the important role that stores and display windows played in the development of good taste, observing that hardly elsewhere was the eye so activated as in the shopping streets of big cities. While the catalog acknowledged that in the past few years the artistic level of displays had been improved overall, the organizers predicted that it would be a long time before entire streets would boast display windows and stores in modern design. The exhibition's *Ladenstrasse*, therefore, was meant to present the possibilities in the development of a "store culture" (*Ladenkultur*) as proposed by Werkbund members and was envisioned by the group as a means of giving a complete overview of the main efforts in that field.[38]

The Cologne exhibition as a whole suffered criticism. Although well attended, it was not a unanimous critical success, and it was condemned for exhibiting expensive luxury items. For example, Theodor Heuss noted that no one below the social and economic rank of schoolmaster or judicial clerk would be able to afford any of the objects on display.[39] Karl Ernst Osthaus's small display, exhibited under the auspices of the Deutsches Museum für Kunst in Handel und Gewerbe (German Museum for Art in Trade and Industry), was called "snobbish" by a critic writing for the journal *Dekorative Kunst* (Decorative art), itself a somewhat elite publication.[40] Architectural critic and Werkbund member Adolf Behne included Hempel's *Ladenstrasse* buildings along with those by Theodor Fischer, Peter Behrens, and Hermann Muthesius in his critique of the Cologne exhibition edifices, viewing them as "indistinguishable from the most bland and bleak utilitarian buildings" to be found in any German city, and deeming the situation especially deplorable in light of the talent and the financial investment involved.[41] Despite the boosterism of the Werkbund's own publications, the *Ladenstrasse* section of the exhibition, especially, was viewed as a failure by critics, including members of the Werkbund itself. For example, member Robert Breuer, in evaluating the street for *Deutsche Kunst und Dekoration* (German art and decoration), noted: "The shops, which were supposed to exhibit impeccable interior configuration and extraordinarily tasteful display windows have only fulfilled their promise to a small degree."[42] Georg Jakob Wolf, in *Dekorative Kunst*, simply called the street "badly made" (*missraten*).[43] The Werkbund, Wolf added, "wanted to exhibit exemplary display window decoration but often was content to do so with cheap arrangements of 'bouillon-soup-cube dummies' [*Arrangements von Suppen-Würfel-Attrapen*] that would shame a main street shop owner."[44] Peter Jessen, criticizing the outcome in the Werkbund's own *Yearbook*, noted that only in a few cases was the desire for model windows fulfilled, otherwise there was a lack of "will and understanding of the task" at hand.[45] Not only was the *Schaufenster* layout lacking; Jessen also noted that there was a dearth of correct goods acting as representative sales merchandise to give the right effect. The street thus represented another occurrence in which the capitalist marketplace could not be persuaded to pay obeisance to Werkbund ideals and ideologies, which were admirable in their intention but ultimately elite, top-down edicts.

Elsewhere in the exhibition, there were many instances in which the arrangement of the material was more reminiscent of a display window than a museum vitrine, for example, in the *Haupthalle*, or main exhibition hall (fig. 2.21). The Haus der Frau—an exhibition building presenting designs by women—featured passages of shop windows, the vitrines of which were designed by Lilly Reich.[46] (Reich, a successful designer of clothing, window displays, exhibition installations, and interiors, was also an early member of the Werkbund, having been invited to join the group in 1912 by its board of directors.) Additionally, the exhibition catalog noted the "strict objectivity" (*strenge Sachlichkeit*) of the Haus der Frau.[47] To that end, the 1914 Werkbund Ausstellung proved a useful built introduction to Werkbund ideas of window design, but one that did not materially measure up to the group's aspirations.

Figure 2.21. *Left*: Richard Riemerschmid, display in the main exhibition hall, German Werkbund exhibition, Cologne, 1914. *Right*: Otto Schulze-Kolbitz, display of textiles for the firm Gustav Cords, main exhibition hall, German Werkbund exhibition, Cologne, 1914.

THE 1910S AND 1920S: COHESION AND ORGANIZATION

Early and multifaceted programs and exhibitions related to store window design were key components of the Werkbund's wide-reaching, overall reform program. However, the greater articulation and follow-through of the various protagonists' ideas and initiatives in the years just before World War I was interrupted by the war itself. After the war, a period of acute political and financial uncertainty followed, culminating in extreme inflation in 1923. When the world of commerce and the flow of capital resumed, the display window was taken up again by Werkbund members; they were joined by a broader array of architects and designers, who added their focused attention to the subject. Over the course of the 1920s, the professional window dresser burgeoned as an occupation, a design specialization that also drew from new expertise in the fields of advertising, technology, and psychology. Interest in the subject brought about a concomitant proliferation of publications devoted to all aspects of the display window; simultaneously art, architectural and trade journals also began to devote numerous feature articles to the topic. These texts, amply illustrated, became a key mode of disseminating modern ideas about the display window. Many of these new window designers and expert authors in the field of window design were members of the Werkbund or sympathetic to Werkbund ideas.

Throughout the 1920s, the Werkbund's new journal, *Die Form*, featured an array of articles on the *Schaufenster* and related topics. A number of highly specific trade journals emerged, and existing publications broadened their reader base. One such example is *Architektur und Schaufenster*, which notably began publication in 1904, making it one of the earliest journals on the topic. Others followed, including *Das Schaufenster: Spezialfachzeitschrift für die Schaufensterdekoration aller Branchen* (The display window: Specialized trade journal for display window decoration of all types; from 1921); *Schaufenster-Kunst und -Technik* (Display window art and technology; beginning in September 1925); *Die Auslage in der Dekoration und in der Reklame: Erstes Deutsches Fachorgan für Ladeninhaber, Schaufensterdekorateure sowie für alle Ladenbau- und Ladenausstattungsbranchen* (Display in decoration and advertising: First German trade journal for store owners, display window decorators, and all types of shop builders and fitters; from 1925 onward); *Laden und Schaufenster: Zeitschrift für die gesamte Einzelhandels-Praxis, Verkaufskunst, Kundendienst, Kundenwerbung, Laden- und Schaufenstergestaltung* (Shop and display window: Journal for general retail practice, art of selling, customer service, advertising, and shop and shop window design; from 1928). These publications were joined by a multitude of inexpensive illustrated books on modern store design, display windows, and advertising, such as the early volume *Der Schaufensterdekorateur: Illustrierte Anleitung zum Erlernen des Dekorierens der Schaufenster* (The store window decorator: Illustrated guide to learning the decoration of display windows, from 1906); Werkbund member Elisabeth von Stephani-Hahn's important 1919 book, *Schaufensterkunst* (The art of the display window), which proved so popular that several subsequent editions followed; and Bruno H. Jahn's 1926 *Reklame durch das Schaufenster* (Advertising through the display window). Jahn's cover featured a stripped-down, modern department store, its windows rhythmically punctuating the facade (fig. 2.22). Devoid of ornament, its architecture was reminiscent of the recently built department stores by Erich Mendelsohn and also very similar to the architectural drawings by Ludwig Hilberseimer, which envisioned a new, rational metropolis.[48] The display windows on Jahn's cover are blazingly illuminated, while the book's title is set in shadow type, projecting outward and literalizing its meaning by illustrating the display window's potential reach beyond the window and into the street. Additionally, many official organizations related to display window designers were founded in this period, such as the Society of Artistic Display Window Decorators (Verband künstlerischer Schaufensterdekorateure, 1913); the German Society of Window Decorators (Verband der Schaufensterdekorateure Deutschlands, 1919); the Association of Berlin Display Window Decorators (Verein Berliner Schaufensterdekorateure, 1920); and the Alliance of German Display Window Decorators (Bund der Schaufensterdekorateure Deutschlands, 1925).[49]

Frederic Schwartz has pointed out the growing importance of the trademark for the Werkbund and for firms in this period.[50] With regard to the strategy of the display window, the Werkbund called for industrial producers to encourage the use of the brand name in the windows of their retailers.[51] According to Peter Bruckmann, writing in the Werkbund's *Yearbook*, brand names could be utilized to whet the consumer desire of the public. The named brand and its trademark, he argued, was particularly helpful in the store window where the public display of the producer's name raised interest not only in the goods on show but familiarized the public with their manufacturer, resulting in a gain for both the store, as intermediary, and the industrial producer.[52] Bruckmann further noted that the Werkbund also had

Figure 2.22. Bruno H. Jahn, *Reklame durch das Schaufenster*, 1926.

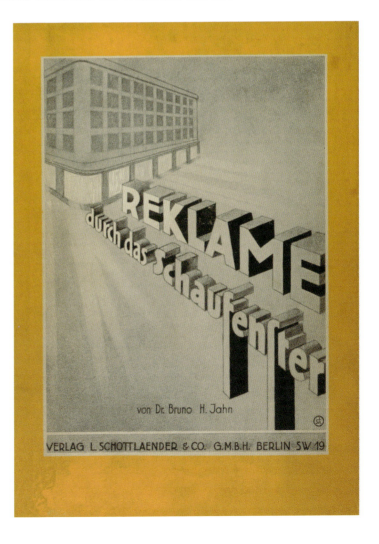

a particular interest in the promotion of brand names when the goods were German, because greater familiarity not only promoted Germany's manufacturing sector, but also German quality.

As an awareness of the value of universal brand recognition emerged, larger firms, desiring uniformity and quality in their window designs, sought to control and standardize the presentation of their products across multiple sales outlets and cities. Firms published enticing booklets, brochures, and pamphlets to bring the trademark message to retailers and to create sets of guidelines for standardizing it. The logo of a particular brand on a signboard, for example, had previously been hand-painted locally by a sign painter, but now guidelines were produced by the parent companies aimed at homogenizing the appearance of logos and trademarks. Simultaneously, firms began producing publications aimed at systematizing and regulating the display of their wares. Under the guise of ideal window display instructions, these small publications gave smaller shopkeepers the tools they needed to create uniform, professional-looking window displays that would feature the branded goods—and related trademarks—of firms. Bahlsen, the parent company of Leibniz Keks, offered store owners a variety of *sachlich* display window ideas for the arranging of their packaged baked goods, for example. Their guidelines reflected Werkbund ideas on the topic, and a rational Bahlsen window display was also featured in the group's *Yearbook* (see fig. 2.12). A small booklet, *H. Bahlsen's Cookie Factory: Gift Packages and Display Window Decoration* of 1912, illustrated many design ideas for display windows, which the accompanying text lauded as "exemplary" or "ideal" layouts.[53] In the illustrations, each variety of cookie package is displayed as a multiple—carefully placed and spaced at measured intervals, laid out in rows, forming simple columnar stacks of goods, or product pyramids. The layout thus celebrated, through the display, the uniformity and rationality of the company's wares, and visually affirmed to consumers that they could expect to find a uniform product within. This is key in a period in which the quality of foodstuffs was still generally uneven and unreliable. The displays also underscore each product's place as part of an overall line of goods; each package can be viewed as an individual unit standing on its own merits yet is also representative of the firm's products more generally—signaling reproducibility, dependability, and consistency. In the suggested illustrated displays, the backdrop always enhances the rationalized presentation; it generally consists of a simple pattern or geometric motif, which visually divides up the background into smaller segments, with the company's typescript bearing the brand name (Bahlsen), product types ("cookies, crackers, waffles," [*Keks, Biscuits, Waffeln*]), and "TET-packaging," the celebrated wrappers that kept the products free of moisture (see fig. 2.12). The descriptive text over each exemplary layout in the booklet repeats the maxim "good display doubles demand."[54] Not only did the firm suggest compositions for the display window, but the booklet featured ways in which the products could be arranged on special shelving and other display apparatuses that the firm offered for direct purchase, priced at less than their own production cost. In exchange for receiving a discounted display stand, storeowners had to promise that they would display only Bahlsen baked goods on it.[55] Given the early standardization of Bahlsen's trademark, company font, and packaging, its employment of artists and designers toward these ends, and its head's membership in the Werkbund, it follows that the modes of display and configuration of windows would also be of utmost concern to this firm and that it would follow the Werkbund's lead. Bahlsen was, as such, an exemplary company for the Werkbund to celebrate as setting the standard for thousands of other German firms to emulate, one in which the display window played a key role.

Krauss metalwares firm, whose managing director was a member of the Werkbund, produced a similar publication in 1926, a booklet titled *Krauss Schaufensterbuch* (Krauss display window book). It instructed retailers on the various ways in which their mass-produced products could be best organized in windows. Photographs were reproduced from a competition held by the firm for the best window design, while other images were produced in-house by Krauss's own marketing department. The accompanying textual descriptions were in line with the straightforward qualities proposed by the Werkbund. For example, the booklet encouraged retailers to construct "simple" (*einfach*), "clean" (*sauber*), and "objective" (*sachlich*) displays, with repetition and symmetry being important qualities therein; it assured shop owners that the clarity of the design would in turn engender consumer confidence in the product itself.[56] The firm, via this display window publication, stressed that little was needed for an effective window, noting that even the window itself need not be enormous; rather, all that was essential was to "let the wares speak for themselves."[57] Once the products were rationally arrayed in the window, only a curtain behind them was needed (dark blue was thought to show Krauss zinc-plated wares to good effect) and lettering forming the brand name (display signs in the brand's font could be borrowed by retailers from the company).[58] Krauss recurrently stressed the importance of displaying the brand name, in the company's own typography, and its trademark, an anchor, in the window, noting that passersby would thus take note and link the goods to the brand name.[59] The two firms of Bahlsen and Krauss, both with close links to the Werkbund, can be seen to be enacting the group's tenets. Instructional booklets and display materials produced in this period resulted in more rational and organized window layouts, and, coupled with close attention to the use of branding and trademarks, began to train consumers. A less cacophonous street-level visual realm for the public also resulted.

TASTE AND THE DISPLAY WINDOW

The didactic task concerning improving "taste" that the Werkbund set for itself more generally also linked directly to the display window, its role in modern architecture, and the selling of modern goods. The Werkbund articulated the architectural quandary the display window presented—the need to display wares in an enclosure and the simultaneous requirement of bringing light into the interior sales space; for the window to blend thoughtfully into the streetscape while still drawing attention to the wares on display. And the group's protagonists acknowledged a difficulty stemming from two "resistant and combative" requirements to be fulfilled, bundled in the word itself—*Schau* (show, display) and *Fenster* (window).[60] However, it was not just a set of formal design questions that the Werkbund sought to address, but those that hinged on less tangible qualities, one of which was the question of taste. The Werkbund's journal *Die Form* used potent language to declare that in modern window design it was not a matter of searching for originality, for sensation, for surprise; but rather for a general and comprehensible simplicity and clarity of form, achieved through the use of color, sublime alignment, and an exemplary handling of the products.[61] Thus, much of its discourse pointed toward qualities related to taste.

For the main protagonists of the Werkbund, it was not enough to promote well-designed objects; there was a need for good architecture to give form to the environment in which these objects were seen. Werkbund leader Karl Ernst Osthaus advised that a display window impinged on the "fate of taste" (*Schicksal des Geschmacks*), and thereby could potentially contribute to the larger regeneration of taste more generally.[62] The modern architecture of Peter Behrens's AEG stores, for instance, which featured refined goods ensconced within ideal display windows, was praised early on for elevating taste. A successful window would not only have an external effect on the buyer and the general public; it was also supposed to work well internally, for example, influencing the store's own personnel, as one Werkbund member noted.[63] This is an important point and large task; the well-designed *Schaufenster* was to do much more than simply sell more products, it was to positively educate its receiving viewers in elements of good taste. But, the Werkbund acknowledged, tasteful small stores were isolated examples and called for a wider application, finding the display window an especially "weak point."[64]

It was therefore all the more important that Werkbund member Elisabeth von Stephani-Hahn, in the first sentence of her groundbreaking 1919 book, *Schaufensterkunst* (The art of the display window), sounded what was more likely a hopeful note than a reflection of reality—that after fifteen years of hard work, "the modern display window as a stage for taste seems to be self-evident to us today."[65] In the next sentence, this notion of "taste" is countered with the economic realities and an acknowledgment of the quandary brought about by the perceived need for novelty: "The businessman, through intense competition, is forced to ever greater publicity."[66] She advises taking into account the aesthetic needs of the public and using the "artistic taste" of the display window as a stimulus for attracting customers. "Merchants and artists, one from a material standpoint, the other from the position of ideals," she noted, see their aims converging in the achievement of the "artistic display window."[67] The window, thus, was the perfect site of Werkbund ideology in praxis, and accordingly the group sought to influence decision makers and practitioners alike with an economic argument aligned with its aesthetic one. Other period commentators used the same terms and related arguments—the economic advantages of tasteful windows—as Werkbund members. For example, in a 1913 article on "The Decoration of Display Windows," the author pointed out that "even goods of middling quality can appear more valuable when they are displayed in a window that has been carefully and tastefully arranged."[68]

The Werkbund was also responding to the prevailing kitsch, a term utilized by its members to describe a populist aesthetic that they set in opposition to "tasteful." Kitsch as a concept has a long and varied history, but in this period it was a useful word employed by Werkbund protagonists to encompass a set of aesthetics and issues that the group was actively fighting—namely, a visual paradigm of garish colors and gaudy decorative motifs applied to low-quality goods and, in window decoration, novelty and sentimentality. One Werkbund member, describing the popular, prevalent windows of the period, noted that the window decorators whose "dexterity" allowed them to "make a waterfall out of handkerchiefs, a winter landscape with sleds out of napkins, a portal from boots, and to fold fabric in an artificial or contrived manner," always failed with regard to questions of taste.[69] Period images abound in this genre, such as a window that showcased a "butterfly" made out of handkerchiefs and a design for a "waterfall" of men's shirts (fig. 2.23). Windows that featured sensation and surprise, often at an overwhelming scale and massing, were popular with the public in this period. They could be monumental in size with a dizzying repetition of product; often one object was agglomerated to create an altogether different product—such as "palm trees" formed of leather gloves or white goods (especially handkerchiefs and linens) folded into a monumental urn of flowers (fig. 2.24).

These novelty windows represented a very different sort of repetition of a single product type from the orderly, spare, and *sachlich* arrangement of objects that made up the tasteful windows that the Werkbund favored. And yet the glove "palm trees" were not dismissed as kitsch. Reproducing the photograph in her book on display

Figure 2.23. *Top*: Window display of a "butterfly" made out of handkerchiefs, N. Israel department store, Berlin, c. 1906. *Bottom*: Design for window display of a "waterfall" made of men's shirts, 1913.

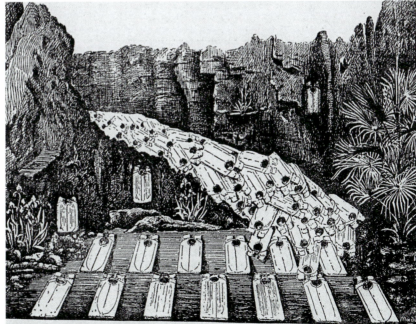

windows, Werkbund member Elisabeth von Stephani-Hahn noted that the design allowed for a clear view of the color and quality of each pair of gloves, and that goods stacked high were always favored by the Werkbund.[70] (The window may have been created by Stephani-Hahn herself—around 1905 she became the artistic director and chief window designer for the Wertheim department store, in whose window the glove palm tree was installed.)[71] Thus the group took a nuanced position—it deemed it essential that the wares on display exhibit clarity in form and type so that they were instantly legible to the viewer. The monumental, over-filled window with a "butterfly" or "flower" motif made out of a seemingly endless supply of folded, indistinguishable linens was much more problematic for Werkbund members. Overly

Figure 2.24. *Top*: Window display of glove "palm trees," Wertheim department store, Berlin, 1919. *Bottom*: Window display of white goods in the form of a flower vase, Berlin, 1913.

showy, these windows did not engender confidence in the educated consumer, who saw through the novelty of their empty content. More elaborate and expensive displays were on view in the metropolis; in 1928 the cultural critic Ernst Bloch reported that Berlin's window displays were "elegant, and often they are rich and striking" but, he quickly followed up, "you do not believe in them."[72] Bloch pronounced them nothing more than "ostentation," or the opposite of subdued rationality and tasteful display that the Werkbund sought. Appealing to notions of "taste" represented a very specific and elite perspective on the part of the group. The resulting window designs did not necessarily attract the attention—or meet the approval—of the general urban population likely to encounter them.

Finally, for Werkbund members, the idea of "taste" with regard to window design was closely aligned with the architectural concept of "appropriateness." In an article on the "principles of modern shop design" in one of the Werkbund's own publications, the author reminded readers that "tastefulness" or "appropriateness" was contextual and related to the object at hand, noting prescriptively that one type of setting, for example, was tasteful for silk blouses, another for metal goods, and that scale was also key—the display of children's toys should be of a scale very different from that of automobiles.[73] Through the 1920s, other period critics joined the Werkbund's call to use modern display to educate and influence the taste of the "buying masses" (*Käufermasse*).[74] Beyond the realm of commerce, the display window was viewed by Werkbund members as an effective arena in which to demonstrate good taste and as a direct, didactic sphere of influence for buyers and window-shoppers alike.

REFORM THROUGH DIDACTIC EDUCATION

In the context of its reform of the display window, the Werkbund launched a sophisticated educational initiative—a multifaceted *Bildungsprogramm*—aimed at small merchants (known as *Kaufmänner*). This was a group that the Werkbund viewed as crucial for reforming the taste of consumers. Werkbund leader Peter Jessen described early efforts in the improvement of taste via the Werkbund's development of an educational program (simply termed *Geschmacksbildung* or "taste-education") for merchants, enticing them with the suggestive promise that following its lead would "turn pennies into silver coins."[75] Already in the first year of its founding, 1907, the Werkbund organized a conference on "The Decoration of Shop Fronts."[76] It ran a lecture series in 1909 titled "Education in the Taste of German Merchants" which was so successful that plans were made to repeat it during 1910–11, with the backing of the chamber of commerce (*Handelskammer*), which planned to support and expand its programming.[77] The Werkbund also worked with the German Association for the Education of Merchants (Deutscher Verband für das kaufmännische Unterrichtswesen), instigating a discussion of the ways in which schools of arts and crafts and museums might contribute to the *Geschmacksbildung* of the German merchant.[78] Meeting reports note that the Werkbund offered suggestions to shopkeepers on a range of topics, including the design of small stores and their windows, advertising posters, printed materials, and packaging.[79] They sponsored a series of popular lectures, with, for instance, Hermann Muthesius lecturing on "The Imperative of Taste-Education for the German Merchant."[80] And they supported the development of the German Museum for Art in Trade and Industry

(Deutsches Museum für Kunst in Handel und Gewerbe), which opened in 1909, didactically showcasing the Werkbund's ideas surrounding good design and display principles. This initiative was bolstered by other Werkbund members working in an informal capacity. In her 1913 essay "The Art of Window Decoration," Elisabeth von Hahn-Stephani praises the artistic nature of Berlin's store windows and the contribution they made to the city's culture, but laments the difficulty of convincing smaller store owners that wares should be displayed not just in a manner intended to encourage sales, but with the aim of improving the public's taste.[81]

In this context, the display window was a crucial element within the Werkbund's multifaceted project to improve German industry and trade: via the reform of objects' design, reform of the consumers themselves, as well as the reform of the purveyors of those goods. In a notable essay on the "Werkbund and Trade" in the Werkbund's 1913 *Yearbook*, politician and political theorist Friedrich Naumann outlined the group's program for the linked involvement of industry, buyers, and sellers, and improvements in advertising, sales methods, and the quality of goods.[82] He advised that the shopkeeper could not be limited to the role of "facilitator" or intermediary, but ought to actively contribute in an artistic way to the streetscape, through his display windows.[83] It was an important role, because, Naumann stated, citizens learned "in front of [the merchant's] glass panes, what beauty is."[84] Naumann acknowledged that sales spaces, their interiors and especially display windows had been an object of recent artistic efforts, with meaningful advances. Though he pointed out that the better department stores and high-end specialty stores had put great effort and care into their outer appearances, he argued that generally more needed to be done.[85]

Display window reform advocates campaigned for a shift away from populism, toward modernism's more lofty goals, such as high quality and good taste. Erich Vogeler, critic and member of the Werkbund circle, writing in 1909 noted the problem of small stores selling a variety of goods—such as fashion accessories or preserved dry goods—who thus felt the onus not only to display every type of ware on offer, but also to fill the window with a multitude of trademark signboards representing these goods, as well as cards listing the prices. The author remarked that in these small stores "everything is still in a sorry state" and declared of utmost importance the promotion of good taste, and especially the promotion of tasteful display windows.[86] Friedrich Naumann offered a solution, reassuring store owners that if one demonstrated via the display that one had good objects, it was unnecessary to display *all* that the store had on offer.[87] This tasteful attrition—showing fewer, but better-designed products—connected with modernism's ideology (fig. 2.25). Members borrowed other concepts from modern architecture. Naumann claimed the forms, terms, and elevated status of art and architecture, noting that the process of designing for the display window was "painting with beautiful objects, an architecture of variformed goods," leading to the emergence of a new profession.[88] Rather than variety or comprehensiveness, designs exhibiting multiplicity and repetition were lauded (see fig. 2.12). Yet the Werkbund was not interested in sheer quantity, nor in bringing "formless and soulless articles" into the marketplace, Naumann was careful to state.[89] For Werkbund leader Hermann Muthesius, too, good "form" was a crucial measure of a culture, while he viewed "formlessness" as synonymous with "*Unkultur*."[90]

"Truthfulness," a key idea in modern architecture, also concerned Werkbund members with regard to display windows and their contents.[91] For example, the group warned against a "false sheen" (*Glanz*) in objects, instead suggesting the objective materiality and the qualities of the products themselves should be their selling point. "Instead of telling stories, each ware wants to be itself," advised Osthaus, regarding objects in windows.[92] Elisabeth von Stephani-Hahn noted that the goods "should recommend themselves, via themselves."[93] These linked to a more expanded version of this set of ideas surrounding representational "truthfulness" or "truth to materials" among Werkbund members. For example, Lilly Reich, in her essay "Questions of Fashion" (1922) for the group's journal *Die Form*, similarly advocated for women to consume genuine German fashion, over domestically produced, inexpensive copies or imports from Paris. Reich called for each woman "to be what she is" and not "to appear as what she is not."[94] At times, the reform ideals of the Werkbund were as much ideological as material or design-driven.

In May 1910, the Werkbund further concretized reform goals by opening a school for window display decoration. It was set up in collaboration with the Association for Mercantile Education (Verein für kaufmännisches Unterrichtswesen) and the Association of Berlin Specialty Stores (Verband Berliner Spezialgeschäfte) and was housed at an existing arts institution, the Reimann School (fig. 2.26). Notably, this initiative was underwritten by the small stores that made up the associations, not by the large department stores, which often sent their employees to the school's evening courses, once the program was in operation.

Technically a *Fachschule*, or trade school, the meeting minutes of the Werkbund refer to it simply as a "school for display window decoration" (*Schule für Schaufensterdekoration*).[95] Taught by leading practitioners in the field, Else Oppler-Legband was named its director, and she hired Lilly Reich, who was already working in clothing display for the Wertheim department store, as one of its instructors.[96] Its course offerings included the history and theory of the store window as well as practical classes on the schematic display of wares, advertising poster design, use of technology, perspective, and instruction in architecture, as it related

Figure 2.25. Julius Klinger, Werkbund-approved window for J. Loewenstein, 1913. From the Werkbund's *Yearbook*, 1913. An example of a pared-down window showing a representative sampling of wares.

to *Schaufenster* design.[97] Students were also taught strategies for improved sales and turnover through window design.[98] By 1914, the Werkbund could satisfactorily report back to its members that the program at the Reimann School, with its twenty-eight instructors, was suitably educating future decorators not only in window design, but also in buying, in customer communications, and in addressing all other "requisite questions of taste in mercantile life."[99]

Werkbund members also supported the growing school's physical plant. Hermann Muthesius had been commissioned to make designs for a new school building, but owing to the outbreak of World War I and then the difficult postwar economy, his plans were put on hold and were never executed.[100] Eventually, in 1926, the school was given an additional 1,000-square-meter space in the Schöneberg town hall, where it installed an instructional interior "street" of display window

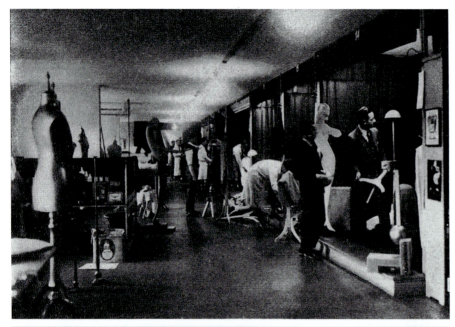

Figure 2.26. Reimann School, view of the window decorating workshop, 1927.

Figure 2.27. Students of the Reimann School, street of display windows (*Schaufensterstrasse*), *Schaufensterschau Leipzig* 1928 exhibition.

spaces ("*Schaufensterstrasse*"), complete with simulated evening lighting (see fig. 2.26). A stockroom was filled with fabric and materials, while additional support came from firms who donated quantities of products for students' use.[101]

The school also organized the *Leipzig Display Window Exhibition* (*Schaufensterschau Leipzig*) in the fall of 1928, in collaboration with the Association of German Window Decorators, Leipzig's Grassimuseum, and the Leipzig State Academy for Graphic Art and Book Design.[102] This extensive exhibition featured design and technology connected with the display window and related event programming. The high point was a "street" of eighteen windows decorated by Reimann School students (fig. 2.27).[103] Reporting on the exhibition, a period critic noted the windows' connection to modern architecture, to *Sachlichkeit* and functionality, and to economic life—hailing them as a spirited link to the age's new style.[104] While many of the Werkbund's lofty ideals did not—or could not—come to fruition, the school for window design was a key example of a successful implementation of the group's reform of the *Schaufenster*, as well as the display window's increasing association with modern architecture.

TOWERING GOODS FOR SALE: OBJECTIVITY AND ARCHITECTONIC AESTHETICS

For the Werkbund, the issue of *Sachlichkeit*—or objectivity—was paramount, both for the design of wares themselves, and in their arrangement in the display window. Werkbund leader Karl Ernst Osthaus, in his 1913 article on the *Schaufenster*, reiterated that rather than being incidental in a narrative, "the new window wants to be *sachlich* [objective]. Each product ... wants to be itself. The display wants to be a display."[105] Osthaus was very prescriptive, advising that "ornament and architectonic partitions should only be used with great caution. The richer the ware, the more neutral the background must be."[106] However, he allowed for harmonious opposition, recommending, for example, that black boots be placed on bright calico. In what he terms "the theory of modern display windows," Osthaus noted that windows do not necessarily function better with fewer goods on display; rather, the type of wares must be considered.[107] As another Werkbund member noted in 1919, the artistic challenge was to identify where the worth of each object lay, and only then, through display, stimulate the eye, drawing the observer in.[108] Windows were no longer to engage in a practice of distraction or wonder, but rather should achieve their effects through the concentration on—and then reproduction of—the single, *sachlich* form or object type. The sober attrition in terms of the circumscribed number and type of goods on display illustrates a specific notion of luxury—that of the artistic paring down of objects so that all that remained was a tasteful grouping, judiciously selected and arranged.

In addition to Osthaus's call for "severe *Sachlichkeit*," the careful interplay of materials was key in the display window. Osthaus was precise in his consideration of the relationships between the wares and their supports—for example, he rejected glass plate shelving because he deemed its immaterial qualities inappropriate. He advised that shelving was never to trump wares and that glass and porcelain objects should be placed on fabric, while fabrics should be displayed on wood or metal racks. He warned that one type of object was never to be placed on top of a differing type—giving the negative example of a tower of glasses crowned by a porcelain vase.[109]

In addition to simply stacking wares upon one another or the utilization of shelving, modern display stands for the presentation of wares were also developed in this period—often taking their forms and aesthetic cues from modern architecture. Period display window literature abounded with images of architectonic elements in miniature, such as asymmetrical or cantilevered stands (fig. 2.28). Diminutive display platforms, a mere 25 cm long, meant for the presentation of small items—such as leather goods, jewelry, or perfume—are strikingly similar to period urban architectural schemes, such as proposals for Berlin's Alexanderplatz by Mies van der Rohe, and others (fig. 2.29).[110] Though these display stands were merely intended to feature wares in display windows, they mimic and reify larger forms and spatial arrangements that were simultaneously occurring at full-scale in the urban architecture of this period.

Perhaps the most *sachlich*, as well as architectural, displays of all were what were termed *Stapelfenster*, literally "stack windows," displays which featured single items piled high into a column or otherwise repetitively stacked (fig. 2.30; see also figs. 2.12, 2.14). Werkbund leaders advised against the meaningless filling of

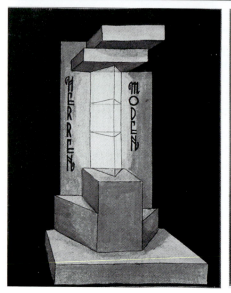

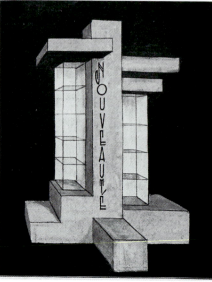

Figure 2.28. Architectonic structures in window displays, 1928. From Emil Baranski, "Architektonische Aufbauten im Schaufenster," *Schaufensterkunst und -Technik* (January 1928).

windows with various types of goods but rather suggested, for the display of goods en masse, a *Stapelfenster*, with empty space left between the stacked-up goods. The artistic appeal, one period observer noted, was in the tasteful and "architectonic" structure of the goods.[111] This principle was sometimes taken to dizzying heights, with the display's effect amplified as the reified goods towered upward. These displays were made possible by the development of larger panes of glass that advances in industrial production brought about, and that architects accordingly inserted in buildings' facades. Thus the burgeoning proliferation of factory-manufactured goods also produced a visually concomitant mode of display. In the architecture of the windows themselves, in the structure of the displays, and in the mass-produced objects as agglomerated individual units, this new kind of window display reflected the material and aestheticized terms of early-twentieth-century industrialized production.

A 1911 Werkbund report noted that the display of piled goods—described as single objects, tastefully, attractively, and cleanly presented in an "architectonic structure"—was sufficient to please the passersby. The report argued that it was this architectonic design, aided by the effects of color, attention to the materials' character, and the technical nature of the displayed wares that achieved the window's success. It posited that buyers were attracted to the "distinguished, tastefully selected arrangement and display of goods."[112] The Werkbund's members especially backed the aesthetics and the concept of the *Stapelfenster* because it mirrored and gave form to their ideas on the rational and objective display of wares. Other period designers, writing general instructional guides to window design, also promoted the *Stapelfenster* and included didactic descriptions on how to most effectively deploy them and what responses they might elicit in the viewer.[113] For example, Hans Bode, in his 1925 text, describes a *Stapelfenster* display that included hundreds of meters of the same fabric. He posits that the passerby would likely react positively to it, believing the

Figure 2.29. *Left*: Elisabeth von Stephani-Hahn, illustration of various display platforms for windows, 1919. *Right*: Mies, competition entry for the redesign of Alexanderplatz, Berlin, 1929, photomontage.

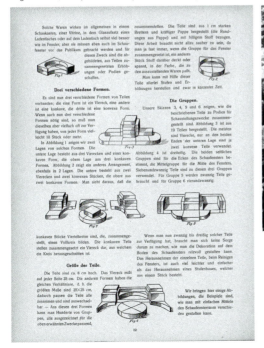
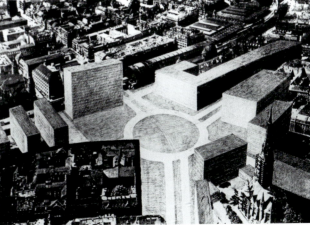

wares to be of good quality and low price owing to the abundant quantities on display.[114]

These displays were very much connected to Werkbund members' interests in the visuality of mass reproduction—a general period excitement on the part of artists, architects, and photographers for the visual representation of the materials and processes of industry, especially the aesthetics of the factory floor and its output. For example, Marianne Brandt's photomontage *Me (Metallwerkstatt)* from 1928 features three stacks of metal Bauhaus lampshades dynamically placed in the foreground, towering over a small standing figure in a lab coat, as well as rows of them receding in the upper right-hand corner (fig. 2.31).[115] Likewise, celebrated period photographer Albert Renger-Patzsch frequently photographed factory goods, often at vertiginous angles, aestheticizing the machinery and the proliferation of identical goods (fig. 2.32).[116] This visual trope was mirrored in the work of other photographers of this period and frequently published in the Werkbund's own journal (fig. 2.33). Art historian Kurt Wilhelm-Kästner, reviewing a photography exhibition in 1929, explained, "*Sachlichkeit* expresses itself as a sharp reproduction of the object through clear articulation and near isolation from surroundings and background, penetratingly even lighting, the banishment of as much shadow as possible or its utilization as a strong outlining element, and above all, a clear, distinct representation of objects with a clearly arranged formal structure."[117] It was these aesthetics that the Werkbund likewise sought in the rational display of goods in windows.

In the *Stapelfenster*, piles of finished goods appeared as if they had been directly transferred from the factory floor: these displays emphasized the repetition and orderliness that was also held in high esteem as a necessary organizing method for rationalized industrial production. Objects no longer seemed like individual wares for sale but rather became part of a spatial ensemble of generalized consumption—like factory workers and their operations, each individual object was a necessary part for the smooth functioning of the whole, each piece contributing toward a totalized effect. Displayed in this manner, the wares appeared even more objective and closer to the rationality of their industrial production processes, yet

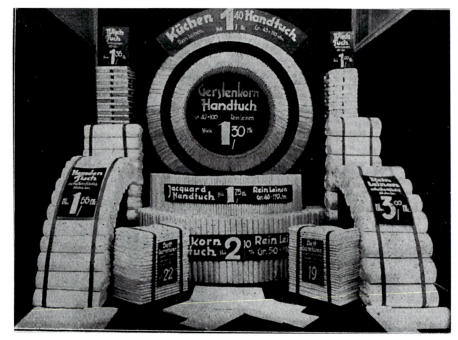

Figure 2.30. "Stack window" display (*Stapelfenster*) of towels, c. 1926.

refined. It was precisely these aesthetics—as well as the processes and changes in society and culture that had brought about a turn from the crafting of the unique object to the mass production of the undifferentiated product—that concerned contemporary critics such as Walter Benjamin. In several essays written in this period, he criticized the objects of *Neue Sachlichkeit* because he saw them as devoid of cultural meaning and lacking social relations.[118] Benjamin observed that "now, to bring things closer to us, or rather to the masses, is just as passionate an inclination in our day as the overcoming of whatever is unique in every situation by means of its reproduction. ... The peeling away of the object's shell, the destruction of the aura, is the signature of a perception whose sense for the sameness of things has grown to the point where even the singular, the unique, is divested of its uniqueness—by means of its reproduction." Benjamin lamented the object photography of this moment that results in "salability" rather than in "any knowledge it might produce."[119] His critical reaction to modernism and to forms of *Sachlichkeit* was not just a concern over aesthetics and a flattening out of the visual environment, but a disquiet about the ways the movement impinged on human interactions in a new, modern society and also in the ways it affected perceptions of interchange between people, objects, and architecture in this period. Likewise, contemporary critic Siegfried Kracauer uses the popular synchronized dance performances, rather than photography, to describe a similar condition in which the participants have "no meaning beyond themselves," they have emptied all the "substantial constructs of their contents." Capitalism is marked by abstraction, notes Kracauer, and this abstract

Figure 2.31. Marianne Brandt, *Me (Metallwerkstatt)*, 1928, photomontage.

mode of thought is "incapable of grasping the actual substance of life."[120] For members of the Werkbund, the rationalized windows of identical goods stacked architectonically performed as positive models by which to celebrate and sell *sachlich* goods to the people; they can be understood in opposition to the sentimental and novel windows that engendered the kinds of bonds Benjamin describes—those narrative sites that connected and drew people in with their popular appeal. The *Stapelfenster* linked the goods for sale to the rationalized aesthetic of factory production, thereby reproducing industrial culture on the city's streets in the self-contained context of the store window frame. This inscribed vision of the infinite replication of goods likely did not diminish the product's salability, rather heightened it, as Benjamin points out. Similarly, Kracauer determined that the commodities that the capitalist production process brought forth were never intended to be "possessed" in any meaningful way, instead "they are made for the sake of a profit that knows no limit."[121] By offering a representation of the conditions of production, the *Stapelfenster* may have negated the viewer's ability to have a knowledgeable and authentic experience with goods, to connect to them in a meaningful way, but that had never been a goal for Werkbund members. Nor was their championing of the *Stapelfenster* purely in pursuit of positive economic outcomes, although they were concerned about the overall health of the German economy. Rather, the Werkbund's protagonists were interested in furthering their agenda of rationality and objectivity in modern design and in supporting the reform of display windows for the positive

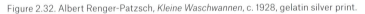

Figure 2.32. Albert Renger-Patzsch, *Kleine Waschwannen*, c. 1928, gelatin silver print.

DAS MASSENERZEUGNIS

Stahlkugeln
Vollkommen gleichartige Gebilde. Schulbeispiel
für die Gleichmäßigkeit und Gleichartigkeit in-
dustriell hergestellter Erzeugnisse

Foto: Dr. H. E. Trieb, Edenkoben

Renger-Foto

Badewannenstapel
Kraußwerke Schwarzenberg i. Sa.
Es werden täglich Hunderte von Badewannen hergestellt und verschickt. Durch die verschiedenen Sorten bzw. Größen
ergibt sich ein Zwischenlager, von dem ein Ausschnitt dargestellt ist

500

Figure 2.33. Page from the Werkbund's journal, *Die Form*, 1929.

effect it might have on developing good taste in consumers and in enhancing the overall appearance of the city.

Modern architecture, the *Stapelfenster*, and the display of modern products of industry come together compellingly in architect Hannes Meyer's *Co-op Vitrine*, an installation resembling a display window, designed in 1925. The *Co-op Vitrine* was a glass cabinet filled with standardized goods—Meyer termed them "Co-op articles"—arrayed horizontally and stacked vertically, simultaneously recalling both the production line processes and the output of a factory (fig. 2.34). Meyer published a photograph of the *Co-op Vitrine* in 1926 as part of an article titled "The New World."[122] He had joined a cooperative society in 1919—the Association of Swiss Consumer Societies—and won the architectural competition to design the Freidorf cooperative housing development for the group, located in Muttenz, Switzerland. He himself lived there until he moved to Dessau in 1926 to teach at the Bauhaus.[123] Freidorf's main community building included a co-op store, also designed by Meyer. The architect articulated what he saw as the difference between the layout of a "private shop" and a "cooperative shop"; the latter did not have a storage room, rather, it was designed so that its products could be centrally laid out and directly accessible to the consumer.[124] At the Bauhaus, Meyer lectured on the topic of the cooperative shop, and notes taken by a student there record his opposition to the "artificial devices" used by private shops to "whet consumer desire"; instead, the cooperative shop was to be designed as "a stockroom in which items fulfilling daily needs are presented in open form to the members of the cooperative."[125]

Meyer's *Co-op Vitrine* can be further linked to the period display window. In the layout of his article "The New World," the published photograph of the *Co-op Vitrine* is set under the heading "propaganda"—a term that did not have the pejorative connotations it carries today, but simply meant "advertising" in this context. The vitrine, as photograph, can be understood as an advertisement for Co-op products, one that celebrated the goods' straightforward nature and rational production. In the same article, Meyer notes, "the display window of today … is display window organization (*Schaufenster-Organisation*) rather than window dressing (*Schaufenster-Dekoration*)," assigning the task a more rationalized title.[126] The vitrine, understood as a display window filled with stacks of standard products serving daily needs (coffee, cocoa, matches, etc.), mirrors the aesthetics of contemporary urban *Stapelfenstern* and their typical products, such as packages of Leibniz butter cookies

Figure 2.34. Hannes Meyer, *Co-op Vitrine*, 1925, photograph published 1926.

and boxes of Tropon protein supplement (see figs. 2.12, 2.14). Similarly, as Meyer notes in his text, "The standardization of our requirements is shown by … the Co-op product, the DIN standard size, and Liebig's meat extract."[127] Meyer considered the conception and design of the *Co-op Vitrine*, as well as the layout of the Freidorf Co-op shop, to be a task for the modern architect, and he connected images of the two directly to architecture in a series of 1925–26 linocuts. *Untitled, Abstract Architecture I*, was the title he gave to his linocut of the *Vitrine*, and he titled his isometric, constructivist linocut of the shop *Untitled, Abstract Architecture II*.[128] In his vitrine layout and in his built cooperative store, Meyer rationally organized the products necessary for meeting daily needs in a manner designed to celebrate the standardization and rationalization of goods (and needs). While he was unable to entirely move away from the spaces of capitalism—a display window and a store—he did seek to subvert it through a cooperative model of production and distribution, and by denying the production of individual consumer desire. Meyer, through his *Co-op Vitrine*, directly addressed the discursive, aesthetic, and capitalist developments of the contemporary metropolis—and the problematic, yet transformative, nature of modern industrial society.

With its stacked products from the Freidorf cooperative, Meyer's *Vitrine* should be viewed in light of the development and discourse of the display window in this period, especially the *Stapelfenster*. Meyer was interested in the rationalization of production processes, as a means of meeting needs, as well as its visual ramifications. There are some key points of conceptual—as well as visual—connection between the *Stapelfenster* and Meyer's *Vitrine*. As K. Michael Hays points out about the *Vitrine*, also applicable to the *Stapelfenster*, the installation drew attention to the "formal problems of the representation of modern industrial society" and alluded to the question "of the ideological nature and function of that representation itself." Hays states, "The commodity, now produced independently of individuals, has lost its subjective aura, and even the arrangement of Co-op products as so many fragments in a glass case indicates this disenfranchisement of individual manufacture. The aesthetic structure of the *Vitrine* is determined by the repetitive and serially structured formation that is the very nature of mass-reproduced commodities and their distribution."[129] Again, the *Stapelfenster* should be understood in these terms, too. Though the Werkbund *Stapelfenster* celebrated the mass-produced objects of industry, it was not wholly engaged with—or celebratory of—capitalist systems. Rather, the *Stapelfenster*, like the *Vitrine*, aestheticized industry's processes and its overall forms, playing down the individual object in favor of the representation of an entire system of production and its larger meaning in contemporary society. However, an important underlying difference between Werkbund windows, especially the *Stapelfenster*, and Meyer's *Vitrine*, is that, as Hays suggests, Meyer is representing the symbolic projection of the fruits of changed relations of production—that is, goods produced by cooperative methods—instead of the standard profit-driven mode of capitalist manufacture.

Meyer's and the Werkbund's attitudes toward capitalism can be further aligned insofar as both were concerned about capitalism's effects—if they could not exert control over them, then at least acting to stem them. Meyer was interested in the idea of the sublation of consumption (and its related effect, consumer desire), via rationalization; likewise, Werkbund leaders such as Osthaus were trying to control production and consumption within capitalism by promoting notions of objectivity and standardization, especially through the rationalization of the display window. Both the *Vitrine* and the *Stapelfenster* blur the lines that might otherwise separate the production from the reception of objects; products are to be received objectively and not beholden to individual subjectivity.[130] The collective modes of production, as Hays argues, had a decentering effect on the individual subject, and on the individual article of consumption, to which "bourgeois individualism, illusionism, and interiority cannot lay claim."[131] Hays reads Georg Lukács's theory of reification (*Verdinglichung*)—a "negative and critical account of rationalization and commodity fetishism structurally related to class"—via Meyer's *Vitrine*, noting that "for the bourgeois, an object is above all a commodity—a fixed, given, immediate thing whose cause is wholly secondary to its consumption—and this static relationship to objects is, of course, but a 'reflection' of the life experience of the bourgeois in the socio-economic realm."[132] The bourgeois subject might buy and consume an article from a *Stapelfenster*, but he or she could not relate to it, and it had no effect on the forces of the period's social production, merely its patterns of consumption.

In light of Lukács's insight, the Werkbund *Stapelfenster*, with its aesthetics of the factory floor and the processes of replication, was seemingly beyond the true grasp of the bourgeois and should have connected with—and held the interests of—the viewing masses on the burgeoning metropolis's streets. Likewise, Meyer's *Vitrine* was an attempt to bring the workers closer to the means of production and the processes at which they labored, as reified in his window installation. Yet these examples of *Stapelfenstern* should instead be viewed as elite—not in terms of their material content but because they lacked appeal to those outside the narrow circle represented by Werkbund members, architects, and proponents of modernism, who would have found them intellectually and visually resonant. Meyer's display, too, was an elite and cerebral presentation that would have appealed to the readers of the magazine in which he published the images, *Das Werk*, a Swiss avant-garde architectural journal; that is, the educated individual and not the common worker. In both the Werkbund's celebration of the *Stapelfenster* and Meyer's *Vitrine*, featuring straightforward stacks of identical goods, the aestheticization and reification of the production process should be understood as another type of elitism—one that was at too far a remove to influence the taste of the common people on the street. By all accounts, those very urban spectators enjoyed the narrative and spectacular window displays offered up by the large department stores. In the rationalized store window, modern designers can be seen as exchanging one kind of visual aesthetic for another, one that was ultimately more top-down and elite than what it replaced.

THE DISPLAY WINDOW AS URBAN INTERVENTION

Werkbund members posited a continuum that ranged from the showcasing of goods to the impact of their display to the improvement of the urban environment. As early as 1909, one critic advocated: "The aesthetic problem of display window design can no longer only be observed with the usual narrowness; it must also encompass a wider viewpoint—not as its own isolated problem, but rather a part of the aesthetic of the entire streetscape."[133] And four years later, Friedrich Naumann, politician and Werkbund member, fervently put forward the idea that with the elevation of the quality of goods and the shop window display of them, the entire appearance of the store, and then the overall appearance of a city, could be uplifted—that is, he noted, with characteristic Werkbund elitist élan—if it were done with "cultivated intention." He, too, argued that the display window was an important part of the city's appearance.[134] Other Werkbund members cited its role in the aesthetics of the metropolis. A window and its contents could have a greater impact than architecture itself, Karl Ernst Osthaus argued, because the *Schaufenster* was observed even more than a building's facade.[135] Whether this could be verified or not, it nevertheless underscores the importance the Werkbund placed on the display window for the greater architectural and urban context.

Between the outside urban environment of the streetscape and the richly material interior world of goods, the display window was an architectural conduit representing a distinct interstitial realm linking the two. A discrete architectural object, the *Schaufenster* was an ensemble of exterior frame and plate glass, and an interior subspace constituted by side walls, a floor area and a backing element (either a floor-to-ceiling wall, half-wall, or other membrane such as a curtain, that separated the window display from the store interior). The display window can be directly tied to larger period developments in modern architecture, especially where it brought together new materials, technology, and visual elements such as display signs using modern typography. As such, the window constituted a scaled-down architectural realm, bound within an architectural whole, but it was also a point of connectivity and in dialogue with the streetscape. This was a key issue for architecture in the period. As a 1930 review of Mies's proposed Adam department store described his building, "Neither wall nor window but something else again, quite new. ... Modern architecture weds a building to the landscape, binds the interior with the space of the street."[136] As glass opened up greater possibilities, this connection between the commercial interior and the urban exterior took on heightened importance, with the display window as the primary point of interchange and the architectural element binding the two.

Two key, and often intertwined, aspects of the display window in the urban environment were their nighttime illumination and advertising.[137] The lighting was especially tied to affluence. Ernst Bloch, writing about Berlin in 1928, observed, "you roam the streets ... observing the rising prosperity, the New Objectivity, the overly lavish lighting of which you have heard so much."[138] Another period description especially noted the illumination of Berlin's luxury stores: "The western center between Wittenbergplatz, Kaiser-Wilhelm-Gedächtniskirche [Kaiser William Memorial Church], and the Kurfürstendamm is essentially the leisure and entertainment quarter. Accordingly, its real character reveals itself best in the artificial light of the evening. Then we see the long rows of brightly lit, broad-fronted luxury shops—the flagship shops of the big firms."[139] For Hannes Meyer, writing in 1926, the display window was a component of the modern synesthetic urban experience, especially lighting and advertising: "Illuminated signs twinkle, loud-speakers screech, posters advertise, display windows shine forth. ... In the display window of today psychological capital is made of the tensions between modern materials with the aid of lighting."[140]

Articles such as "The New Building Style and Advertising" of 1928 stressed the importance of cohesion in the advertising components of the facade and the relationship between the structure and the window groupings, especially their silhouetting, which was critical for how buildings would appear at night.[141] Similarly, a year earlier Max Landsberg had discussed "Illuminated Advertising in the City" and noted, "The most beautiful cityscape, the most beautiful edifice disappears at night behind its lights. The commercial city already has such a different appearance by day and by night, that one can speak of an urban architecture for the day, and must demand one for the night."[142] Moreover, lighting effects were to contribute to the *Sachlichkeit* of the advertising as well as the harmony of the building's mass. In articles such as "The Influence of Modern Architecture on the Display Window," lighting was considered a "new architectural material."[143] The criticality of night illumination was also underscored with the suggestion that the company's name appear on the building's facade and in illuminated lettering at night, but never on the window itself, which, it was advised, should be entirely without any lettering.[144] A good visual example of how this might be achieved is the Leibniz Keks facade in Berlin, in which the firm's name was highly legible, even more so when illuminated at night (see fig. 2.1).

In the display window, the architectural and business realm were poised to come closer together, especially as advertising and architectural intervention in the city intersected. As Kathleen James-Chakraborty has pointed out, in the Werkbund's search for an "aesthetically compelling and economically profitable relationship between architecture and marketing," advertising "emerged as a source of artistic effects that were realized almost exclusively through technology."[145] Erich Mendelsohn's architecture particularly addressed this goal; especially against the cacophony of the modern city, he ensured that the store name and the display windows were highly legible. His flat, rectangular display cases were praised in the period for allowing maximum flexibility for the window designer.[146] For example, Mendelsohn's store for C. A. Herpich Sons allowed for the choice of a contiguous display across multiple window bays, or individual window designs, each confined to one bay (see fig. 2.11). During the day, light flooded into the store because the steel frame allowed for large windows, while still presenting an elegant travertine-clad facade accented with bronze hoods and sills.[147] Mendelsohn's store windows, too, were designed for optimum effectiveness when illuminated at night.

Illuminated advertising signage and display window lighting had become so important by the late 1920s that not only were many books or sections of books exclusively devoted to it, but an exhibition for the sake of public education, *Illuminated Advertising and Display Window Illumination* (*Lichtreklame und Schaufensterbeleuchtung*), also took place in 1928 at the Applied Arts Museum in Basel.[148] On major streets and transportation thoroughfares, it was recommended

Figure 2.35. False and correct lighting, 1928. From Albert Walter, *Das Schaufenster und sein Schmuck: Ein kurzer Leitfaden für die Praxis* (Leipzig: G. A. Gloeckner, 1928).

that windows be illuminated through the entire night.[149] The task of lighting was seen not as the responsibility of the window designer, but of the architect, yet most period texts on the topic of the display window included extensive sections devoted to effective—and ineffective—lighting techniques.[150] A soft, even light from a covered source, especially soffit lighting, was advised (fig. 2.35).[151] Multiple solutions for hiding the light source from the viewer were suggested during this period, with gas and electricity allowing for differing options and effects.[152] Other designers were not opposed to visible light sources, but suggested the use of reflectors, covers, and varying placement options for lights.[153]

The Werkbund, in various articles in *Die Form*, stressed that advertising on buildings cost very little but brought in income, seeing it as a positive enlivening of the architecture, as natural and appealing when properly applied, and even describing advertising signs as "architecture-forming," showing, among several examples, a photograph of the Leibniz Keks shop facade (see fig. 2.1).[154] However, badly integrated advertising presented a problem on city streets, this same article noted, providing as an example a photograph in which the signage covered up elements of a building's facade (fig. 2.36).[155] A positive effect of having the branding of the store placed via signage attached to the entire facade of an older building, noted the author, was that the new, modern signage could connect the entire building to a street-level, ground-floor shopfront that had been modernized. The author was at pains to point out, "It is no longer that the advertising fits the existing architecture after a fashion, conversely it is, that the architecture is formed by the needs of advertising. … In the night it is generally only the illuminated advertising that constitutes architecture: as the building itself recedes into darkness, its lines remain. It becomes a type of suspended architecture that is completed through the moving figures, through skywriting and images, an illusionary magical world—the fitting

Figure 2.36. German Werkbund, example of badly integrated advertising, c. 1928, photograph as published in Wilhelm Theodor Schnarrenberger, "Reklame Architekturbildend," *Die Form* 3, no. 9 (September 1928): 269.

frames for the city's night."[156] Other texts on modern store design suggested the means by which the outward appearance of individual shopfronts and even whole shopping streets could be made more lustrous or gleaming, for example, through the use of materials such as Nirosta.[157] Nirosta was a non-rusting, non-tarnishing metal, available in a range of tones from silver-white to gray-platinum, from highly polished to matte, manufactured by Krupp and marketed as a material for a building's facade.

This relationship between the viewer, the street, the architecture, and its display windows was also emphasized in other publications, which offered suggestions for the renovation or reconfiguration of stores in order to heighten the display opportunities and draw consumers to the windows.[158] Period literature advised on the rebuilding of existing shops to allow for the windows to project out into the sidewalk, or display cases could even be placed as stand-alone elements, entering the realm of the pedestrian.[159] The possibilities for improving existing stores seemed almost infinite, especially as advances in glazing allowed for curving glass so that display windows were not limited to rectilinear corners, but rounded edges could entice viewers to encircle the wares or be led around the display cases and into the store (fig. 2.37).

Two 1926 designs by Bauhaus master Josef Albers for renovations to stores for Ullstein sewing patterns, published in the journal *Offset*, exemplify this trend (fig. 2.38). In Albers's first design, which he published simply as "Design for a Store Renovation" (although the design's signs identify it as "Ullstein Schnittmuster"), he uses dynamic lines and color to project the building into the street. Jutting out from the building's center, a corrugated sheet metal canopy was intended to aggregate potential customers in front of the display windows while protecting them from the elements.[160] Placed at the front edge of the canopy, a sign made of glass letters announced the name of the store, and to the right, a second, vertical sign

Figure 2.37. Display options for shop windows, 1926. From Bruno H. Jahn, *Reklame durch das Schaufenster* (Berlin: Verlag L. Schottlaender, 1926).

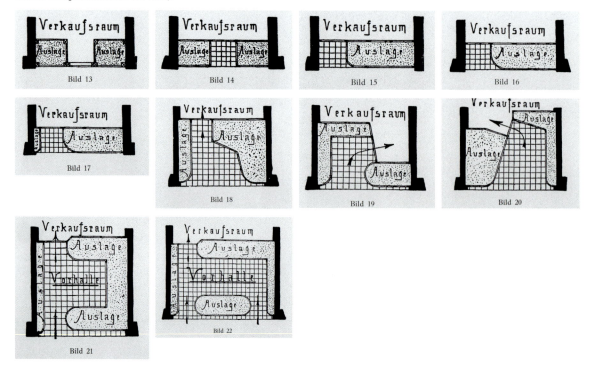

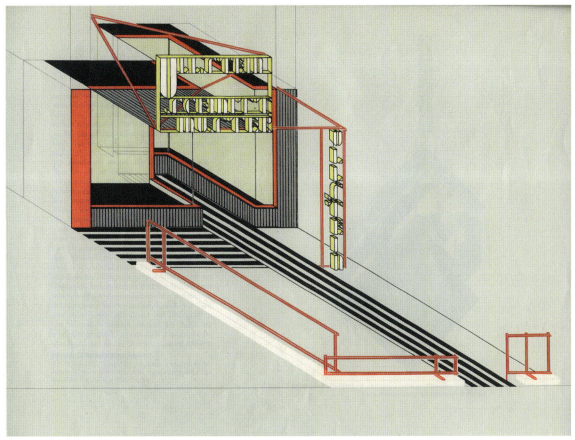

Figure 2.38. *Top and bottom*: Josef Albers, designs for a remodeled storefront for the Ullstein sewing patterns stores, 1926.

with the firm's name also projected out into the forecourt. This advertising signage, which could be illuminated at night, was well integrated with the architecture and reached dynamically into the realm of the pedestrian. From the street, a striped path brought passersby up to the display windows and led them into the store. By placing the entrance door in deeply, Albers was able to devote a significant area to the display windows on three sides. A large, deep, square display area to the left was oriented to the street and would have caught the eyes of passersby, while a small space in the middle and a long, narrow display space along the right side were designed for viewing the available patterns up close, leading potential customers along the window and into the shop. Albers stated that he placed the display windows at knee-height so that shoppers could freely approach and gaze at the patterns from a comfortable distance.[161] But in the interior, just behind the glass, the floor of the display case was lowered slightly to maintain the impression of a contained interior space and for the optimal viewing of the clothing (made from the sewing patterns) modeled by the mannequins. Albers specified glass corners in order that the samples on show could be examined from the front, side, and back.[162] The modern materials selected by Albers contrasted with each other in a dynamic way. The overall flatness and transparent effect of the display windows and the semitransparency of the white glass of the illuminated lettering were in contradistinction to the wavy ridges of the corrugated sheet metal used for the canopy and the facade's cladding.

Albers's second store redesign was for a shop located on the corner of Berlin's Friedrichstrasse and Leipziger Strasse. This design, a worm's eye view published in black and white, relied less on projective geometry and instead simply encased the small, kiosk-sized shop in display windows on two sides and similarly clad the building with corrugated sheet metal. A modest overhang offered some protection from the weather and provided the surface on which to identify the store. Both designs are representative of how developments in modern architecture—such as the use of new materials, integrated advertising, provisions for night illumination, and even dynamic new modes of illustrating the designs—came to bear on the modernization of stores, and especially an understanding of the importance of the display window.

The allure of the display window as an urban fixture and how subjects interacted with them—phenomenologically and contemplatively—in the metropolis can be charted in street scene paintings by Ernst Ludwig Kirchner and August Macke, both of whose work prominently featured windows as key elements in their depictions of the exuberance and allure of the ever-changing Berlin streetscape of this period.[163] Kirchner's *Five Women on the Street* (*Fünf Frauen auf der Strasse*), painted around 1913, for example, depicts women, likely prostitutes, gathered around an illuminated display window (fig. 2.39). Their interest in the window's contents is superficial and fleeting. In other paintings, the windows are a prominent repeated urban motif, as with *Street at Schöneberg City Park* (*Strasse am Stadtpark Schöneberg*), 1912–13. More than a decade later, Kirchner's *Street Scene at Night* (*Strassenszene bei Nacht*), 1926–27, offers a composed view of a codified, yet vivid 1920s Berlin evening street, in which the urban elements are prominently celebrated—crowds, automobiles, signage, illuminated advertising affixed to buildings and several large, well-lit display windows. This latter scene is vibrant, yet the city appears ordered—represented by elemental, geometric forms and planes that supersede each other, as the signs recede down the street and figures are carefully silhouetted by the illuminated shop windows. August Macke's protagonists are depicted more intimately and contemplatively engrossed with the urban display window. In the painting *Fashion Store* (*Modegeschäft*), 1913, window-shoppers are framed by display windows on one side and a freestanding vitrine filled with hats on the other (fig. 2.40). The shoppers are outside the store, one with her parasol still open as she gazes at the display window. It is unclear if the window-shoppers intend to enter the store—they are in an indeterminate space, still in the public sphere of the street and yet already being drawn in, under the spell of the entrancing windows and vitrines. Macke depicts a range of windows and contents in the series of paintings he executed in this period. In *Large Bright Display Window* (*Grosses helles Schaufenster*), 1912, a woman stands motionless, transfixed by the cacophony of colors and forms. *Hat Shop* (*Hutladen*), 1913, consists of a simple, *sachlich* store facade, entrance doorway, and single plate

Figure 2.39. Ernst Ludwig Kirchner, *Five Women on the Street* (*Fünf Frauen auf der Strasse*), 1913.

glass window with five hats tastefully arranged on hat stands, set against a plain background and with no other accoutrements. A tastefully dressed shopper serenely gazing at the goods completes the composition, in effect, a visualization of Werkbund ideals regarding store window reform in this period.

————

The display window initiative was an important part of the multifaceted programming that the Werkbund developed and sponsored. Unlike other schemes, such as the book of Werkbund-approved goods, the 1915 *Deutsches Warenbuch*, its short-lived foray into promoting German fashion, its programming in schools, or its promotion of the modern architecture of the new dwelling, *Schaufenster* reform had the potential to successfully reach, and impact, the average shopper on the street. But did it? Were objective displays of wares stacked as factory production line output or simple, non-narrative windows effective at not only holding the attention of shoppers but waking their consuming desire? Could they develop "taste" in their gazers and cause consumers to look for German "quality"—if they could even afford it? Joan Campbell has pointed out that the consumer education program of the Werkbund was aimed at the educated urban elite (the *Gebildeten*) and that the bourgeoisie purchased

Figure 2.40. August Macke, *Fashion Store* (*Modegeschäft*), 1913.

handcrafted, custom-made designs and furniture and were generally resistant to machine-made goods, instead favoring luxury wares. Notes Campbell, in making their case for modernism, at times members of the Werkbund promoted the previous bourgeois styles as models in their promotion of good taste: for Paul Schultze-Naumburg the model was Biedermeier of around 1800, and for Hermann Muthesius it was the English country house.[164] Key here was the emphasis placed on the bourgeois elite as the bearers of traditions of taste and quality, simplicity and well-made goods that the Werkbund sought to renew on a greater scale, and in modern design. This luxury of objectivity, of spare and tasteful design, was thus built on an earlier but well-established tradition of well-designed, pared-down domestic goods promoted by an elite class, the wealthy bourgeoisie. In the Werkbund window, objectivity remained a luxury.

Berlin and other metropolises of this period represented a truly electrifying and eclectic mix of elements: of peoples, social classes, occupations, modes of transport, shopfronts, dwelling districts, desires, scales, visualities, and tempo. The display window, with its alluring contents, was one space that had the potential to attract the attention of both the elite society lady and the working-class shopgirl on her way home from work. The Werkbund, too, with its emphasis on *Geschmacksbildung*, sought to educate store window designers and then an eventual audience of consuming eyes with their ideas. Janet Ward has convincingly described the "surface culture" of 1920s German urban visual culture.[165] But here I might also propose that the window represents deep divisions between people and things, even as the period put certain maneuvers in place to mitigate—at least superficially—these stark differences.

Werkbund endeavors extended widely in relation to the display window's potential role in ongoing efforts in the arenas of "taste," "culture," and "objectivity"—reform to be enacted through the visual culture of everyday life, with architecture (broadly defined) playing a major part. Through their theorization of objective store window design, the Werkbund was also able to integrate two key elements—objects and architecture—into its overall reform program. The sheer abundance of machine output had been given visual lucidity in the *Stapelfenster*; translated into form, that is, it becomes an architecture representing mass production. Goods, displayed in patterns and in great numbers as part of a *sachlich* formation, especially in the case of the *Stapelfenster*, were denied individual status and their own discrete materiality, subsumed as they were into the group. In a kind of circularity, the display window was also an enclosure in which objects for sale—carefully ordered—could in turn become their own self-contained spatial ensemble, objects becoming architecture. To this end, the display window can be understood as both an object with architectural qualities and an architecture with objectlike qualities. Architecture could oversee and aid the ordering of objects in the window, and the ordered objects within could help constitute the window as architectural container.

To spread reform downward and influence mass taste, the Werkbund thus looked to retailers and shopkeepers and created outreach programs aimed at street-level consumers. Certainly in the burgeoning metropolis such a project had merit and potential, postulating a necessary corrective to out-of-control expansion and the effects of capitalism in the urban environment. Yet the order and refinement of the tastefully decorated Werkbund window remained an unreal fantasy, an exception to the rule, not reflective of the actual chaotic situation of the metropolis of Berlin,

Figure 2.41. George Grosz, *Friedrichstrasse*, (illustration from *Ecce Homo*), 1918.

with its lack of pared-down, spare modernity. Georg Grosz's 1918 *Friedrichstrasse* presents a more realistic, if somewhat overwrought, image of the city (fig. 2.41). Grosz's representation should be considered against the rational urban calm of the Werkbund's images of street facades, photographed such that they were emptied of window-shoppers, active consumers, and urban cacophony. As much as the Werkbund members wanted to reach the average citizen with their foray into window layout, they also seemingly wanted to keep the masses at bay—rejecting, in their window design, the fascination of kitsch, of narrative, of moving parts, or of dizzying feats of decoration. The window typology they advocated was meant to bring consumers closer to the mass-produced realities of the origins of the goods, to make modern products more comprehensible, and to help order the city, but were these types of windows actually poised to do so? While Grosz presents something more akin to the authentic experience of Berlin in 1918, it is distant from the Werkbund's ideal organization of a city. The Werkbund's project was elite and top-down; the group hoped that capitalism and consumerism could be instrumentalized to combat rampant capitalism and consumption, and even that the architecture of rational display could reorder the city. In a privileged approach, members of the Werkbund, especially architects, were focused on control: of the window, the building, and the street. They sought to engage and elevate the masses without pandering to them, to encourage careful consideration of wares but not rampant capitalism as a result of uncritical buying. Via the containment of the *Schaufenster*, the Werkbund sought to control and rein in capitalism.

The Werkbund remained an elite, fighting the inevitability of the results of the period's flow of capital into major German metropolises. Its members were not as effective as they wished to be in countering the growing population who readily spent their earnings as quickly as they acquired them, and rarely on well-designed, high-quality goods. *Sachlichkeit* was necessarily elite, with its emphasis on good taste rather than mass taste, nonnarrative rather than narrative, staid windows that used repetition and patterning rather than glamour and *Glanz*. Objectivity represents luxury precisely because it favored the few over the many, elite taste over shop-girl taste, high art (even for everyday products) over mass art and kitsch. The Werkbund and its *sachlich* windows remained in the realm of luxury not only in this area of taste, but also in the erudition behind it all, the premise that taste could be taught via consumption and that the tide of consumption could be turned. Moreover, the group's premise was essentially top-down—a circle of artists, architects, politicians (and Werkbund members who would soon enter politics), and industrialists who sought to influence the taste and buying habits of Germans at home and, in their aims for the export market, potential consumers abroad. The Werkbund was a bold project, not just in how it manifested itself at the level of the shop window, but in its overall premise, of which the *Schaufenster* initiative was just one manifestation. *Sachlichkeit*, or objectivity, remained in the realm of luxury.

CAPITAL

"Can't you help me to find capitalists?" wrote Walter Gropius in the early years of the Weimar Bauhaus in an appeal to Lily Hildebrandt, wife of art historian Hans Hildebrandt. "There's no money to relieve the terrible conditions of the students. … I try to raise funds but I am not gifted at it."[1] Over the course of the next few years, Gropius would hone his fund-raising skills with a wide variety of "capitalists" who contributed sums of money, materials, and products to the Bauhaus's efforts. In the same period, Bauhaus-member Oskar Schlemmer worried aloud about the effects of capital on art in the pamphlet designed for the Bauhaus's 1923 exhibition—a document that was quickly withdrawn by the school—writing, "Mathematics, structure and mechanization are the elements, and power and money are the dictators of these modern phenomena of steel, concrete, glass, and electricity. Velocity of rigid matter, dematerialization of matter, organization of inorganic matter, all these produce the miracle of abstraction. Based on the laws of nature, these are the achievements of mind in the conquest of nature, based on the power of capital, the work of man against man. The speed and supertension of commercialism make expediency and utility the measure of all effectiveness, and calculation seizes the transcendent world: art becomes a logarithm."[2]

The Bauhaus in 1923 was pulled in many directions: a dire need for financial support as government backing—and its funding—was being withdrawn; a resulting new turn to capitalism to assist it in meeting the economic crises of the day; an ambiguous position with regard to the priority of craftsmanship, technology, and industry; and a radical redefinition of the role of art and the artist in an age of mechanical reproduction. At this economically desperate moment in Germany—the height of the post–World War I inflation that caused the bulk of the population extraordinary economic distress—the school was eager to "collaborate" with capitalist industry, setting the direction that would continue for the length of Gropius's tenure as the Bauhaus's director. At the same time, these circumstances dramatically altered the society for which the Bauhaus was designing.

The Haus am Horn, a seemingly modest, single-family show house constructed to communicate ideas and design fostered by the Bauhaus at its initial large-scale public exhibition in 1923, was the first concrete example of architecture to emerge from the school, which famously did not have a formalized program or department of architecture until Hannes Meyer was appointed to succeed Gropius in 1927 (figs. 3.1, 3.2).[3] This key architectural exemplar seemingly demonstrates all of the concepts that modernism proclaimed—functionality, technology, hygiene, the use of modern materials and construction methods—and was built using the latest materials—plywood, plate glass, rubber flooring. The Haus am Horn marks a turning point from the more romantic, socialist, and expressionistic post–World War I origins of the Bauhaus to a representation of the school's practical and visual move away from utopianism and craftsmanship toward a stated desire to produce for and cooperate with (capitalist) industry, concretized in Gropius's concurrent slogan, proclaimed at the exhibition's opening: "art and technology—a new unity." But it was laboriously designed at great cost for a specific use and place and never put into mass production. It was, in short, a singular object of expensive luxury.

At the Haus am Horn, not only was the reproducibility of its architecture limited by its costly fabrication and materials, but it failed also in the more general sense that, despite the school's ideological and social project, it remained an inaccessible luxury object appropriate only for the period's wealthy. The house spoke mainly to an upper echelon of industrial patrons and their circle, whose taste and favor it sought to cultivate, rather than to a wide base of potential dwellers for whom it was nominally intended. Understood as an elite object, a product of 1920s industrial capitalism more than of any revolutionary social program, the Haus am Horn illuminates the disconnect between modernism's ideals and the realities of the reigning economic structures. Completed at a moment of runaway inflation, it is less a visionary conception of a house of the future than a compromise with the realities of capitalism, albeit under the peculiar and dramatic circumstances of the German currency's collapse. Under these conditions, the Haus am Horn was less a vehicle for a collaboration with industry, as Gropius had espoused, than an uncritical showcasing of its output. It represents an improbable application of industrial capital to

Figure 3.1. Georg Muche, Walter Gropius, and the Bauhaus Siedlung GmbH, Haus am Horn, Weimar, 1923.

Figure 3.2. Muche, Gropius, and the Bauhaus Siedlung, Haus am Horn, living room work niche. Desk by Erich Dieckmann; chair by Marcel Breuer; rug by Gunta Stölzl.

design and a very early and noteworthy example of the role capitalism could have in determining architecture, a relationship that would come to its fullest fruition following World War II.

BAUHAUS BEGINNINGS

That the school, under Gropius, would find itself in a position to construct the Haus am Horn in 1923 was not self-evident. The forerunner to the Bauhaus was Weimar's School of Arts and Crafts, led by the Belgian architect Henry van de Velde. Though it had begun as an arts and crafts school, by 1907, it had shifted its emphasis from handicraft instruction toward industrial prototypes. The school offered practical training in its workshops, instruction in design, and classes on subjects such as color theory. Its instructors advised journeymen and master craftsmen on how to prepare their newly developed prototypes for production.[4] As a foreigner, van de Velde was forced to resign once World War I broke out. In April 1915, he listed Gropius as one of three potential successors. Although the school closed in July 1915, Gropius's contact with those in charge of the school placed him in a good position to make his proposal for a new kind of institution after the war.

In the years leading up to World War I, the young Gropius had been very much involved in the modern design community in Germany, not only as a practicing architect, but as a designer of goods related to modern industry, from train engines to car interiors. He had achieved early acclaim in 1910 for the design, with Adolf Meyer, of the Fagus shoe last factory in Alfeld-an-der-Leine. His full-scale model office building and factory was on display at the 1914 Cologne Werkbund exhibition. With Peter Behrens, in 1910, he published "Memorandum on the Industrial Prefabrication of Houses on a Unified Artistic Basis," which evidenced Gropius's early interest in using modern industrial techniques to solve housing problems. During this period, he also published frequently and was an active public lecturer.

In these pre–World War I years, Gropius was interested in the potential of the industrial machine and its uses in architecture. He asserted that it was the artist who "holds the responsibility for the formation and further development of form in the world, only by sensibly coming to terms with the most powerful means of modern formal design, the machine of all types, from the simplest to the most complicated, and by pressing it into his service."[5] Gropius fully believed in the rationality, utility, and inevitability of the machine in art, architecture, and society at large. In 1913, he published an article in the Werkbund's *Yearbook*, titled "The Development of Modern Industrial Architecture," in which he asserted that designers should become more involved in industry and machine-made products. He advocated, "The modern architect must develop his aesthetic repertoire from forms stamped with precision, with nothing left to chance: clear contrasts, the ordering of the members, symmetry and unity of form and color—this is what the energy and economics of public life require."[6]

Gropius was a reservist and so was called up immediately when World War I broke out. In August 1914, he began dangerous reconnaissance missions and also served in the trenches on the western front. The modern machine in its many forms played important roles in the war effort on both sides—its power harnessed for destruction. Technology had produced efficient machine guns and rapid-fire field artillery guns, and also aided more effective aerial attacks with tactical bombing and the use of zeppelins. The war expanded the industrial potential of European economies; the efficient mobilization of industry and labor by the German war machine represented a new collaboration between industry, the army, and labor.[7] This use of machines for destruction and death caused many to doubt the Hegelian telos of progress and the ability of advanced technology to improve the human condition. For many, Gropius included, the war shattered the optimism of the machine age.[8]

Gropius was much changed upon his return to Berlin after the war—his expectations of progress brought by the machine in the prewar days had been obliterated by what he had seen during the war and Germany's dire situation after it. He significantly altered his mode of thinking, and this, in turn, heightened his urgency to create a school where he could put new ideas to the test. He attributed his idea for the Bauhaus to a "blend of profound depression resulting from the lost war with its breakdown of intellectual and economic life, and the ardent hope and desire to build up something new from these ruins."[9] Gropius had been mulling over the idea of taking on the directorship of a school for a number of years before the opportunity arose. In a letter to Karl Ernst Osthaus in 1918, Gropius announced, "I am working on something entirely different now, which I've been turning over in my head for many years—a *Bauhütte*! With a few like-minded artists … I ask you to keep quiet about it until I have spoken with you face to face, otherwise the idea, which requires gentle discretion, will be trampled in the economic turmoil before it's able to live."[10]

In conceiving of the Bauhaus, Gropius was not merely looking back to the arts and crafts, Jugendstil, or pre-Werkbund ideology of twenty years earlier; rather, he was reacting to the postwar political and social situation and a common belief in art's potential for rebuilding German society. Emerging from the horrors of World War I, anti-technology sentiments abounded in society at large. Collectively, these feelings contributed to an environment in which Gropius's proposal for the Bauhaus could be approved by the new politicians of the Weimar Republic. Moreover, Gropius had been actively involved in postwar political and artistic movements in Berlin, such as the Novembergruppe (November Group) and Arbeitsrat für Kunst (Workers' Council for Art), and was cognizant of similar movements throughout Germany and across Europe, which influenced his vision for the school. As an institution, the Bauhaus very much represented an amalgamation of artistic and political currents of the early years of the Weimar Republic.

Gropius rejected his earlier embrace of machine rationality and the Werkbund circle in favor of guilds and other premodern modes. In 1919, in a statement that he would have been less inclined to make in 1910, Gropius decried ugliness as the product of "our function-cursed age."[11] In an early speech to Bauhaus students, presumably in reference to himself, Behrens, and other members of the Werkbund, Gropius noted that before the war artists and architects "created artistic ashtrays and beer tankards and wanted to move upwards towards the large building gradually. Everything by means of cool-headed organization. That was a presumption on which we came to grief." He went on to propose a new mode of organization and rationale, "What will develop are not large, intellectual organizations but small, secret, closed associations, lodges, guilds, cabals which preserve a secret, a core of belief and wish to create artistically until a general, great, productive, intellectual and religious idea emerges from the individual groupings, an idea which must ultimately find expression crystallized in a great, total work of art. And this great total work of art, this cathedral of the future, will illuminate the smallest things of everyday life with floods of light."[12]

Early in 1919, Gropius was appointed director of Weimar's Arts and Crafts School and its Academy of Fine Art, which he merged into one school, the Staatliches Bauhaus (State Bauhaus).[13] The result was an institution very different from its two constituent parts—Gropius eliminated all formal academic requirements and accepted pupils regardless of gender, financial position, nationality, religion, or philosophical beliefs.[14] Initially, the Bauhaus offered craft training at three levels: apprentice, journeyman, and junior master, with students laboring under two instructors, a form master (a visual artist) and a craft master (a craftsman in charge of technical and practical training).

Gropius sought to elevate the crafts to the status of fine arts, seeking a new spiritual and social integration. In these early, idealistic years, he sought a different kind of postwar society, one that would benefit from reform in art education and the joining of craftsmen, artists, and sculptors together in order to build. The school's name, Bauhaus, confirmed on April 12, 1919, was a neologism that derived its significance from an amalgamation of sources, rich in associative meanings: *Bau*, meaning "a building"; *Bauhütten*, the name for guilds of the Middle Ages; and *bauen*, meaning "to build, construct, or to grow a crop."

The first large-scale collaborative project completed by the nascent Bauhaus was the Sommerfeld House, commissioned by Adolf Sommerfeld and completed in 1921 in the Berlin suburb of Dahlem (fig. 3.3).[15] Sommerfeld, a timber merchant, acquired the teak lining of a wrecked warship and hired Gropius to design a house out of the materials. Gropius and Adolf Meyer's design evokes a vernacular German typology using traditional wood construction techniques and a tall, peaked roof. The house also shows the influence of Frank Lloyd Wright's prairie style in its geometric forms, the overhang of the roof, and the use of natural materials. In the same period, Gropius wrote an article praising wood as the "building material of the present," appropriate "to the primitive beginning of our newly developing life."[16] Far removed from the rationality of his prewar commissions, such as the Fagus factory designed with Meyer in brick and glass, the Sommerfeld House—with its handmade decorative elements and high quality of craftsmanship—was an expression of the beauty and utility of craftsmanship, as well as the cooperative spirit Gropius wanted to foster at the Bauhaus. Handicraft came to the fore as Gropius subcontracted out the interior fittings and furnishings to the workshops of the Bauhaus. In the interior, the zigzag and other motifs in the wood carvings by Joost Schmidt and the stained glass

Figure 3.3. *Left*: Gropius and Adolf Meyer, Sommerfeld House (destroyed), entrance facade, Berlin, 1920–21. *Right*: Exterior, garden side.

windows by Josef Albers referenced an earlier time, abandoning any prewar ideas of industry and standardization (fig. 3.4). Other students and masters collaborated on the interior, which featured appliqué textile hangings by Dörte Helm and chairs by Marcel Breuer.

BUILDING BLOCKS FOR INDUSTRY

The Haus am Horn, produced a mere two years later, thus represented a very different direction for the school. It was designed and marketed as a scalable, flexible, mass-producible dwelling within a planned settlement. Although artist Georg Muche is credited as the architect, members of the Bauhaus and Gropius's private architectural office shared the design. Muche won the competition held at the Bauhaus; Gropius's architectural office took over the execution of the design, with Adolf Meyer in charge of the project (fig. 3.5). The Gropius proposal was less modest, with two more stories of additional rooms for working and sleeping, but likewise consisting of small rooms ringing a central, double-height living room.[17] Muche's plan and elevations for the Haus am Horn were a modification of a system of modular building block units that Gropius had been working on since 1911. With the assistance of Fred Forbát, a young architect recently brought into his office, Gropius had returned to his modular block idea, exhibiting it at the Bauhaus in June 1922 and again in the "Exhibition of International Architecture" held within the Haus am Horn during the 1923 exhibition.[18] The system was composed of different basic blocks intended to form variable, two- to three-story single and multifamily houses; mass-produced elementary forms were combined, and the results were labeled simply a "serial type-house" (*Typenserienhaus*) (fig. 3.6). Standardization was to be attained via a single module used in conjunction with a set of molds for concrete casting.[19]

In reference to the underlying concept of these expandable units, Gropius used the terms "honeycomb construction" (*Wabenbau*), which helpfully aligned the conceptually useful modular principle in beehive construction with the term "structure"

Figure 3.4. Gropius and Meyer, Sommerfeld House (destroyed), entrance hall. Interior design by Joost Schmidt; furniture by Marcel Breuer.

Figure 3.5. Muche, Gropius, and the Bauhaus Siedlung, plans submitted for the Haus am Horn construction permit.

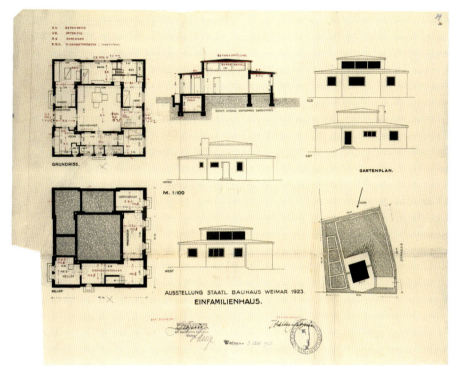

Figure 3.6. *Left*: Gropius, serial type-house (large-scale building blocks), 1922. *Right*: Gropius, variable floor plan of the serial type-house, 1922. Both as published in Adolf Meyer, ed., *Ein Versuchshaus des Bauhauses in Weimar*, 1925.

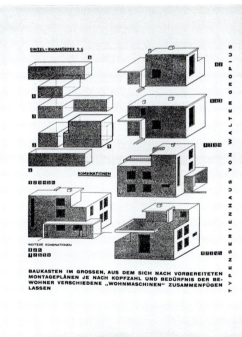

or "building" (*Bau*). The elements themselves he termed "large-scale building blocks" (*Baukasten im Grossen*), referencing elementary and easily mass-produced children's building blocks. A flexible combination of forms and sizes for variably numbered dwellers and their needs, yet still appropriate for industrialized, serial production, these units or "living machines" (*Wohnmaschinen*), as Gropius referred to them, were designed to be assembled together according to a prepared installation plan.[20] Gropius's goal was "dry-assembly construction … that would make it possible to order a house from the factory inventory as one orders a pair of shoes," with "savings to be expected from constructing houses in this way at 50 percent or more compared to traditional methods."[21] Realizing such a design would have required a true collaboration with industry of the sort often associated with the Bauhaus. The underlying intention with this building block system was to produce a socioeconomic gain through the development of housing made economically feasible via industrial production methods—and that could be backed, moreover, Gropius hoped, by capitalist enterprise.

INCORPORATED PLANNING: THE BAUHAUS SIEDLUNG GMBH

In order to realize these aims, the Bauhaus undertook an organizational innovation, the Bauhaus Siedlung GmbH, a limited liability holding company registered by the Bauhaus for the purposes of creating a planned housing development in Weimar. This was the first in a series of such companies that the Bauhaus would found in an ultimately unsuccessful attempt to formalize ties between design at the school, industry, and the wider market.[22] The Bauhaus Siedlung GmbH was established in April 1921 (and granted legal status in May 1922) to create affordable housing for Bauhaus members and to cultivate food for the Bauhaus cafeteria.[23]

Figure 3.7. Gropius, plan of the Bauhaus Siedlung, Weimar, 1922.

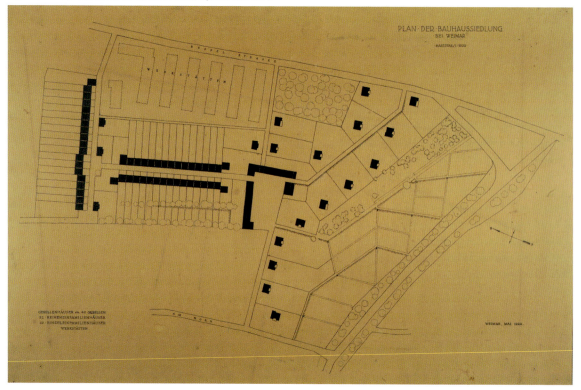

The Bauhaus housing estate idea was not a new one; as early as October 1920, Gropius asked the masters and students of the Bauhaus to come up with ideas for a planned community.[24] From 1920 to 1922, organizational meetings were held and an executive committee formed; interested parties—members of the school and of Gropius's office—gave sums of money toward the project; and the intended site was divided into plots. In June 1921, Gropius wrote to the Thuringian Finance Ministry asking for a lease to the land.[25] One year later, he requested a plot of land for ninety-nine years, rent-free, as well as a 5 million–mark loan for the construction of dwellings (which were to be sold with inexpensive mortgages, rather than rented) and the development of the Bauhaus garden. Gropius carefully made the case to the Thuringian officials that the Siedlung-plan represented an architecturally and economically new, flexible building plan—in contradistinction to the "usual one-sided template" for planned housing communities—addressing a variety of needs.[26]

The intended site was a sizable plot of land in a residential section of the city surrounded by large, single-family villas, overlooking the Ilm Park, situated between the streets Am Horn and Besselstrasse. The plan by Gropius, Forbát, and other members of Gropius's office comprised a mix of housing types: nineteen freestanding family houses (intended for masters), fifty-two single-family row houses, school dormitories for forty students, as well as additional workshops and school buildings (fig. 3.7). Perhaps tellingly, the single-family homes on the slope, intended for the masters, were deemed, in Forbát's recollection, the "most urgent and my first commission [was] to plan these."[27] Many of the designs featured, like the Haus am Horn, a central living room surrounded by bedrooms, the kitchen, and other service rooms. As early as mid-July 1922, four house designs merited building permit applications.[28] Although Gropius exerted much effort in attaining rights to the land and financing for the development, the political situation ultimately deteriorated, and the financial crisis and period of hyperinflation caused the development to become unfeasible.

The Bauhaus Siedlung GmbH, albeit unsuccessful, was an important step in formalizing Bauhaus initiatives within market economic structures, in a pragmatic attempt to eliminate the middleman, and in controlling the intended development site from not only an architectural but also a financial standpoint. Likewise, it points to Gropius's particular take on how housing operated in the market. There was an interest in industrial means of production across a wide spectrum from the political left to the right, from capitalism to communism. Architects such as Hannes Meyer were equally interested in economical building and industrialized techniques, but toward socialist ends, without an engagement with capitalism. The decision to build single-family houses over high-density apartment blocks and to sell rather than rent demonstrates Gropius's interest in capitalism on the consumptive side, rather than the most efficient, cost-sensitive, productive side.

TAKING FINANCIAL STOCK: THE HAUS AM HORN AT THE 1923 BAUHAUS EXHIBITION

The 1923 Bauhaus exhibition and its accompanying celebratory "Bauhaus Week," which brought an initial wave of visitors to Weimar, was deeply tied to the financial status of the school and its future economic outlook. The exhibition represented an attempt at accounting for the state funding and at the promotion of public relations for the school in hopes of continued state—and new external—support. In 1922, the Thuringian government agreed to give an additional loan for the expansion of the workshops under the condition that the school put on a comprehensive exhibition.[29] The Bauhaus was a state institution funded primarily through the regional parliament, where political parties were divided with regard to continuing its funding. Generally in support of the Bauhaus were the workers', socialist, and communist parties, and against it were the bourgeois and right-wing parties.[30]

Emerging out of World War I, the German economy was in shambles, a condition made manifest in the everyday visibility of the destitute, the severely disabled, the widowed, and the unemployed. The economic upheaval caused by the war generally, the loss of the Alsace and Lorraine regions, war reparations, and faltering industry left citizens and the country bereft.[31] The devaluation of currency had already begun by the Bauhaus's opening in 1919; in proposing his initial budget, Gropius noted, "the momentary financial situation does not promise favorable working conditions. … The value of money today amounts to only about 1/3 to 1/4" of its prior worth.[32] Gropius urged state officials to "put the school into a viable condition" by including the "estimated sum in the state budget." Though the school was allotted an annual budget, Gropius regularly made additional appeals for sums of money and other support, in writing and in person at the parliament. The German economy worsened as inflation rose, reaching its peak precisely during the exhibition dates. Thus the worth of the annual budget would drastically fall as hyperinflation ensued. Schlemmer described the dire situation: "This exhibition, which will decide the fate of the Bauhaus, is so much at the mercy of attacks from right and left, shortage of money, and the spirit of the times, that it becomes a question of survival, of victory or total destruction."[33]

The school sprang into action, organizing an exhibition committee that met regularly and that carefully organized publicity in order to maximize its impact. By November 1922, for example, the school had already designed an ink stamp with the text "Bauhaus Exhibition Summer 1923," which Gropius declared should be placed on all outgoing mail.[34] The exhibition was also advertised on the sides of trains and in major train stations.[35] The economic opportunity posed by the

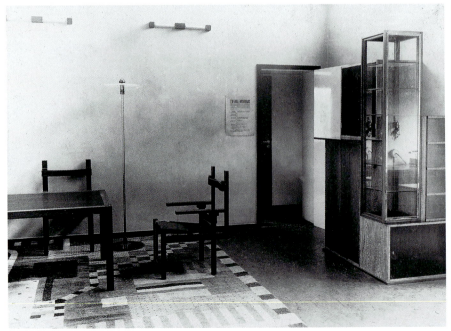

Figure 3.8. Haus am Horn, living room. Furniture by Marcel Breuer.

exhibition was never far from discussions that went into its planning; March 1922 meeting minutes, for example, record the desire, through exhibitions generally, to find "individuals who would economically support the Bauhaus."[36]

In meetings held throughout the fall of 1922, it was also decided to offer objects for sale at the exhibition, the aim being to draw attention to their designs in order to sell more goods in the future, to try to arrange contracts for products, and to drum up more government support as well as space for a permanent Bauhaus exhibition in the city museum.[37] A flyer available at the exhibition underscored—in bold type—the degree to which all wares on display were for sale: with regard to the workshop wares, copy stated "all of the objects are for purchase or available for later orders"; about the Haus am Horn it was noted, "house and interior available for purchase"; and with reference to the Bauhaus exhibition installed at the Weimar Landesmuseum, "all works are for sale."[38] Exhibition sales did in fact raise 4,500 gold marks (less than had been hoped, and only a little more than half of which was actually collected), which was earmarked for use in setting up a corporation to keep the workshops in supply of working capital (*Betriebskapital*).[39]

In September 1922, it was decided that "at least one house" from the Bauhaus Siedlung should be constructed, furnished, and made accessible to the exhibition's visitors. Rather than the idea of a single show house encompassing the ideals and products of the school, the emphasis was on an exemplary dwelling within the context of the planned community.[40] The flyer available at the house alerted visitors that the overall site plan for the Bauhaus development was completed, noted that the government lacked the necessary financial resources, and called for interested parties to support the project.[41]

Figure 3.9. Haus am Horn, woman's bedroom. Furniture (bed, chair, vanity table) by Marcel Breuer.

In comparison to the Sommerfeld House, the modestly scaled Haus am Horn was straightforward in its design and seemingly devoid of superficial ornamentation. Instead, the use of new materials and building techniques gave it its distinguishing characteristics, namely, a machinelike precision that belied the costly provision of industrial products and mechanical systems. The interior comprised a central living room lit from above by atrium windows and one ground-level set of windows in the work niche, while three small bedrooms (a guest room and two separate bedrooms for husband and wife), a large children's nursery, and the kitchen and dining room ringed the other three sides (fig. 3.8; see also fig. 3.5). The light-filled work niche featured an expansive wooden desk upon which sat a telephone; attached to the wall above it was an adjustable metal light fixture designed by Carl Jacob Jucker in 1923 that both extended outward and pivoted sideways on hinges (see fig. 3.2). New materials were celebrated—an elegant plate of glass installed above the radiator provided a convenient shelf, while glass baseboards ran along the floor and the door featured Gropius's sleek metal door handle. Overall, the interiors featured a mixture of industrially produced elements such as exposed metal radiators, steel window and door frames, and modern appliances, along with modern-appearing but hand-made, mainly wooden, furniture from the Bauhaus's workshops, exemplified by pieces such as Marcel Breuer's armchairs and bedroom dressing table (fig. 3.9). The furnishings, however, were unstinting in their use of luxury materials—Breuer's dressing table was made out of lemon and walnut wood with two swiveling mirrors, one of which was on a nickel-polished armature, in a period in which nickel was an expensive detail.[42] Color was an important aspect of this emerging modern aesthetic; its use in the interiors further emphasized the house's rarified modern materials, from the black glass baseboards ringing the bedroom's cream white walls, to the red, white, and blue rubber flooring of the dining room, to the black frames around the African plywood doors.[43] The furnishings, in particular, were expensive; for example, the constructivist women's dressing table by Marcel Breuer was valued at 350 gold marks, the divan in the living room with cushions and covers at 290 gold marks, the glass cupboard at 550 gold marks, and the desk in the niche at 520 gold marks.[44] The total sales price for all Bauhaus-produced furnishings was 6,692 gold marks.

The kitchen, designed by Benita Otte and Ernst Gebhardt, featured a light-filled space with windows that tipped open, white opaque glass backsplash surfaces, a modern radiator, a ventilation fan, ample work surfaces, storage units, and two sinks, one with hot running water made possible by a small gas hot water heater installed above the sink (figs. 3.10, 3.11). The electric stove was commended for alleviating the former necessity of wood or coal transportation and of lighting it, and for being both adjustable and extinguishable.[45] As famous and forward-thinking as this kitchen appears—it predates the 1926 Frankfurt Kitchen, which was successfully mass-produced—in reality it represents the acquiring and insertion of industrial materials and technical objects in a modern layout. Beyond the simple cupboards, shelves, and counters, the only other items of design from the school were Theodor Bogler's stoneware storage jars, supplied by the Steingutfabriken Velten-Vordamm, which were never produced again in the period. In an environment where the newest hot water heater and stove could be celebrated next to the pared-down storage jars, a

Figure 3.10. Haus am Horn, kitchen. Interior design by Benita Otte and Ernst Gebhardt.

modern aesthetic emerged. But whereas the technical products from existing firms were readily available, the Bauhaus objects were not and did not, in any case, align with factory owners' notions of potential consumer desire. It was largely these *outside* products that gave the house a seductive, modern patina.

In its provision with technologically advanced amenities, the house was indeed innovative. Specific instances are numerous: the house prominently featured an "in-house laundry facility" connected with gas for heating the hot water and electric motors (fig. 3.12).[46] Costing 1,260 gold marks, its technical specifications included a "full-steam" washing machine and a "spinning dryer."[47] Archival records detail an extraordinary number of mechanical apparatuses and appliances at the Haus am Horn—electric belt pulleys, hot water heaters, vacuum, toaster, electric coffee machine, iron, hair dryer, curling iron, and electric cigar lighter, all supplied by the AEG and totaling 1,700 gold marks.[48] For 580 gold marks, three telephones were installed, including an extra bell so that the ring could be heard in the kitchen.[49] The critic Paul Westheim wrote enthusiastically in October 1923 about the house's showcasing of objects produced by industry, citing specifically the bath facilities, electric iron, vacuum cleaner, and electric cigar lighter as "splendid," advising that they should be adopted more widely.[50]

52

Figure 3.11. Haus am Horn, kitchen. Interior design by Benita Otte and Ernst Gebhardt.

KÜCHE   AUFWASCHTISCH, SCHRANK, ARBEITSTISCH

ENTWURF: B. OTTE UND E. GEBHARDT, STAATLICHES BAUHAUS. GEFÄSSE. MODELL: T. BOGLER, STAATLICHES BAUHAUS; FABRIKMÄSSIGE HERSTELLUNG DURCH STEINGUTFABRIKEN VELTEN VORDAMM G. M. B. H., VELTEN-BERLIN GLAS-KOCH- UND -BACKGEFÄSSE. DURAXGLAS, SCHOTT & GEN., GLASWERKE JENA

But in this, it was out of step with the economic realities of the time.[51] Corporate sponsorship—an important strategy for obtaining the desired materials and technical objects, many of which were newly introduced to the market—entailed product placement at the Haus am Horn, rather than the school's true collaboration with industry.[52] In exchange for partially underwriting the cost and installation of goods such as flooring, radiators, windows, mirrors, door handles, and light fixtures, all of the firms' names and wares were listed in the exhibition's accompanying publicity materials and prominently posted on a wall placard in the living room (see fig. 3.8).[53] The bathroom, for example, featured walls and ceiling covered with white opaque glass from Deutsche Spiegelglas AG, bathroom fixtures from the Triton-Werke AG Hamburg, a gas hot water heater from Junkers & Co. in Dessau, and rubber flooring supplied by the Harburger Gummiwaren-Fabrik (fig. 3.13). The wares were sourced from firms across Germany: radiators came from the Berlin-Burger Eisenwerk AG; the cast bronze, nickel-coated door handle designed by Walter Gropius and Adolf Meyer (in 1922) was manufactured by S. A. Loevy, Berlin; the plywood (Koptoxyl panel) doors came from B. Harras GmbH, Böhlen; and lighting fixtures were supplied by the AEG in association with Osram.[54] These materials and goods were also thoroughly described in the Bauhaus Book on the house, *Ein Versuchshaus des Bauhauses in Weimar*

Figure 3.12. Haus am Horn, gas and electric laundry facility. Supplied by J. A. John AG.

WAND- UND DECKENBEKLEIDUNG: WEISSES OPAKGLAS. DEUTSCHE SPIEGELGLAS-A.-G., FREDEN AN DER LEINE

JUNKERS & CO. DESSAU

GASBADEOFEN IM BADEZIMMER

KÜCHE BAD WARMWASSER VERSORGUNG

JUNKERS & CO. DESSAU

KÜCHE:
PROFESSOR JUNKERS SCHNELL-WASSER-ERHITZER
BAD:
PROFESSOR JUNKERS KUPFER-BADEOFEN (VERNICKELT)

äußerst geringer und sparsamer Verbrauch an Gas
glatte organische Nutzform
Zeit- und Arbeitsersparnis für die Hausfrau
geringe Raumbeanspruchung
Siehe Abbildung Seite 48, 50

KÜCHENHERD
IMPERIAL
GAS-BRAT- UND GRILLHERD
DOPPELBRATER
D. R. P. UND D. R. G. M.

glatte, abwaschbare Nutzform
bequeme Hantierung für die Hausfrau
kein Feueranzünden
kein Holz- und Kohlentransport
größte Ausnutzung des Heizmaterials, da bequem
regulierbar und abstellbar
Siehe Abbildung Seite 53

INDUSTRIEWERKE VOGEL, KOMMANDITGESELL-
SCHAFT AUF AKTIEN, BÜNDE IN WESTFALEN

Figure 3.13. *Top and bottom*: Haus am Horn, bathroom.

(An experimental house by the Bauhaus in Weimar), which featured all of the participating firms, who paid for their inclusion. Hastily and quite late in the process, in May 1923, Gropius organized the publication of this book about the Haus am Horn—in which advertising for all of the participating firms was foreseen as a way to help underwrite costs, noting internally that it was "self-evident" that the firms would have to pay for the publicity.[55] The book reads accordingly like advertising copy, rather than underscoring any actual collaboration between modern architecture, industry, and technology, as Gropius's famous proclamation of "art and technology—a new unity" at the exhibition's opening suggested; it does, however, highlight his acumen for enlisting capitalism's prerogatives for the school's financial benefit.

INFLATION, INDUSTRIALISTS, AND THE BAUHAUS

The Haus am Horn was thus a very concrete example of working within the reigning capitalist economic system of the early Weimar Republic in a period of desperate financial crisis and absolute insecurity of the banking and monetary system (fig. 3.14). Gropius's biggest foe in raising funds for the house was the period of hyperinflation that mirrored the time span of the Haus am Horn's conception and construction. Inflation had been a fact of daily life from the beginning of the Weimar Republic, but hyperinflation began in June 1921 and in earnest in 1922, until the mark's value had finally fallen to the point of 4.2 billion marks to the dollar in November 1923.[56] (The printing of money could hardly keep pace; contributing to the effort, Bauhaus artist Herbert Bayer designed banknotes in denominations of 1, 2, 5, 10, 20, 50, 100, and 500 million mark notes, issued by the state bank of Thuringia in August 1923.[57]) The Rentenmark (RM)—backed by bonds linked to the gold mark and hard assets such as Germany's real estate—was finally introduced on November 16, 1923, replacing the old Reichsbank mark, stabilizing the currency.

Against this backdrop, Gropius sought to raise money for the house. From November 1922 through February 1923, he wrote a series of letters translated into English by Lyonel Feininger to Henry Ford, John Rockefeller, William Hearst, and Paul Warburg—labeled in the school's own records as the "dollar kings"—which described the school, its aims, organization, and activities and asked for money to build the Haus am Horn, noting that $3,000 was needed, which varied (at that moment) between 30 million and 60 million marks or 12,000 and 13,000 gold marks.[58] American industrialists, for Germans in general and Gropius in particular, represented the success of capitalism, and their dollars had obvious appeal in the context of the inflation. Nothing came of these appeals, however, but a similar letter campaign addressed to German industrialists successfully raised 100 million marks by the time of the house's opening. Carl Benscheidt Jr., who had hired Gropius to design the Fagus Factory, gave 1.5 million marks.[59] Adolf Sommerfeld initially loaned him 20 million marks, interest free, to be paid back when the house sold.[60] Hermann Lange, an industrialist in the silk industry who would later commission Ludwig Mies van der Rohe to design his home in Krefeld, gave the Bauhaus 6 million marks.[61] These donations underscored the extent to which many industrialists, unlike the rest of the population, were doing extremely well during this period—even as the real value of the funds raised continued to diminish.

Archival documents note that Gropius reestimated the Haus am Horn construction prices to be at 100 million marks in March 1923, but by August, the recently opened house had cost 450 million marks, with Sommerfeld having ultimately contributed 208 million marks.[62] The Bauhaus had to contend with a 150-fold debasement of the currency from March to September 1923, a difference that left it with a 1.5-billion-mark deficit for the house. As a result, the business manager of the Bauhaus, Emil Lange, wrote an unsuccessful letter to Sommerfeld in September asking him for an additional billion marks.[63] The Bauhaus's own workshops also faced a 10- to 15-million-mark shortfall for their contributions to the house.[64]

Wherever possible, Gropius arranged the materials purchases so that the cost was fixed to the delivery date's price, taking further pains to arrange prices below the market rate.[65] And generally the firms were willing to wait to be paid until the house was finished.[66] The hyperinflation led to complicated payment schedules. For example, for the ordering of the wooden doors, the following arrangement was detailed: on the date of delivery, the firm was to note the day's wood price and what percentage rebate was going to be in effect (given the publicity the firm would receive though its product placement); the firm was to be paid when the house sold at the exhibition's close (at the latest on November 1), at which point a higher or lower percentage of the bill was to be paid out, depending on whether the price of wood had risen or fallen.[67] The terms of sale for the workshop pieces and artworks of the exhibition also reflected the daily devaluation of currency—the Bauhaus stipulated that prices be calculated for the day of receipt of payment, not sale date.[68]

Figure 3.14. Children using money as building blocks during the German inflation crisis, 1923.

The contributing firms lent materials and money for the house's construction, with the intention of its being recuperated through the Haus am Horn's eventual resale. For example, the glass manufacturer lent 5 million marks and agreed to put off billing for the glass until the house sold, agreeing to bill at cost.[69] Archival sources reveal many letters from participating firms beseeching the Bauhaus to pay overdue bills.[70] After much correspondence, following the exhibition's closure and as the mark's value continued to plummet, Sommerfeld's firm finally authorized 18 billion marks so that the school could pay the other firms.[71]

In 1921, Schlemmer had noted Gropius's business acumen: "Gropius is an excellent diplomat, businessman, and practical genius."[72] But Schlemmer's diary from November 1922 reveals the disquiet the new direction caused for him and the difficulties he foresaw for the school: "Handmade *objets d'art* in the age of the machine and technology would be a luxury for the rich, lacking a broad popular basis and roots in the people. Industry now provides what the crafts once provided, or it will when fully developed: standardized, solid functional objects made of genuine materials. ... Technological progress has resulted in bold innovations. ... I do not believe that craftsmanship as practiced at the Bauhaus can transcend the aesthetic and fulfill more serious social functions. 'Getting in touch with industry' will not do the trick; we would have to commit ourselves and merge completely with industry." He concludes, "But we cannot make that our goal; it would mean turning our backs on the Bauhaus."[73]

LUXURY AT THE HAUS AM HORN: THE PERIOD RECEPTION

How can we understand the Haus am Horn in relation to the intersection of architecture and capitalism—in terms of both its utopian aspirations about dwelling anew and its concessions to economic realities? The materials (rubber flooring, plywood) and technology (electric washer and dryer) it utilized have now attained an everyday quality, part of what is often expected of even a minimal dwelling. But the extraordinary amenities of the house during a period of uncertainty and economic chaos must be seen in the context of the relationship between industrial capitalism and housing needs of its time.

The period response to the house was mixed, and criticism often focused on the house's ambiguous position vis-à-vis the economic realities of its day. It was unclear if the house was meant to be a realistic solution for typical middle-class dwelling as part of a larger housing plan or if it was a show house for an idealized future. The school was careful to chart a middle course. For example, Muche, in his essay about it, specifically points out a desire to ensure that machine production of furniture and interior fittings would not result in the "barbarism of formlessness."[74] Gropius, too, would talk of the "uncultivated formlessness of a parvenu," suggesting a need to maintain an elite standard of design in the face of its anticipated diffusion.[75] He also sought to maintain a nuanced, critical position on the relationship between living, design, art, and business: "Our informing conception of the basic unity of all design in relation to life was in diametrical opposition to that of 'art for art's sake,' and the even more dangerous philosophy it sprang from: business as an end in itself."[76] This disavowal of "business" and his talk of collaboration with the more neutral "industrial production" might be seen as an attempt to mask his intensive engagement with the powers of German industrial capitalism.

But to the observers and critics, regardless of rhetoric, it was clear that the house was not within reach of the average family of the period. As one reporter pointed out, "only a dollar-man" (that is, only someone possessing hard currency) would be eligible to live in this housing development, quipping that it would be very welcome if the Bauhaus succeeded, in its next exhibition, in meeting local conditions and terms of livability.[77] Bruno Adler, writing for *Das Volk*, noted that the "small house, in which no man could work," is "for millionaires—gold mark millionaires—admittedly, those who are doing so badly that they, for example, can't keep servants anymore. It doesn't provide any solutions to real dwelling problems. As pleasant as all the comfortable furnishings surely are, and to furnish a house attractively may well be a delightful task, but surely in our time there are more worthy ones. Dwelling problems of the industrialists ought to be laid aside for a few decades."[78] Architectural critic Adolf Behne similarly found the house to be both irreproducible and unable to meet people's needs: "The Bauhaus affirms the typification and normalization of the dwelling. … They flirt with machine exactness, but simply *everything* here turns out oblique, false, hollow, artificial, for each individual object, like the whole, lacks necessity, an internal law, a human will of its own!"[79] In another review, Behne articulated the unconvincing, contradictory nature of the house, commenting that it "stands among all these difficulties as somewhat uninteresting and unknowing. It is half luxurious, half primitive; half postulation of an ideal, half product of its time; half handicraft, half industry; half standard-type, half idyll. But it is in no sense pure and persuasive, but again an aesthetic, papery affair."[80] Ernst May commented that despite some fine individual solutions toward the rational management of the household, the rich use of "precious materials … that stamp the building as luxury housing" contradicted the efficiencies; he called for attention to problems relevant to "not just 5% but rather 95% of all Germans."[81] In reviewing the show, one newspaper reporter pointed out, in discussing the laundry facilities and their electric dryer, that the designers were clearly most concerned with utilizing all of the products of modern technology, and especially through the heavy use of electric power, to make a home that would be as easy as possible to run: "The aim was thus not to create a low-cost house, but rather a house with the most comfort possible."[82]

And although he continued to subsidize the house's construction, Sommerfeld wrote to Gropius on May 8, 1923, of his own doubts about its aims—"I would like to urgently ask you to rein in your fantasies."[83] And in September, he again raised his concerns: "What now remains is a strange [*seltsames*] house that one can argue about if one likes, but that, when observed as a sales object, poses great difficulties and that costs many times more than what a solidly built, normal house would cost in comparison."[84]

————

Indeed, more than a vision of bourgeois middle- or upper-class single-family living, the Haus am Horn demonstrates the results of the school's ardent desire to work within the strictures of capitalism, however flawed they were in this period: to convince industry to cooperate with the Bauhaus by making available its products and its financial support, in return for which the Bauhaus showcased industry's products in the context of its own exhibition. Occurring at a moment of rapid impoverishment of German society, the result is ambiguous and anachronistic. The house was a product of its time, itself manifesting the contrast, and contradictions, between the Bauhaus's social ambitions for design and its ideas of reformed "everyday" dwelling, on the one hand, and the house's status as a luxury object in its time and a distant, unrealistic, utopian hope, on the other. Unattuned to the needs of the day, the experimental Bauhaus house exhibited expensive industrial products and materials, which were not readily available to the many and certainly not objects of everyday life. To be sure, they were products of industrial innovation and mass-production processes, but their development answered to the imperatives of a capitalist industrial economy, not to any collaboration with the artists and designers of the Bauhaus nor to any pressing social needs.

Read unforgivingly, the Haus am Horn was a project doomed to failure, its desire to mix the luxury of avant-garde approaches to design with Taylorist efficiencies inherently naive. Read generously, one might argue that the school under Gropius sought to cultivate the social potential that might be found within the economic system of its time and with the support of its industrial protagonists. Even though this search did not come to fruition, and although the specific material and design solutions the Gropius-led Bauhaus proposed were out of touch with the needs and means of those for whom it claimed to want to design, some observers of the 1923 Bauhaus exhibition and the Haus am Horn were able to find promise in this apparent contradiction, perhaps seeing in it the potential to harness capitalism toward socially oriented design. Critic Fritz Wichert wrote, "Now there is space for ideas, for inspiration, for being moved. It's almost as if one could see the thoughts and feelings appear like something sculpted on this bare writing table. The force from within, the creative interior life of the human being, regains the upper hand."[85] As another critic noted, "Only one thing is key: the inner life, the fruitful possibility of an enterprise [*Unternehmen*]. For the Bauhaus, talented people will work with inner participation, honesty, and commitment. The results of this work are just a beginning. ... But there is a spirit within, which is infused with trust."[86] The Haus am Horn is a cogent instance of the modern architectural movement's deep engagement with industrial capitalism to come. It can be seen as a hopeful "house of the future," as a possible radical, utopian plan of a luxurious world yet to be normalized.

PRODUCTION

Objects produced at the Bauhaus occupy an uneasy juncture between the canonical history of modern art and architecture, period culture, and issues such as the production and consumption of modernism.[1] In 1923, Walter Gropius articulated the aims of the Bauhaus with the proclamation, "art and technology—a new unity," which advanced the use of new materials, more stripped-down forms, and a spare, functional aesthetic. His successor Hannes Meyer pronounced, "people's needs instead of luxury needs" (*Volksbedarf statt Luxusbedarf*)—but would he have been moved to make such a declaration if Gropius had successfully carried out his stated aims? The failure of Gropius's Bauhaus to merge art and technology—to move from the production of individual, luxury objects to mass reproduction—is the subject of this chapter, specifically the objects produced under Gropius from 1923 to 1928, the period of his overtures to industry.

This repertoire of specialized objects—including silver and ebony tea services, individual tea infusers, modern chess sets, and children's toys, to name just a few canonical works—represents a paradigmatic example by which to examine the relationship between modernism's discourse and its material results. Expensive in their day, original Bauhaus products are now art objects displayed in museum vitrines as individual works of art (fig. 4.1). Often hailed for the mythic merging of forward-thinking ideas and modern production techniques, they are asked to illustrate modernism's unflinching belief in the powers of industry. And they are presented as objects of discourse, the material evidence of a series of debates on taste, handcraftsmanship, machine production, and seriality (fig. 4.2).

This chapter considers and contextualizes the ways in which the Bauhaus produced its modern objects and the extent to which, despite its egalitarian ideals, the school ultimately spoke to—and designed for—an elite. The products of the Bauhaus, ostensibly intended for mass production, were expensive, difficult to fabricate, and never sold on a widespread basis, reflecting the economic realities of producing and purchasing modern objects. Essential to this discussion is the problem of reproduction itself. Engaging Walter Benjamin's essay "The Work of Art in the Age of Its Technological Reproducibility," this chapter recognizes that, ideologically, the Bauhaus protagonists were willing to call the status of the objects the Bauhaus produced into question—to sacrifice their "aura" and status as "art" in order to achieve their mass reproduction; yet, in practice the Bauhaus was unable to do so.[2] This failure was due to the limits to the reproducibility of Bauhaus objects—themselves a product of their place in the Weimar Republic social order that they also sought to transform.

LUXURY OBJECTS

At first glance, two small teapots, ME 8 and MT 49, designed and executed in 1924 by Marianne Brandt at the Bauhaus, evince all of the concepts that modernism proclaimed—*Sachlichkeit*, functionality, hygiene, and the use of modern materials and construction methods (fig. 4.3; see also fig. 4.1).[3] To all appearances they are thoroughly modern objects. Surface decoration has been eschewed in favor of pared-down, machinelike geometrical shapes that form the round lids, the semicircular handles, and the crossed bases. But although they suggest machine production, they were laboriously hand-wrought in the Bauhaus's workshop at great cost. They are fabricated out of expensive materials—both diminutive pots are made of silver, while the small knobs (which differ slightly from each other) attached to the lids and the handles are ebony. Out of the numerous objects designed at the school, the ME 8 teapot was one of only twelve products selected in 1925–26 for inclusion in the Bauhaus GmbH product catalog, the *Katalog der Muster*, which suggests that it was deemed representative of the Bauhaus (fig. 4.4).[4] Yet, it could not be inexpensively mass-produced in these materials, nor was it intended to be; as the catalog notes, it featured "exacting handcraftsmanship" (see fig. 4.3). In any case, its smooth form and the meticulous joins of its body to its spout and base lacked the surface ornamentation that hid imperfections that occurred in cheaply produced factory goods of this period, resulting in an object that would have been very difficult to industrially fabricate with precision. Thus, it could be serially produced by hand in the metal

Figure 4.1. Marianne Brandt, Tea Extract Pot (MT 49), 1924. Silver and ebony.

Figure 4.2. Otto Rittweger and Wolfgang Tümpel, Stands with Tea Infusers, 1924. German silver. Photograph by Lucia Moholy, 1925.

Figure 4.3. Brandt, Tea Extract Pot and Strainer (ME 8), 1924. Silver. From Bauhaus GmbH, *Katalog der Muster*, 1925. Graphic design by Herbert Bayer.

Figure 4.4. Bauhaus GmbH, *Katalog der Muster*, 1925. Graphic design by Herbert Bayer.

workshop in limited quantities, but it was not—in form, material, or price—suitable for mass reproduction. It was, in short, a luxury object in need of an elite consumer—and not only one who could bear its expense, but one who understood both its modern form and its underlying ideas.[5]

Bauhaus goods were also highly legible expressions of affluence. Though the Bauhaus proposed to utilize industry to make goods that even the masses could afford, it played to a privileged audience—especially members of the industrially orientated (*Wirtschaftsbürgertum*) or classically educated (*Bildungsbürgertum*) upper middle class. Despite the rise of German industrialism, accompanied by the ascension of technical firms such as the AEG, Siemens, and numerous smaller rivals, the objects produced by the Bauhaus were not items associated with the machine age, such as advanced electrical goods. Equally revealing, the school's products did not advocate an entirely new way of living, unlike designs of its contemporaries, such as Grete Schütte-Lihotzky's mass-produced Frankfurt Kitchen of 1926 (a small modern kitchen designed for maximum efficiency that limited the number of steps needed to perform tasks following the scientific principles of Frederick Winslow Taylor) or Hannes Meyer's Coop-Zimmer (a radically pared down single room supplied with standard elements to meet the absolute minimum needs for dwelling). Gropius's stated aims for the workshops, from about 1923 onward, reiterated the Bauhaus's desire to develop "standard types for all practical commodities of everyday use."[6] And yet, given this charge, why were there no Bauhaus forks, an ordinary product that could be easily molded or stamped out in large quantities at low cost? Instead, the school remained committed to producing the types of traditional, conventional objects—chess sets, teapots, tea services, tea containers, ashtrays, and armchairs—that already had a place in upper-class homes (fig. 4.5).

Bauhaus objects employed a straightforward vocabulary of forms while reducing applied ornament; the result was an object that was modern and yet familiar.[7] One can see this process at work in Wilhelm Wagenfeld's 1924 Bauhaus design for a set of sphere-shaped jugs, which rework some Werkbund *Warenbuch*-endorsed silver versions available at least as early as 1915 (fig. 4.6).[8] The earlier jugs featured delicate, reed-covered handles and a hand-hammered arts and crafts finish; the Bauhaus counterparts were simplified and more geometric but had the same general form and function. Material costs were reduced in the Bauhaus versions by employing silver-plated brass and German silver (*Neusilber*, as it was called in German, an alloy of copper, zinc, and nickel)—which, tellingly, maintained the appearance of real silver. But older, luxurious materials such as ebony and silver also remained part of the Bauhaus repertoire throughout the 1920s. A Bauhaus egg cooker from 1926 had an ebony handle, for example. A number of objects, such as Brandt's tea service with water pot (ME 24) and tea extract pots (MT 49, ME 8), were advertised in silver, obviously a luxury material (fig. 4.7; see also figs. 4.1, 4.3). Already expensive because they were handmade, objects in finer materials raised costs significantly, allowing quality to take precedence over the goods' accessibility to a broader public.

In other words, the Bauhaus did not reinvent products but simply introduced known objects in new "modern" forms and occasionally new materials. It did not wish to alienate its potential consumers with modernism, but rather to accommodate their perceived needs and already articulated desires for a certain repertoire of goods, which were then given a modernist treatment. Under Gropius, even through the late 1920s, the school introduced very little that was unfamiliar and relied on established, traditional luxury objects prevalent in the upper echelons of culture. Rather than overwhelm its audience with wholly new ideas and goods, the Bauhaus created its new market through consensualist means, remaining committed to designing the types of weighty, representative objects that the bourgeoisie might be enticed to buy.

In doing so, the Bauhaus appealed to what Walter Benjamin described as the authority of traditional art objects, that is, the authority that they retained through their relationship to a tradition and in the context of established social rituals. Traditional decorative arts objects such as the tea service with its array of accoutrements (tea infuser, water pot, creamer, sugar bowl) maintained this autonomous authority through their role in the customs that guided patterns of life in bourgeois homes (see fig. 4.7). These social rituals continued to maintain a distance between the object and its user—the aura—the "unique apparition of a distance, however near it may be" that sustained traditional authority. Technological reproducibility, on the other hand, "emancipates the work of art from its parasitic subservience to ritual."[9] For the Bauhaus to have engaged in successful mass reproduction of standard objects of everyday use, it would have been necessary that objects—rather than shoring up their withering aura through an appeal to tradition—instead be produced in such a manner that they successfully reached the masses.

Bauhaus goods were also prohibitively expensive. To put their prices in perspective, it is important to note that the average income for a working-class (*Arbeiter*) family in 1927 was about 64 marks per week and for a white-collar (*Angestellten*) family, around 91 marks per week.[10] Marcel Breuer's "Wassily" chair,

Figure 4.5. Vitrine of Bauhaus objects, as shown at the *European Applied Arts Exhibition* (*Ausstellung Europäisches Kunstgewerbe*), Grassi-Museum, Leipzig, 1927.

not in leather but merely in fabric, cost 60 marks, about a week's wages for a worker.[11] The silver Bauhaus cookie tin (*Keksdose*) cost 160 marks, the teapot cost 90 marks, and the five-piece tea service in German silver cost 180 marks—three times a worker's weekly wage (see fig. 4.7). As Bauhaus artist Otto Rittweger noted in 1926, "Today it is more difficult than ever for the vast majority of people who would like to possess such a [Bauhaus] service to actually afford one."[12] Comparatively, a non-Bauhaus, generic nickeled coffee set cost only 10 marks. Bauhaus objects were not consumed by the masses; even if they could have afforded a Bauhaus lamp, in 1925, 81 percent of the inhabitants in Berlin's working-class areas lived without electricity.[13]

Figure 4.6. *Left*: Wilhelm Wagenfeld (designer, executed by Josef Knau), Sphere-Shaped Jugs, 1924. Silver-plated brass, German silver lids and hinges. Photograph by Lucia Moholy, 1924. *Right*: German Werkbund, Silver Jugs, c. 1915.

Figure 4.7. Brandt, Tea Service with Water Pot, 1924. Silver with ebony handles. From Bauhaus GmbH, *Katalog der Muster*, 1925. Graphic design by Herbert Bayer.

Indeed, the start-up costs of mass production or the high projected sale prices often kept goods from ever being produced. On several occasions, Gropius commented that the costs for producing the objects were higher than what the market could bear and that the selling price of Bauhaus goods was artificially high in order to meet costs associated with balancing the Bauhaus budget and the purchase of raw materials in small quantities rather than in bulk.[14] Objects from the metal workshop were especially unaffordable, as both labor and material costs were high, but goods from the other workshops were also costly, and it was often the more expensive objects that were promoted. For example, there were two categories of Bauhaus chess sets designed by Josef Hartwig, the standard version (*Gebrauchsspiel*, or "everyday utilitarian") and a "luxury" set (*Luxusspiel*), which was made by hand or in small batches, using rarer and more costly types of wood, including walnut and pear (fig. 4.8).[15] While the standard wood chess set was priced at 51 marks, the walnut version cost 155 marks.[16] The *Luxusspiel* was marketed early on through a series of postcards, two of which featured the word *Luxus* prominently in the advertising copy (fig. 4.9). Hartwig also designed a small table with an integrated chess board and an accompanying armchair; the table's contrasting colored chess squares were made of inlaid mahogany and oak.[17]

Gropius had to contend with the accusation that the products of the Bauhaus were simply another form of expensive, artistic luxury similar to the output of other

Figure 4.8. Josef Hartwig, Bauhaus Chess Set, luxury version, c. 1923. Photograph by Lucia Moholy.

Figure 4.9. Postcard advertising Hartwig's Bauhaus Chess Sets, 1924. Graphic design by Joost Schmidt.

schools of the applied arts.[18] He was careful to articulate that the Bauhaus was involved in creating artistic objects within the present economic paradigm, but asserted early on that its work was not involved in "artistic luxury affairs" (*künstlerische Luxusangelegenheiten*).[19] László Moholy-Nagy, around 1928, conceived of a dialogue between a "well-meaning critic" of the Bauhaus and a "representative of the Bauhaus." In it, the critic charges that Bauhaus objects have become luxury objects, accessible only to a few.[20] To this, the representative of the Bauhaus replies that during the initial phases the objects were so expensive that only a few wealthy people were able to buy them but that the luxury product itself was merely an intermediate link in the development toward becoming an object of everyday use.[21] This intriguing line of reasoning—that the objects were part of an evolution from luxury to accessibility—does not appear to have gained wider currency. During Gropius's tenure, a tension existed between concurrent realities: the production of serial objects by hand, the ideal of the prototype, and the desire for mass production. By never fully reaching the mass production stage, owing to their cost and nature, the Bauhaus's products ultimately remained luxury objects.

Following Benjamin's formulation, the very act of the mass reproduction and dissemination of Bauhaus goods—rather than small, serialized production of multiple copies made by hand—would have allowed them to be brought out of the rarified realm of luxury and tradition: "It might be stated as a general formula that the technology of reproduction detaches the reproduced object from the sphere of tradition. By replicating the work many times over, it substitutes a mass existence for a unique existence. And in permitting the reproduction to reach the recipient in his or her own situation, it actualizes that which is reproduced."[22] The cost and exclusivity of Bauhaus objects were related to the fact that they were turned out in small batches, mainly to fill specific commissions, in a workshop system. As Benjamin observes, "In principle, the work of art has always been reproducible. Objects made by humans could always be copied by humans. Replicas were made by pupils in practicing for their craft, by masters in disseminating their works, and, finally, by third parties in pursuit of profit. But the technological reproduction of artworks is something new."[23] At the Bauhaus, the move to industrial reproduction would have necessitated the object's overcoming of its tradition-grounded formal qualities so as to be determined instead by its inherent reproducibility; in Benjamin's words, "the work reproduced becomes the reproduction of a work designed for reproducibility."[24] Thus, in terms of the Bauhaus project, the fact that Bauhaus objects were visually modern is less important than the fact that they were never reproduced in any significant numbers.

BAUHAUS MODERN ON DISPLAY

The design of Gropius's new school building in Dessau not only brought together all of the school's necessary operating components—workshops, auditorium, cafeteria, and dormitories—but showcased its ideas (fig. 4.10). In its spare white walls, flat roof, raised bridge, and glazed curtain walls, the new hallmarks of modern architecture were celebrated. Its dynamic pinwheel design delineated and separated its key functions (work, eating, sleeping), while the light-flooded main staircase brought the school's diverse faculty and students into regular contact with each other. The expansive, open-plan workshops benefited from the natural light of fully glazed

Figure 4.10. Walter Gropius, Bauhaus Building, Dessau, 1925–26. Photograph by Lucia Moholy.

Figure 4.11. Gropius, Bauhaus Building, director's office. Photograph by Erich Consemüller.

Figure 4.12. Gropius, Bauhaus masters' housing. Photograph by Lucia Moholy.

Figure 4.13. Gropius, Bauhaus masters' housing, interior of Moholy-Nagy House. Photograph by Lucia Moholy.

exterior curtain walls and were outfitted with new, technical equipment. Thus, the school building offered the spatial, technical, and social potential for new, collaborative modern design. Gropius's director's office—located on the central bridge, with its view of the street leading up to the school, the front doors, and the glazed corners of the workshops—gave him a distinct vantage point from which to oversee the school's activities. His office was carefully outfitted as an additional means of presenting the school's products (fig. 4.11).

Additionally, the nearby houses of the school's masters were on view and played a very public role in setting the context for Bauhaus objects, eliciting interest by the media and the public alike (figs. 4.12, 4.13). Like the Bauhaus objects, Gropius's director's house and the three double masters' houses advertise an aesthetic of mass reproducibility but in fact are also examples of limited serial production. It is not insignificant that their inhabitants often referred to them as "villas"; they represented a rarified form of dwelling and were meant to function as lived-in showpieces for the school's theories and ideals, allowing the Bauhaus to exhibit the products of its workshops in an instructive and architecturally appropriate domestic setting.

Ise Gropius's diary charts an unending stream of important visitors representing an elevated, educated segment of the population—from trade organizations and cultural groups to politicians, modern architects, artists, cultural critics, period intellectuals, and professors.[25] Even a year after they had been completed, there seemed to be no indication that interest in the houses was waning, as Lyonel Feininger wrote exasperatedly to his wife in the fall of 1927: "What is going on here is beyond belief and almost beyond endurance. Crowds of idlers slowly amble along Burgkühnauer Allee, from morning to night, goggling at our houses, not to speak of trespassing in our gardens to stare in the windows."[26] According to Dessau Mayor Fritz Hesse, between 1927 and 1930, the Bauhaus buildings received more than twenty thousand

Figure 4.14. Gropius's maid demonstrating automatic soap-infused sprayer for the dishes and pass-through cupboards from kitchen to dining room. Film still, *Neues Wohnen*, from *Wie wohnen wir gesund und wirtschaftlich*, Humboldt Film Company, filmed 1926, released 1928.

visitors.[27] This indicates that their modern design and contents were not quickly assimilated into the general culture but remained objects of fascination.

The director's house, in particular, functioned as an "exhibition house," playing a very public role. As Feininger wrote to his wife, "Gropius's house, of course, is miraculous. The furniture and the entire setup are intended as representative."[28] The house boasted an appliance-filled kitchen with labor-saving conveniences, such as an automatic soap-infused sprayer for the dishes, an early clothes washer, and a centrifuge dryer. But these devices were for the hired help, an expected domestic arrangement for a couple of their social standing (fig. 4.14). Period films celebrating the house depict a uniformed maid at work washing dishes or putting them away in the convenient pass-through cupboards (which provided sliding-door access from the kitchen to the dining room) while Ise Gropius drinks tea with friends in the living room "tea corner" (fig. 4.15). Serviced by hot and cold running water and an electric teakettle, it aptly illustrates the merging of bourgeois habits and precious objects with modern technology and convenience, with little pretense toward universal application. The dining room featured Bauhaus furniture made out of costly nickel-plated tubular steel, an adjustable plate warmer, and other electrical appliances that could be plugged in directly to the floor outlets conveniently placed in the center of the room, adjacent to the table. A fan installed in the living room was connected to the central heating system behind the wall, so that warmed, but fresh, air could be brought in during the winter. Gropius's 1930 book, *Bauhausbauten Dessau*, acknowledged that this feature, like many others in the house, was an extravagance, noting "today a lot still functions as luxury," but he predicts that much "will be the norm the day after tomorrow!"[29] At a time when modern architects looked to mass production for interior fittings, and when mass-produced, plain porcelain sinks were readily available, Gropius's bathroom featured a luxurious, richly marble-veined double sink, flanked by glass-lined walls (see fig. I.1, left). The *Bauhausbauten* book

Figure 4.15. Gropius House, tea corner, Dessau, 1925–26. Photograph by Lucia Moholy, 1926.

erased the marble veining from the sink to make it appear more industrial and less luxurious (see fig. I.1, right). Perhaps tellingly, Gropius employed a chauffeur, and his house was the only one with a garage (the masters' houses were supplied with small bicycle sheds). Generally, the house was not portrayed for what it really was—a prohibitively expensive design for the powerful director of the Bauhaus.

PRODUCTIVE OPERATIONS

As early as April 1922 and continuing into 1923, the Bauhaus masters and Gropius had discussed the necessity of organizing the workshops into a productive operation, a *Produktiv-Betrieb*, and indicated that they viewed the school itself as a *Produktiv-Apparat*, a locus of productive operations.[30] Gropius envisioned products from Bauhaus prototypes, reproduced via methods of standardization and large-scale sales as the only way that goods could be offered at a reasonable price.[31] The Bauhaus's embrace of an industrial means of production was the result of external political and economic as well as internal pressures. This proposed shift in the activities and overall orientation of the workshops, clearly articulated by Gropius, was founded on an astonishingly immodest premise: to sway the industrial powers of 1920s Germany.[32]

Although factory production was the stated desire after 1923, throughout the entire history of the school, small orders were filled for specific patrons in response to requests via correspondence and personal visits to the Bauhaus.[33] From small objects to furnishings for entire apartments, original pieces were produced, not just in the Weimar period as might be expected, when original crafts were the mainstay, but throughout the Dessau period too.[34] Students were expected to spend a specific number of hours in their chosen workshop with a portion of that time devoted to formal instruction and the acquisition of technical skills, but orders for Bauhaus goods also had to be filled. A general lack of production capacity in the workshops because of labor, financial, and materials shortages meant that orders were constantly delayed or only partially supplied.

In 1924, the Bauhaus manager Emil Lange wrote Gropius a long letter containing recommendations for making the workshops economically sound.[35] Lange does not suggest reviewing the overall design process, the internal production costs, or whether the products were appealing to potential buyers; to the contrary, he expresses frustration with the caprice of buyers and the unpredictability in their ordering patterns, apparently showing little acumen about the market and tools of selling. This lack of attunement to consumer desire was a continual problem. But more important, the Bauhaus continued to be oriented toward workshop production rather than to what successful mass reproduction would have had to entail.

During 1924 and 1925, the Bauhaus took important measures to shore up its finances and implemented some basic operations to organize its fairly autonomous workshops into a more comprehensive entity for the purposes of selling designs. The first mention of a "Bauhaus AG" appears in conjunction with the possible uses of profits from the school's 1923 exhibition.[36] In January 1924, Gropius began lengthy proceedings with the government over the founding of a separate Bauhaus company, the Bauhaus GmbH.[37] In a long meeting on February 18, 1924, Gropius laid out plans for an economically feasible Bauhaus corporation, discussing its relationship to the workshops and provisions for student employment and payment—either by piecework or wages.[38] At this stage, the general plan was not to outsource production to other companies, but rather to internally organize the labor and productivity of the workshops according to what Gropius called the "free market" (*freie Wirtschaft*). An agreement template was drawn up that gave the Bauhaus GmbH the rights to all objects made at the school and stipulated that the designer was not to make similar objects on his or her own.[39] In return, the company would pay for every approved design and give the designer up to 30 percent of the resulting profits.[40] The company hired a business manager, Walter Haas, to act as a conduit between the Bauhaus and industry, to market the prototypes designed in the workshops, and to oversee the reproduction of objects. The Bauhaus printed up stationery and invoices for the GmbH, which was legally a separate entity.

Under the aegis of the Bauhaus GmbH, the school began to organize its products into one comprehensive sales catalog, known as the *Katalog der Muster*.[41] There are two versions. A double-sided sheet, designed by László Moholy-Nagy, appeared with just four selected products, perhaps those viewed as most marketable (fig. 4.16). A multipage, orange-and-black version, designed by Herbert Bayer with new photography by Lucia Moholy, appeared in November 1925 (see figs. 4.3, 4.4, 4.7).[42] This catalog was a loose-leaf booklet, organized by workshop, in which each product or product group could be removed and function as a stand-alone information sheet. A separate price list, which could be periodically updated, possibly accompanied it. The objects could be ordered individually from the Bauhaus GmbH, although the hope was for mass production through the company itself.

Presented as single objects on individual leaflets, the products in the *Katalog der Muster* are not offered as part of a comprehensive Bauhaus collection, in that the objects are organized by workshop rather than by use or intended room. The images project the clean, clutter-free ideal of modernism, but the design also reflects the straightforwardness of standard product catalogs of the period. There is a careful estrangement of the objects from their surroundings. The images, through their

Figure 4.16. Bauhaus GmbH, *Katalog der Muster*, 1925. Single sheet, front and verso. Graphic design by László Moholy-Nagy.

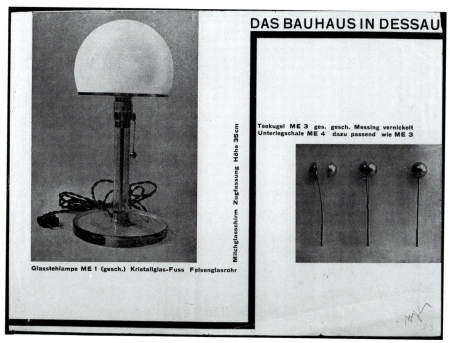

coldness and detachment, highlight the alluring surface qualities of the individual objects rather than their potential for use.

Whereas in an earlier period the workshops had been guided by an ideal of working in tandem to create an integrated interior—as took place in the 1920 Sommerfeld House or the Haus am Horn exhibition house in 1923—the *Katalog der Muster* represents a shift to the pursuit of the single object, or type-object, for wider production. As Gropius stated unequivocally, the workshops' mandate was to create standard types for practical commodities. Yet the objects selected for the catalog represent some of the school's most elite designs and arguably many of its least practical ones—a full silver tea service, the tea container and tea balls, the chess set, and several ashtrays that, among other objects, would not have been easily stamped out or otherwise mass-produced by machine. Furthermore, several descriptions note the items' "most exacting" (*genaueste*) or "finest handcraftsmanship" (*feinste Handarbeit*), calling into question whether some of the objects in the catalog were ever intended for mass production. The "Inventory of Work and Ownership Rights of the Workshops," serves as a good indication of what the Bauhaus had produced by April 1925 and lists the objects that it theoretically could have selected from when assembling the *Katalog der Muster*.[43] Simpler, arguably more easily mass-producible objects on the list, such as tablecloths, pillows, scarves, or drapes being produced in the weaving workshop, are notably absent from the catalog.

Another method by which the Bauhaus sought to draw German industrialists to its goods was through participation in trade shows, especially the twice-yearly Leipzig Trade Fair, at which the school exhibited objects regularly from 1924 to 1931, selling goods and taking orders to be filled by the workshops.[44] As with the *Katalog der Muster*, the Leipzig activities underscore the ambiguity of the Bauhaus's program: the products represented special, one-off goods to be sold for profit as well as prototypes intended for mass production. In 1927, four years after Gropius's turn to industry and his proclamation "art and technology—a new unity," the Bauhaus was selected to represent Germany at the *European Applied Arts Exhibition* (*Ausstellung Europäisches Kunstgewerbe*), held in conjunction with the regular Leipzig fair (see fig. 4.5). Chosen not as a producer of modern, rational goods intended for industry but rather for their fine craftsmanship, the handmade, luxurious nature of the goods comes to the fore. Bauhaus objects, including a hammered, silver-lined fish-poaching dish, were put on display in the same room as Meissen porcelain and other expensive goods made in Germany. This conjunction illustrates the Bauhaus's difficult position of trying to be modern while existing within the context of applied arts education (*Kunstgewerbe*), with the skilled training in the traditional crafts that it required. The workshops continued to occupy an unclear position between their role as producers of the unique art object and as designers of prototypes for mass reproduction.

Although industrial production and the formation of an alliance between the Bauhaus and industry was a carefully articulated goal, even an underlying principle, which Gropius reiterated in speeches and writings and which is implied in the "industrial" aesthetics of the objects, there is little evidence beyond the *Katalog der Muster* and trade fair exhibitions that clear steps toward the formalization of relations with industry were taken.[45] As years passed, the situation began to appear dire, as Moholy-Nagy admitted in 1928: "Designs for vessels and appliances, with which we have been occupied for years, have so far not been sold to industry."[46] Outside visitors, such as art theorist Rudolf Arnheim, similarly noted: "Certainly the Bauhaus has not yet come so far as to be able to supply industry with conclusively standard patterns."[47] A contract finally materialized in 1927 with the metalworks factory Paul Stotz AG of Stuttgart to manufacture and distribute the glass lamp, although it was not fulfilled.[48] Later, relations with the manufacturers Körting & Mathiesen and Schwintzer & Gräff brought lighting to the market in significant numbers for the first time in the Bauhaus's history.[49] In the end, only four workshops were ever able to deliver models to industry—carpentry, weaving, metal, and wall painting—and Gropius's ideal of working closely with manufacturers never materialized.[50] Only three firms began negotiations during his tenure; the rest came during that of his successors, mainly Hannes Meyer.

Practically speaking, Bauhaus objects were not mass-produced in any number, nor picked up by industry in general. It is important to differentiate between objects that were genuinely mass-reproducible and the visual propagation of an idea of modern, reproducible products. This idea of reducing objects to their essences appealed to students and masters at the Bauhaus as a visual and conceptual task—though outside the school the objects met with limited success. Bauhaus objects did not transform function but rather attempted to distill the object's essential function, as in the visually pared-down tea extraction pot that was refined until it poured well (see fig. 4.1). Yet, designed to make a very strong cup of tea, its contents needed to be diluted with hot water from yet another vessel—resulting in the proliferation, rather than reduction, of household objects. What remained important to the Bauhaus, if not the consuming public, was the aesthetic of simple, machinelike forms, the elevation of function, and the *idea* of mass reproduction.

Buyers, in any case, were skeptical. Even though Gropius stressed that the Bauhaus workshops were addressing the "necessities of life of the majority of people" and viewed the home and its furnishings as "mass consumer goods," and though the school wanted to limit designs to "characteristic, primary forms and colors, readily accessible to everyone," the masses themselves did not embrace the modern goods.[51] Convincing them to value a teapot's severe reduction in form and decoration for its attendant Bauhaus ideology was arguably as much of a hindrance as its price tag. These objects were not received with wide enthusiasm outside an elite of left-wing artistic and intellectual circles, the members of which understood the principles of the school and its objects, or what was sometimes termed the *Intellektuell-Sachliches*—even among those who could afford them.[52] A list of workshop commissions completed in 1926 notes mainly avant-garde art galleries as patrons.[53] Photographs of industrialists' interiors, for example, reveal homes amply laden with modern paintings and sculpture yet virtually no modern design objects. Surprisingly, modern interiors, such as those by Marcel Breuer, do not feature Bauhaus objects on their tables or shelves with any frequency either.[54] It is very difficult, outside of its *own* buildings and photographs, to find the products of the Bauhaus in domestic settings. As Grete Lihotzky, in her important 1927 essay "Rationalization in the Household," ends her devastating critique, "Years of effort on the part of the German Werkbund and individual architects, countless articles and lectures demanding clarity, simplicity, and efficiency in furnishings, as well as a turn away from the traditional kitsch of the last fifty years, have had almost no effect whatsoever."[55]

Other sources, too, indicate that Bauhaus objects were estranged from public taste; according to a critic for the *Frankfurter Zeitung*, the Bauhaus was "even further from the general taste of the public than the Werkbund."[56] The legacy of the Bauhaus's products lies more with an idea and a few canonical objects than with any widespread material reality or mass adoption of modern objects.

PRODUCTION/REPRODUCTION

How then should these issues of production figure in the assessment of the Bauhaus's significance? Should the Bauhaus be viewed as an entity that failed to produce objects that buyers wanted to consume or that manufacturers wanted to produce? Should Bauhaus objects be understood as unique, authentic works of art—which may be their historical fate, judging by their scarcity and their status in art museums today? Walter Benjamin's postulation that "what withers in the age of the technological reproducibility of the work of art is the latter's aura" is useful for reflecting on the status of these objects within the conditions of production of their time.[57] The status of art and art objects, including objects intended for use, in such an age was precisely the question that Gropius faced at the Bauhaus. As proclaimed by his slogan "art and technology—a new unity," his emphasis was on both *art* and *technology*, and specifically their relation to each other.

The nineteenth-century heritage of applied arts education (*Kunstgewerbe*) and its post–World War I revival shaped the school's earliest incarnation, which explicitly attempted to recover that heritage via the high-quality art object produced by a craftsman. This heritage continued to influence subsequent activities at the school, although Gropius carefully sought to elude what he termed "dilettantism of the handicrafts" (*kunstgewerblicher Dilettantismus*).[58] Simultaneously he worked to counter the ersatz and low-quality products of an industrializing Germany. The potential for degradation of Bauhaus designs through the reproduction process was of continual concern to Gropius, who offered the reassurance that a decline in the quality of the product's material and construction, as a result of mechanical reproduction, would be countered by all available means.[59] Gropius thus sought to mass-produce well-designed objects by industrial methods without ever wholly freeing the school from its *Kunstgewerbe* legacy—the design of the singular work of art produced in small numbers. According to Benjamin's theory, given the reality of small batches in the workshops, these objects would have safeguarded their own, autonomous authority, grounded in tradition, and resisted being taken up and appropriated by the masses. However, a loss of aura and authority would necessarily have resulted if the Bauhaus had succeeded in factory mass reproduction.

These issues of production and reproduction of art, architecture, and objects were a subject of period concern among theorists and critics, such as Benjamin and the architectural critic Adolf Behne, artists such as Moholy-Nagy, and architects such as Gropius.[60] Each had different, specific ideas, but the terms and the overarching concern—the relationship of the authentic art object to the modern means of production—formed an important commonality of discourse. In his 1917 essay, "The Reproductive Age" ("Das reproduktive Zeitalter"), Behne argued that, unlike the circumstances attached to earlier authentic artworks, technological reproduction caused the essential effect—*Wirkung*—of the original to be lost, and yet the aesthetic values of the work of art were transferred to the reproductive process itself.[61] Moholy-Nagy's 1922 essay, "Production-Reproduction," written with Lucia Moholy, went further, specifying the goal of making reproductive processes useful for creative activities.[62] Benjamin identified the loss of authenticity and aura and the turn to mass reproduction as inevitable consequences of the modern transformation in conditions of production, which nonetheless bore great artistic and political potential, while Moholy-Nagy, and the Bauhaus generally, actively endorsed mass reproduction as an art practice.

Perhaps the Bauhaus should be assessed not in terms of production, but reproduction—the stage at which it failed most visibly to realize its aims.[63] As Gropius shifted the emphasis of the Bauhaus toward mass reproduction, along with other basic operations he instituted, he was not reacting to a change in the availability of industrial technology but rather to a change in ideas about process. In an attempt to broaden consumption, the Bauhaus needed to move from concentrating on *production* (where it arguably did well, generating many functionally and aesthetically successful designs in a relatively short period of time) to *reproduction*. As this examination has shown, reproduction, as both a practical process and a theoretical construct, is precisely where a material and economic failure took place; at the same time, this historical episode has much theoretical significance.

In evaluating the Bauhaus, it is the emphasis laid on the process of reproduction that is important and imbued with social significance in the context of the period. As K. Michael Hays has pointed out, Benjamin's analysis reveals that as one approaches those mediums that are inherently multiple and reproducible, not only does the authenticity of the object, its here and now, lose its value as a repository of meaning but also the reproductive technique *as procedure* takes on the features of a system of signification. Meaning arises from the multiple forces of social practice rather than the formal qualities of the auratic art object.[64] Thus the potential significance of the Bauhaus project under Gropius lies less in the produced objects themselves but rather in the Bauhaus's grappling with the problem of reproducibility. The members of the Bauhaus saw their larger project not just as art practice but as a part of *social* practice, as Moholy-Nagy wrote: "We hope that from the inspirations of the Bauhaus, such results will come forth as will be useful to a new social order."[65] This social function, for Benjamin and for the Bauhaus, occurred when the art object was reproduced in such a way that what it would lose in aura it would make up for by reaching society at large, becoming available for its use. For Benjamin, the social function of art was revolutionized as soon as the criterion of authenticity ceased to be applicable to artistic production.[66]

The actual objects designed by the Bauhaus, however, were not consonant with what was needed to achieve its goals for reproduction, as their elite qualities stymied the social project. In their relationship to society, the object-types the Bauhaus produced—such as silver tea services—were insufficient; their luxury character limited their reproducibility, perhaps equally as much as their costly fabrication and materials. As a result of this disjunction, Bauhaus objects can be read as material indices of the social problematic of mass reproducibility.

Benjamin pinpoints the transformation that occurs in the modern age from the autonomous authority of the art object itself to its social determination by its inherent technological reproducibility. That Gropius's Bauhaus embraced mass reproduction as a system and a goal is meaningful even if it was unable to realize this goal to any significant, material degree. As Josef Albers noted, "The greatest success of the Bauhaus was to win over and interest industry. We realized this aim only to a small degree."[67] Indeed, the *idea* of a relationship with industry remained the Bauhaus's greatest achievement, even if it was hardly realized. The Bauhaus inserted itself into this system of signification through the ideal of reproduction, and it was willing to sacrifice the auratic or authentic qualities of its objects to do so. An essential legacy of Bauhaus objects is the mythical aspiration of good design for the masses achieved through an alignment with industrial production. And meaning can be derived from this ideal even if it never occurred at the level of actual Bauhaus products. Through their very failure as objects of reproduction and mass consumption, the products of the Bauhaus paradoxically retained both their authenticity and their aura, for, in an age of mechanical reproduction, that is, of the definitive withering of aura, an individual Bauhaus object, such as a Brandt teapot, remains a work of art. To acknowledge this by conceding these objects' elite, luxury status, however, calls into question the received, mythological account of the Bauhaus's contribution to the trajectory of modernism. It also re-poses the question of what designing objects for mass reproduction—and socially transformative use by society, by the masses—might entail.

SUBJECTIVITY

Architecture's materials have always been an essential component of understanding every other constituent element—what a building wants to convey or elects not to convey about its structure and cladding, its context in time and locality, its aspirations, and its realities. As substance and as surface, materials were tasked in the first part of the twentieth century with demonstrating the modern movement's ideas, via physical, built manifestations, realizing and representing its conceptions of a new, modern world. As Walter Curt Behrendt pointed out in one of the earliest histories of modern architecture, his 1927 *The Victory of the New Building Style*, modernism was "in a very distinct way a *material* style, that is, a style that uses the material—be it steel, glass, ceramics, and so on—for the sake of its materiality or refined material beauty."[1] Within that paradigm, the luxurious materiality of Ludwig Mies van der Rohe's buildings and interiors stands apart. The materials of Mies's modern architecture are striking, whether in their stark, unadorned plainness (white linoleum) or via their technical virtuosity (descending walls of glass) or in their visual allure through the showcasing of new materials (nickel and chromium plating), visual access to previously concealed materials (exposed steel beams), or traditional materials newly deployed for modernism (flat planes of travertine, marble, and onyx) (fig. 5.1).[2] As found in Mies's houses, especially their interiors, and in the exhibition house projects, most of which he designed in close collaboration with Lilly Reich, these forms of modernist materiality represent another facet of luxury in modern architecture.[3] Whether in the design of large-scale family villas or in showcasing modern dwelling ideals through exhibitions for the general public, Mies, together with Reich, expressed his ideas about modern housing through individual materials—giving careful attention to their substance and their surfaces alike.[4] Emphasizing a rigorous solidity in the materials selected and precisely placed, Mies simultaneously contrasted their firm presence with thin surface treatments of veneer or metal plating. He also celebrated the immateriality and the ephemeral qualities of materials—from spare, blank walls to the transparency or semitransparency of varieties of glass, to the arresting voids created by his sinkable windows. Invoking the materiality of modernism, from the glass curtain wall to the intricately veined onyx slab, from the shimmering cruciform column to the solidity of a travertine floor, from mobile, sinkable windows to stable, heavy furnishings, this chapter examines how Mies's material choices were meaningful in their expression of modernism itself.

Rather than using materials to express concepts of mass production, industry, or technology, as many of his peers did, Mies's materials were statements of modern elegance and luxury.[5] The idea of luxurious materials was neither new to architecture nor to the bourgeois interior. However, Mies utilized these materials to deploy luxury within the visual and theoretical paradigm of modernism and toward social and cultural—as well as architectural—ends.[6] While designers such as Adolf Loos, Josef Hoffmann and members of the Wiener Werkstätte in Vienna, Peter Behrens, and other artists at the Mathildenhöhe artists' colony in Darmstadt used luxury materials in their architecture and applied arts objects created during the first two decades of the twentieth century, the luxurious materiality of Mies in the context of 1920s and early 1930s Berlin is demonstrably different.[7] In Berlin, Mies was involved in a circle of avant-garde architects and artists, as part of the interdisciplinary circle that produced the journal *G* and the group known as The Ring.[8] These groups' members privileged stark, *sachlich* modern design—and yet his was an architecture that utilized luxury materials within this context. The social status and taste of Mies's clients, who generally came from an upper-class group made up of commercial and industrial magnates (*Grossbürgertum*) and the educated elite (*Bildungsbürgertum*), was reflected in his choice of elite materials for their dwellings, illustrating the ways in which objects, through their materials, could be aligned with subjects. It is without question that this had always been the case with regard to an elite clientele and their architectural representations, from Louis XIV's Hall of Mirrors at Versailles to Karl Friedrich Schinkel's pavilion at the Schloss Charlottenburg. However, in addition

Figure 5.1. *Below*: Ludwig Mies van der Rohe, Tugendhat House, main living area, Brno, Czech Republic, 1928–30. *Opposite*: Detail, column base on travertine floor in reception area.

to traditional meanings, the materials used in the modern period reflected new tasks for architecture and the ways in which dwelling subjects, in turn, might relate to architecture.

Moreover, beyond the visibly costly materials showcased by Mies, such as onyx and travertine, even seemingly common materials, such as metal and glass, were costly to acquire, refine, install, and maintain. The mass production of architecture, and its attendant reduction in costs, never emerged on a large-scale basis during the Weimar Republic; that was to come in the post–World War II period. This state of affairs was often noted by modernism's critics as well as lamented by its proponents. By 1932, the international architectural critic Karel Teige could aptly, if polemically, articulate the central paradox of the luxuriousness of modern architecture's materiality, especially in the German context:

> Bored, the modern bourgeoisie is casting about to find its own "modern" luxury style. Nor should it be forgotten that academic architecture always propped up the show of wealth by using luxury materials, such as marble, granite, bronze, and so on, regardless of their cost; in the same way, the modern rich … do not mind spending large sums on construction and maintenance, squandering money on the need to heat superfluous glass halls, and paying their servants to polish, clean, and mop the glass and chrome that so fascinate the modern snob architect and his clients. Just as the Secession made a fetish out of ceramic tile decorations not long ago, so today glass has become the modern luxury material of choice—a new fetish, embraced by Gropius, Breuer, Mies van der Rohe, and others too numerous to mention here.[9]

Teige was not alone in his bald criticism of the excesses of modernism's materials and their associated costs—which included an initial high acquisition price for raw natural substances, the industrial application and installation of manufactured materials, and their compounded upkeep thereafter. However, his assessment does generally run counter to the received ideology of modern architecture in the period itself and in its mainstream historiography thereafter: namely, that modernism in

for himself and his family.[14] He lived alone from the latter half of 1921 onward (the same year in which he modified his last name), although he never divorced his wife. She and their three children moved first to Bornstedt, near Potsdam, and then embarked on a peripatetic life, never settling in one place for very long. On one hand, Mies's exercise of individual freedom is symptomatic of the Weimar period in its shrugging off of social constraints, including marriage.[15] Yet Mies's public persona and his lifelong concern for his own position in society should also be understood in relation to the circle of clients he worked for, and the materials he used and how he deployed them in the dwellings he designed in the 1920s and early 1930s for these clients.

MATERIALITY AT THE HERMANN LANGE AND THE JOSEF ESTERS HOUSES

Despite positioning himself within avant-garde architectural circles whose other protagonists, such as Ludwig Hilberseimer, proffered stripped-down housing intended for the masses, through the late 1920s Mies's architecture and interiors became increasingly luxurious. This was commented on by Mies's critics with ever greater regularity, reaching a crescendo in evaluations of his contribution to the *German Building Exhibition* in 1931.[16] His best-known commissions, large villas with expansive interiors in affluent city neighborhoods, demonstrate Mies's interest in lush materiality and in pushing the limits of technology, not only for spatial and material effect, but for richness of experience. It is easy to account for the select nature of these commissions given the aspirations and budgets of the clients; this was a group accustomed to original and luxurious interiors, and generally Mies's clients were trading a Jugendstil or an elaborate nineteenth-century historicist dwelling for an equally rarified modern one. Luxury in Mies's architecture was the sum of many material and technical components working in concert—shimmering cruciform columns, large-scale windows that could be entirely retracted down into the basement, commissioned items of furniture designed for specific placement in these interiors, and high-level finishes such as zebrawood trim.

As modern architects looked toward the techniques of mass production, the promise of technical advancement, and the language of industry, they had to contend with the reality that the use of new technology and materials was often prohibitively expensive in this period. Mies did not shy away from this association between technology and luxury; rather, he transformed technical elements into luxurious details by sheathing them in gleaming, new materials—for example, plating his sinkable windows in nickel or chromium, thereby visually highlighting them. Even his stationary windows expressed opulence via their large size and in the shimmer of their metal framing. After freeing his internal walls from the task of carrying weight through the utilization of load-bearing steel beams, he could now, with expressive aplomb, veneer non-load-bearing room dividers in rare tropical woods and stand sheets of costly stone upright. In example after example, at the Barcelona Pavilion, the Tugendhat House, in exhibition architecture, and elsewhere, the use of new technology both enlivened the visual appeal of modernism and made it possible for Mies to put luxurious materials on show.

The complicated relationship between architecture and issues of materiality, technology, and bourgeois dwelling first came together in a major commission—Mies's

Esters and Lange houses, designed and built from 1927 to 1930 (figs. 5.2, 5.3). Although Mies's drawings are labeled "country house," specifically "Landhaus Dr. Esters" and "Landhaus Hermann Lange," they should be understood as urban villas, given their location on adjacent lots surrounded by other large, single-family homes in an affluent neighborhood of the small city of Krefeld, near Düsseldorf.[17] The pair of houses for the two textile industrialists Josef Esters and Hermann Lange and their families display many hallmarks characteristic of the period's modern architecture—flat roofs, horizontal bands of windows, roof terraces, and easy access

Figure 5.2. Mies, Esters House, exterior, northwest view, Krefeld, 1927–30.

Figure 5.3. Mies, Lange House, Krefeld, 1927–30.

between inside and outside. With few external details, they both evince an overall rational appearance, with doors and windows seemingly punched into their facades, and each with a simple cantilevered overhang replacing the traditional porte cochere. Both display the product of Mies's attention to surface and substance, resulting in rich experimentation with materiality. This play of materials would reach its apotheosis in the next designs by Mies, the Tugendhat House and the Barcelona Pavilion. The Krefeld houses are of special interest in that they can be read as a step in Mies's process of material refinement, involving an experimentation with a plethora of contrasting materials and at times an uneasy compromise between his modern ideals and the realities of his clients' needs.

While modern architects and their chroniclers hailed the advent of industrial materials in the home—steel beams allowed for ever-larger glass window spans and open interior plans—Mies's architecture of this period can be seen as equally deeply engaged in the use of natural materials, especially in the Krefeld commissions (fig. 5.4). The two houses feature sumptuous purple-red bricks, wide zebra-striped macassar ebony wood, and oak herringbone and parquet floors (fig. 5.5). The laborious technical and complex structural means that allowed these materials to be showcased were often masked. Hidden beneath unbroken courses of exterior bricks and placid white interiors, numerous steel beams carried the load. These innovations allowed for large, spanning lengths, which appear as pure space and the apparent absence of technology. Thus long expanses of white walls in the interior spaces could be celebrated, but they simultaneously dematerialized before the eye, enhancing the materiality of the room's details—the baseboards, door frames, and radiator coverings. Mies varied the materials from room to room; macassar ebony was featured in the baseboards and radiator coverings in one room, golden oak in the next. This had the effect of highlighting the individual materials of each room, illuminating

Figure 5.4. Mies, Lange House, open plan and descending window.

them for visitors who moved through the spaces. Travertine window seats, wooden wall partitions, bookshelves inserted into walls, and prominent wooden paneling (used to frame windows and conceal radiators) all insistently highlighted their constitutional materiality.

The expressive material presence of individual elements heightened the viewer's awareness of them as architectural objects. For example, the widely veined macassar ebony wood of the front doors emphasizes each door as *wooden front door*. The everyday character of a common wooden door is here amplified via the dark and light striations that give the impression of oversized wood grains, a radical representation of the materiality of an otherwise very commonplace object (fig. 5.6). Inside, in the kitchen of the Lange House, the rich wooden worktops, cupboards, and sink cabinetry in teak stand out as distinctive elements from the white tiled walls and light floors, rather than visually integrating these elements, as was the case in the all-white kitchen of the Haus am Horn or in Mies's Tugendhat House (fig. 5.7, see also fig. 3.11). Throughout the ground floor of each house, deep oak or macassar window jambs, wide travertine sills, and exposed shiny metal window frames all use uncommon materials to highlight each architectural element, while also serving to delineate an unambiguous, materialized border between individual architectural objects.

Shifting valences of materiality are at play between the solids and frames within the Krefeld houses. When the oak pocket doors between the dining room and the children's playroom of the Esters House are slid closed, for example, what had been a frame becomes a visual solid (fig. 5.8). At the Esters House, especially, the floor-to-ceiling pocket doors provide a substantial visual and physical barrier when closed. But when they are slid back open, receding completely into the wall, what had been

Figure 5.5. *Left*: Mies, Lange House, main floor: door frames in zebrawood; oak herringbone and parquet floors. *Right*: Main floor: travertine window sill; radiator cover and baseboards in zebrawood; oak herringbone floors.

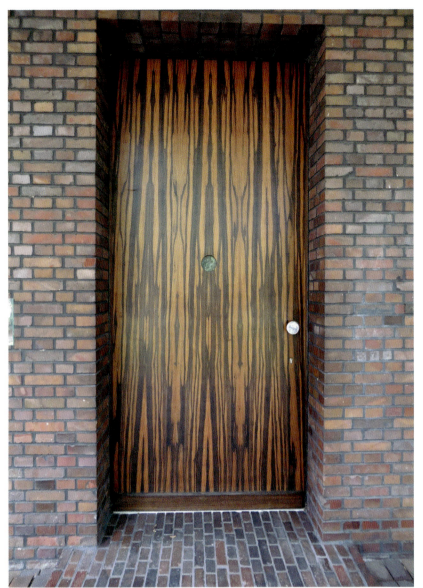

Figure 5.6. Mies, Lange House, front door.

Figure 5.7. Mies, Lange House, kitchen.

solid gives the impression of having been dematerialized (fig. 5.9). Similarly, the four-panel wooden structure in the Lange House's dining room gives the impression of a solid wall, but it is not solid; it is demountable, allowing the dining room to be combined with the central hall during large social events (fig. 5.10).[18] In both examples, the wood has a distinct presence in the room, drawing attention to the materiality of the richly solid double door (Esters) or four-panel divider (Lange) as they materialize in the room. When the door is again slid back into the wall or the divider removed, the rooms are optically and haptically opened back up again.

Figure 5.8. Mies, Esters House, children's playroom, pencil on tracing paper.

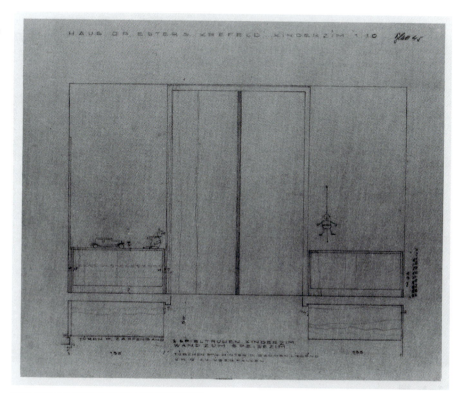

Figure 5.9. *Left*: Mies, Esters House, view from dining room into children's playroom, through to women's sitting room. *Right*: View from women's sitting room into children's playroom, through to dining room.

Throughout the ground floors of both houses, in contrast to the white-painted wood trim upstairs, baseboards in oak or macassar starkly delineate the herringbone parquet flooring from the white walls. Doorways are framed in walnut and oak, not precisely lined up as in an enfilade with a single vanishing point, but staggered slightly with frames visible to the left or right (fig. 5.11; see also fig. 5.9). This placement emphasizes the rich wood of the baseboards and door frames while offering a view across several thresholds, connecting and visually opening up these spaces.[19] Another effect of the staggered alignment is that the frames are highlighted between successive rooms, not just accentuating the multiple white planes of the modern architectural interior, but the materialist breaks in those planes.

On the exterior, the green-gray painted steel of the window casements, terrace doors, and door frames introduces another material substance that represents a strong, liminal, yet patently hard, material boundary (figs. 5.12, 5.13). When viewed from the outside, the steel mediates between the substantive planes of brick and the transparency of the large glass windows and doors. The terrace doors, which give direct access to the rear garden, are composed of a single sheet of glass inserted into steel frames with a half-circle metal disk for the door handle hardware. In contrast to the appearance of opaque solidity of both houses' front doors, the transparency of the rear facade invites the crossing of thresholds.

Elsewhere, through his strategic use of materials, Mies's architecture suggests that what gives the impression of solidity can turn out to be mere surface, and what appears as only surface can be substantial. The finely pointed purple-red exterior brick, installed exactingly by skilled masons, displays boldly variegated colors that appear stolidly solid. And yet the external walls are not quite as substantial as they appear; rather, these exterior bricks (partially glazed Bockhorn bricks) are set as cladding over larger, rougher bricks (fig. 5.14; see also fig. 5.12).[20] These clinker bricks can be considered surface decoration and, as such, they can be read as a "veneer" on the rougher bricks, in the same manner that wood veneer is applied to

Figure 5.10. *Left*: Mies, Lange House, dining room, showing the demountable four-panel wooden enclosure. *Right*: View of the demountable wooden structure from the entry hall.

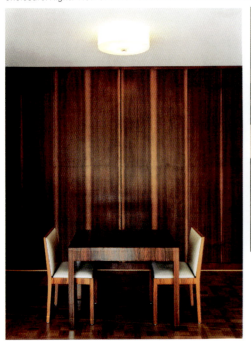

Figure 5.11. Mies, Esters House, view of the staggered door frames and windows folded back and open.

a lesser grade, structural wooden substrate. Returning to the massive Lange and Esters front doors, their oversized, zebra-like graining similarly, exaggeratedly proclaims the essential, solid, material presence of wood (see fig. 5.6). Yet, this graining is not evidence of the solidity it projects; it too is just a thin veneer, a surface materiality. Where the same bookmatched macassar wood veneer is used indoors at the Lange House, in the baseboards and the paneling that encloses the radiator, the effect is the same, a surface material standing in visually and physically for solidity. In comparison, a plain but genuinely solid oak door would have announced itself much more subtly, less substantially, but more truthfully, than does the bold macassar veneer.

In yet one more play of opposites, the windows in both houses call attention to themselves via their generous size and the mechanics by which they are opened, either folding back onto themselves or descending into the wall (fig. 5.15; see also figs. 5.4, 5.11). The windows' weight seems almost unsupported, and their substantial expanses of glass create an openness that negates their material presence; they are at once both object and dematerialized mirage. The windows, when fully sunken or doubled back on themselves, create a void in the architecture. In these houses especially, planes and frames provide borders and openings—a study in contrasts made manifest through their material presence. It is clear that, for Mies, spaces are necessarily bounded and the elements of architecture are weighty and substantial, and yet even in their solidity emphatically material elements can shift and open. Materiality, in short, can be deceiving. It is not fixed, nor is it stable.

Figure 5.12. *Below and opposite:* Mies, Lange House, rear facade.

Figure 5.13. Mies, Esters House, metal terrace doors.

Figure 5.14. Rough interior bricks exposed during restoration of the houses.

Figure 5.15. Mies, Esters House, view of the dining room with windows folded back and open, also the built-in wall cupboard.

BOURGEOIS LIVING AS ADMIXTURE OF MODERN
TECHNOLOGY AND TRADITION

Many of the technological innovations that Mies became renowned for in his subsequent buildings originated at the Lange and Esters houses, at least in some part. The technical complexity behind the straightforward-appearing houses is revealed in their intricate and exacting structural engineering; the Lange House required 88 pages of structural calculations, 124 pages for the Esters House.[21] Large, open spans of the interiors represent an instance of luxury provided by technology, namely, in the use of steel beams concealed in the walls that made this open space possible—there were 350 steel beams in the Esters House alone.[22] At the Lange House, motorized, sinkable windows that lowered to the basement for a complete opening to the garden in both the study and the living room predated the more famous examples at the Tugendhat House. At the Esters House, the casement windows were framed and hinged at 180 degrees so that they folded all the way over onto themselves when open, thereby nearly disappearing.[23]

There is every indication that the clients were enthusiastic about the technological advancement represented by the pair of houses. Certain technical conveniences were planned by the owners; for example, Esters wrote to Lange (who was coordinating the details of both commissions with Mies's office) in October 1928 to specify the positioning of telephones in the women's parlor, in the study, and adjacent to the front door, and requested a gas stove for the kitchen rather than a coal stove.[24] (This was a period in which an electric stove would have been viewed as the most luxurious and modern convenience.) Other modern amenities were installed: the stairwell of the Lange House was designed for music equipment with an accompanying cupboard fitted to hold record albums and, on the second floor, a room was set up as a photography darkroom.[25] Hermann Lange had a large modern art collection, around which his main living space was designed (fig. 5.16). For the rotation of the paintings in that space, a 3-meter slot was placed in the room's floor so that artworks could be lowered directly into a basement art storage area.[26]

However, the houses were not always rational demonstrations of modern technical prowess. At times, the showcasing of materials trumped that technology. A common lament in the period was that domestic warmth was being lost in the move toward rationality, specifically through cold, technical materials. In an elegant maneuver that highlighted the expensive encasing materials, Mies covered the radiators at the Esters and Lange houses with a vertical plane of oak or zebrawood and topped it with a thick slab of travertine. This must be understood as an abrupt departure from modern architecture's usual celebration of technological objects such as radiators, and in contradistinction to those exposed and wall-mounted radiators placed by Walter Gropius at the Bauhaus Building in Dessau in 1926. Gropius's design, too, was more about appearance than function: because heat rises, silver-painted radiators mounted at eye level on the walls proved an effective visual embellishment in celebration of technology that in reality functioned poorly in terms of heat distribution. Rather than a functionalist program of modern rationalization, the instances of new technology in the Krefeld houses should be viewed in terms of individualistic, modernist luxury. Rather than through technology laid bare, Mies gave sense to his architecture via a rich materiality.

The materials of the Krefeld villas, and as showcased in other buildings by Mies, also signal the triumphs of markets and industries. Mies's clients, here and elsewhere, were not simply capitalists, but captains of industry—or, as in the case of Lange and Esters, involved in the highest levels of the management of modern industry. As such, the lives that they lived in their modern domiciles were familiarly bourgeois, and, despite their unconventional surroundings, were not especially modern. With their expanses of glass and the liberation of many load-bearing walls, the two Krefeld houses appeared more materially, technically, and spatially radical than their bourgeois neighbors. Yet they functioned in a traditional manner in terms of dwelling, bolstered by conventional gendered room divisions such as separate bedrooms for the husband and wife, sitting rooms for the ladies of the house, and studies for the men. Materials used at the houses such as painted steel and vibrantly striped macassar wood can be seen as surprising, in light of the houses' otherwise traditional and deeply conservative context. To this end, the materials, in fact, might be the most modern aspect of the two houses. Along with the commissioning of a modern dwelling, the materials on display projected a certain self-representation on the part of the clients. The design was singularly equipped to handle the tension between clients' bourgeois patterns of dwelling and Mies's ideas for modern architecture; his use of unusual or rich materials toward modern ends can be seen as a point of connection between the two. Mies did not revolutionize the home in terms of challenging how his clients might live in it.

In Krefeld, and in other commissions, Mies's modern designs did not work against the predominant social customs of a typical bourgeois home. New amenities that

Figure 5.16. Mies, Lange House, view of the art collection in the front hall.

were by that period often found in modern interiors, such as an open pass-through to the kitchen (a feature present in all of the masters' houses of the Bauhaus), are notably absent. Of the intersection of space with the daily patterns of life, Hermann Lange's daughter Christiane recalls, "The structure and internal organization of Lange House satisfied all of the demands of a traditional, representative way of life. A servant and a housekeeper were in constant attendance; visitors were only received in the vestibule."[27] And the *bürgerlich* qualities of the Krefeld houses were also acknowledged in the period. "A bourgeois twentieth-century 'Sans Souci,'" is how the art dealer Alfred Flechtheim, from whom Hermann Lange bought art, characterized his client's house.[28] Initially austere appearances notwithstanding, in the Esters and Lange houses, photographs illustrate the ways in which Mies's interiors

Figure 5.17. Mies, Lange House, men's study. Photograph showing family furniture.

Figure 5.18. Mies, Esters House, entry hall.

were subsequently domesticated by their inhabitants, revealing a myriad of typical activities in keeping with period expectations. Lace doilies and oriental rugs abound, and most rooms were furnished with the families' Biedermeier and other antiques (fig. 5.17). On the Esters's travertine windowsill, a motley row of house plants in small pots are visible through the diaphanous silk curtain; in the distance, an assortment of flowers in vases and fruits and nuts in bowls can be seen lined up along the marble-topped walnut veneer dining room sideboard (fig. 5.18). All would have been overseen by the woman of the house, in keeping with the types of household tasks associated with a lady of Hedwig Esters's or Marie Lange's class and status.

Each Krefeld house included a women's sitting room (*Damenzimmer*) into which the proprietress of the house could retreat to enjoy a space of her own and to entertain female friends. Like the reception room, this nineteenth-century room type was disappearing by the late 1920s. Eliminated from the Tugendhat house plan, in Krefeld it represents another instance of bourgeois tradition (fig. 5.19). Via correspondence with Mies during the planning stages, for example, it was noted that Marie Lange did not want the heater placed under the window in her sitting room but rather along another wall because she desired to put flowers and plants on the windowsill.[29] (She did not prevail; the radiator is beneath the windowsill.) These popular domestic pastimes—the care of houseplants, the arranging of flowers in decorative clusters—point to a pattern of conventional bourgeois living rather than modern dwelling reconceived. The Lange family kept a fruit and vegetable garden, and Mies provided them with a greenhouse.[30] In his windowsills, generous

Figure 5.19. Mies, Lange House, women's sitting room. Furniture by Mies and Lilly Reich.

to houseplants, and built-in display cabinets for collections, Mies created interiors that were radical in appearance, luxurious in the use of materials, but accommodating of those bourgeois activities normally encouraged by—and reflected in—traditional upper-class spaces. His remarkable attention to detail allowed for an overall modern interior, yet one that operated smoothly in a manner sensitive to the bourgeois inhabitants' desired domestic life.

Significantly, both the Lange and Esters families elected to bring the majority of their own furniture into their new homes. Mies and Reich thus only designed furnishings for the two dining rooms and the women's sitting room of the Lange House. The families' interiors consisted mainly of historicist pieces, including carved tables, desks, chairs, and stuffed wing chairs, accented by oriental carpets and lace doilies.[31] This thoroughly bourgeois assemblage expressed the stability and timelessness of the domestic life contained within the house. Though the external shell was modern, with its unarticulated courses of bricks, pared-down facades punctuated by large expanses of glass, flat roof, multiple points of access to the outside, and extensive terraces, much was done on the interior to mitigate the effect of modernism, especially in the more private areas of the house.

The most public rooms were thus also the most modern. In the Esters's front entry hall, for example, a threshold for the many who had business with the household but who would not be invited further into the house, visitors were not presented with the family's antiques (see fig. 5.18). In keeping with the house's modern exterior, they would encounter its most modern furniture. Four modernistic chairs (not designed by Mies or Reich), were grouped around a small round table, a stripped-down version of a style formerly popular in the Biedermeier period. The richest or most modern materials were also on display for the more public rooms of the Lange House. The entry hall contained heavy-set leather armchairs, oriental rugs of various sizes scattered at angles, and Hermann Lange's art collection, which featured sculpture placed on Mies-designed, dark, polished-wood plinths and travertine wall-mounted blocks (see fig. 5.16).[32] From the Esters's front hall, visible through the doors to the right, the dining room could be glimpsed with its grand piano, and the Mies-designed dining table, chairs, and sideboard. A long buffet—itself a staid bourgeois furniture type—in walnut veneer casing with a marble top, was built into the wall in each of the houses' dining rooms. Also part of the more selective, but still public, social function of each house were the women's sitting rooms. That Mies and Reich were commissioned to design the furniture for Marie Lange's parlor reiterates how emphasis was placed on showcasing modernism in the most accessible parts of the house (see fig. 5.19). By contrast, Hermann Lange's corresponding gentleman's study did not contain furniture by Mies and Reich. His space was not as public as the other rooms on the ground floor—Lange would most likely have seen his business associates at his firm's office and worked alone at home, while Marie Lange would be expected to entertain friends and family in her sitting room. It is not surprising that the spectacular front doors, the most public aspect of the house, were in visually arresting macassar, and interior ground floor door and window frames were in macassar, oak, and walnut. But in the more private areas, such as along the Langes' second-floor hallway, the door frames were painted white, masking a lowly substrate material. This dyad of modern public rooms and more intimate, traditional family spaces was one that was set up by the family, not Mies, who would have preferred to design all of the interior furnishings to accompany his architecture.

From the point of entry, the visitor was introduced to the basic character of the house—the materials and tropes of modernism were presented clearly via the expansive open spaces made possible by supportive steel beams, through the large expanses of glass, and in the select representative pieces of modern furniture. However, traditional signs of affluence were also on display from the earliest point of entry, via materials, as evidenced in the leather chairs, the showcasing of rare types of wood, and the travertine window sills and sculpture plinths, and in the prominent, public display of the art collection. Modernism and what may be considered typically bourgeois elements—such as the lace-covered table in the Langes' entry hall—greeted the visitor as an ensemble, presenting an interior that was new to Krefeld's elite and, at the same time, reassuringly traditional. From the front entry hall and public main spaces, to the upstairs level with its family bedrooms, each threshold of the interior introduced the guest to a successive level of intimacy, and a concomitant layer away from modern design to one more deeply tied to traditional modes of dwelling.

Although Lange and Esters selected Mies as their architect and allowed him to follow through on many of his plans for the houses, they resisted a number of his newer ideas. Most notably, Mies designed a nearly continuous glass wall for the garden side of the Esters House. Although never built, it is noteworthy in that it presaged the glass wall of the Tugendhat House. An earlier plan with fewer interior walls, including a design for the entry hall to be completely opened up to the dining room, was also rejected by the clients. In Krefeld, the agency of the two patrons, in this case powerful industrial businessmen, often prevailed, resulting in a dwelling that represented constant negotiation and compromise. While the houses that Mies produced in Krefeld did not fully exhibit the modern architecture that he was capable of in this period, as the Tugendhat House or the Barcelona Pavilion would amply validate, he did successfully demonstrate his mastery over materials and the effects that materiality could engender. Removed from the avant-garde of Berlin, different from a modern *Gesamtkunstwerk* as represented by commissions such as the Tugendhat House, and far from the works of other modern architects such as Gropius's masters' housing in Dessau, the expansive Krefeld houses can best be understood in terms of modern architecture's relationship to modern capitalism. The Krefeld exemplars represented a convergence of affluence, luxury, and materiality, coming together to form a consensual, stable, bourgeois environment.

FORM AND MATERIALS AT THE TUGENDHAT HOUSE (1928-1930)

Diverging from his earlier, traditional, and classically orientated Berlin villas, as well as the consensual Krefeld houses, the seemingly unornamented modern design of Mies's Tugendhat House represents an apex in the luxury of his form and material aesthetic.[33] Begun in 1928, the Tugendhat House was completed by 1930 for Grete and Fritz Tugendhat and their young family in Brno, an industrial city on the eastern border of the Czech Republic. Designed in close collaboration with Lilly Reich, the house's materiality is constituted by Mies's merging of modern form with materialized surface.

This steel skeleton and concrete house was built into the hillside, allowing for commanding views over Brno, on an expensive plot of land (around $200,000 in today's currency for the plot alone) in an enclave of upper-bourgeois homes built decades before, generally in historicist and art nouveau styles.[34] Steel was a costly and uncommon material for a domestic building in this period. The exterior spare, white planes, flat roof, large windows, and accessible terraces presented a by-then familiar modern architecture, akin to other examples that had been built at the Weissenhof Housing Settlement in 1927 (figs. 5.20, 5.21). It is on the inside that the viewer experienced a modernism of lavish materials and new conceptions of space. Approaching the house from the street, visitors entered the vestibule via a front door out of immediate view, located behind the curving milk glass panels that encased the main stairs. From the front door, it was also possible to continue around to the main terrace at the back of the house, with its sweeping vistas over the large rear garden and the city center below. Once inside the front door, the materiality of the Tugendhat house immediately presented itself—in the floor-to-ceiling rosewood partitions and closets that lined the entryway, the travertine window sills and flooring, and the small seating group comprising a table set between two tubular steel chairs with leather spanning (fig. 5.22). Bypassing the family's bedrooms that were arrayed along the corridor behind the vestibule, visitors would immediately be ushered down the stairs to the main level of the house (fig. 5.23). There, the expansive space featured a magnificent onyx wall, a curved macassar wood dining room partition, large sinkable windows, and a glazed conservatory, punctuated throughout with shiny cruciform columns (figs. 5.24, 5.25; see also fig. 5.1). Although an open plan, these material objects clearly delineated the space into living room, office, library, dining room, and conservatory. The kitchen and quarters for the household domestic staff were also located on this level, but sequestered away from the main living space. Operating in the same manner as the sinkable windows, a dumbwaiter in the pantry served all of the house's floors, but was primarily used to hoist trays of food from the kitchen to the floor above, where the children and nursemaid ate their evening meal in daughter Hanna's room.[35]

At the Tugendhat House, Mies's use of costly natural materials—travertine and onyx—in vast quantities, as well as expensively refined modern substances such as chrome and nickel, should be viewed in light of both the aesthetic and intrinsic value of those materials. The house also featured dramatically veined, exotic wood veneers, including macassar ebony, palisander, rosewood, pear, and zebrawood (fig. 5.26). Although most of the richest materials are to be found in the more public, main living spaces of the house, a notable exception was the bedroom for the oldest child, Hanna. There, Mies used a deeply striated zebrawood veneer for the floor-to-ceiling door, numerous cupboards, and the bookshelf (fig. 5.27).

The use of luxurious materials was, of course, an old trope in the bourgeois interior, itself preceded by aristocratic and royal models. However, Mies employed these rarified materials in conjunction with the pared-down forms and flat surfaces championed by modern architecture. Even the walls took on a new materiality; as one observer from the period noted about the house, "the surfaces of the facade and the interior walls did not have any 'color' but instead appeared as 'material.'"[36] As early as 1933, the Tugendhat House was characterized by a

Figure 5.20. Mies, Tugendhat House, street facade.

Figure 5.21. Mies, Tugendhat House, rear facade.

Figure 5.22. Mies, Tugendhat House, reception area.

Figure 5.23. Mies, Tugendhat House, view of stairs leading from reception area to main floor.

Figure 5.24. Mies, Tugendhat House, main floor.

Figure 5.25. Mies, Tugendhat House, dining area.

Figure 5.26. Mies, Tugendhat House, wooden dining partition in macassar ebony veneer.

Figure 5.27. Mies, Tugendhat House, zebrawood in daughter Hanna's room.

critic as taking pleasure in new forms and new materials and singled out as being apart from modern architecture's "compulsion toward thrift" (*Zwang zur Sparsamkeit*).[37]

Introducing cruciform columns into the interior also represented luxury—both the luxury of the expansive space that resulted from the columns' structural contribution and the luxury of the materiality of the columns themselves.[38] This surface ornamentation was very costly—in Mies's earliest experiments with these columns, the steel was plated in nickel, but beginning with the Tugendhat House, the nickel-plating was superseded by the slightly less expensive chrome.[39] Although the price paid for chroming the Tugendhat columns is unknown, they would have cost about the same amount as Mies's other columns of this period. The projected price for the chroming of a single cruciform column intended for the Nolde House in 1929 was RM 690 (and four were intended) and RM 475 each for the Henke House addition in 1930.[40]

Columns have always held signification beyond their load-carrying function, and Mies's are no exception.[41] His served a decorative role in their visual punctuation of the space, in their shape, and in the high luminosity of their surfaces. Bare steel columns would have appeared technical and functionalist—the cruciform was a structurally unnecessary but compelling form; likewise, the application of the shiny outer coating served merely aesthetic purposes, domesticating the column through its reflection and refraction of the interior shapes, materials, and colors.[42] In a sense, the chromed columns alternately deflected and absorbed the interior, rather than competing with it. Observed closely, the intrinsic beauty of the chrome complemented the traditional luxury materials of onyx, marble, and travertine, joining their elite ranks. Paired with black leather, white parchment, and the ruby-red velvet of the Tugendhat's chairs, this modern metal contributed to the exalted status of the interior.

At the Tugendhat House, the interiors comprised a complex interplay of gleaming onyx walls, travertine floors, thinly chromed columns, and extravagant cuts of macassar and other costly types of wood, hardly representative of the ideology of modern architecture with its cost-effective, stripped-down materials and aesthetic. The luxury of the materials employed does not accord with the "skin and bones" architectural ideas for which Mies is best known.[43] Furthermore, two dictums that have been attached to the architect, "less is more" and "truth to materials," can also be problematized in light of his materials here. The materials on display in these interiors were often mere surfaces composed of wood veneer or chromium plating, set upon a less costly substrate. What "truth to materials" is thus being presented? The materials seem truthful and entice the viewer with their majesty, but what is really at work is the lure of luxury, not representative of any particular material truth.[44] The curved dining room wall, for example, is not "truthful," but rather a veneered, ornamental surface decorating the form to which it was adhered; it is a thin representational surface—representative, that is, of luxury itself. Moreover, these highly refined materials were selected and enhanced to overwhelm via their natural details that come to the fore—the wood graining, the rich veins of the marble and onyx, the pocks of the travertine. Rather than seeking to make a direct connection to nature for the subject, the materials are presented at a clear remove from their origins in quarries and forests, and highly reworked. Not directly representative of nature, the materials signal its potential opulence—nature as refined into a luxury product. Far from bringing into being a minimal or essential experience of space as such, these interiors constitute a subjective setting in which inhabitants would be drawn to—and connect to—these rarified materials, provoking a new awareness of self within the space. With an emphasis on materiality, surface luminosity, and the refined technology of modernism, these materials pronounced the Tugendhat interior as luxury.

MIES'S MATERIALS AND MODERNISM: LUXURY AT ANY SCALE

From large, family-sized villas to the redesign of small apartment interiors to the creation of temporary exhibition spaces, Mies worked at differing scales with regard to the size and terms of his commissions in his later Berlin period. When Mies ceased to attain larger projects as a result of the financial crises of the late 1920s, he did obtain commissions for a series of apartment interior renovations and furnishings. In light of his more patently luxurious houses, the preciousness of these smaller commissions underscores the design attention that Mies placed on all of his interiors. They illustrate the degree to which he created conditions for the showcasing of materials without regard for size, scale, or location—whether in a house in a leafy bourgeois enclave or a city apartment. Despite variations in use—he also produced several exhibition spaces that had only a representational use value—most of the ideas and material elements remained consistent across these examples, including the smaller commissions, in which luxury was likewise materialized.

Mies's apartment renovations contained almost all of the same elements as his villas, albeit without the large-scale windows and commanding open space (although whenever possible he did remove nonstructural interior walls). These designs provide insight into the consistency of his ideas for interiors—his maintenance of an elegance that was not particularly modified for smaller spaces or budgets. The rich materiality of the elements, the combination of furnishings in dialogue with each other and in relationship to the rest of the space, the effects of shimmering metal against matte materials and of highly manufactured materials against natural substances, combined with the use of a palette that alternated between vibrant and muted colors, all represent the powerful distillation of key aspects of Mies's modernist materiality in this period.

A typical example of a small-scale commission is Mies's 1930 transformation of the top two floors of a characteristically *bürgerlich* Berlin building into a modern, six-room apartment for Stefanie Hess.[45] An independent woman, Hess was the president of the German section of the League of Human Rights.[46] The apartment, built about 1910, was located in Wilmersdorf, a leafy, affluent section of the city, more given over to single-family houses than apartments. Photographs of several of the apartment's rooms as well as drawings in the Mies Archive attest to its similarity with other Mies interiors of the period (fig. 5.28).[47] Mies removed a non-loadbearing wall to turn two rooms into a large living-dining space and eliminated all traces of the typical plaster decoration from the walls, resulting in a sleek, horizontally oriented open space with smooth modern walls. The entire apartment was light-filled, an effect enhanced by painting the walls white, installing a light-colored floor material, and fronting the wall cupboards with large mirrors. The apartment featured rush matting and two sets of curtains: an outer, light-colored, semi-transparent curtain for the daytime and thicker, heavier curtains hung on the inside, to be drawn at night. These floor-to-ceiling drapes gave the visual impression that the windows were much larger—and thus more modern—than they actually were. In the living-dining room, the furnishings consisted of the same major pieces found in Mies's villas: Barcelona chairs and an ottoman, a leather couch, and a floor lamp were placed around a small coffee table to form a conversational group in the living room section, while nearby the dining area was furnished with a round wooden table, cantilevered chairs, and a sideboard. The couch, or "Klubsofa," was described by Werner Gräff in his 1933 how-to book on modern interior design as being made of yellow Moroccan leather, and it was a substantial expense, costing RM 1,050 in 1933 or $4,570 in today's dollars (RM 1,050 represents about a half year's salary of a white-collar worker in the period).[48] With the exception of the chromed metal in the room, the materials derived from and celebrated the natural world—rush flooring, leather, wood, and caning. The domestic objects captured in period photographs underscore the apartment's habitability: plants in pots and flowers in vases, small art objects scattered about the rooms, a prominently placed telephone, and casually placed books slanted in and on top of the shelf and the coffee table. The apartment is both representational of bourgeois respectability and demonstrates a modern sensibility. It hints at a life of the mind and of a free-thinking, single female dweller—an autonomous late Weimar denizen. Overall, the apartment illustrates a combination of elegance and bourgeois comfort representative of Mies's interiors of this period—luxury in the careful combination and deployment of rich materials.

Figure 5.28. Mies, renovated interior of the Stefanie Hess Apartment, Berlin, 1930.

In the 1920s, Mies also renovated the interior of his own Berlin apartment, which was located in central Berlin, in a circa 1860s apartment building. His daughter Georgia began her description of the apartment with the observation, "Mies lived luxuriously."[49] Her vivid account of the apartment notes the rich contrast of materials that are found in his other commissions of the period, including white linoleum floors and dark blue, heavy Shantung silk drapes, which were hung across the entire row of windows in the manner of a theater curtain.[50] The living room, where guests and clients were received, and the Ring collective of architects met, was furnished with Barcelona chairs, a rosewood veneer dining table, four chairs with white leather parchment seats, and a sideboard.[51] The apartment was similarly described by other period chroniclers as luxurious. For example, the American architect and critic George Nelson, in a 1935 article introducing Mies to an American audience, summarized Mies's domestic circumstances: "The luxuriously simple apartment in Berlin is in no sense a garret, and for this ample, well-fed German the meager life holds no attractions."[52] After visiting him in 1933, James Johnson Sweeney described Mies's materials as well as the relationship between the corporeal Mies and his furniture designs, noting that the Barcelona chair "just comfortably accommodated his breadth. … The glass and chromium steel table near which he was seated, which we had always thought strangely high in proportion to its width, now looked perfectly in scale with its designer. Even on the first visit, I realized Mies's love of space, scale and quality of material."[53]

Mies's 1930 addition to the Henke House in Essen provides another good example of luxury at a smaller scale (fig. 5.29). The spaces resulted from an extended dialogue between Mies and his clients concerning the materials and interior fittings. Director of the Rhine-Westphalia Electrical Works in Essen, Ernst Henke, like many of Mies's clients, was on the forefront of the new industrial economy. Primarily meant to house his expanding art collection, a two-story L-shaped wing by Mies was added

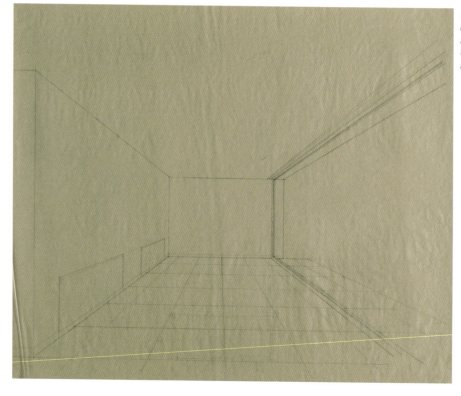

Figure 5.29. *Left*: Mies, drawing for Henke House addition, 1930. *Opposite*: Henke House addition, Essen, 1930.

to an existing dwelling as a gallery and sunroom.[54] The interior was representative of the open, visual simplicity of modern architecture, and outfitted with many custom-designed furnishings in refined materials. For example, Mies and Reich's furniture for this space included a cupboard in rosewood with elegant mouse-gray glass shelves, and an additional cupboard, also in rosewood, which was purpose-built for a radio. Glass-topped, chromed tubular steel was used for a series of low tables intended for flowers.[55] Roman travertine was specified for the floors and baseboards. In the art gallery, drapes in a light tulle were hung for daytime use, paired with dark blue raw silk—a color, Mies noted, that underscored the hues in the Henkes' paintings.[56] Hung in front of the hard materials of the metal and glass window wall on a polished metal curtain rail, the effect of these two drapes would have been to envelop and soften the interior, especially at night when both curtains would have been drawn. The result was an interior that contrasted elegant natural materials with highly reflective, new materials.

Technological prowess and its sheen also prevailed. Mies celebrated the new possibilities of large glass windows in a domestic setting, opening the interior space directly onto the garden. Because an entire wall was given over to the single window, when it was lowered, a dramatic impression of the room's opening up to the outside would have been made—perhaps even more dramatic than in the larger living space of the Tugendhat House, in which only every other window descended. The Henke window, like Mies's others of this period, was especially rarified because of the added technical luxury of an electric mechanical system that allowed the window to be lowered into the house's basement. This should be viewed in contrast to the more basic, less elegant mechanism designed by Walter Gropius to simultaneously open small sets of windows along the walls at the Bauhaus, which was operated by a hand-cranked wheel (fig. 5.30). Each Mies-designed window of this type had to be custom-made to his measurements, carefully fitted, and connected to motors.

Although it might have eventually reduced costs, Mies never standardized his electrical windows, usually subcontracting the work to a local firm. For the Henke window, as at the Lange House and elsewhere, Mies even gave his attention to the design of a switchplate that had three buttons and sans serif lettering denoting the window's functions: "up," "down," "stop." For Henke's immense, sinkable window—it was 7 by 3 meters (22.9 ft. x 9.8 ft.)—two framing options were proposed: a less expensive iron with bronze guide rails (RM 4,800) or bronze with bronze (RM 5,930), which Mies suggested having either burnished, the result of which would be a more sedate, darker frame, or sanded and polished, which would have produced a gleaming appearance.[57] In addition to the selection of elegant stone, glass, wood, and fabric for this commission, Mies also showcased a rich assortment of highly polished metals: bronze, brass, and chrome. Seemingly no detail was overlooked—for mounting the windows, bronze screws were ordered. Mies also designed a grille for the window, 9 meters by 3 meters (29.5 ft. x 9.8 ft.), which could be raised to safeguard the art collection when the Henkes were not in residence.[58] Mies also ordered 18.9 running meters (62 ft.) of metal from the Berliner Metallgewerbe so that Henke could have coordinating metal picture frames made.[59] The curtain rails were in chromed brass. For the doors to the new addition, bronze bands were specified, and Mies custom-designed white-bronze door handles with brass locks.[60] Overall, this combination of refined technology and the use of elegant materials illustrates the means by which Mies imbued even his more modest commissions with a materialized luxury.

A final example of a smaller scale commission evincing the rich materials of Mies's work in this period is his renovation of Philip Johnson's New York apartment, which he did from his Berlin office (fig. 5.31). Mies obtained the project in 1930, when the twenty-four-year-old Johnson was in Germany conducting research for the book *The International Style*, which he was writing with Henry-Russell Hitchcock.[61] Johnson recalled that he met Mies during this particular trip to Germany, where he toured Mies-designed buildings as well as visited some of the apartments that Mies had renovated in Berlin.[62] In a 1930 letter to J.J.P. Oud, Johnson writes, "After seeing some of the rooms that he had decorated here in Berlin, I got the idea of getting him to do my rooms in New York for me. I went

Figure 5.30. Walter Gropius, windows of the Bauhaus Building. Photograph by Erich Consemüller.

to call on him with my best friend, a German, Jan Ruhtenberg."[63] Johnson signed a contract in September, and, using floor plans of the New York apartment, Mies was able to complete the commission quickly, resulting in about twenty-nine items being shipped to New York on December 16, 1930. A final list of the furnishings, organized by room, suggests the intended destination for each article of furniture, and Mies also provided detailed floor plans delineating the arrangements.[64] Archival documents indicate their material richness: a rosewood chest of drawers, a leather-topped writing desk, a rosewood couch frame with steel legs and a leather cushion, caned chairs, leather chairs with chrome-plated metal frames, as well as a Chinese silk counterpane, and 65 meters of raw Honan silk intended for floor-to-ceiling drapes.[65] Two chromed Barcelona chairs and a daybed were upholstered in a light, white-yellow pigskin, (see fig. 5.31, bottom), and in the dining room, the four armchairs were in calfskin.[66] From his Berlin purveyor, Mies ordered and shipped 80 meters of rush floor matting.[67] Two chromed Mies-designed door handles

Figure 5.31. *Top*: Philip Johnson Apartment, New York City, 1930. Interior furnishings by Mies and Reich. *Bottom*: Two chairs, daybed, and table.

were reworked to fit American size standards.[68] Mies ordered the furnishings through the same firms that customarily supplied his German commissions; the metalwork was executed by the Berliner Metallgewerbe, the woodwork by the firm Richard Fahnkow, and the upholstery by the firm Günther & Co.[69] The total cost, including Mies's honorarium of RM 2,000 was RM 10,240, in which the most expensive items were the bookshelf at RM 1,020, the couch at RM 750, and the Barcelona chairs, which cost RM 535 each.[70]

Johnson later reminisced about Mies's careful design of his apartment: "In 1930 he had only my apartment to do. He did it as if it were six skyscrapers—the amount of work he put into that apartment was incredible."[71] Johnson's hyperbole aside, the architectural consideration of this apartment does indicate the consistent level of care that Mies gave all of his commissions. In the same period, Mies refused to respond to entreaties for work in several other cases, causing the potential clients to withdraw in anger.[72] But when he did take on a commission, perhaps in this case during a period of exceptional financial duress, he lavished it with the exacting attention that marked all of his design. In 1935, in reference to the Johnson Apartment, George Nelson neatly summed up Mies's work with regard to luxury: "Mies's fondness for simplicity and solid luxury is well exemplified here. The heavy leather of the chairs and their sturdy frames, the use of quantities of material to produce an effect of richness are all typical of Mies's decorative treatment which distinguishes him from his imitators."[73]

Far from the ideal of the mass reproducible, standardized interior, almost all of the elements of Mies's interiors were uniquely conceived as single, or small-batch, entities and intended for specific commissions. The overarching characteristic of Mies's work in this period, even as the economic situation in Germany worsened in the early 1930s, was one of highly refined luxury and a rich material presence. Even the technology utilized was elegant and, notably, custom-designed for each commission. Windows especially, as designed by Mies, demonstrated both technological luxury and brandished a glimmering, almost ephemeral materiality. In this view, custom, sinkable windows were as luxurious as pigskin Barcelona chairs—or more

Figure 5.32. *Left and opposite*: German Werkbund, cover and inside page from the brochure for *The Dwelling* (*Die Wohnung*) exhibition and Weissenhof Housing Settlement, Stuttgart, 1927.

so. Coordinated to work in concert with the rich materials of the interior space as a whole—and also as gleaming, independent, material objects—Mies's windows, walls, and chairs were designed to demonstrate the refined, rarified possibilities of modern architecture.

MATERIALITY ON DISPLAY: THE EXHIBITION HOUSES

Modern architects strove not only to win an aesthetic battle with the public; they needed to fight the real (and perceived) notion that modernism stood for costly luxury furniture, objects, and architecture. Exhibitions were effective and popular opportunities for educating the public about modern design. Modern products were put on display for close-up viewing, and attendees could walk through full-scale show houses. Groups such as the Werkbund used exhibitions to promote modern goods and modes of living, especially gaining ground as the price of some modern furniture and technical products eventually began to drop in the later 1920s. Still, the brochure produced by the Werkbund for its 1927 *The Dwelling* exhibition in Stuttgart had to explicitly deny the presence of luxury in the modern goods on display (fig. 5.32). Addressing the modern domestic objects, the advertising leaflet categorically proclaimed: "Not a trade show! Rigorously chosen for viewing! Selected for worth, *however, not luxury*! Simple, functional forms, dignified materials, clean finishing, and value have determined the selection. *Cost-reducing* serial production."[74] Despite this frank assertion of the exhibition's aspirations for the products it showcased, reviewers such as the critic Paul Westheim noted the costliness and luxuriousness of the objects on display: "In principle there remains nothing to be said against it when a rich man, who can afford it, acquires luxury for himself. He is also not to be rebutted, when he states, precisely this taste, which for us is not taste, heightens his pleasure and enjoyment of the dwelling. From the side of the cultural, the moral, the political-economic and the artistic, one can argue against it; but eventually one must leave each to the right of his quirky taste, when he will and can afford it."[75] Even though the Werkbund's objective for the exhibition was to highlight

new housing solutions for the masses, as well as new ideas for modern interiors, from the perspective of critics and the public alike, the project fell short in many ways, especially in terms of affordability. And the allure of luxury associated with modern goods remained.

Mies was able to showcase many of his ideas about materiality and dwelling more exactingly in full-scale exhibition architecture. He was, in a sense, his own client. Exhibition houses were demonstrative yet did not have the constriction of client taste or domestic habits, and thus left the architect and his design partner Lilly Reich more freedom to present their ideas about modern living.[76] Though the Barcelona Pavilion might be viewed as the signature example of luxury in Mies's architecture in terms of materials and furnishings—and non-use, as a structure of pure representational value with no pretensions of utility—these materialist qualities came to the fore in other exhibitions, too.

The *German Building Exhibition* of 1931, whose theme was "The Dwelling in Our Time" (*Die Wohnung unserer Zeit*), can be seen as the culmination of Mies and Reich's ideas about dwelling as they connected to materiality.[77] For the exhibition, Reich was appointed artistic director and participating architect. Before walking through the full-scale architectural contributions, visitors were led through a large mezzanine exhibition space given over to the "Material Show" (*Materialienschau*) organized and designed by Reich. It featured displays of interior and building materials such as furnishing textiles, varieties of glass, floor coverings, and wood specimens, which were hung or laid out on stands, display panels, tables, and vitrines

Figure 5.33. Lilly Reich, exhibit of wood in the Material Show section, *German Building Exhibition*, Berlin, 1931.

in a sophisticated, elegant manner that showcased each product's materiality.[78] For example, in the wood section of the exhibit, massive logs and stacked, plain-sawn planks were laid directly on the floor, demonstrating their mass and a rough-hewn materiality (fig. 5.33). In contrast, Reich affixed long, thin pieces of veneer directly to the wall, accentuating their flat surface materiality. By presaging the architectural contributions with this show of materials, Mies and Reich foregrounded the importance of materiality for modern architecture—as space generating, form giving, and as eye-catching visual surface.

Mies presided over the housing section of the *German Building Exhibition*, coordinating the display of full-scale show houses. The exhibition showcased the work of many modern architects, including Hugo Häring, the Luckhardt brothers, Marcel Breuer, Walter Gropius, Ludwig Hilberseimer, and Lilly Reich. Reich's Ground Floor House featured a luxurious and highly impractical bedroom furnished with a sumptuous white carpet, a light-colored upholstered chair, a tubular steel bed, and a glass-topped, tubular steel bedside table (fig. 5.34). Mies's own contributions to the exhibition also seem woefully inadequate to the general needs of the period, given the acute housing shortages at that time in Berlin, but they do allow subtle insight into his refinements for domestic spaces. His House for a Childless Couple (also known simply as the Exhibition House) and the Apartment for a Bachelor, were both widely regarded as luxurious (fig. 5.35). Together, they represented his last chance to build in a way that expressed his ideas, unfettered by the economic and political systems crumbling around him.

Figure 5.34. Reich, Ground Floor House, woman's bedroom, The Dwelling in Our Time section, *German Building Exhibition*, Berlin, 1931.

The House for a Childless Couple was a large-scale, one-story dwelling of 3,400 square feet (with a total footprint of 8,000 square feet, including its outside space).[79] It featured an open plan with a living-dining area that had three glass window walls, of which one window could be lowered into the ground, as at the Tugendhat House.[80] The flowing, open plan was bisected by a large, veneered partition wall. The internal space could be further closed off by heavy curtains, while diaphanous semitransparent drapes were placed in front of external windows. It was the rich material objects—the dark wooden wall partition, reflective chrome columns, and furnishings (including Brno, Barcelona and MR cantilever chairs)—that delineated and organized the space into a dining area, a living room, and two bedrooms. The bedrooms opened to the elegant exterior courtyard, which had a reflecting pool and a sculpture by Georg Kolbe.

Mies's Apartment for a Bachelor was a more modest studio unit. Yet a rich materiality prevailed in its furnishings too: in the carefully considered built-in wardrobe, room-dividing bookshelf, square dining table with four dark blue, caned cantilever chairs, small round table placed between two MR roll-cushioned lounge chairs, and, in the bedroom area, a single bed, night table, desk, and chair. As in the Henke House addition, dark blue silk and white tulle drapes were installed in front of the exterior windows, and interior curtains divided the bedroom from the bathroom. Although small in scale, the furnishings bespoke a pared-down elegance, an appropriate dwelling for an elite bachelor.

Elsewhere in Berlin a counter-exhibition, the *Proletarian Building Exhibition* (*proletarische Bauausstellung*) was mounted during the same period as the official

Figure 5.35. *Below*: Mies, House for a Childless Couple, *German Building Exhibition*, Berlin, 1931.
Opposite: Mies, Apartment for a Bachelor, *German Building Exhibition*, Berlin, 1931.

German Building Exhibition. This exhibition unsubtly—or "crassly," in the eyes of one Werkbund reviewer—displayed apartments of the poverty-stricken next to luxury apartments.[81] Yet, transparent as the aims of this mode of exhibition may have been, it is against this backdrop that Mies and Reich's exhibition must be read. In their architectural exhibits, as well as in those of several other participating architects, the modern amenities, materials, and the overall opulent lifestyle put on display were in stark contrast to the domestic reality of the majority of Berlin's dwellers. This was foregrounded in both the laudatory and declamatory reviews of Mies's spaces.

Philip Johnson appraised Mies's contributions in detail, in two separate reviews of the 1931 exhibition. In the first, he described the elegant results: "The interior of this house shows the simple device Mies uses to achieve his effects—the contrast of chrome steel posts against the plain white plaster or richly grained woods, blue silk hangings and the leather upholstered chrome chairs on a dark brown carpet. There are no patterns anywhere, nor any molding on the wooden panels. There are no windows, only glass walls. The materials themselves and the contrasts give elegance and beauty."[82] This description is in contradistinction to his account of Gropius's contribution, demonstrating Mies's distance from other modern architects of this period. As Johnson noted, "The development of Gropius through constructivism and Bauhaus *Sachlichkeit* is evident in his preference for painted wood and artificial materials like oilcloth, linoleum, rubber, and Trolit (the brand name of a cellulose nitrate plastic)."[83] Albeit in plainer materials, it should be noted that Gropius's display was still elite—the artificial materials were not inexpensive in the period, and his contribution consisted of elegantly furnished common rooms—including a swimming pool ringed with chaise longues, a well-equipped gymnastics area, a library,

and a coffee and dance terrace—intended for a high-rise apartment building.[84] In a second article, Johnson reported that "Mies has long since passed the stage where the house is regarded by the architect as the cheapest, best-planned expression of the needs of the family. The Mies home is admittedly luxurious. For this reason Mies is disliked by many architects and critics, especially the Communists. On the other hand, the public still apparently wants beauty in its everyday surroundings. … Ornament is absent in the Mies house, nor is any needed. The richness of the beautiful woods, the sheets of plate glass and the gleaming chrome steel posts suffice. The essential beauty of the house lies in handling the walls as planes and not as supporting elements."[85] Thus, Johnson adeptly summarized Mies's work in this period: the use of luxurious materials, contrasting textures, and various registers of luminosity, which resulted in an expansive materiality and transformed the experience of the space.

Johnson also addressed the controversy over Mies's exhibition house, noting the German critics' objections to it, and reiterating the luxurious nature of Mies's contribution: "partly because of lack of money, partly on political grounds, there has grown up a faction of young architects who believe that architecture, to be of value, must be directed to a social end. Mies's house does not fulfill such a proposition. It is admittedly luxurious."[86] Johnson is responding to critics such as Karel Teige, who, in *The Minimum Dwelling*, condemned Mies's architecture in terms of its lack of social function and its inability to meet what Teige considered to be the standards of dwelling. Teige writes of the 1931 exhibition, "The architecturally most interesting objects in the hall were also the most reactionary in their social content. For example, the house designed by Mies van der Rohe is not even a genuine villa but a more or less irrational adaption of the German Barcelona Pavilion transformed into a dwelling: all he did in this adaption of this pavilion … is to add a toilet and a bathroom—and presto, the villa of the future has arrived. The whole concept is supremely impractical and governed by formal sculptural intentions, which, in turn, are based on purely abstract notions of space composition—*Raumkunst*—executed with luxury materials. … This is theater and sculpture, not architecture—snobbish ostentation, but not a dwelling."[87]

Other critics focused on the fact that in his expansive and expensive House for a Childless Couple, Mies failed to take on the issue of minimal housing needs—his design neither addressed the *Kleinwohnung* (smallest apartment unit, generally intended for workers) nor the wider question of *Existenzminimum* (subsistence-level living; literally "the minimum required for living") that other architects of the period sought to fulfill. Although only a small-scaled unit, Mies's Apartment for a Bachelor could not satisfy the critics, because of its luxury. Werkbund member Wilhelm Lotz pointed out that both Mies and Reich would have "nothing more to do" with the problem of designing small apartments for workers and reported a general puzzlement on the part of the exhibition's public that such a "modern luxury building" would be displayed in close proximity to a nearby proletarian floor plan.[88]

The sumptuousness of Mies and Reich's contributions, especially the design of a house for a childless couple that featured individual bedrooms for the husband and the wife, and impractical furnishings such as thick white rugs and white chairs, were especially jarring to viewers because Berlin was undergoing a housing crisis at that time. The proceedings from a conference on "Dwelling and Building," held in conjunction with the *German Building Exhibition*, starkly illuminated the dire situation in Berlin: "There is a steady increase in the number of those waiting for and entitled to dwelling accommodation in Berlin. The last available statistics (1929) show the number of new residents entitled to dwelling accommodation as exceeding 35,000, and it is anticipated that the figure for 1930 will be even higher. At the same time these statistics do not by any means suffice to illustrate the severity of the housing shortage in Berlin. At the present time there are approximately 360,000 dwellings in Berlin that consist solely of one room and a kitchen and consequently cannot be classed as suitable dwellings for families. More than 11,000 families are still accommodated in barracks and emergency dwellings. More than 7,000 families are housed in old buildings that are waiting to be pulled down, and over 36,000 families are living in houses that will have to be pulled down under any circumstances within the next ten years."[89] Against the backdrop of severe housing shortages and dire living conditions, and as Germany began to experience more severe financial crises, exacerbating the problem, Mies's architectural visions appeared more and more jarringly luxurious and elite.

FURNITURE'S MATERIAL PRESENCE

Most modern architects who designed furniture and architects who were well known for their furniture designs, such as Marcel Breuer, did so either early in their careers prior to obtaining important built commissions or as ancillary—although directly related to—their architectural work. Furniture designed for specific built projects often appeared far along in the process, usually after the most arduous portion—the design of the building itself—was completed. However, for Mies, working closely with Reich, furnishings were a primary task, a part of the overall design process. Significantly, as Philip Johnson pointed out in reference to the Tugendhat House, "The relation of one piece of furniture to another, of one group to another, and of the groups to the walls and partitions is so carefully calculated as to seem inevitable. No other important contemporary architect cares so much about placing furniture. Mies gives as much thought to placing chairs in a room as other architects do to placing buildings around a square."[90] As Howard Dearstyne, who studied with Mies at the Bauhaus and later taught with him at IIT (the Illinois Institute of Technology in Chicago), has noted, Mies placed his furniture carefully in relation to his interior layout, using it to direct the flow of domestic traffic and—with the freestanding chairs, couches, and tables—to accentuate its spatial character.[91] Although a few key pieces of furniture, such as the Barcelona chair, would be specified for multiple commissions throughout his postwar career, in this period Mies's furniture was overwhelmingly designed for specific commissions, planned and placed in dialogue with the open space of the room.[92]

The furnishings themselves and the attention to their arrangement in his spaces, their structural aesthetics, and the materials, colors, and textures all played a crucial role in the *Gesamtkunstwerk* that Mies and Reich's interiors represented. (To note again, the furniture and furnishings, especially the textiles and rugs, when not Reich's design outright, were very much indebted to her input and their collaborative design process.) Preliminary drawings illustrate Mies's thinking as he conceived of views and sections, which included the placement of furniture, especially shelves, along with the designations of walls and windows. That Mies made this a single process—instead of first designing the interior spaces and then populating them with furniture—underscores the significance he placed on his interiors and, within that paradigm, shows the furnishings to be an integral part of the design process and eventual architectural outcome. Bookshelves and smaller glass cupboards were often built into the walls—not simply attached to the masonry as fixed elements of the room's structure, as was common for built-in furniture from the 1910s onward. Mies's built-in components necessitated careful planning and structural calculations, rendering them effectively immobile and thus a stable element of the house's materiality. These shelves and cupboards were set deeply into the walls, most notably in the Esters and Lange halls (a bookshelf, inserted into and thus flush with the wall) and dining rooms (a walnut veneer and glass cupboard inserted into the wall to hold wine and liqueur glasses and a buffet set two-thirds into the niche) and in Marie Lange's parlor (a glass display case, set one-third into the wall) (see figs. 5.15, 5.16, 5.19). Even smaller apartment commissions featured dramatically set-in cupboards.

Against the widespread aspiration for mass production professed by modern architecture's protagonists in this period, Mies's level of specificity in his interiors underscores his interest in the unique over the universal interior solution—the single design without mass dissemination. From about 1927 to 1935, the period in which he was actively designing furniture, Mies did not call for the mass production of furniture. Instead, he was careful to quietly patent his designs whenever possible and worked out independent arrangements with the small workshops that made his furniture to order. It does not appear that he sought out large manufacturers before 1931. Unlike Gropius's 1923 call for the Bauhaus to work with industry, Mies's furniture utilizes the sheen (or *Glanz,* the Weimar-period term) of machine production, suggesting that it was a product of modern industry, when in fact it was carefully handcrafted and mainly intended for specific commissions.

Mies had a working relationship with a small metal shop, the Berliner Metallgewerbe run by Josef Müller, through whom he would order his furniture for individual clients—it was probably not created in advance and stocked although the Berliner Metallgewerbe eventually produced a small flyer of available furniture designs. The tubular steel furniture relied on metal rods, made by a process introduced by the Mannesmann works in 1886, which were not only extremely light but also highly resilient and could be bent by hand, making the production of furniture possible even in blacksmiths' shops.[93] By the late 1920s, this process was no longer new, but the use of metal tubes for furniture still appeared innovative. As Mies acquired large-scale commissions outside Berlin, he generally continued to rely on Berliner Metallgewerbe to supply the cantilevered chairs and other furniture. He would commission the large metal window frames and other metal components from local metalworkers; likewise, items such as built-in cabinets and bookshelves would be given to local woodworkers to execute. Although other workshops appeared to have copied Mies's MR line of tubular steel furniture, the Berliner Metallgewerbe boasted the rights to make it.

In 1931, Adolf Bamberg, the technical manager of the Berliner Metallgewerbe, took over, renaming the company Bamberg Metallwerkstätten.[94] The new firm had a Mies-designed showroom that displayed furnishings in small, domestic tableaux in the same manner as department stores and furniture stores of the period. Bamberg Metallwerkstätten produced a catalog sheet with the entire collection of Mies and Reich–designed furniture, each piece depicted in outline, accompanied by a listing of the available colors, metals, materials, and prices (fig. 5.36).[95] The new firm was able to lower prices slightly; for example, the standard Mies chromed cantilever chair in black leather cost 74 marks from Berliner Metallgewerbe in 1927, but at Bamberg Metallwerkstätten it was listed at 68 marks by 1931 (with armrests it cost 117 and 115 marks, respectively).[96] Seating coverings were available in a range of materials, including cowhide and pigskin, as well as the iconic caning and the more pedestrian two-cord yarn fabric, and in plain and checkered linen; tabletops were available in rosewood, plywood, and in clear and black glass.[97] An "MR" or "LR" prefix code identified the designer as Mies or Reich. Period documents suggest that Mies much more often opted for nickel- or chrome-plating when ordering the furniture for his own commissions, rather than the more pedestrian painted metal versions that the workshop could also supply.[98]

This arrangement with the Bamberg Metallwerkstätten was short-lived, evidenced by the important contract with Thonet that Mies signed in November 1931. The first Thonet catalog to include Mies furniture was published in July 1932; the contract included a base annual salary of 2,500 marks and 5 percent royalties on the retail price of sold items (with a guarantee of 7,500 marks over the course of the contract), as well as first refusal by Thonet for new designs by Mies.[99] Thonet produced just three pieces of furniture by Lilly Reich—a bed and two couches—which only appeared in their first catalog and were credited to Mies.[100]

The relationship between Mies's architecture and his furnishings can be seen as a dialectic in which each furniture piece functioned as an independent, unique, and modern object and, simultaneously, as part of the whole. A particularly apt

Figure 5.36. Bamberg Metallwerkstätten, illustrated products and price list of furniture designed by Mies and Reich, Berlin, 1931.

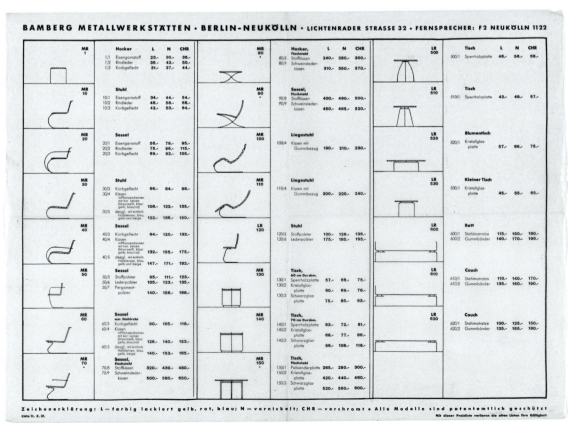

example is the furnishing plan of the Tugendhat House, in which every item was of a striking form, color, and texture. Upholstery was crucial in this context. The commission included a total of twenty-four Brno chairs covered in white vellum, a black pear wood dining table, Tugendhat chairs covered with silver-gray Rodier fabric, Barcelona chairs in emerald green leather, and a chaise longue with a ruby red velvet cushion, and, in Grete Tugendhat's bedroom, a cherry-red leather Brno chair and matching red Barcelona ottoman (fig. 5.37; see also fig. 5.1 left).[101] Thus the materials of these furnishings were as singular as the house's onyx and macassar walls, further connecting the two—furniture and architecture—via rarified, luxurious materiality. Each item of furniture was an object-exemplar in keeping with the luxury of its greater surroundings, each piece representing a nexus of surface, structure, and material.

In the Tugendhat's seemingly spare main space (in part owing to the lack of domestic clutter and small objects), the furniture defined the room. It reads as both discernible, individual elements, even events, in the space, but it also resonates collectively, as visual points of connection are formed between the pieces of furniture, linked materially and spatially across the open plan. The distinctive chairs of the dining area, living area, sitting area near the milk glass wall, and the library were connected in their use and materiality (shiny metal legs and rich surfaces), yet distinguished by the diverse materials, colors, and uses intended by these differing areas. Moreover, the elemental form and chrome of the chaise longue and chairs related to the shiny bases of the other pieces of furniture, the cruciform chromed columns, and also to the tubular safety railings and the rectilinear edging of the window frames. Although each piece made a strong statement on its own, the color, texture, and placement of every item of furniture also worked in tandem with the others to create a distinctive whole. Each piece can been seen as an

Figure 5.37. Mies, Tugendhat House, Grete Tugendhat's bedroom.

independent object, designed for a particular purpose—yet it is the furniture that creates the room designations in the context of the open plan. For instance, two cantilevered chairs and a small table by the front entrance form a reception area upstairs, while six chairs positioned as a conversation-generating area in front of the onyx wall designate this section of the living room as one intended for more elegant and formal entertaining.

The specificity of Mies's furniture placement vis-à-vis the architecture was understood by his clients, who were carefully consulted in each step of the process via correspondence as the commission unfolded, and who later rigorously followed his original furnishing plans. While the official photographs of the Tugendhat House show all of the objects in their intended spaces, more important, the informal family photographs taken by Fritz Tugendhat over a subsequent eight years capture the interiors candidly, in the manner in which they were actually lived.[102] These photographs document that Mies's vision was preserved. In other cases, such as at the Barcelona Pavilion, the civil servants charged with maintaining the pavilion throughout the duration of the fair very conscientiously inquired into the possibility of being sent a diagram that would indicate Mies's exact desired placement of the chairs and stools, which were regularly displaced by visitors over the course of the day. The same letter notes other difficulties at the pavilion, including the fact that visitors regularly walked into the glass walls if the red curtains were opened in the manner Mies desired.[103] These examples demonstrate an understanding of the exacting nature of his interiors by his clients, and the degree to which Mies was able to successfully convey that the integrity of his interior spaces depended on their remaining as he had designed them. The individual pieces of furniture and the architectural whole, held in tension and distributed in space, resulted in a dialectic that was a crucial element of the overall materiality of Mies's work in this period.

SURFACE MATERIALITY: RE-CODING THE LUXURY OF ORNAMENT

To various modes of luxury represented by materials, another key reading can be layered in—the role of surface itself in Mies's work, in relation to the underlying materiality creating the effects of that surface. While flatness in modernism has been much discussed, and the supposed banishment of ornament from modern architecture was celebrated in the period, Mies's surfaces can be understood as ornament, and ornament as yet another example of luxury.[104] Mies's treatment of materials often emphasized surface, rather than solidity, as exemplified by the luminous milky planes of his frosted glass walls, the vibrant stripes of his wood veneers, or the high reflectivity of the metal coating of his columns. Each of these materials was aestheticized through its surface treatment. Moreover, the gleaming surfaces of the columns both attracted attention and diverted it from the gravity of their weight-bearing task; even structural columns are made to appear more surface than object.

In his sketches, Mies noted the direction of the marble grains so that stone slabs could be laid in such a way that they would explicitly contrast with adjacent surfaces, for example, where travertine flooring met flat glass walls, according to Sergius Ruegenberg, who worked for Mies in this period.[105] Veined stone slabs were bookmatched, which accentuated their surface and its repetitive patterning. This also served to emphasize, once again, the stone as a slice of material, rather than a solid block with depth. The stone slabs were not placed directly abutting one another—which would have been feasible given that stone does not contract and expand—but were installed with a small reveal or gap, further highlighting the slabs as slices, rather than as thick solids.

In modern architecture generally, and in Mies's work of this period especially, a reverse coagulation occurred—one in which decorative masses of an earlier architectural era dissipated to thin surface, agglomerated or imitative forms took on a geometrical regularity, and an overall simplification occurred. This was a fusing of surface materials to architectural form, rather than forms emerging from the materials themselves, as traditionally had occurred, for example, in carved marble pediments. In Mies's modernism, what might be termed a "surface materiality" was applied to forms—materials were showcased at the surface, in celebration of surface itself. The richly applied decorative details of the nineteenth century, so beloved by the bourgeoisie and masses, were reappropriated and differently coded in the twentieth century, so that the luxury they represented was repositioned under modernism. This phenomenon is captured well in a period description, which refers to walls "decorated with decoration-free surfaces."[106] Period critics raised a series of problematics surrounding transformations in materiality taking place at this time, including the reduction of ornament. They were concerned about the flattening out of surfaces and the disarticulation of ornament in objectivity (*Sachlichkeit*). For example, the modern architect Hans Poelzig raised the fear that in prohibiting ornament in modernism, the architect would instead begin to play with the limitless possibilities of construction methods, which he termed "an expensive game."[107] He noted that the play of ornament, surface, and decoration was at present "forbidden" but that valuable materials—glass, metal, and stone—had replaced hand-wrought and machine-produced ornaments. The interplay of ornament had been substituted by the interplay of different surfaces, Poelzig pointed out perceptively. Traditional ornament, by this formulation, had been transposed into material and surface, which ultimately performed the same function, and was afforded the same status: ornament as luxury.

In Mies's interior architecture, surface was arguably as important as form. In addition to their functions in dividing and supporting the interior, Mies's cruciform-shaped columns, the appealing curve of the Tugendhat house's dining room wall, and the decision to bisect the main living space with a rectangular onyx wall added much visual interest, in comparison with Mies's more ascetic peers, such as Walter Gropius or Marcel Breuer. But it was the treatment of these forms' surfaces that was their most noticeable feature at the Tugendhat House. Through the application of thin material—chroming, wood veneering, and the high polish given to the onyx stone (which had already been selected for its surface of notable veins and dramatic coloring)—a surface materiality predominated. The visual qualities of those already unique materials were given further surface enhancement—in the intensely reflective chrome-plating, the dramatic zebra-striping of the macassar, and in the polishing of stone. In opposition to the thickness of the preceding generations' applied ornament, in modernism a thin resurfacing took place, in delicate tension with the substratum form. In Mies's work this surface materiality should be read as modern luxury—deployed in various registers of luminosity and reflectivity, and through the use of rare, expressive materials.

FLUID LUXURY: THE MATERIALITY OF TEXTILES

The fluctuating, subjective effects of materiality, as surface and as space-defining medium, receives perhaps its purest expression in Mies and Reich's use of textiles. Via drapes, they created the possibility for interior structure within the open plan. As the Tugendhats' daughter noted, "The spacious main room … could also be further divided into smaller spaces by black and white velvet and Shantung silk curtains. My parents made frequent use of these draperies."[108] The rich materiality of the fabrics was in large part dependent on the expertise of Reich, who had maintained her own clothing atelier since 1914.[109] The pair often double-hung a thin, semitransparent floor-to-ceiling silk curtain directly in front of a window, followed by velvet or opaque dark drapes, resulting in an interior that created an intimate feeling of contained space, *Raumgefühl*, while simultaneously enveloping the dweller, literally and figuratively, in material luxury. The drapes of the Tugendhat House functioned in this manner. They added subtle surface texture and spatial definition to the already surface-filled interior, recalling Poelzig's reevaluation of ornament as the interplay of differing surfaces. At the Tugendhat House, a white velvet curtain was placed between the entrance area and the library beyond, while a black Shantung silk curtain was hung in front of the conservatory; a black velvet curtain was placed beside it; and a silver-gray Shantung silk was hung along the main glass wall (see figs. 5.24, 5.25).[110] By the late 1920s, artificial silks were readily available on the mass market, seemingly democratizing access to "silk." Concurrently—and in contrast—expansive swaths of nubby, raw silk were to be found in the interiors of the Tugendhat house, an expressive and expensive detail. Thus, a luxurious—yet subtle—surface materiality came into play via the sheen of the thin raw silk against the thickness of the velvet curtains' pile. This was noted by Philip Johnson: "At night raw silk curtains cover the glass walls from floor to ceiling, enhancing the luxuriousness of the interior by their color and texture. … The elegance of this room derives not only from its size and the simple beauty of its design, but from the contrast of rich materials and the exquisite perfection of details."[111]

The Tugendhat House's elegant floor coverings likewise played up their material effect via subtly differing surfaces. In the hand-woven, light-colored wool carpet laid on white linoleum in front of the onyx wall in the main living space and in the interplay of white lambskins placed on travertine upstairs, surface texture was of paramount importance. While in some instances the contrast in materials was subtle, often it was vividly distinctive—between hard and soft materials, or vibrant and muted colors. Each material was seemingly a part of the whole, yet was also legible as an independent, distinctive element within the interior. Overall, the Tugendhat House's rugs, curtains, and furniture coverings may have been impractical in many ways: in terms of color (pale grays, whites, and a soft pink), in terms of longevity (given the danger of permanent staining to fair colors), in the use of difficult-to-clean materials, and the fragile quality of materials such as silk. But this only heightened the luxury expressed by the interior fabrics.

The rich structure-giving quality of textiles and interplay of surface materiality was also exploited by Mies and Reich in their design of the Velvet and Silk Café. Installed at the 1927 *Women's Fashion Exhibition* in Berlin, both the structure and the enclosing space were ceded over to enveloping, draped lengths of velvet and silk fabric (fig. 5.38).[112] Akin to the extravagant travertine and marble Mies was using

Figure 5.38. *Top*: Reich and Mies, Velvet and Silk Café, *Women's Fashion Exhibition*, Berlin, 1927.
Bottom: Color rendering by Enrique Colomés and Gonzalo Moure.

in other commissions, here in this temporary installation, the refined fabric harked back to an earlier period, in which velvets and silks signified aristocratic wealth. To form the café, fabric literally became curtain "walls" in draped silk (gold, silver, lemon-yellow, and black) and velvet (black, red, and orange). Similar to the undulating materials that made up the café's walls, visitors did not sit on a solid seat or cushion, but on the spanned material itself that formed the seats and backrests of Mies's cantilevered chairs. The rich materials were carefully detailed in period reviews, which praised the beauty, value, and intimacy evoked by them, while lauding the clarity and straightforward nature of the design.[113] The overall effect was that nothing was fixed—a fluidity constituted and defined the architecture of this space, resulting in a subjective architectural experience constituted by the delicate interplay of material surfaces.

SURFACES IN SPACE: UNFOLDING SUBJECTIVITY AS ORGANIZED BY MATERIAL OBJECTS AT THE BARCELONA PAVILION AND THE TUGENDHAT HOUSE

Perhaps the most manifest instance of the shifting subjectivity of material form and surface in Mies's work is to be found in the materials and planes of the German Pavilion, more commonly known as the Barcelona Pavilion, Germany's contribution to the 1929 International Exposition in Barcelona, Spain (fig. 5.39).[114] As can be experienced in the now reconstructed pavilion (1986), the interconnecting planes of stone and the cruciform supporting columns together create a loose enclosure, yet the resulting space can as easily be read as a profligate display of surfaces. This is especially intensified by the reflections in the varied types of glass (gray, green, white, translucent); the gleaming metal (which reflected the room's contents and cast shimmers of light onto the ceiling); the water of the reflecting pools (which reflected the sky and the surrounding architecture); and by the stone (green marble, onyx, travertine), whose decorative qualities were heightened by Mies's expert selection of specimens that had extravagant natural veining and patterning, subsequent dramatic bookmatching, and polishing (figs. 5.40, 5.41). Architectural critic Justus Bier, in reviewing the Barcelona Pavilion in the journal *Die Form*, observed that his description was "only able to intimate the sumptuous impression of the building, and the care and certitude of the selection of materials, with their conscious escalation in the inside."[115] In fact, these striking materials prompted so many inquiries from the public that the *Ministerialdirektor* beseeched Mies to provide information regarding the source of the marble, travertine, and other substances.[116] Famously over budget by at least 300,000 marks, these expensive, expansive surfaces formed a purely representational space, far from modernism's ideals of mass reproducibility and functionalism.[117]

The high legibility of surface and form in Mies's work of this period closely connects to his use of the open plan, especially at the Barcelona Pavilion, but also at the Tugendhat House. It is his material objects' placement in space that calls attention to the openness, even infiniteness, of the surrounding space (see figs. 5.26, 5.40). Mies highlights open space and then counteracts it by punctuating it with columns and freestanding walls; he also frames it at intervals (usually in shimmering metal-encased glass) and gives it intermittent borders (terminating boundaries of stone or more ephemeral ones in glass). In this context, both form and surface material stand

5.39. *Top*: Mies, German Pavilion, exterior (reconstructed), Barcelona, Spain, 1928–29.
Bottom: View of the interior (reconstructed).

Figure 5.40. Mies, German Pavilion.

Figure 5.41. Mies, German Pavilion.

out. This is best represented in Mies's sketch of the pavilion, in which he has rendered the material forms and surfaces in detail, rather than the enclosing space (fig. 5.42). As Mies himself remembered, "One evening as I was working late on the building I made a sketch of a freestanding wall, and I got a shock. I knew it was a new principle."[118] In his open interiors, the cruciform columns, freestanding slab walls, and metal window frames appear to stand out and even project toward the viewer, as material objects more than architecture (see fig. 5.41). The slab walls, especially, articulate form and surface because they read clearly as detached elements in the open plan. Already intensified through an emphasis on surface and the deployment of unconventional, luxurious materials, the open surrounding space thus heightened the expressive effects of Mies's materiality for the viewer.

Likewise, the highly reflective cruciform columns at the Barcelona Pavilion, the Tugendhat House, and elsewhere, reflect, refract, and also distort both the surrounding interior spaces and subjects moving through them. The interior, as reflected back at the viewer, appears to be in continual motion and flux—a destabilized yet dynamic space always experienced subjectively. There is an indeterminacy to these columns, as objects. Although they punctuate the open space, they challenge being viewed as fixed. More often they reflect the unfolding space around them, nearly dissolving (see figs. 5.1 right, 5.41) Thus, they read less as structure than as status-shifting, alternately materializing and dematerializing objects.

K. Michael Hays describes the specific materiality of the Barcelona Pavilion:

Because there is no conceptual center to organize the parts or transcend our perception of them, the particular quality of each material is registered as a kind of absolute; space itself becomes a function of the specificities of the materials. … The normal system of expectations about materials, however, is quickly shattered as materials begin to contradict their own nature. Supporting columns dissolve in an invasion of light on their surfaces; the highly polished green Tinian

Figure 5.42. Mies, German Pavilion, interior perspective, crayon and pencil on illustration board.

marble reflects the highlights of the chromium glazing bars and seems to become transparent, as does the onyx slab; the green-tinted glass, in turn, becomes an insuperable mirrored screen; the pool in the small court—shielded from the wind and lined in black glass—is a perfect mirror, in which stands Georg Kolbe's "Dawn." The fragmentation and distortion of the space is total. ... The work itself is an event with temporal duration, whose actual existence is continually being produced.[119]

At the Barcelona Pavilion, and in other works by Mies in this period, the viewer was constantly being made aware of—even confronted by—the materiality of the building. Overall, the dynamic and open-ended nature of the free plan served to heighten the subject's awareness of forms, surfaces, and materials. Most important, the vital interplay between viewer and materials—which distort, confuse, change with the light, and with the movements of the viewer—resulted in interiors in which the significance of materiality and the viewer's own privileged subjectivity was revealed.

Taken together, the interior architectural objects, with their distinct materiality, create the means by which to mark the passage of time. To subjects, they introduce an unfolding, durational quality in the interior. At both the Barcelona Pavilion and the Tugendhat House, for example, time can be marked through the charting of the light as it passes dramatically through the main space from dawn to dusk, and into night. Breaking with earlier bourgeois dwellings, the open plan allows for, and encourages, subjects to meander at their own will, rather than follow a prescribed room sequence. At the Tugendhat House especially, it is the material objects that act as the organizing elements within the space; open-ended as they seem, they define and divide the dining room from the living room, the living room from the library (see figs. 5.24, 5.26). It is around these objects—fixed entities in stone, metal, and wood—that subjects had to navigate and organize themselves. And it is against these surfaces and forms that the activities of daily life unfolded, such as dining, familial interaction, play, solitary reading, and evening activities. Each material seemingly participated in—or formed a backdrop to—the subjective actions of the dwellers, as Fritz Tugendhat's photographs attest. Family members are captured refracted in the metal, reflected in the polished stone, or as shadows cast against the wooden partitions. It is against these seemingly set objects—objects that are rare, auratic—that the dweller's subjectivity and the subjective quality of Mies's architecture is made manifest.

The result is a space of varying conditions offering an ever-changing experience, as augmented by the window walls of glass, shimmering columns, white floors, time of day, and external weather and seasonal conditions. In earlier, comparable representational interiors, certain tasks were assigned to specific rooms and utilized at distinct periods of the day: breakfast room, reception room, ladies' sitting room, male study, living room, and dining room. The open plan, by contrast, afforded a heightened awareness, throughout the day, of the changing subjectivity of the space as a whole, as measured against its interior objects, the activities of its inhabitants, and changing external stimuli. The dwellers' subjective interactions with each other, enabled and amplified by the space and its materials, further served to highlight the unfolding and durational aspect of this interior. Through materiality Mies permitted the dwellers or visitors to encounter the spaces in an open-ended, flexible manner, which allowed for a changing, subjective interaction with both the material forms of the interior spaces and with others—comfortably situated amid the luxury that this materiality afforded those subjects.

GLASS'S MATERIALITY

Glass defined and gave material form not only to Mies's major spaces such as the Tugendhat House and the Barcelona Pavilion but to many of his smaller commissions. It served to organize the interior, most cogently in the framed, glazed partition walls that formed his and Reich's Glass Room, a full-scale installation in the main hall of the Werkbund's 1927 Stuttgart exhibition, *The Dwelling* (fig. 5.43). The Glass Room was a project initiated by Mies, who then approached the Association of German Glass Manufacturers for sponsorship. Although known as the Glass Room, in actuality it took the form of a four-room, sparsely furnished dwelling. Its sequence of glazed, open-ended spaces without doors loosely comprised an entryway, dining room with table (but without chairs), living room (containing three white cube club chairs, a red club chair, and a low table), library-study with book-filled shelves, and two enclosed courtyards, one containing a large sculpture, the other with oversized potted plants. Striking glazed walls were composed of white milk, mouse gray, and olive green glass.[120] Because of these colors, the glass panels read as materialized architectural objects, rather than window-like voids. Mies compounded this effect by setting the glass in highly-polished, nickel-plated metal frames, further accentuating the material presence of the glazed panels. Both the metal and the glass exerted a strong materiality, demarcating and shaping the space for visitors.

The experience of the Glass Room was dominated by the continually changing and shifting material presence of glass, as both the light and the visitors themselves were reflected and refracted in and through it. While transparency was a crucial phenomenon in Mies's use of glass elsewhere, here he used the opacity of glass to illustrate its distinctive effects and reflections. Early evidence of his interest in glass's

Figure 5.43. Reich and Mies, Glass Room, *The Dwelling* exhibition, Stuttgart, 1927.

reflective quality is found in a 1922 article published to accompany his Friedrichstrasse skyscraper, in which he wrote about his use of glass, "[I]t is not an effect of light and shadow one wants to achieve but a right interplay of light reflections."[121] In his and Reich's 1927 Glass Room, these characteristics were especially on display—via the fluctuating reflections and registers of transparency afforded by the different types of glass and its varying levels of opacity. Photographs from the period illustrate how in some instances visitors would have been able to see through the glass from one space to another, for example, outward to the first courtyard, where a sculpture on a plinth was clearly visible through the glass, or to the large potted plants in the courtyard off of the living room. In other areas, the glass formed an entirely opaque wall, particularly where dark glass was used, and in these spaces only the contents of the room itself were reflected in the glass. In these rooms, varying degrees of reflection and refraction heightened an awareness of the rooms' sparse contents, the other visitors to the space, and oneself. As Siegfried Kracauer would describe the space and its effects in the *Frankfurter Zeitung*, "A glass box, translucent, the adjacent rooms penetrate it. Every gadget and every movement in them creates a magical play of shadows on the wall, disembodied silhouettes that float through the air and mingle with the mirror images from the glass room itself … intangible, glassy ghosts, changing like a kaleidoscope."[122] Glass here represents Mies's deep engagement with materiality and its shifting surface effects, illustrating the way in which glass could engender a response in the surrounding space, causing a heightened awareness in the visitor toward architectural objects.

Following the 1927 Glass Room, Mies used a myriad of types and hues of glass in other work, replicating many of the same effects. The Barcelona Pavilion, which featured a range of differing types of glass, is a notable example (see fig. 5.40). A critic reviewing the pavilion in 1929 observed, "Some of these glass planes are of somber and neutral tint, reflecting people and other objects, and what you see through the glass mingles with what you see reflected on it."[123] In addition to the varying colors and transparencies of glass, in Barcelona Mies introduced a new element: at one end of the pavilion he installed two wide, floor-to-ceiling, white frosted glass panels, fitting lighting units between the panes so that the whole installation could be illuminated. Like the other glass panes, this opaque matte surface reflected the room's contents in varying registers by day, but when lit at night it became non-reflective, transforming into a luminous, but solid, white wall. The thick slabs of glass on Mies's tables, pushed directly against the walls, acted as mirrors, further reflecting the surfaces of the room.

As with the experience of the Glass Room and the Barcelona Pavilion, at the Tugendhat House glass complicated the interiors, especially via the large glass windows of the main living room and the interior and exterior glass window walls forming three sides of the conservatory. At the bottom of the stairs of the main space of the Tugendhat House, adjacent to the dining area, Mies installed a similar illuminable frosted glass wall, placing a table and four chairs in front of it (see fig. 5.26). Additionally, many of the Tugendhat House's doors were glazed in frosted glass, producing effects of milky reflectivity.[124] Small interior objects further broke up the light and mirrored images outward, such as the glass-topped coffee table in front of the onyx wall, the prominent glass flower vase on the piano, and the glass lamp on Fritz Tugendhat's desk, which was filled with water (see fig. 5.24).[125]

This use of glass was far from the dramatic, speculative quality of Mies's glass skyscraper proposals or the more straightforward urban shopping experience offered by large plate glass store windows. In the late 1920s, for the dweller or exhibition viewer, Mies complicated and enriched the already complex materiality of his architecture by using glass in an optically sophisticated manner. While a dematerialization of the demarcation between inside and outside resulted from the use of large, transparent glass windows, Mies simultaneously used the reflectivity of semitransparent and opaque glass to intensify the sense of his interiors' objects and materials. Dependent on the differing colors of the glass and its varying registers of transparency, translucency, and opaqueness, the effects of the types of glass offered a modulation in experience. The human subject was not only organized by the material of these resulting spaces, but intersected and interacted with them in a changing and variable way, further heightening his or her modern subjectivity.

REINSCRIBING ARCHITECTURE'S MEANING:
CONNECTING FORMS AND MATERIALS TO LIFE

While the use of unusual and lavish materials came to define Mies's interiors in this period, the luxury of this endeavor should be read not only via the symbolic and real worth of his materials, but as a key element of the experience itself that Mies's work advanced. Laying himself bare in a diary entry from 1928, Mies reveals both a lament and a radically new way of thinking when he writes, "We want to give meaning again to things. Who still feels anything of a wall, an opening? ... We want to give sense again to things. ... Steps, spaces. One has lost the meaning of this language [of space], one feels nothing anymore."[126] Most important, Mies sought to reinscribe meaning into his architectural objects; materials were to play a key role in this effort and the impact he sought. In this period, he had begun to search for a way to connect the form-giving process of his architecture to subjects in an authentic and profound manner. The loss of connection between the subject and object was a pressing concern for Mies by the late 1920s—as evidenced by a series of passages that he had underlined in *Von heiligen Zeichen* (*Sacred Signs*, 1922), a book by the Catholic philosopher-theologian Romano Guardini, whose writings were particularly important for Mies in this period.[127]

It is essential to underscore two elements about Mies's remarkable diary passage. First, he believed that architecture only has meaning if its forms and spaces connect to us, that is, if humans are able to feel something for their surroundings. This runs counter to the period's dominant trend in which architects strove to rationalize and mass-produce housing in order to achieve the greatest number of units for the lowest cost, the results of which were often viewed as aesthetically cold and distanced from individuals' lives. Ludwig Hilberseimer's 1924 skyscraper projects for Berlin are emblematic of this approach (fig. 5.44). One way that Mies began to reforge connections between people and architecture was through his use of rich, unexpected materials (at least for modernism), in order to engender a subjective response. Through their unique materiality—onyx, travertine, highly polished metal—Mies's architectural objects invited users to be drawn to and feel something again for a wall, for steps, or a column (fig. 5.45; see also figs. 5.23, 5.41, 5.42). Mies used luxury materials to reinscribe meaning into modern architecture via the senses, both haptically (in the smoothly polished stone, the craggy pocks of the travertine, and the uneven, artisanal bricks) and optically (in the rich veining of the stone, in the dazzling shimmer of the columns, the exaggerated grains of zebrawood). Second, for Mies, it was architecture's fundamental components that were to act as the points of connection between people and their surroundings, not a change in conditions of architecture per se. He sought to evoke feeling for—and thus give meaning again to—the basic constitutive parts of which architecture is formed: walls, openings, steps, spaces. His rich materials were central in that aim, drawing in and conveying sense—"sense" understood as "sensation" and also "meaning"—to the encountering subject. Sensuous, rarified materials especially served this goal. To this end, the luxury used in Mies's interiors of this period did not merely represent an ostentatious display of social status, as was often charged against Mies and his clients. Rather, his interiors presented the opportunity to, in his words, "give sense again to things" by heightening awareness, offering the prospect of tactile sensation, and raising cognizance of the subjective conditions of space—as a mode by which to reestablish meaning in architecture for its subjects.

Throughout 1927 and into 1928, Mies's attitude toward what was most imperative for architecture shifted greatly. He began to seek out a manifest interconnectivity between life and architecture. Up until about 1927, his work had been either highly speculative, as exemplified by the brick and concrete houses, the Friedrichstrasse skyscrapers, and other unbuilt projects, or celebratory of rationalization and technocratic construction, as seen in his apartment buildings at the Weissenhof Housing Settlement in Stuttgart and the block of apartments on Afrikanische Strasse in Berlin. In precisely the same period as he was designing the Tugendhat House and the Barcelona Pavilion, his most canonical works in terms of material virtuosity, he was conceiving and writing (in his terse, laconic manner) about his pursuit of reestablishing meaning in architecture, especially connecting architectural form with life. This can be first glimpsed in the foreword that he wrote for the 1927 Werkbund exhibition catalogue, *The Dwelling*: "The problem of rationalization

Figure 5.44. Ludwig Hilberseimer, High-Rise City (*Hochhausstadt*) project, Berlin, 1924.

and typification is only part of the problem. … The struggle for new housing is only an element of the larger struggle for new forms of living."[128] In 1928, in a statement about what he wanted to convey in his exhibitions, he posited (again laconically) that "the central problem of our time—the intensification of life" needed to be showcased, in order to "bring about a revolution of our thinking."[129] In the same year, in an article titled "We Stand at the Turning Point of Time: Building Art as the Expression of Spiritual Decisions," he stated, "Building art is not the object of clever speculation, it is in reality only understandable as a *life process*, it is an expression of man's ability to assert himself and master his surroundings."[130] This thinking about the direct connections between architecture and life appeared in other published writings, where he stressed an interrelated need for intensity and authenticity in internal life in order to arrive at intensity and authenticity in form. Mies writes, "Form as a goal results always in formalism. For this effort does not aim toward something internal but toward an external. But only a vital inside has a vital outside. Only life intensity has form intensity. … Authentic form presupposes authentic life. … We value not the result but the starting point of the form-giving process. … This is why the form-giving process appears to me so important. Life is what matters. In its entire fullness, in its spiritual and concrete interconnection."[131] In his diary of 1928, in his telegraphic style, Mies would write a condensed version: "New demands: Connections with real life. New man. Form relationship to surroundings. Not rejection but mastery."[132] Mies's shift in outlook was also noted by his peers. Hans Richter, the filmmaker and Mies's fellow editor at the journal *G*, wrote that the "old architect has nothing to give his time anymore" and contrasted this outdated figure to Mies, whom he called a new type of "building master," more concerned with "creating actual relationships than mere symbols standing for them. … The new building master has to reckon with a new sensuousness."[133] Mies's interior spaces were sensuous; he drew people in with his resplendent materials—from silk, velvet, and leather to zebrawood, chromium, and travertine. Materials, to be directly encountered by the subject, were key to

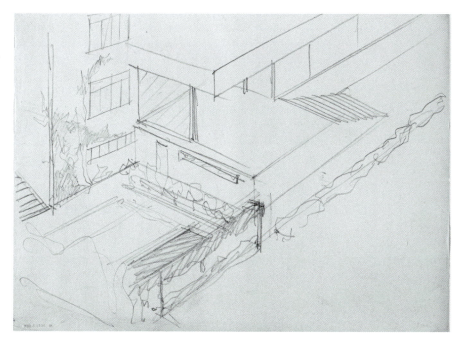

Figure 5.45. Mies, Tugendhat House, partial aerial perspective from southwest, pencil on paper.

Mies's stated desire to engender intense and authentic relationships between lives and surroundings.

Highly aware of their representative potential, Mies viewed architectural objects and interiors as bestowed with differential value and dignity. As he would write, "Things have their own life and a dignity arising out of their intrinsic nature. The things are not the same, but different not only according to their intrinsic nature, but also according to the type and rank of their dignity."[134] He continued, now linking the experiencing subject to the object, while also reiterating his earlier points: "There is a hierarchy of things, and they are not readily accessible but only if, in stepping in front of them, one is as they demand and assumes a position that relates to them. To the hierarchy of objects corresponds a hierarchy of levels of perception on which the perceiver stands and on which he must stand if he wants to relate to the object. There is an awareness attitude assigned to each object. … Things also are subject to a hierarchy. So it is that each object has a corresponding awareness attitude that stands with it on the same level of rank. Much as there is a hierarchy of objects, there is a hierarchy of awareness attitudes."[135] Thus, to Mies, objects resonated, aided by their "intrinsic nature," of which materiality was an important component. It was equally important to him that the perceiving subject experiencing the object could read and make a hierarchical differentiation between things. Opulent materials were especially self-evident in this hierarchy—onyx, travertine, and marble were highly legible in their luxurious, rarified materiality, which in turn aided the reading of architectural form. In this context, steps in travertine and walls in onyx made the viewer aware of an object's intrinsic nature; this materiality was the conduit by which the subject could once again, in modernism, connect to and have a meaningful relationship with the objects of architecture.

The Barcelona Pavilion is a useful example of this in praxis. The extraordinary display of luxurious materials included travertine, onyx, and two types of polished green marble; three colors of plate glass framed in metal; shimmering cruciform columns; a sumptuous, black wool carpet; and red curtains. The "intrinsic nature" of the materials that made up the pavilion—the green marble and white travertine, for example—were highly legible to the perceiving viewer as valuable. Indeed, its rich materials, and their effect on visitors, was amply noted in the period; the materials were seen as articulating and enhancing the pavilion's forms, the functioning of its parts, and its architectural effect as a whole, especially in the interior. Critic Justus Bier argued that the pavilion's materiality aided the understanding of its architectural forms, describing the Barcelona Pavilion's "rare interplay of rooms, which function like a noble vessel, without opulence, via the rigorous austerity of the forms. It is essential that the richness of the materials used does not impair the architectonic clarity; to the contrary, each of the building organism's individual members is bestowed with a clear function." Perhaps most important, Mies's materials seemed to provoke a subtle awareness in the experiencing subject. A "singularly impalpable materiality" was how Bier described the glass walls that constituted the space. He enthused that walking through the sequence of spaces of the Barcelona Pavilion, its spatial parts as well as the constructed whole, made "an extraordinary impression upon the visitors, speaking to their spirit [Geist]."[136] Another period critic similarly noted the effect of the pavilion on the emotions of the visitor, stating that "all the materials and even the geometry" seem to give in to a sentimental tendency. "[I]t might appear surprising to discover something sentimental in a work of a very modern and very technical architecture; but we must recognize that architecture can hardly elude the social influences which give it its root."[137] At the Barcelona Pavilion, Mies was able to again renew the meaning of architecture's constituent parts, to give sense to things, to make space once more expressive.

In the Tugendhat House, too, objects in rarified materials provided points of visual and tactile connection between a given space and its potential inhabitants. The deep pile of the sheepskin rug or the cherry red leather Brno chair in Grete Tugendhat's bedroom allude to a hierarchy of materials and things (see fig. 5.37). The Tugendhat's central, non-load-bearing onyx wall was freed from architectural usefulness and from performing a function; it could serve as a material object onto which to attach meaning. Its role seems to hark back to Mies's diary entry and quest to give "meaning" and "sense" again to things; to feel something for a wall, an opening. The onyx wall seemed to present such an opportunity. In addition to its rich materiality, it was highly polished; thus its reflective qualities meant that it was continually changing, acting as a central point of magnetism for the main space of the house. As the setting sun illuminated this semitranslucent wall, light would penetrate it, causing it to glow red on the reverse side.[138]

Images of life in the Tugendhat House, captured by Fritz Tugendhat, demonstrate not only the spatial and material experience of it, but the way in which its constituent objects were indeed meaningful and meaning-giving for its inhabitants. Photographs of family members shown at close range in front of the alluring macassar and onyx walls, where daily lives unfolded, illustrate how the house's inhabitants' lives were connected to its objects and materials. A young Ernst Tugendhat is seen ineffectively gripping the metal handle to a typically tall Miesian door, and is pictured, jubilant, on the travertine stairs. Ernst and Herbert in the living room sit transfixed by the raindrops falling down the glass wall. These images aptly reflect Mies's quest, as architect, to give meaning to things—to walls and steps—and the ways in which subjects might form relationships to their material surroundings. Simple steps, such as those descending into the Tugendhat's rear garden, are given potency via travertine's association with a Roman past; onyx and rare wood may similarly resonate with an elegance of preceding ages, without abandoning the visual paradigm of modernism. By means of an expansive materiality that linked his modern spaces and surfaces to architecture's past, Mies's forms could be inscribed, or reinscribed, with historical meaning. Or to echo his words once more, "Life is what matters. In its entire fullness, in its spiritual and concrete interconnection."[139]

MEANINGFUL ABSENCE: OPENINGS, FRAMED VOIDS, DEMATERIALIZED WALLS

In addressing the question of "who still feels anything of a wall, an opening?" Mies's architecture of this period unlocked the possibility of not only experiencing walls anew, but openings—via unenclosed spaces, via various processes of dematerialization, and by key modes of articulating materiality's absence.[140] As Mies would note, "And what finally is beauty? Certainly nothing that can be calculated or measured. It is always something imponderable, something that lies in between things."[141] He not only gives a sense to things via rich material insertions, but to the spaces in between his objects, by making the ephemeral architectural elements more perceptible to subjects. For example, while his shimmering cruciform columns contributed to an awareness of the surrounding open plan, they also punctuated the space, acting as a linear counterpoint to the wide, stone slab walls. In this placement, he makes the spaces and openings between these two elements—column and wall—that much more resonant. The semicircular wall of the Tugendhat dining space also functions in this manner, calling attention to the striking curve as architectural form, but also very much allowing the dweller to become aware of and feel the resulting hollowed-out space.

These openings were important points of connection to the experiencing subject. Mies's transparent glass walls would naturally seem to disappear—as windows that lowered into the ground (as at the Tugendhat House) or as fixed glass walls (as at the Barcelona Pavilion) (see figs. 5.25, 5.39 bottom). Yet Mies heightens the effect by emphasizing the void—framing it in gleaming chrome. The opening is given boundary and shape, via the materialized frame; it is made perceptible, so that the subject might feel something for that resulting absence. It is also an assertion of mastery over the act of framing the view, by architect and inhabitant alike.

In contradistinction to the striking material presence of Mies's freestanding walls in stone or wood, a process of dematerialization was also occurring—not only through the use of glass and windows but also in Mies's planar white walls, which recede in the co-presence of other surfaces and frames. At the Lange and Esters houses, white walls were bordered by striking bookmatched zebrawood baseboards, oak and zebrawood door frames and jambs, and wooden window casings (fig. 5.46; see also fig. 5.9). The result was a shifting dialectic between rich materiality and dematerialization, made especially manifest by framed borders.

Fritz Neumeyer has described how one finds in Mies's work a "viewing frame" in which the "objective structure of the frame became an instrument of perception."[142] In examining Mies's structural and internal frames, Neumeyer connects them to the phenomenological effect of the subject moving through the building. In his reading, the "perceptual frame … constructs the viewer by arranging a set of frames and sequential spaces, the building now appears in a morphological transformation whose complexity is revealed only by passing through and strolling around. The sublimity of stepping aside engenders a new kind of awareness of the whole— a process of discerning the world and the self as one."[143] In addition to reading the frame in this manner, as a mode that unites subjects to a world of objects,

Figure 5.46. Mies, Lange House, view of baseboards in bookmatched zebrawood.

the materiality of that frame might also be considered a direct method of connecting the two, making the perceiving subject aware, too, of the artifice—or construct—of that world. This can be seen, for example, in Mies's Henke House addition of 1930 (see fig. 5.29). Mies's windows there are not only instantiations of the idea of transparency, or of the act of dematerializing the wall, but also part of his quest in this period to reinscribe wall, window, and void alike with meaning. This is done through the dematerializing function of glass but also via a distinctly materialized frame. Harking back to his earlier, questioning thoughts of 1928, but now, from his vantage point in 1933, Mies could write with conviction of his glass walls: "They are genuine building elements and the instruments of a new building art. … Now it becomes clear again what a wall is, what an opening, what is floor and what ceiling. Simplicity of construction, clarity of tectonic means, and purity of material reflect the luminosity of original beauty."[144]

———

Reflecting back on this period in his career, Mies himself highlighted the role of luxurious materials in the reception of his architecture: "When one thinks of my European work, the Tugendhat House is preeminent, but only because it was the first modern building made out of rich materials—and of great elegance."[145] Whether it is true that the Tugendhat House was indeed the first such building is not important, but the significance of Mies's materials in the trajectory of modern architecture is. His choice of luxurious materials intimated quality and timelessness, proffering immediate readability as extravagant insertions into the intimate domestic realm. At large-scale exhibitions, Mies offered up modernism as aspirational luxury. Understanding his use of materials is crucial for insight into the bourgeois system of values that his work engendered, particularly the legibility of capital. At a time when other architects were experimenting with new materials, in his furniture and interior finishes alike, Mies showcased such ostentatious natural materials as ebony, zebra, and pear wood; travertine, marble, and onyx. Certainly, the visible surface qualities of these materials were of paramount importance in Mies's system of representation, but the signification of their material worth was not inconsiderable. His use of expensive materials in his interiors should not only be viewed in light of the intrinsic value of those materials, but also in terms of the connotations of related vast fortunes still dependent on natural resources.

Mies's interiors in this period evidenced a conspicuous, potent materiality. His materials dramatically celebrated the raw material of the natural world as an architectural resource available to be tapped—the zebrawood or macassar veneers had seemingly magnified wood grains, and the marble and onyx slabs were carefully selected for their large, dramatic veins. Commodious, yellow pigskin Barcelona chairs did not try to disguise their animal origins. Heavy, dark silks displayed the large slubs characteristic of unrefined, natural silk fibers in stark contrast to the prevalent rayon of the period, with its preternatural smoothness and its slippery draping qualities. Moreover, the carefully specified wool rugs emphasized the natural colors and unevenness of a raw material. In the same interiors, this overstated materiality contrasted with the processed evenness and repetitiveness of other natural materials, such as the rush chair caning and the rice-straw matting, as well as the thin, almost translucent, white daytime drapes. But crucially, Mies's designs unequivocally held nature at bay, exhibiting an extravagant mastery of nature, used for maximum effect. His emphasis on natural materials was telling, as if designed to counter the superficiality of the ever more prevalent and present industrial production taking place beyond—and propping up—the usual bourgeois interior.

At the same time, in contrast to the seeming stability of these materials, Mies's use of reflective cruciform columns and glass gives the effect of dematerialization. Expected and manageable borders, such as window frames, become shimmering metal chimera. Floor-to-ceiling windows could withdraw altogether by descending into a house's depths, dematerializing an entire wall. The reflective qualities of the nickel-plating and chroming, especially in the cruciform columns, mirror—but also distort—the room, further giving moments of disorientation. Metals—iron, steel, bronze, brass, chrome—used in the furniture, fittings and details served to highlight some of the room's elements; for example, the patterning of floor coverings or floorboards was reflected upward on the flat legs of the Barcelona chair, allowing a manifest material presence where one is not normally to be found. Simultaneously, the materials dematerialize the element itself; in Mies's metal-legged, glass-topped coffee table, for example, the legs, again, pick up and distort specific surrounding elements while the glass top dematerializes the very notion of the table itself. In Mies's interiors, a dependence on process and refinement resulted in certain spatial effects and visual outcomes. The sanding, polishing, veneering, burnishing, plating, or chroming of varying materials—some modern and some long-established (although perhaps not for architecture)—allowed for interiors that reflected back to the viewer, or that could be absorbed. In all of these privileged uses of distinctive materials, Mies sought to elicit and to reestablish feeling for architecture—both by emphasizing its basic elements, such as steps, walls, and spaces, and by drawing constant attention to the more subjective, auratic materiality of architecture and its ability to shore up the subjectivity of the individual dwelling in its midst. Luxurious materiality allowed Mies's modern architectural objects to engage, foster, and reinforce the new species of architectural subject that his modernism was in the process of inventing.

If, subsequently, as K. Michael Hays has argued, in Mies's postwar North American work the architect sought to "desubjectify the aesthetic phenomena" of architecture to the "abstraction that almost every analysis of Mies ends up declaring," and to "displace the subject-centered categories of experience, consciousness, [and] interiority … with the elementary bits and pieces of the object world itself—and [also displace] the commitment to produce aesthetic experience," then the earlier period of work in 1920s and 1930s Germany should be viewed as one in which Mies, in contrast, first sets the subject into meaningful dialogue with the materials, experiences, and aesthetics of that object world before—perhaps—finding ways to dismantle that dialogue.[146] Pivotal for understanding Mies's work of the 1920s and 1930s is his engagement of rarified materials for objects such as steps and walls, curtains and doors, which acted as points of connectivity between the perceiving subject and Mies's modern architecture. Abstraction in form and meaning, fused with the image of technology, have long been viewed as the hallmarks of modern architecture and design, especially in Mies's late German works. These emphases are belied by the luxurious materiality of Mies's environments and objects from this time—through which this Miesian modernism sought to reinscribe dwelling space with meaning for its subjects.

INTERIORITY

In the face of the swirling activity of the modern city, Ludwig Mies van der Rohe designed houses for the affluent bourgeoisie of modern capitalist society. In doing so, he was singularly affirmative of settings that carved out spaces autonomous from the city and from society at large (fig. 6.1). Mies was not un-committed to the modern city and its capitalist enterprises; for it, he designed office buildings, banks, and department stores—while exerting scant effort on mass housing for modern workers (fig. 6.2; see also fig. 2.16). For many ar-chitects of the modern movement, and for the more circumscribed group constituting an avant-garde, the pressing question of the period was "the housing question," namely, how to adequately and inexpensively house the urban masses. Modern architects were at the forefront of the movement: Walter Gropius, Hans Scharoun, Bruno Taut, Hans and Wassili Luckhardt, and Erich Mendelsohn, among others, realized important projects during this period.[1] Given the interest among these architects in multifamily dwellings' suitability for fulfilling the demand for mass housing, Mies's lack of interest in this problem indicates his markedly different design priorities. With little effort, Mies could have translated his commercial building and skyscraper projects—with their many stories, amenities located in the core, and repetition—into multi-unit housing for the masses. But by the 1927 opening ceremonies of the Weissenhof Housing Settlement, an exhibition showcasing new housing ideas built in Stuttgart for the German Werkbund under Mies's artistic direction, this was no longer Mies's question, if it ever had been.

Figure 6.1. *Left*: Walter Ruttmann (director), film still from *Berlin: Symphony of a Metropolis* (*Berlin: Die Sinfonie der Grossstadt*), Berlin, 1927. *Right*: Underground station at Potsdamer Platz, Berlin, 1924.

Modern consumers had a dizzying array of choices available to them in this period, and while decisions were made for aesthetic, practical, social, or ideological reasons, these are not the only ways to think about the relationship of interiors to their inhabitants, or modernism to its predecessors. This chapter builds on the previous one by examining the functioning and meaning of modern interior space in, and set apart from, the modern city, as exemplified by Mies's Tugendhat House, read here through the lens of period discourses on modern dwelling.[2] Mies's level of specificity in his domestic interiors underscores his interest in the unique over the universal interior solution—the select, individual design without mass dissemination. This chapter argues that the space of the interior was designed by the architect as an opportunity for the inhabitants to express themselves, to enclose themselves, and to create the conditions for an interiority that was opposed to the modern metropolis. This condition is read as luxury, the luxury of that interiority that was made possible for select members of society by the efforts of a modern architecture that placed its dwellers uniquely at a remove from the fast-changing world around them. Interiority can be understood as that abstract quality that allows for the recognition and definition of an interior, a possible condition of control—in an action of both exclusion and inclusion, enabled by containment, privacy, and protection; interiority reveals itself as, to a great extent, elitist and selective, a setting of a minimally porous boundary between the self and the world.[3]

In his house designs, Mies appears to have been uninterested in everyday life as it was lived by the many, nor does he seem to have been invested in a model for housing with a potential for scalability or replication, akin to Gropius's experiments with modular building block units or as the early Bauhaus had envisioned with the Haus am Horn. That Mies was designing for a very specific, elite clientele certainly allowed him latitude in terms of the size and overall cost of his housing designs, but he was also frequently fettered by his patrons' tastes or defined needs, a continual negotiation that often interrupted his design process. In this period, Mies's architecture, materials, and furniture appeared strikingly modern and new but continued to appeal to traditional bourgeois values. From the reserved (for their

Figure 6.2. Ludwig Mies van der Rohe, Concrete Office Building project, 1923.

time period), bourgeois interiors of his early Werner House (1912–13), Urbig House (1915–17), and Eichstädt House (1921–23) to the modern-appearing but equally elite interiors he designed for the Wolf (1925–27), Esters (1927–30), Lange (1927–30), Tugendhat (1928–30), and Lemke (1932–33) families, Mies's pursuit of modernism can be seen in his opening up of forms and spaces, and yet traditional bourgeois cultural values remained solidly intact. Despite the modern architectural fabric of the houses, these designs still allowed for modes of living that reinforced period bourgeois practices.

The final years of the Weimar Republic represented the apotheosis of a wide range of changes that had been accumulating at breakneck speed throughout the twenties—including evolving ideas surrounding the "new woman," new visuality as a result of avant-garde art and architectural movements, the rise of mass entertainment encompassing many different cultural spheres, and new groups such as the numerous modern office workers who had leisure time and income to spend, as well as members of the burgeoning worker movements and trade groups. However, even against this varied and changing landscape, it was also a period of stability and even retrenchment into family and interior life. Though the trappings of domestic life changed dramatically in some instances, through new technology and materials (to name just two well-known shifts in this period that affected architecture), the underlying values among the elite did not. Notably, while modern villas were commissioned by those select members of the affluent bourgeoisie daring enough to build in a new way, they still tended to construct them in traditionally exclusive areas of the city, surrounded by conventional, conservative dwellings.

Thus, a distinction between living in a modern house and living a modern life must be made. Berlin's most ostensibly "modern" dwellers—such as the typical young office worker who, as vividly described by Siegfried Kracauer, slips out to cafés in the afternoon with her boss and who wears out a pair of shoes each month dancing in nightclubs with him—most likely returned home at night to an old apartment building of the 1880s with a shared toilet on the stairs.[4] Grete Tugendhat did not lead such a life. She was a private person, concerned with the management of the household and the stable domestic life lived within the unconventional walls of the extraordinary house built for her and her husband and their family by Mies.[5]

MODERN ARCHITECTURE AND BOURGEOIS LIVING:
THE TUGENDHAT HOUSE, 1928-1930

Though stylistically and spatially removed from his interiors of the 1910s and early 1920s, Mies's late–Weimar era interiors mark a continuation of his thinking about the types of spaces making up a home, the spectrum of activities to be conducted in it, and the range of fittings, materials, and furniture befitting his elite, upper-class clients. The patrons Fritz and Grete Tugendhat both came from well-to-do, Jewish, industrial families involved in the textile industry. The elaborate and expansive modern house they commissioned for their family in Brno was sited on a plot of land located in a bourgeois, residential neighborhood with a view of the Špilberk Castle and the city below.[6] Although the house appears as a modest one story on the street facade, in the rear it is cut into the hill on the backside of the plot—allowing for two large dwelling floors and a full basement (figs. 6.3, 6.4). The street-level story contains the family's bedrooms, while the main living floor is below. This main floor is distinguished by an open plan, with cruciform columns and dividing walls carefully placed at junctions, allowing for the division of spaces. A wall of glass windows, two of which could be fully lowered to the ground, further contributed to an interior that appears strikingly modern. Mies and Lilly Reich designed nearly all of the furniture. Like the interior spaces of the Lange and Esters houses, the house was divided into formal, austere spaces for entertaining on the main floor and more intimate, private rooms upstairs, such as Grete's small bedroom, which contained a cozy sheepskin rug, a bed, and a daybed (see fig. 5.37).

By leaving the main living room open and the areas loosely defined, Mies, on first glance, was breaking apart bourgeois notions of room use in which entry into a certain space corresponded to a specific activity (figs. 6.5, 6.6; see also fig. 5.24). Yet, despite the open plan, traditional bourgeois room designations and their implied activities remained: the space was divided into a clearly defined formal living room, dining room, library, music area with grand piano, plant-filled conservatory, and a reading area with chaise longue. The dining room area, delimited by a curved, ebony-veneered wall, was unconventional in form and materials. There, Mies quelled initial concerns regarding the smell of food and the sounds of its preparation by employing the traditional device utilized to sequester a dining room—the hanging of a thick, velvet curtain (see fig. 6.5). This allowed the space to adhere to the bourgeois conventions expected of it. Indeed, curtains throughout could be called into service to seclude each of the living spaces or to envelop the entire perimeter of the open space from the outside (fig. 6.7).[7]

Here, bourgeois life continued, less in a highly delineated, room-specific fashion, but rather in a more flexible way. While in a traditional bourgeois household reading might be done in the library, photographs of Grete Tugendhat show her reading in a variety of spaces—in her husband's room upstairs, on the main floor in the red velvet chaise longue, and one imagines that she would have read in the house's library area as well (fig. 6.8). For the most part, however, traditional room designations and their implied activities remained—even without actual walls to definitively separate them. Structured by metal and glass, the Tugendhat House included many of the features of a traditional nineteenth-century home—a dark-paneled library (period photographs reveal a decorative lace doily on the table), a houseplant-filled conservatory, formal and informal entertaining spaces, a grand piano, a chaise longue, and yards of velvet curtains. Mies's remarkable attention to detail allowed for an interior that initially appeared different from period conventions yet functioned in the expected bourgeois manner. For example, his plan does not provide for a reception room, generally a separate room adjacent to the front door where visitors on business would wait to speak with a member of the household. This nineteenth-century tradition was already dying by the 1910s, but Mies still provides a furnished reception area by the entrance (see fig. 5.22). Similarly, the Tugendhats had separate bedrooms, a convention that was waning in this period. Likely, they themselves requested separate rooms of Mies; their inclusion provides another example of the ways in which a typical bourgeois life was lived within this elegant modern shell.

By all accounts, the house was very comfortable to live in, aided by its new technology. Fritz Tugendhat wrote of its functioning: "Technically the house has everything that modern man could possibly wish. In winter the house is easier to heat than a house with thick walls and small double windows. Thanks to the floor-to-ceiling glass wall and the high placement of the house the sun shines deep into

Figure 6.3. Mies, Tugendhat House, entrance facade, Brno, Czech Republic, 1928–30.

Figure 6.4. Mies, Tugendhat House, rear facade.

Figure 6.5. Mies, Tugendhat House, view of living room area toward dining area. Photograph by Fritz Tugendhat, 1930s.

Figure 6.6. Mies, Tugendhat House, view of the living room area, music area, and library.

Figure 6.7. *Top and bottom*: Mies, Tugendhat House, main living space with curtain partitions.

the room. In clear freezing weather we can lower the panes and sit in the warm sun and look out at the snow-covered landscape just as though we were in Davos. In the summer the sunshades and electric air conditioning provide comfortable temperatures."[8] Like the tea corner in Gropius's house in Dessau, Mies's modern interiors featured technological amenities; these accorded well with the interior's new industrial aesthetic, as exemplified by furniture such as a chaise longue in tubular steel. These features provided extra comfort and convenience, while bolstering, rather than altering, traditional modes of living—they did not break the prevailing class norms and activities of Mies's upper-class clients.

In the interior of the Tugendhat House, Mies created a modern, open-ended framework for living that let the individual dwellers assert themselves within it while also permitting them to sustain conventional patterns of life. The range of activities that the Tugendhat children participated in reveal a thoroughly charming but very traditional upbringing, as opposed to that of the Bauhaus members' offspring or even Mies's own three children. Overseen by their mother, and also often in the care of the family's beloved nursemaid, in period photographs the Tugendhat children are seen watering the plants, celebrating holidays, and playing on the travertine terrace, illustrating the degree to which the house was thoroughly "lived" in. Likewise, Grete Tugendhat is captured reading, watering in the conservatory, and involved in activities with her children. Though the Tugendhats had the added novelty of electrically controlled plate glass windows, their lives—like those of their peers—were not unusually "modern"; rather, their daily routine was much more akin to that evoked by Walter Benjamin in *Berlin Childhood around 1900*, his vivid portrait of upper-class domestic rhythms of the 1880s.

WOMEN AND AUTONOMY

Within the context of Mies's open plan and the position of the dweller as an autonomous individual therein, a consideration of the changing role of women in the home is of relevance. Although never an aspect that Mies specifically addressed, women's roles were being reexamined by architects and architectural critics of this

Figure 6.8. Mies, Tugendhat House, library area. Photograph by Fritz Tugendhat, 1930s.

period and have bearing on an understanding of his interiors.[9] As the various roles women could perform were rapidly expanding, particularly in urban areas at the height of the Weimar Republic, new conceptions of the role of women at home were being formed by modern architects and their circle.[10] Women were taking up new positions on the factory floor, in office typing pools, in the arts, on the stage, as writers and critics, and in other professions. Simultaneously, the role of the housewife was also being reinvented. Articles, books, films, and scientific studies promoted the idea that women should take an authoritative stance in the running of their households. A more autonomous role for women was at the forefront of architectural thought, evidenced by books such as Bruno Taut's 1924 *Die neue Wohnung: Die Frau als Schöpferin* (The new dwelling: The woman as creator) or Erna Meyer's 1926 *Der neue Haushalt* (The new household). In this literature, women were presented as active agents in the household, running it efficiently and embracing new modern machines, objects, and organizational methods. In many of these texts, the house was conceived as a factorylike space and was to be run with factorylike efficiency, aided by designs such as Grete Schütte-Lihotzky's efficient "Frankfurt Kitchen," which was mass-produced and organized to reduce the number of steps within the kitchen, among other time-saving elements. Unlike the factory worker or office typist, who labored under constraints imposed on her to which she had to adhere or risk the termination of her position (by not laboring swiftly enough, for example), the modern housewife was viewed akin to a manager—she was to efficiently direct the activities in her home, often with a staff acting at her behest. She also had some autonomy in the sourcing and selection of household equipment; customers at the AEG's elegantly appointed Berlin stores were as likely to be women as men. Likewise, advertisements in this period also seem aimed at women as well as men. Walter Gropius left the equipping of his director's house kitchen to his wife, Ise, who lamented how difficult it was to find the kind of "scientific" equipment for her kitchen that she desired.[11] However, the design of work-reducing modern amenities was reserved by the period's architects and designers, as well as engineers employed by large manufacturers, for themselves. Mies, for example, wrote in his notebook during this period, "To simplify the household is a technical problem; not the housewife but the technician will solve it."[12] The role of the housewife was to efficiently run the newly simplified domicile, leaving the design of modern interiors and labor-saving devices to experts.

This was also reiterated in several period films that sought to introduce and popularize modern architecture to the general public. In these films, the woman of the house, usually elegantly dressed and wearing impractical high heels, effortlessly demonstrates the modern house's features, as is the case in both *Die neue Wohnung* (The new dwelling, 1930), directed by Hans Richter, and *Neues Wohnen* (New living), part of a series of films on modern living, *Wie wohnen wir gesund und wirtschaftlich?* (How can we live healthily and economically?, 1928). Stop-motion photography was used to show windows, doors, and furniture drawers opening and closing in a manner that intimated an efficient, more automated future—the house as a machine for living—one seemingly requiring little human intervention. In other scenes, children readily slide open wall partitions, again underscoring the ease of operating a modern dwelling. In *Neues Wohnen*, Ise Gropius was depicted as the manager of the interior domain; her famous husband, the designer of most of the home's features, is entirely absent from the film. Underscoring Ise Gropius's managerial role, a domestic servant is shown at work, operating a number of the house's modern machines and accoutrements (see fig. 4.14). Households that could afford expensive, modern appliances and conveniences generally had the where-withal to employ domestic help. In many of the modern interiors depicted in these films, it was made clear that the housewife would run the household, including the staff, not dispense with domestic help altogether.

Likewise, in the rarified realm of Mies's upper-class domiciles, it was intended that the woman of the house would manage the staff, not participate in domestic labor herself. This intention is reflected in the layout. Notably, the kitchen, wholly conceived as the domain of the domestic servants, was not integrated in any way with the living spaces as would become common in postwar open plans. Even the labor-saving "pass through" openings between the dining rooms and the kitchens of all of Gropius's masters' houses are entirely absent from Mies's interiors—his kitchens were completely sealed off from the dining rooms. Mies's kitchens were not the efficient, diminutive spaces being popularized in the period known as reform kitchens (*Reformküchen*), where a smaller footprint was intended to save the number of steps necessary to complete tasks.[13] Instead, the kitchens and laundry rooms at the Lange, Esters, Wolf, and Tugendhat houses were very large spaces where many people could work at once to serve the needs of the household. The Tugendhats employed a nursemaid (who was treated as a member of the family), a chauffeur, a cook, and two chambermaids. Likewise, the Langes had servants, gardeners, and a chauffeur. Even Mies's more modest modern dwellings, such as the one-bedroom Lemke House, included a bedroom for the domestic help. It was intended that the staff would perform the work to keep the house running smoothly, with the wife at the organizational helm.

MODERN DWELLING AND THE AUTONOMOUS INDIVIDUAL

Modern architects were conceptualizing anew what it meant to dwell and what role inhabitants might play in new interiors, as well as in society and communities. In the same period, philosophers and cultural theorists gave careful thought to how social and material environments constituted their inhabitants—these were questions that were discussed by thinkers such as Bertolt Brecht and Walter Benjamin, Martin Heidegger, Helmuth Plessner, and Ferdinand Tönnies.[14] For architects in the period generally, and in Mies's interiors more specifically, the autonomy and agency of the individual subject was an important aspect of "new living" or *Neues Wohnen*.

Mies adhered to a moral philosophy of autonomous will and a belief in self-definition. He read widely in this period, including in the fields of philosophy, sociology, aesthetics, religion, and economics. His was a philosophy of *Gesellschaft* (society), of autonomy and even anonymity, over *Gemeinschaft* (community) and common points of orientation. This ties into the critical reception of his work: Mies was praised for being antifunctionalist and anti-Marxist, yet he was criticized for displaying "luxury and snobbism" and viewed as representing the completely isolated individual being.[15] Period conceptions and concerns about the role of the autonomous individual in society—and the relationship of the dweller to new modes of dwelling and new spatial types—were reflected in the criticism of Mies's architecture, especially the interiors and their contents.

The Tugendhat House, particularly, faced scrutiny. In a series of articles and subsequent responses in the journal *Die Form*, critics and defenders of the house weighed in on the question of whether the house was even habitable.[16] Period critics charged that the house was ostentatious, rarified, and that it, in effect, *suppressed* its dwellers. Justus Bier, launching the controversy in his infamous article "Can One Live in the Tugendhat House?," indicted it for preciousness, excessive display, and pretentiousness, which he felt would force the inhabitants into a life of ostentation against which they would rebel internally.[17] In response, Fritz Tugendhat pointed out that the patterning of the marble and the natural graining of the wood did not take the place of art; rather, they participated in the art of the space, and "'art' is permitted to take on a special importance … just as our personal lives do—more freely than ever. … It is true that one cannot hang any pictures in the main space, in the same way that one cannot introduce a piece of furniture that would destroy the stylistic unity of the original furnishings—but is our 'personal life repressed' for that reason?"[18] In her reply, Grete Tugendhat asserted that she had never thought of the spaces as being precious, but as "austere and grand—*not in a way that oppresses, but that liberates.*"[19]

Overall, the family was, in effect, freed of the weight of history, of family heirlooms, of precious items on every shelf requiring attention and care (see figs. 6.5, 6.6). Instead, their main living space was pared down to Mies and Reich's careful selection of specific materials, furniture, and objects, and family members were left to live as they pleased; they were thus granted a new degree of personal autonomy—within the home. Their private life was represented by their interactions with each other and the activities that took place within the spaces, not their familiar material goods—by their *actions* and not their *possessions*.

It was the inhabitants' mode of dwelling, their high degree of autonomy within their home, that resulted in rich conditions of interiority at the Tugendhat House. As the critic Paul Westheim noted in 1927 about Mies's interior plans, "the character of a single room does not come from the manner of its outfitting and furniture, but rather from its determination through *being lived in*."[20] That modern architecture was essentially about a manner of living initiated by the inhabitants was promoted by enthusiasts of modern design and Mies alike. Westheim rejected the idea that there might be a particular way to live in a modern interior or that the interior itself might dictate behavior, as other critics proclaimed, arguing in favor of the dweller's autonomy. Later, when asked what kind of house he would design for himself, Mies responded, "I would build a simple but very large house, so that I can do inside what I like."[21]

This principle of individual self-realization, set within a unique and opulent space, represented a new form of luxury for those members of the upper class who could afford these dwellings. The architectural critic Roger Ginsburger noted the "immoral luxury" of the Tugendhat's interior, "but this awe and bemusement is exactly what takes hold of us when we enter a church or a palace. … The aim is the same: to give the impression of affluence, of particularity, of something never experienced before."[22] Critic Walter Riezler pointed out that, as opposed to the machine for living, the Tugendhat was a house of pure luxury; and as such it was not meant to restrict life in any way, but rather expanded "the sense of what could be." He argued that what counted as luxury was a complete realization of each and every "singularity."[23] In the context of modern architecture, a new conceptual formulation for luxury was emerging, one that was not limited to magnificent scale, opulence, or rarified craftsmanship. Luxury was seen as having its own telos and its own self-contained logic. To the qualities already connected to luxury in modernism, such as rarified technology, lavish materials, or an abundance of space, an added layer is evident in the Tugendhat House. Its luxury is expressed in its being a site for singularity itself—the singularity of its architecture and the singularity of the individual dweller; it offered the subject conditions that allowed for self-realization and autonomy.

Grete Tugendhat specifically addressed the issue of individuality with regard to architecture, giving credence to the idea that it facilitated the autonomy of the individual, noting, "I believe that the needs of people are determined practically as well as esthetically ... by their individuality and the personal outlook on life, and will therefore always differ."[24] In 1928, Mies wrote of building a new order that "permits free play for the unfolding of life."[25] He touches on the subject again in 1932: "[I]t is our hope that genuine arrangements will be found with a reality content so large that authentic life can unfold in them: but life that—vitally secured—permits space for the unfolding of the spirit."[26] While Mies laid out a series of spaces, filled them with rarified materials and technology, and carefully placed furniture at precise junctures within the rooms, it was the dweller, through his or her own agency, who completed the space.

The effect of Mies's interiors—that they were set up as a background for the actions of the autonomous individual—was noted in the period. The possibilities for thought and self-determination in these kinds of new spaces was commented on by others, too. One critic writing in 1930 noted:

> The interior as home has gained a new, a different meaning of living. It is no longer satisfied with being merely a closed room. ... The human being of today wants freedom, air and light; he needs distance for his thoughts and ideas. The furniture, beds, and almost all furnishings disappear in the wall. The room becomes empty, allows movement and liberates in contrast to a time where it was only possible, with the utmost dexterity, to find one's way through "living rooms" darkened by multiple door and window curtains and crowded with knick-knacks and furniture of all styles. In the whitewashed, almost empty room there stands today the minimum of absolutely necessary furniture, as if one were outside.[27]

In rejecting the *Gesamtkunstwerk* of the preceding period, Mies created a realm for his inhabitants to be free-thinking and free agents, unlike the interiors of Henry van de Velde or Peter Behrens before him, whose interiors were so well orchestrated that the two architects, like others in the period, even designed "artistic" dresses for their wives so that they would harmonize with the interior architecture. Mies's dwellers were the protagonists and the space merely a setting.

This is something that the Tugendhats, especially Grete Tugendhat, understood well. Influenced in part by her reading of Heidegger, she noted, "It is extremely important that client and architect should both share the same basic feeling of being, that in their principles and on a human level they should be in fundamental accord with one another."[28] Soon after the house's completion, she wrote eloquently of the experience of living in the main space as one in which the inhabitants were not absorbed by it but rather compelled into action as differentiated individuals. She noted that the austerity forbade merely passing time by "relaxing and letting oneself go" but rather forced the inhabitant to do something constructive, which Tugendhat viewed as a liberation. She discussed how each individual flower in the room is seen in a fresh, new way owing to the striking nature of the interior, and compared this effect to the manner in which, similarly, a person at the Tugendhat House appears, both to himself and to others, to be more clearly set off from his surroundings (figs. 6.9, 6.10).[29] This phenomenon, of the inhabitant set apart from his or her surroundings, was a particular effect of Mies's interiors—the dweller and visitor alike became keenly aware of the placement of the self in relationship to the other objects in the room and the space overall (fig. 6.11; see also fig. 6.5). Mies's belief in the autonomous individual led him to create a space where the subject could be showcased against the object, in this case the stable elements of the room. In ebony and onyx, Mies created immobile, timeless fixtures. Furniture in equally stable, ponderous materials appeared similarly anchored. Against this inert, fixed background, human forms and activities appeared particularly highlighted as the inhabitants went about the tasks of daily living with the self-awareness of autonomous individuals.

REINSCRIBING THE HUMAN: WALTER BENJAMIN AND MEANINGFUL MODERN DWELLING

Period critics, writers, and theorists focused their attention on the new buildings and interiors designed by modern architects—on view in department stores, in lavish magazine spreads, and at the many large-scale exhibitions of the period—and considered the larger ramifications of these new modes of dwelling in light of the preceding period's interiors. A key set of questions revolved around the impact of new materials and types of living spaces—how meaningful connections between subjects and objects, dwellers and modern interiors, could be retained in the face of seemingly growing anonymity, especially in the urban context. For example, in 1900, the sociologist Georg Simmel had already noted with disquiet: "Modern man is so

Figure 6.9. Mies, Tugendhat House, poppies in front of the onyx wall. Color photograph by Fritz Tugendhat, 1930s.

Figure 6.10. Mies, Tugendhat House, living room. Photograph by Fritz Tugendhat, 1930s.

Figure 6.11. Mies van der Rohe at the Tugendhat House, 1930s. Photograph by Fritz Tugendhat.

surrounded by nothing but impersonal objects that he becomes more and more conditioned into accepting the idea of an anti-individualistic social order—though, of course, he may also oppose it. Cultural objects increasingly evolve into an inter-connected enclosed world that has increasingly fewer points at which the subjective soul can interpose its will and feelings. And this trend is supported by a certain autonomous mobility on the part of objects. ... Both material and intellectual objects today move independently, without personal representatives or transport. Objects and people have become separated from one another."[30] A lament over the perceived breakdown of the connection of people to their surroundings and objects continued into the 1920s and 1930s. The cultural theorist Walter Benjamin thought critically about these issues, and his writings articulated the problems he saw arising in modern architecture's interiors.

The work of Benjamin, where it considers the human and the historical in the domain of the material, is useful for its analysis of how the affective, communicative, and sensual uses to which all humans arguably put things is shaped by a particular moment.[31] Benjamin closely followed his age's burgeoning modern architectural developments and the associated discourses occurring in print, in public lectures, and in informal discussions among his peers. For Benjamin, an overwhelming prob-lem of modern life was the inability to get close to things, as distinct from the earlier era he describes in *Berlin Childhood around 1900*, in which he recounts his personal connection to the bourgeois objects, interiors, and special Berlin places of his youth.[32] In *The Arcades Project*, he considers the past relationship between subjects and their objects, citing Simmel: "During the first decades of the nineteenth century, furniture and the objects that surrounded us for use and pleasure were relatively simple and durable ... [resulting in] people's attachment, as they grew up, to the objects of their surroundings."[33] Benjamin attributes to Simmel several reasons for the waning of this attachment, first, "the sheer quantity of very specifically formed objects make a close ... relationship to each of them more difficult"; second, "changes in fashion disrupt that ... process of ... assimilation between subject and object"; and third, the problem of "the multitude of styles that confronts us when we view the objects that surround us."[34]

Benjamin writes evocatively of an afternoon spent with Bertolt Brecht, in which Benjamin focused on what he called his "favorite topic," dwelling (*das Wohnen*). Here he explicates their dialectical viewpoints:

> Brecht's starting point was a "sympathetic" [*mitahmend*] dwelling. This is a mode of dwelling that "shapes" its environment, arranges it in a suitable, adaptable, and compliant way—a world in which the dweller is at home in his own way. Brecht contrasted this with a different approach: the habit of always behaving like a guest. Such a person refuses to take responsibility for what he makes use of; he feels invited by the chair on which he sits, and when he gets up he feels himself to be disinvited. At this point, I set out to explain a different dialectic of living. I managed to convince Brecht that my account was not just a paraphrase of his own views. I made a distinction between a way of dwelling that gives the inhab-itant a maximum of habits, and a way of dwelling that gives him a minimum. Both extremes are pathological. The probable difference between this approach and the one outlined by Brecht is that the attitudes he described tend to diverge, whereas those I defined tend to converge. The mode of dwelling that reinforces

habits is the one imagined by the landladies of rented accommodations. For them, a human being becomes a function of the activities that the furnishings require of him. The person inhabiting a dwelling has a completely different relationship to the world of things from the relationship involved in "sympathetic" dwelling. The objects are taken seriously (whether or not they are "property" in the legal sense), whereas for "sympathetic" dwelling they have roughly the same meaning as a stage set. We might even say that one mode takes place in a stage set; the other, in an interior. What is less easily defined is the element of habit in "sympathetic" dwelling, whereas for living as a guest, it is completely captured by Nietzsche's statement, "I love ephemeral habits." Last, the fourth mode of dwelling—the dwelling that gives you the fewest habits—is just simple lodging [*Hausen*]. This idea, too, appears best-developed in the mentality of landladies. At its center are the idea of the bad lodger and the concept of wear and tear. For simple lodging is destructive dwelling—a mode of dwelling that undoubtedly prevents the development of any habits, because it constantly clears away its basis: the objects.[35]

Important here is Benjamin's linking of habits to objects.[36] To live well, according to Benjamin, one must acquire a certain number of meaningful objects, which, in turn, allow for a commensurate number of habits, neither too few nor too many. These habits are differentiated by the type and meaningfulness of the dweller's relationship to the objects of an interior, whether an object-filled nineteenth-century-style apartment, a spare interior of modern architecture, or bare-bones lodgings. Benjamin's description of the tension between the maximum and the minimum number of habits offered by an interior is a revealing way to think about the concept of living in Mies's spaces. No longer beholden to a preponderance of possessions or habits, in a Miesian interior, the modern individual is freed up and allowed to dwell, to pursue a new life within. Mies carefully considered the activity of dwelling; in his copy of Friedrich Dessauer's 1927 *Philosophie der Technik* (*Philosophy of Technology*), the following passage is underlined: "[T]he technical aim of building is not the house but *dwelling*, just as the goal of machine making is not a locomotive but its ride."[37] Mies wrote in his notebook around the same period: "We can only talk of a new building art when new forms of living have been formed."[38] Ideas surrounding "new forms of living" were key to many of modernism's protagonists; important here is how they put these conceptions into design practice—namely, how new dispositions of objects and spaces might free the individual for new modes of living. Mies presented his inhabitants with interiors containing far fewer discrete objects than the older interiors to which they were accustomed; in doing so, he offered an environment ripe for autonomous individuality and living in a purposeful manner.

Benjamin seemed to require a certain number of objects in his interior to make dwelling therein meaningful. He compared the interiors of his childhood, which both suffocated and alienated him (but for which he nonetheless retained a certain amount of affection), to those of the modern dwelling, which he found too vacant. Introducing the concept of the trace to his notion of the habit, Benjamin postulated that the overwhelming accumulation of habits in past interiors was connected to opportunities for leaving traces.[39] In the modern dwelling, this was eliminated, allowing a measure of freedom. Benjamin used the Bauhaus as his example, but he could have equally been writing about a Miesian interior: "What is possible among the pieces of furniture of the Bauhaus is no more than a bare housing [*ein Hausen*] when compared with life in a bourgeois dwelling, whose interior compels the inhabitant to adopt a maximum number of habits; and indeed these habits are better calculated to celebrate the interior in which he lives than to do justice to himself. … The modern style of building, whatever else may be said of it, has now created rooms in which it is hard to leave such traces (this is why glass and metal have become so important) and which make it almost impossible to acquire habits in the first place. This is why the rooms are empty and often adjustable at will."[40]

Benjamin read modern interiors against their nineteenth-century, bourgeois forebears, proclaiming them free of the heavy traces that permeated the older interior spaces. Though these new spaces were problematically empty for Benjamin, without traces or habits, he acknowledged that the dweller now had the freedom to modify or change them. It is not surprising that Mies removed anything that could interfere with interior autonomy from the space of the dwelling. The objects and the interiors designed by Mies and Reich allowed for a new exercise of the will of autonomous individuals. But Benjamin raised the question of whether they really could exercise this will.

Although Mies created sumptuous modern interiors that granted their inhabitants a radical amount of independence, at least from the weight of the past, these spaces also left open the possibility that dwellers would not be able to leave their own imprint on the house. In practice this fear was allayed. The Tugendhat family, for example, wrote evocatively of their connection to its objects—for example, the way in which the onyx wall glowed on its reverse side with the setting of the sun or the descending windows that allowed for warm winter sun to shine in—they felt absolute freedom and autonomy in the house Mies designed for them. Photographs by Fritz Tugendhat likewise capture his family seemingly connected to the house's objects—quiet moments of his wife and children in front of the onyx and macassar walls and portraits of family members very much at home in the expansive Barcelona chairs. Benjamin and Mies theorized two different, yet not ultimately incompatible, versions of the relationship of inhabitants to their dwellings: for Benjamin, the activity of inhabitation was related to acquiring habits and being able to leave traces, while Mies created conditions of freedom within the interior that finally allowed for full and active inhabitation through variations on conventional patterns and habits. These theories come together in the open-plan interior and the architectural objects of the Tugendhat House, via the onyx wall, the furniture, and other elements against which the family contentedly conducted the activities of their daily lives. Where Benjamin feared the ramifications of an interior vacant of objects, Mies gave the inhabitants meaningful surfaces and materials. Protected from the outside world, the Tugendhat family fully inhabited their spaces. Through the conditions of interiority that Mies created within their house, they were free in their manner of dwelling and also connected meaningfully to their objects in a Benjaminian sense.

INTERIORS OF GLASS, AURA, AND THE CRITICS

Certain materials used in modern architecture galvanized the opinions of theorists and architectural and cultural critics—the expansive and new role of glass was one such point of discussion and contention. Glass, as material and as symbol, proved to be a fulcrum for respondents to modernism more generally. Glass had not been seen at such expansive scales in a domestic context until modern architects, especially Mies, began to introduce large spans into dwellings and exhibition houses.[41] For critics and theorists, glass raised materially and socially contingent sets of concerns related to subjectivity and the modern dweller.

Adolf Behne, an important and early architectural critic who authored one of the first books on modern architecture, *The Modern Functional Building*, in 1923 (published in 1926), wrote on glass architecture as early as 1919. In examining Paul Scheerbart's 1914 book, *Glass Architecture*, as well as considering glass's materiality, Behne specifically makes a case for glass's positively transformative—and activating—potential for man: "No material overcomes matter to such an extent as glass. Glass is a completely pure [*reines*] material; to produce it, matter has been melted down and transformed. It has the most elementary effect of all the materials we possess. It reflects sky and sun, it is transparent like water, and it has a wealth of possibilities as regards color, shape, and quality that are really inexhaustible and to which no one can remain indifferent."[42] Behne's positive enumeration of glass not only includes what he views as its defining material characteristics but its relationship to subjects, namely, people's attachment to it, their inability to "remain indifferent" to it, and how it engenders a response. He argues for glass as a transformative and redemptive material for humanity: "The European is right when he fears that glass architecture might lose its coziness [*ungemütlich werden*]. Certainly, it will be so. And that is not its least advantage. For first of all the European must be wrenched out of his coziness. Not without good reason the adjective '*gemütlich*' [cozy] intensified becomes '*saugemütlich*' [swinishly comfortable]. Away with comfort [*Gemütlichkeit*]! Only where comfort ends, does humanity begin. … Glass architecture rules out the dull vegetative state of jellyfish-like comfort in which all values become blunted and worn, and it substitutes a state of bright alertness, a daring activity, and the creation of ever fresher, ever more beautiful values."[43] Behne concludes: "Glass architecture is going to eliminate all harshness from the Europeans, even where it is hidden, and replace it with tenderness, beauty, and candor."[44]

For a material that was often held up as the embodiment of modern architecture's functionalism and rationality, this is a surprising description, but it accords perfectly with the inhabitants' stated experience within the Tugendhat House as being uplifting and productive. Throughout the text, Behne espouses his belief in glass architecture's ability to elevate and markedly change people by wrenching them out of bourgeois comfort for a more activated and humane existence. The account of a transformed human subjectivity resulting from an interaction with glass's materiality is especially striking.

Other period critics similarly understood glass in modernism as a subjective, impressionable material with diverse qualities. For example, Arthur Korn, in his 1929 book, *Glass in Modern Architecture,* wrote eloquently on the new use of glass in modern architecture. He described its effects as "noticeable yet not quite visible. It is the great membrane, full of mystery, delicate yet tough. It can enclose and open up spaces in more than one direction." The subjectivity of the material is evident in Korn's description: "Its peculiar advantage is in the diversity of the impressions it creates."[45] This subjectivity is also embedded in his use of terms such as "delicate," akin to Behne's utilization of the word "tender" to describe how glass affects people.

In a sustained, yet diverse set of writings, Walter Benjamin honed in on the use of glass in the modern domestic interior, contrasting its effects to those of the earlier architecture of the nineteenth century, returning once again to the idea of the trace.[46] In the bourgeois room of the 1880s, Benjamin observed the owner's traces as inscribed everywhere: in the ornaments on the mantelpiece, the antimacassars on armchairs, the screen in front of the fire. Ornament in the Jugendstil house, according to Benjamin, was like the signature of a painting: an expression of the individual, a last, desperate attempt to "express" one's personality, representing both the "consummation" and the "shattering" of the interior.[47] He writes, "The étuis, dust covers, sheaths with which the bourgeois household of the preceding century encased its utensils were so many measures taken to capture and preserve traces."[48] In the bourgeois apartment, "the traces of its inhabitant are molded into the interior."[49] But in modernism, in what Benjamin termed "adjustable, movable glass-covered dwellings," the glass, "a cold and sober material," a hard, smooth surface onto which nothing could be fixed, resulted in rooms in which dwellers could no longer leave traces.[50] He observes, "Objects made of glass have no 'aura.' Glass is, in general, the enemy of secrets. It is also the enemy of possession."[51] Here Benjamin situates glass in terms of the dweller and holds the material responsible for keeping the inhabitant from making an imprint, leaving a trace or even possessing objects, in contrast to the auratic object-filled rooms of the previous period.[52] In these new interiors, it was impossible to form habits or for dwellers to imprint themselves upon the interior, thus contributing to the anomie of modernity. He cites Scheerbart: "[W]e can surely talk about a 'culture of glass.' The new glass-milieu will transform humanity utterly. And now it remains only to be wished that the new glass-culture will not encounter too many enemies."[53] For Benjamin, the coldness in modern objects was fraught with danger: "Warmth is ebbing from things. Objects of daily use gently but insistently repel us. … We must compensate for their coldness with our warmth if they are not to freeze us to death, and handle their spiny forms with infinite dexterity if we are not to bleed to death."[54] Benjamin believes that technical culture is to blame: "With this tremendous development of technology, a completely new poverty has descended on mankind. … We have become impoverished. We have given up one portion of the human heritage after another, and have often left it at the pawnbroker's for a hundredth of its true value, in exchange for the small change of 'the contemporary.'" He nevertheless understands that his present modern age, however impoverished he believes it to be, will continue, thanks to the attachment it demands from its enlightened populace: "A total absence of illusion about the age and at the same time an unlimited commitment to it—this is its hallmark."[55]

Benjamin strives to come to terms with the impact of modern architecture on the modern subject, as individual, and on humanity as a whole. Along with his examination of the architecture that defined his period, which was poised to house more and more of his era's inhabitants, he brings to the fore the complicated, sometimes fraught, relationship between modern subjects and new interior spaces. Benjamin expresses the subjectivity of modern individuals as dwellers who maintained the desire to warmly connect to their spaces, rather than be repelled by their forms, by their cold materials, and by the surfaces upon which no trace of humanity could be left. Ironically, traces, in the form of fingerprints, could in fact be left on every surface in a modern interior—on shiny cruciform columns and glass tabletops and windows, but these digital traces, Benjamin might say, are incapable of bearing meaning. Rather, he articulates the desire for rich spaces of interiority—auratic spaces upon which one could leave one's own substantial mark, and where one could dwell in a meaningful way.

Concern over the phenomenon of a widening gap between people and their surroundings—or, as Mies framed it, our ability to form a relationship to, and master, our surroundings—as one linked to conditions of modernity, was being expressed by other key thinkers in post-Wilhelmine Berlin. Philosopher and critic Ernst Bloch expressed a set of similar concerns about the period and the impact of new architecture on dwelling subjects in a diverse and sustained manner, beginning with his 1918 essay, "The Creation of the Ornament."[56] Bloch exchanged ideas and visits with Benjamin, including a meeting in the summer of 1935, following the publication of Bloch's book *Heritage of Our Times*, which had made extensive use of Benjamin's motifs.[57] Bloch, like Benjamin, took up the issue of modern architecture, expressing concerns about its potential for shallowness and emptiness, a theme he later reexamined in "Building in Empty Spaces" (written 1938–47): "Although during its creation, modern architecture was basically oriented toward the outside, toward the sun and the public sphere, there is now a general increasing desire for an enclosed security of life, at least in the private sphere. The initial principle of the architecture was openness; it broke the dark cave. It opened vistas through light glass walls, but this will for balance with the outside world came doubtlessly too early. The de-internalization [*Entinnerlichung*] turned into shallowness."[58] Bloch wrote of architecture's new abstractness, contrasting it, like Benjamin, to the nineteenth century. What was falsely promoted as "unadornedness" and the "facade-character" of modern architecture, with its "dreadful emptiness," were, for Bloch, the price that the late-bourgeoisie had to pay for demythologization and for the renunciation of the bombast of the nineteenth century.[59] Architecture "appears as surface, as something eternally functional," he argued, "even with the greatest transparency, it shows no content. … To be sure, this abstractness connects superbly with glass … emptiness in air and light, newly cosmic from nothingness."[60] At times, it almost seems that Bloch is critiquing an interior by Mies. "To be objective [*sachlich*]," he notes acerbically, means to "make life and its things as cool as they are light. … Nothing is expressed in this except emptiness … the emptiness is so nickel-plated that it gleams and captivates"; it distracts "with shining veneer."[61] In *Neue Sachlichkeit* (new objectivity) Bloch saw the despiritualization of life, the process of human beings and things becoming commodities, yet "polished up," so that objectivity's diversion would be undetectable and its distraction would be read as "honest" form. In Bloch's Marxist critique, this "diversion" was but a "naked, apparent, overbright" tool of late-phase capitalism, which attempted to fill in the "hollow space" created by the collapse of bourgeois culture.[62] It is from this deception that "chrome-plated misery" results.[63] Bloch lambasted *Sachlichkeit* for being "sheer facade" in both ideology and economy, arguing that behind the built-in rationalities, the simplified and standardized implements, the serially produced machine products, and the "steely rooms"—"which would seem almost classless if they were not so expensive"—the total anarchy of a profit economy remained.[64]

Often paired with the problem of coldness in modernism, the potentially redemptive role of the human in architecture comes frequently to the fore in period commentary. Using Le Corbusier's "machine for dwelling" as his example, Bloch characterized the new architecture as "out of touch with real human beings, home, comfort."[65] Bloch, like Benjamin, was wary of the "technological coldness" of modern architecture, where "nearly everything looks empty" and "nobody knows anymore how to live permanently and has forgotten how to keep his home warm and solid."[66] Of the period's architecture, he wrote that the "house without an aura, the city map made of affirmed lifelessness and distance to people … corresponds to the machine that no longer resembles the human being. Functional architecture reflects and doubles anyway the icy realm of commodity world automation, its alienation, its labor-divided human beings, its abstract technology."[67]

In Bloch's opinion, "Architecture cannot at all flourish in the late capitalist hollow space since it is, far more than the other fine arts, a social creation and remains that way. Only the beginnings of a different society will make true architecture possible again." Thus he yet saw some possible redemption in this modernist landscape. For Bloch, the abstractness of modernism might endure, but it would have to make itself available to the human dweller for reinvention and coordination with the patterns of life. "The utopia of the glass building needs shapes that deserve transparency," he argued, in words that recall Benjamin's. "It needs configurations that retain the human being as a question." Architecture, for Bloch, should remain "the attempt to produce the human home—from the given purpose of dwelling to the appearance of a more beautiful world of proportion and ornament."[68] From modern architecture, Bloch demanded a return to the human question over the coldness of the technological machine, content over shallow emptiness, the recovery of an aura for the spaces in which life was to be lived.

Bloch and Benjamin's critical reaction to modern architecture centered on human interactions, modes of dwelling, and habits and objects in a new and changing society. They believed in humanity's need for domestic comfort. Each of them, too, recognized a potential in glass for a transformation of humanity. Benjamin pinpointed the problem of modern materials such as glass as one in which the lack of aura and the inability to leave traces resulted in a disconnect between the dwelling subject and his modern surroundings and its objects. What Benjamin felt was the cold sobriety of modern materials such as glass, coupled with the removal of meaningful possessions from the domestic interior, dramatically changed not just the visual environment but also affected perceptions of dwelling and interchange between people, objects, and architecture in this period. Benjamin famously expounded: "What is aura, actually? A strange weave of space and time: the unique appearance or semblance of distance, no matter how close it may be."[69] Or, in his "Work of Art" essay, aura is "the unique apparition of a distance, however near it [the object] may be." He observed a "social basis" for the aura's decay: the masses' desire to " 'get closer' to things, and their equally passionate concern for overcoming each thing's uniqueness."[70] This was a key problem for modernism. It can be used to understand Mies's renewed interest in this period in reestablishing the real or perceived distance between subjects and auratic objects, giving meaning and feeling back to things. This can also explain his move away from mass housing solutions toward unique, material-filled spaces for his select dwellers. When Benjamin states that glass is something to which nothing can be affixed, a cold, sober material that has no aura, and when Bloch describes the "house without an aura," both are describing similar conditions under modernism that vexed Mies but which he thought modern designs could overcome. Mies bemoaned that "one feels nothing anymore," lamenting the loss of meaning and feeling in architecture, and proclaimed that "we want to give meaning again to things … we want to give sense again to things."[71] Mies, like

Benjamin and Bloch, yearned for a time when things carried meaning, and a key question was how to reinscribe modernism with meaning, how to once again meaningfully connect subjects and objects, people and things.

Mies came to insert exceptional materials into his modern architecture via a very personal process of carefully selecting and overseeing the cutting of each stone or wood specimen, then showcasing these select materials against a backdrop of modern glass and white planar walls. His late Berlin period works—private villas and exhibition houses alike—were auratic spaces, singular propositions for a uniquely modern mode of living, not mass-reproducible modernism. The representational luxury and unique nature of each material on show—rarified varieties of onyx and marble—resulted in spaces that can be understood to be as non-reproducible and as auratic as an original work of art described by Benjamin in his canonical essay; Mies's spaces are modern yet radiate aura in a Benjaminian sense.[72] Benjamin's insight is also that "the uniqueness of the work of art is identical to its embeddedness in the context of tradition."[73] While other scholars have examined the basis of tradition in Mies's architecture, from ancient Greek precedents to Schinkel, here it may suffice simply to highlight the effects of his very specific use of travertine and marble, two materials inseparable from architecture's noble past. Although the masses had access to modernism via technically reproduced images, cheap mass-produced department store products, or, with increasing frequency, via mass-produced apartment units, none of these possibilities created singular experiences. The attention commanded by unique zebrawood partitions, unevenly pocked travertine floors, or thick slabs of veined marble and onyx gave the dweller—following Mies—a renewed feeling for a wall, an opening, for space itself. Through materiality, a modern interior could be inscribed with meaning. But these physical materials represent luxury, and access to this materiality itself and the interiority and autonomy it fostered was also an extraordinary luxury in the setting of the modern city. In an age with the potential for technological reproducibility in architecture, as well as of art, Mies can be understood as imbuing his architectural objects with meaning by deploying a singular materiality in the service of an auratic spatial and psychic interiority.

INDIVIDUALITY AND THE CITY

Period thinkers conceptualized what the new urban experience might mean for individuals and their manner of living, as well the role of luxury therein. Mies did not seem to see any potential conflict between the aims and modes of industrial capitalism and life in the city; rather, in the context of his elite designs, there was the potential for an expansion of autonomy through the luxury of their materials and the opportunities they allowed for enhanced independence and interior life in the home. Mies was influenced, too, by Oswald Spengler's *The Decline of the West*, which warned of an increasing bureaucracy that threatened to overpower creative pursuits, and of "civilization" replacing "culture."[74] Spengler argued that the individual subject found freedom in the subjectivity afforded by modern dwelling and in the wider metropolis, as Francesco Dal Co has noted. Sharing an interest in the "redemption of subjectivity," Dal Co points to a clear convergence between Spengler's thought and modern architecture's goals.[75] Taking a slightly different tack, the sociologist Werner Sombart, writing on the modern city in the same period as Spengler, according to Dal Co, identified a continual *objectification* brought about by the need for luxury as this emerged and became a reality in the post-medieval city. The modern city is, in fact, the milieu in which luxury loses its public character and becomes an object for private consumption. ... The process of objectification renders luxury self-continuing, subjecting it to the transformations and variable dictates of fashion. ... The handicraft product retains a ritual quality inasmuch as it is a direct image of the organic relationship between the working hand and the intimate norm governing its movements; on the contrary, in the luxury object reproduced in a linear manner for the continuity of consumption ... luxury finds its place in the home. ... The urban home and metropolitan dwelling, therefore, no longer retain any ties to the original idea of place. ... The bourgeois residence, in the age of consumption's and fashion's dominance, is the driving force behind "the dissemination of luxury"—a relentless process of objectification that brings to culmination the definitive "secularization of life conduct."[76]

The sociologist Georg Simmel, who famously diagnosed the crisis of the individual in the midst of the overwhelming metropolis (see fig. 6.1), did not regret the loss of *Gemeinschaft* (community) but rather looked to the city, specifically Berlin, for new, life-affirming modern values capable of responding to that crisis.[77] As early as 1903, Simmel opened his important essay "The Metropolis and Mental Life" with a problematization of the individual in the modern environment: "The deepest problems of modern life derive from the claim of the individual to preserve the autonomy and individuality of his existence in the face of overwhelming social forces, of historical heritage, of external culture, and of the technique of life." In seeking to understand modern life and its products, Simmel looked to the metropolis as a structure that mediates between the individual and what he terms the "super-individual contents of life."[78] In examining the psychological conditions of the city, Simmel defined the metropolitan type—who, he was careful to point out, existed in a thousand individual variants—and who devised manifold modes of self-protection from the city's external environment. Yet, Simmel observed, the money economy reduced all quality and individuality to a simple exchange value.[79] As a result of the blasé attitude that the metropolis's inhabitants developed, a more general mental phenomenon arose: the individual was granted an amount of personal freedom not available under other conditions. Simmel identified two types of individualism in the metropolis, individual independence and the elaboration of individuality itself.[80] As the city of individuals grows—according to what Simmel charts as the urge for the most individual personal existence—he warned of a regression in the culture of the individual with reference to spirituality, delicacy, and idealism.[81] This, too, concerned Mies, and he sought to fulfill a perceived need with his call for *geistlich* existence, as well as autonomy in which the individual would be granted mastery of his or her own space.

Simmel was attempting to resolve the antinomy of the individual and society, while Mies might be viewed as attempting to resolve, through the maintenance of bourgeois interiority, the antinomy of the individual and the city. For example, in the essay "Freedom and the Individual," Simmel writes, "Throughout the modern era, the quest of the individual is for his self, for a fixed and unambiguous point of reference. He needs such a fixed point more and more urgently in view of the unprecedented expansion of theoretical and practical perspectives and the complication of life, and the related fact that he can no longer find it anywhere outside himself."[82] Simmel, in various essays, asks the broad question of how the fragmented and isolated phenomena of modernity could be redeemed by their participation in a present or future totality.[83] Miesian interiority can be read as an attempt to address the same conundrum. Using the very phenomena of modernity, its materials, and its surfaces, Mies sought to create a totalized design environment, away *from*—but in many ways as a reaction *to*—the city.[84] He lavished exacting attention on the interior in an uncharacteristic way for modern architects of his period. Mies can be seen as gathering up the fragments of the metropolis and sealing them indoors in purified form, while still allowing the dweller access to the outside world from his domicile, albeit mediated via a descending glass wall or the limited edges of a travertine terrace.

SUBSUMING THE METROPOLIS

Mies's interiors both assimilated the city and created an escape from the onslaught of its sensory experiences. Given the cultural transformations taking place beyond the thresholds of Mies's dwellings, the extent to which they shut out the city and excluded mass culture is significant. Unlike the ideology of the Bauhaus or the position of other modern architects who gestured to the masses even though their objects and buildings were often beyond these people's financial reach, Mies's architecture and interiors, as unique solutions, were ideologically very different from those of his peers. When Mies considered the role of the masses, he saw them as potential capitalist consumers, stating that "each of the many has a right to life and goods."[85] He did not view them as society's unfortunate poor who needed to be provided for, but rather as self-actualizing figures who were to exercise power over their own actions and destinies.[86] Across the social, political, and financial spectrum, he called for a mature economic energy—a deep engagement with capitalism—and linked it to the self-assertive individual.

Mies's domestic commissions take into account human subjectivity and individuality, which the modern metropolis was thought to negate on many levels. His work can be seen as specifically reacting to the experience of the modern city, forming two different architectural solutions—one for dwelling and one for working. In his designs for tall office buildings, banks, and urban plans, he relegated the employees to units of undifferentiated, unrelenting sameness (fig. 6.12; see also fig. 6.2).[87] Yet, with just a few exceptions, Mies, unlike his peers, hardly ever envisioned large buildings with multiple units for dwelling. Although he was bound by the commissions he received, mostly single-family houses, he did not envision projects comprising urban dwelling units akin to Ludwig Hilberseimer's High-Rise project (*Hochhausstadt*, 1924), which Hilberseimer further elaborated on in his book, *Metropolis Architecture* (*Grossstadtarchitektur*, 1927)—a vision of the modern metropolis as elementary cells that could be multiplied to form multitudinous dwelling units, ultimately expanding to create a whole urban organism (see fig. 5.44).[88] Hilberseimer, in addition to working on urban form as an architectural project, thought deeply about the subject's practical relationship with the city and its amenities, particularly the workers in relation to their living spaces, and ideas of flow and transportation.[89] Mies was much less engaged with the workings of the city generally, and with the relationship of its inhabitants to it. The worker was a cog in the economic wheel, visualized by repetitive office floors in buildings, whereas the dweller at home was granted an individual

Figure 6.12. Mies, Friedrichstrasse Skyscraper project, Berlin, 1923.

solution. In Mies's formulation, the captain of industry retired home from overseeing his dominion of office units to the open expansiveness of the unique private residence. George Grosz described the city as a rushed, noisy place of nerve-grating, doubtful amusement, with a fake sparkle designed to "rev up tired businessmen," whose crowning achievement was a big villa in a safe place, a place of "ghastly materialism and boredom."[90] Mies's architecture can be situated in this oppositional formulation between the frenetic city and the calm oasis of the private, bourgeois dwelling.

In the late 1920s and early 1930s, especially in commissions for single-family houses, Mies had the opportunity to scale down and internalize many of the ideas that he had earlier devised for urban buildings. While the Brick Country House and Concrete Country House projects found built translation in the Wolf House or the Tugendhat House, major aspects and elements from his skyscrapers and office building, too, are in evidence. Mies's work may be viewed as a process of first isolating the forms and ideas, materials and movement of the modern metropolis, and then domesticating them by transposing them into the space of the interior. Period critic Paul Westheim described Mies's construction of an interior as akin to designing the city, organized around circulation so that one might conduct one's life in an orderly and frictionless manner.[91] Taking the materials of the city, Mies inserted a visible urban language into his comfortable, bourgeois commissions, in effect domesticating the city. Whereas in the city, friction was inevitable, in the interior it could, in theory, be eliminated. His large expanses of glazing, in some cases floor-to-ceiling windows, represent a predominant form in the new Weimar city—the plate glass window—being transferred to the domestic realm (fig. 6.13).[92] By this period, the Werkbund's ideal of the spare store window with its contents organized in a straightforward and *sachlich* manner had gained currency. Mies translated this idea to the large glass windows of his living rooms, in which the carefully organized furniture and fittings inside replicated the effect of the display window's contents, incorporating a newer visual component of the city into the interior and vice-versa—the outside world reduced to a display to be contemplated from the sanctuary of the home. Metal, in the refined form of the chromed cruciform column, was similarly domesticated. While importing the shiny surfaces of the city to the interior, Mies left behind its superficiality, tempo, and chaos.

Mies also addressed the plethora of new urban surfaces described by period observers, critics, and theorists. Cities in the late Weimar Republic exhibited a significant number of new, flat surfaces, from the modern apartment houses—either recently renovated to remove their turn-of-the-century stucco decoration or wholly new—to plate glass display windows, advertising kiosks, and cinema screens. Most of Mies's interior surfaces and furniture display a similar flatness, particularly the planes of the windows and dividing walls, as well as his cube-shaped tables, rectilinear desks, sideboards and cupboards, and other furniture. As a result, the interiors might initially seem empty or plain—especially in comparison with the overstuffed bourgeois interiors described by period observers such as Walter Benjamin; however, the elaborate patterning of the onyx wall or the zebra stripes of the macassar ebony veneer panels displayed much visual activity, not unlike the busyness of a Weimar advertising kiosk.

The interiors of the Mies villas and apartments alike can be read as enabling a paradoxical withdrawal from modern society: an avowal of society that was premised on the domestication of—and isolation from—that same society. This escape from the metropolis, while still within it, was reassuring for the individuals who lived in these spaces. Mies's interiors affirmed a sense of control, timelessness, and stalwart bourgeois stability in a bewildering period. The city was kept at arm's length, beyond the sealed plate glass window, where the individual's autonomy was not threatened by the others upon whom capitalism depended.

AUTONOMY AND AGENCY: CAPITALISM AND THE AUTONOMOUS INDIVIDUAL

Beginning around 1927, Mies noticeably curtailed his earlier style of rational, *sachlich* writing and began to engage in discussions that bespoke an immersion in the philosophers and theorists of the period.[93] Moving away from his earlier short, technocratic statements and articles, he began to consider the role of the autonomous individual in a modern *geistlich* (spiritual, also in the sense of *innerlich*, or interior) society, and the role of economy and technology in light of ideas of quality and the advancement of art.[94] By 1930, he had specifically rejected functionalism.[95] And he embraced capitalism as a means toward self-defined autonomy, specifically as a way for individuals to control nature and assert themselves over their surroundings.

Mies began describing a process of detachment by the modern individual from the community, and he saw the individual as having a sense of self-actualization and autonomy.[96] He stated his new position in an important lecture of 1928, "The Preconditions of Architectural Work," where he rejected the communal aspects of the past in favor of the detached, autonomous individual of the present by laying out a historical trajectory: "Whereas man in the Middle Ages was committed, internally and externally, to the community [*Gemeinschaft*], now takes place the great

Figure 6.13. Mies, Tugendhat House, living room with chaise longue. Photograph by Fritz Tugendhat, 1930s.

detachment of the individual, who conceives himself entitled to advance his talents and develop his forces. The development became the basis for spiritual [*geistig*, also mental] freedom, for the will to think autonomously and search independently."[97] He argued that the individual now took precedence and that his relationship to the art of building [*Baukunst*] represented a means by which humans could demonstrate their mastery over their spatial environment.[98] Prodding the individual to preside over the economic and the technical, while calling for a more human and mindful existence in doing so, Mies continued, "We do not need less science [*Wissenschaft*, knowledge], but a science that is more *geistig* [human, mindful]; not less, but a more mature economic energy. All that will only become possible when man asserts himself in objective nature and relates it to himself. ... It must be possible to solve the task of controlling nature and yet create simultaneously a new freedom."[99] Here Mies was taking a position of opposition against *Technik*, bureaucracy, and the technicalization of human existence—and calling for a renewal in creative, economic powers and the Promethean power of life.[100]

This belief in the economy, and in quality and luxury, was not universally embraced by his audience. For example, a critic for the *Berliner Tageblatt* reviewed the lecture negatively, as demanding "material quality without giving up quantity. Sublimation without loss of volume, these are the themes advanced by him. This luxury consumption in ever larger format is to deliver the basics for the new building style and new art forms in general."[101] By 1926, Mies was already looking to the broader, capitalistic society as a generator of the new, rather than to the technological or the architectural avant-garde, arguing, in effect, that the economy was the underlying force behind architectural changes, and other changes to contemporary life. Mies detailed this belief in the ability of economic underpinnings to foster cultural change in a 1926 lecture, asserting, "Transformations within cultures, too, depend on transformations of their economic structures. ... They change the living conditions of a particular people, and this in turn leads to a change of formal expression." Mies strove to demonstrate the ways in which building design and the economy were linked, noting that "the degree to which life before the war was already tied to the economy only became clear to us in the postwar years. Now there is only economy. It dominates everything, politics and life. ... I did not plan to hold forth on the history of economic or building development, but wanted only to show to what degree building is intertwined with living and the degree to which transformations in life find their expression in the transformations of our building forms."[102]

In the same lecture, he intimated a presumptively free-market, capitalist stance, stating, "Those who assume the right to interfere in the lives of individuals and the community in a regulatory way should first of all acquire adequate knowledge of things and their interconnections. Only superior abilities and real mastery entitles one to authority."[103] Mies asserted the primacy of the architect in making authoritative architectural decisions, rather than regulatory bodies, and he favored the expertise of the individual in making determinations for the community, rather than government agents. Mies's notebook, too, makes reference to the relationship between architecture and economic growth; he writes in his typical terse form, "Concretization of the idea to an object. Mass object. Transition from building art to building economy. The actual work field of organizers."[104] Most telling, perhaps, are the handwritten final sentences to his 1926 lecture, where he moves further away from technical solutions to the delineated problem by asserting that "building art is not the realization of specific formal problems, no matter how much they may be contained therein. But it is always, I repeat, the spatial execution of *geistig* decisions."[105] Here and elsewhere, Mies moved away from purely technocratic answers, with increasingly frequent references to *Geist* and "life" as generators of form. Furthermore, he had very clear ideas on the precedence of "life" over "form." Mies rejected the nineteenth-century position that saw art as autonomous and relocated it in the material world of industrial capitalism.[106]

This shift in Mies's theoretical writings—which can be loosely described as a move from a stated belief in technology to one in capitalism—also finds a counterpart in his architectural oeuvre. For example, the "Five Projects" that announced him to the world as an avant-garde architect are all buildings that distinctly represent capitalism and enterprise—two skyscrapers intended as offices (see fig. 6.12), a concrete office building, and two large country houses most appropriate for affluent clients. Although their radical forms and advanced technological aspirations precluded their critical reception as agents of capitalism, these structures overwhelmingly embraced free enterprise. America's seemingly unchecked growth and its economic success were observed closely by German architects during this period; they were especially interested in Henry Ford and Fordism, as well as in the overall financial environment that supported the skyscrapers and other manifestations of American technical and industrial might. Although Mies did not directly cite the example of American individualism, the "self-made" American, or the founding myth of American self-determination, his interest in the individual's ability to advance "his talents and develop his forces" and assert himself as a "master" of his environment should be viewed in light of ideas being exported from America.[107] Frank Lloyd Wright has been cited as an important influence for the two country house projects and on the free-flowing interior space of Mies's work in the late 1920s.[108] Wrightian interiors—with their open plans, careful use of fine materials, and space-defining furniture—might have figured prominently not only as representations of architectural form for Mies, but can also be related to Mies's engagement with American-style capitalism and self-determinism.

Unlike many of the other avant-garde architects of his circle, Mies was not prescriptive about how lives should be lived, instead believing in the autonomy of the individual and the modern capitalist as the agent and motor of positive change. He argued that transformations within cultures depended on transformations of their economic structures.[109] Across the social, political, and financial spectrum, Mies looked to this economic energy—a deep engagement with capitalism—and linked it to the self-assertive individual.

INTERIORITY AND MODERN SPACE

Mies's modernism provided spaces bounded by both physical architecture and intangible boundaries, such as bourgeois codes that assured that only a few people would be allowed past the threshold. Beatriz Colomina has noted Nietzsche's 1874 claim that modern humankind is modern by virtue of the unprecedented split between our interior and exterior, and the "remarkable antithesis between an interior which fails to correspond to any exterior and an exterior which fails to correspond to any interior."[110] Mies's modernity, too, can be seen to stem from a similar antithesis between his exteriors and his interiors. Although much has been written about the material relationship between the inside and the outside of his architecture—for example, the continuity of the interior flooring materials that extend out onto terraces—phenomenologically, the interiors are very distinct spaces.

The exteriors of Mies's buildings can be read as an architecture of structure, of surfaces and planes, cut by glazing, whereas their interiors are an architecture of structured, three-dimensional forms. This "architecture of integral objects," as Detlef Mertins has termed it in his examination of Mies's early skyscraper project, corresponds as well to Mies's interiors of the 1927–33 period, such as the Tugendhat House, in which the overwhelming transparency of his ever-larger windows is mediated by the highly legible spatial volumes of the interior rooms.[111] Within the spaces themselves, the large "forms" created by the interior volumes are populated by smaller, elemental "blocks" that make up the interior: bookshelves, sideboards, and tables—especially as tubular steel table frames give way to veneered, wooden cube-shaped tables. As glimpsed through the plate glass, these integral objects formed an essential component of the experience of interiority generated by the architecture. Mies employed a number of operational details that actively remind the subjects that they are entirely immersed within the interior—in the meticulous design and placement of the furniture, in the materiality of the slab of onyx and the curve of the dining room wall punctuated by the cruciform columns, and in the thick, floor-to-ceiling drapes. As Grete Tugendhat would recall to her daughter, she and her husband would frequently make use of the curtains that divided the rooms, "creating and delimitating their own private space at will … this experience of space was an essential quality of life in the house: while providing seclusion and privacy there was a feeling of belonging to a larger totality at the same time" (see fig. 6.7).[112] The larger world was conspicuously kept at bay. The resulting interiority—self-contained and carefully structured—was a domain unto itself, formed by period notions of bourgeois propriety, flexibility in the interior architecture, and Mies's allowing for the autonomous individual's multiple possible modes of bourgeois dwelling.

It is in this period that Mies's plans called for opening up the interior spaces, albeit to the limits of what his clients would allow. He saw the open floor plan as an essential unifying element of his architecture. The Brick Country House project (1924), as Barry Bergdoll has noted, was an early rejection of roomlike enclosures in favor of a sense of space flowing between rooms and around freestanding walls and L- and T-shaped partitions.[113] For the Esters House, Mies proposed leaving the ground floor interior space open, with the dining room flowing out from the entry hall, a plan that was rejected by the family, who insisted on a closed dining room. At the Tugendhat House, Mies generally abolished space-enclosing walls, employing curtains to partition rooms. Furniture became a crucial method of demarcation between otherwise indistinguishable spaces. Details took on more significance, as evidenced by the careful design of vent covers, doorknobs, door nameplates, and furniture upholstered in evocative colors—Lilly Reich's contribution.

As the multiroom dwelling slowly transformed into a single living space, the relationship of different areas to each other—as well as the relationship of different pieces of furniture to one another—became more important (see fig. 6.6). The outfitting of a single room, which earlier might have been organized and decorated according to the room's function, such as a library or a dining room, represented an altogether new problem: in an open plan, multiple functions and furnishing types needed to coexist in one space, and in relationship to each other. Thus, the open plan changed the experience of the interior by generalizing it into one space. The viewer ceased to evaluate the interior by room designation; instead it became a single entity with many highlighted aspects—bookshelves signaling a library area, or a single chair as a reading nook. The room itself, to a certain degree, recedes, and instead the furnishings and fittings are emphasized as signs of the possible activities to be carried out in each area. But overall, the open plan offered the modern subject a new degree of autonomy; it was an interior in which action was conceived of as open-ended and self-determined.

These were interiors into which Mies's privileged modern urban subjects had the luxury of retreat. Compared with the outside "surface city," or what Janet Ward has identified as "Weimar surfaces," Mies's interiors are anything but superficial or ephemeral. As Grete Tugendhat reported, "Though the connection between inside and outside is indeed important, the space is nonetheless entirely enclosed and self-sufficient; in this sense the glass wall functions completely as a boundary. If it were otherwise, I myself feel that one would have a sense of restlessness and exposure."[114] Mies's interiors were highlighted by means of the architecture, inclusionary objects, and space-making techniques, creating settings of luxuriously modern interiority. The space of the interior is necessarily a bounded condition, but not a fixed one. Interiority is an explicit manipulation of an environment to achieve and construct a desired space, including the incorporation of mechanisms of control.[115] Temporality is a condition of interiority, for as boundaries move and change, they determine the interiority's potential extent.[116] Sinkable windows at the Henke, Tugendhat, or Lange houses radically transformed the construction of interiority, a situation that could be manipulated at will at any given moment by either opening up the room to the exterior or reinforcing interiority by drawing the velvet curtains.

———

Mies, at the Tugendhat House especially, conceived of a modern interior that gave the subject personal freedom and imbued dwellers with a sense of purpose within its confines. Interiors in which inhabitants felt consequential and purposeful were ones in which conditions for interiority were successfully achieved by the architect. These interiors can be connected back to Mies's aspiration, in the same period, to "give sense again to things."[117] In creating conditions for interiority at the Tugendhat House, chromed steel columns shimmered, and bright expanses of glass were sheathed in diaphanous, semitranslucent silk, coupled with thick, impenetrable velvet for nighttime privacy. Drapery runners allowed nearly every section of the space to be partitioned off, adding to the possibility of containment, or, as Fritz Tugendhat noted, providing the inhabitant the ability "to completely shut oneself off."[118] At the Tugendhat House and elsewhere, Mies's interiors were flexible yet static; it was up to individual inhabitants to complete them, to make their mark on the world, to shape their own destiny. For Mies, modern life was created by the individual, and his or her individuality was sustained by being shielded from society.[119] The harshness, the rush, the noise, the very "everydayness" of the urban exterior was negated in the interior; linoleum or rice-straw matting ensured noiseless steps; heavy Barcelona chairs and couches implied permanence and stasis, as did the materials used: calf leather, vellum, velvet.

The Tugendhat House and other examples seem to offer up the opportunity for a new modern autonomy. This autonomy of the modern individual in society, as championed by Mies, revealed itself to be premised, paradoxically, on possession of the means to withdraw oneself from—and insulate oneself against—society. Mies devised spaces that produced the sensation in their inhabitants that they could be manipulated at will, at a necessary remove from the relationships and encounters of the city beyond the plate glass windows. Unburdened by the past, the inhabitants were ostensibly free to create their own meaning and develop their own habits—and yet Mies's interiors, furniture, and materials were instantly recognizable in their connections to the recent bourgeois past. There may have been fewer macassar objects in a Mies living room than in typical 1880s interiors, but Mies still employed wood macassar veneer. Similarly, the deep red velvet curtains of an earlier era were replaced by a red velvet chaise longue. Mies acknowledged the changing economic and social realities of his day but sought to enable the autonomous individual in a private realm. The masses, and their world, were kept out. He embraced capitalism and its bourgeois protagonists as a means of fostering innovation and of furthering culture. And he rewarded them with serene dwellings that left no doubt about the financial means and cultural standing of the inhabitants. This was the luxury of modern interiority—one of the many luxuries of architectural modernism—that served to shore up the autonomous subjectivity of certain, privileged dwellers of the modern city.

LUXURY'S LAST MANIFESTATIONS

Luxury in German architecture and design came to an apotheosis in the spring of 1930. More even than Mies's Barcelona Pavilion, Germany's contribution to the Paris exhibition of the Société des artistes décorateurs—known as the *Section allemande*—was conceived as a didactic, comprehensive display of the ideas behind German modernism, representing both a selection of what Germany's architectural and design realm had produced to date and designers' visions for future developments (figs. 7.1, 7.2, 7.3).[1] In a strikingly clarion manner, this small, five-room display coalesced in a compact presentation the very objects, institutions, firms, and protagonists that this study has examined in depth. It brought together modern materials, such as Trolit (a cellulose nitrate plastic) and linoleum, with technology and expertise from companies such as the AEG and Siemens, along with products that had been designed at the Bauhaus and elsewhere. German modernism's key avant-garde protagonists—Walter Gropius, Marcel Breuer, László Moholy-Nagy, Herbert Bayer, Ludwig Mies van der Rohe, Bruno and Max Taut, Marianne Brandt, Wilhelm Wagenfeld, among many others—provided the architectural exemplars, furniture, and domestic objects on display.[2] The *German Section* favored an aspirational version of modernism, one that emphasized new media and technology, new materials, and new modes of living. As such, modern luxury permeated the exhibition: in its display of a rich and gleaming materiality, its showcasing of multimedia and technology housed in sleek modern casings, its appealing rows of modern goods simulating the plenitude of serial production, its eye-catching full-scale displays of alluring modern interiors, and through the arresting installation of photographs of recently built architecture.

The French invitation was significant because it was the first time Germany had been invited to exhibit in France since World War I, having been excluded from the important international decorative arts exhibition in 1925, the Exposition Internationale des Arts Décoratifs et Industriels Modernes. The German Foreign Office awarded the commission to the Werkbund in 1929; the group selected Gropius as the artistic director, and he, in turn, formed an exhibition team by extending invitations to Breuer, Moholy-Nagy, and Bayer.[3] The five rooms comprising the *German Section* featured full-sized, highly modern interiors (Rooms 1 and 3), lavish displays of objects and architectural models housed in sparkling metal and glass vitrines (Rooms 2 and 4), and modern chairs and large-scale photographs of modern architecture, both mounted to the wall in an unconventional manner

Figure 7.1. Walter Gropius, entrance to the *German Section* (*Section allemande*), exhibition of the Société des artistes décorateurs, Paris, 1930.

Figure 7.2. László Moholy-Nagy, Room 2, *German Section*, Société des artistes décorateurs, Paris, 1930.

Figure 7.3. *Top*: Herbert Bayer, Room 4, utensils display, *German Section*, Société des artistes décorateurs, Paris, 1930. *Bottom*: Display of unique and standardized goods.

Figure 7.4. *Above and opposite*: Moholy-Nagy, Room 2, *German Section*, Société des artistes décorateurs, Paris, 1930.

(Room 5). Highly reflective modern materials, such as Trolit panels in a range of colors and shimmering nickel-chrome framing elements inset with glass, created a structural pathway for visitors to follow, predominantly laid out by Herbert Bayer in a manner that anticipated his design for the Museum of Modern Art's 1938 Bauhaus exhibition.[4] Several works that would become transformative in the oeuvre of their designers debuted at this key exhibition, among them Moholy-Nagy's Light Prop for an Electric Stage (later renamed the Light-Space Modulator). For Room 2, Moholy-Nagy organized a display of modern lighting, designed a cinema area in which he projected slides of post–World War I Germany (from Deutschland Reportage), and installed a full-scale modern post office counter (fig. 7.4).[5] The room also incorporated avant-garde ideas for the theater, such as Moholy's Light Prop, an electrically run object intended to create diverse visual effects. A model of Gropius's Total Theater—a variable and highly modifiable elliptical theater design with a mobile auditorium floor and stage—was featured in a stand-alone vitrine, and Oskar Schlemmer's Triadic Ballet costumes were displayed on full-size mannequins. Bayer's installation of large-scale photographs of modern architecture, suspended at tilted angles from floor to ceiling, not only introduced visitors to German modernism, but also presented his sweeping vision for a new mode of exhibition display—one that sought to activate the full range of optical angles of the viewer's eye (fig. 7.5).[6]

This dazzlingly installed exhibition portrayed a glamorous modernism that included alluring objects, high-rise housing with lavish communal spa and gym facilities, rooftop gardens, and other elegant spaces. Although it purported to display the organizers' stated interests in standardization and mass production, as laid out in the exhibition catalogue, it was bereft of low-cost objects and workers' interiors; for example, neither Gropius's Törten Housing Settlement in Dessau nor Ernst May's low-cost housing in Frankfurt were represented. A notable exception to the dearth of inexpensive interiors and objects was the simple wooden furniture—desk, chairs, and cabinets—developed by Gropius in 1929 for the B. Feder department store, on display in a corner at the far end of the vitrines and textiles of Bayer's Room 4 (see fig. 7.3 bottom). In any case, this furniture, which had been shown at exhibitions such as *The Cheap and Beautiful Apartment* (Berlin, 1929), was criticized in the period as being beyond the financial means of workers.[7] The exhibition's objects and installations were more appropriate for a well-off modern urban denizen—an active participant in the professional and economic realm of modern life with leisure time to relax in the common rooms of a high-rise dwelling and partake in the realm of high culture outside the home. Overall, it was a carefully edited, opulent installation designed to whet desire for modern architecture and its attendant objects.

Setting the material and visual tone of Germany's contribution, the first sight visitors had of the *German Section* was a framed view into Gropius's well-appointed, full-scale gym and spa facilities, enclosed behind glass plates mounted in gleaming metal supports (see fig. 7.1). Room 1's generous amenities, including an elegant interior swimming pool, exercise equipment, bathing facilities, and a chaise longue intended for massages, illustrated the kinds of communal activities that Gropius proposed for the inhabitants of his high-rise buildings (fig. 7.6). Set against a shiny wall of black Trolit panels, the sleek installation featured polished metal fixtures

Figure 7.5. Bayer, Room 5, Architecture Exhibition, *German Section*, Société des artistes décorateurs, Paris, 1930.

and tubular steel railings as well as an illuminated, three-section, metal-and-glass fish aquarium.[8]

From the spa area, visitors ascended a galvanized steel lattice structure (a product referred to in the exhibition materials by its brand name, "Tezett") for a view of the entire exhibition from above.[9] They took in the main communal room, a space structured by the same metal frames and glass inserts and located directly across from the spa area (fig. 7.7). In the center of the room, Gropius situated a small dance area and a lounge with a semicircular bar, ringed with tall leather and chrome stools. The area in front of the bar featured a sofa and three small square tables set on a rug of shaggy white fur; lining the other side was a row of three round glass tables and three tubular steel arm chairs. At the far end of the room Gropius placed a bank of leather sofas and small, round, glass tables and, to the left above them, installed what he termed a "news wall" with mounted, large-scale maps, newspaper racks, and notice boards. A sleek Siemens electric clock, featuring non-numeric indicator marks, hung down from a ceiling mount.

To the side, a staircase led to a mezzanine-level library with a small reading area, featuring tubular steel bookcases, chairs, and small tables (fig. 7.8). The stairs and structure of the library were made of Tezett, with a Luxfer prism glass floor that allowed light to trickle to the spaces beneath. Three carrels, tucked under the library structure, were each dedicated to specific activities: work and correspondence (a desk was installed with a telephone, writing implements, and a typewriter that swung out on a metal plate); playing board games; and listening to music on a gramophone and a radio.[10] Marcel Breuer principally designed the furniture of these

Figure 7.6. Gropius, Room 1, Communal Rooms for a Ten-Story Apartment Building, *German Section*, Société des artistes décorateurs, Paris, 1930.

Figure 7.7. *Top*: Gropius, Room 1, Communal Rooms for a Ten-Story Apartment Building, *German Section*, Société des artistes décorateurs, Paris, 1930. *Bottom*: Detail, bar/lounge and "news wall."

rooms, with much of the elegant, nickel-plated, tubular steel furniture produced by Thonet.[11] Notable exceptions include the bar and high tables designed by Gropius, and a single caned cantilever chair by Mies van der Rohe, placed in the listening carrel. To complete the space, Gropius distributed houseplants, potted flowers, and cut flowers in elegant, round glass vases throughout the room.

On the other side of the steel lattice viewing platform, Breuer's dwelling rooms (Room 3) put a new style of living on display—one that was sleekly modern. Breuer's rooms were intended for a "residential hotel" (*Wohnhotel*), a 1929 project, with Gustav Hassenpflug, made up of two twelve-story apartment blocks, for which the pair envisioned ground floor communal spaces (including restaurants, common rooms, and other services), a roof garden, and four different apartment typologies.[12] In Paris, Breuer displayed a "Type 1" apartment, a configuration containing a woman's bedroom/sitting room and a gentleman's bedroom/sitting room, both connected to a central shared entrance vestibule, well-designed modern kitchenette, and bathroom (figs. 7.9, 7.10). Breuer's configuration also featured a separate work/office space, the "Type 4" prototype.[13] Built-in flexibility guided Breuer's thinking; he envisioned that inhabitants could rent additional, connected work or dwelling rooms, and later shed them when they no longer needed them.[14] The elegant rooms, as set up and furnished, appear ready to house the new cosmopolitan urbanite, whom Gropius's common rooms also addressed. In the man's room and office, upon elegant, tubular steel tables and desks, Breuer placed a telephone, Dictaphone, typewriter, globe, and bound volumes. Likewise, he furnished the woman's room with modern tubular steel furniture, including a wheeled tea cart, adding a spherical glass vase of flowers, a portable record player, and magazines. In both bedrooms and in the office, the filing cabinets on wheels, bookshelves, and cupboards underscore a seriousness of intent envisioned for the prospective dwellers.[15]

Gropius and Breuer's installations were meant to be understood in tandem with each other. The catalogue notes that Breuer's living quarters would be served by common amenities as exemplified by Gropius's spa and lounge in Room 1.[16] After

Figure 7.8. Gropius, Room 1, Communal Rooms for a Ten-Story Apartment Building, view showing library and carrels, *German Section*, Société des artistes décorateurs, Paris, 1930.

viewing the full-scale interiors, in the next room (Room 2), visitors encountered a model of a ten-story, steel construction "apartment hotel" project designed by Gropius, intended to show the architectural context for his common rooms. The design had developed out of an earlier competition entry by his office in 1928 for high-rise housing in Berlin, which included a series of twelve-story towers and associated amenities (daycare centers, schools, shops).[17] Gropius's office reworked this project in 1929–30: they lowered it to ten stories and commissioned cost assessments to gauge its feasibility. It proved excessively expensive, especially because of the steel construction (uncharted territory for contractors), elevators, and the effects of the additional height on the foundations and heating; as Winfried Nerdinger points out, given these cost analyses from contractors, "Gropius' concept was economically untenable and purely ideological."[18]

THE MATERIALITY OF LUXURY

The use of new materials—not only their intrinsic cost but also their visual qualities, especially their luminosity—helped convey a sense of opulence in the interiors. In the materials that made up the exhibition infrastructure itself, this was exemplified by the polished shine of the nickel-chrome alloy of the metal frames that divided the rooms and directed the flow of visitors, in the nickel-plating of the display cases and furniture, the luster of black Trolit, the rippled glass sheets in the pool basin (simulating water), the Luxfer prism glass in the library floor, and the generous use of crystal glass and mirrors throughout.[19] This luminosity contributed to the reception

Figure 7.9. Marcel Breuer, Room 3, Dwelling Rooms for a Residential Hotel, *German Section*, Société des artistes décorateurs, Paris, 1930. Aerial view of the woman's and man's bedroom/sitting rooms, kitchenette, bathroom, and vestibule.

Figure 7.10. *Top*: Breuer, Room 3, *German Section*, Société des artistes décorateurs, Paris, 1930. View of the man's bedroom/sitting room. *Bottom*: View of the woman's bedroom/sitting room.

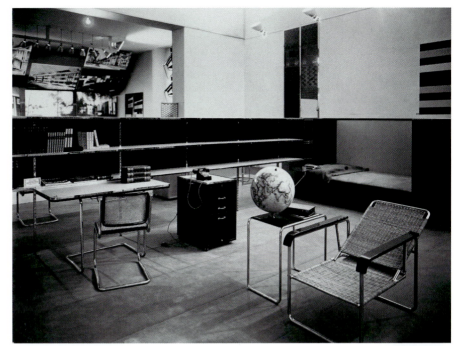

of the full-scale installations, as critic Wilhelm Lotz, writing in *Die Form*, reported: "[T]he German rooms give an impression of lightness and freedom which is the expression of an absolutely modern feeling."[20] The display cases also bespoke luxury. Herbert Bayer's specially designed large vitrines in Room 4, which held small domestic products, had graceful, rounded glass corners that were both complicated and costly to fabricate (see fig. 7.3 bottom). In addition to the smoothly undulating glass wall in Moholy's Room 2, his rectilinear, freestanding display cases had metal three-corner profiles, creating a flush and nearly seamless transition between the beveled glass edge and its frame, resulting in an especially refined effect (see fig. 7.2).[21] The display cases, dividing screens, and exhibition panels had polished aluminum metal structural elements that affixed them to both the floor and to the ceiling, while in other instances, the cases featured a trusslike base. The result does not appear overbuilt, but rather, throughout the exhibition, the display structures and their contents reified modern architecture at its most luxurious—elegantly refined and executed in gleaming metals.

The expense of the materials and the detailed construction did not go unnoticed. In reviewing the rooms, a critic charged that the "luxury materials"—specifically noting the Trolit, glass, and chrome-nickel alloy—and the "luxury execution" of the objects were still expensive for general use and had no grounding in practicality; rather, they represented an "ideal solution" without any "basis in reality." The critic concluded that the exhibition lacked "the table, the chair, the armchair and the wardrobe" to match the monthly income of the bus conductor.[22] Although it may not have been apparent to visitors, the stair, ramp, and elevated Tezett walkway in Gropius's display comprised the single most expensive item of the installation, costing 24,000 RM, or more than ten times the annual salary of a German white-collar worker in 1930 (or about $81,100 today).[23] Of Germany's display, a period critic asked whether it "was not an ideology on a technical basis. To put it bluntly: a mannerism of the supposedly entirely unmannerist?"[24] In fact, not much had changed since the Haus am Horn. Here, once again, a new mode of living was promoted along with new materials and expensive objects in a manner that was estranged—aesthetically and ideologically as well as financially—from its target audience, prompting a similarly reactionary response from the public and critics.[25] And with a budget of 150,000 RM, as with the Haus am Horn, the *German Section* in Paris was incredibly costly to mount.[26]

In addition to the materials used to construct the architecture of the exhibition, the materiality of the objects on display also contributed to the opulent effect. In Bayer's Room 4, the supposedly everyday wares that filled the vitrines tended toward the more elite end of the spectrum, even though the stated goal of the room was to display "German standard wares" and demonstrate "the principle of serial production."[27] The objects placed in the curved glass and metal vitrines, laid out in multiples to underscore the serial nature of their making, were in fact rows of jewelry, men's ties (and various silks appropriate for making ties, umbrellas, and parasols), elegant watering cans, a large soup tureen, and cutlery featuring a new, corrosion-free metal, Nirosta (see fig. 7.3).[28] In the period, metal composites, like the Krupp firm's "Nirosta," marketed in its lavishly appointed showrooms, were associated with luxury and exclusivity.[29] Although these objects might have been standardized and serially produced, two important goals of modernism, they would not have been ubiquitous in average German homes of this period.

LUXURY'S LIFESTYLE

For all the discussion in the late-1920s about "minimal dwelling" needs, housing the masses, and the use of standardized, mass-reproducible objects and parts, this exhibition was not about sheltering people as efficiently as possible, but featured instead a luxury space for a rarified life. In Paris, Gropius presented a very different type of architecture, and architectural aesthetic, from what he had been articulating in his articles and lectures—which stressed the imperative of building economical, technically inflected dwelling out of standardized, mass-produced parts; urged the use of new, space-saving methods and economizing on materials; and promoted rational building processes through the industrialization of construction.[30] The desire to bring modern design to everyone was expressed by Gropius in his text for the catalogue and in other writing in this period, as well as in the quotes from Gropius and other designers in the front section of the exhibition catalogue, a point that Wilhelm Lotz reiterated in his review.[31] Lotz also differentiated the German contribution from the French displays, which he characterized as "valuable, luxurious individual pieces of work."[32] Yet, as design for the masses, the objects and architecture on display in Paris were far from being economically realized or aesthetically embraced.

Indicating the elegant lifestyle envisioned in these spaces, the amenities and appliances associated with an elite were in abundant supply in the *German Section*. For example, Gropius's bar featured Meissen porcelain, a gleaming espresso machine for producing specialty coffee, and a Siemens mixer for cocktails.[33] In his minutes from a planning meeting, Gropius noted that the bar could be put into operation during the exhibition and serve, he suggests, not coffee, but wines from the Rhine valley, beer from Munich, and "good German liquors."[34] The luxurious nature of Gropius's spa and gym would have been read as such by visitors, as Paul Overy underscored: "In France the new cult of the body, sport and fitness was almost invariably presented as a component of a luxurious and exclusive leisured modernity."[35] Technical amenities, such as the typewriter, telephone, Dictaphone, and gramophone also hinted at the elite nature of these spaces and the status—and potential needs, as conceptualized by the designers—of the intended dwellers. The presence of a globe in Breuer's room and the world maps on the walls of Gropius's "news wall," nodded toward the worldly nature of the residents. Far from an *Existenzminimum*, and distant from other examples of communal modern space that had been developed in this period, such as workers' clubs, the modernism that was on display was patently leisured while also conveying the elevated status—and the important daily business—of its inhabitants. Paris was not an isolated case. The following year, at the 1931 *German Building Exhibition* in Berlin, Gropius designed a similar series of common rooms, likewise intended for a high-rise. Altering the program slightly, he reinstated much of the furniture and architectural elements from the Paris exhibition. In the Berlin iteration, Gropius designed a roof terrace, a separate café (which reused the curved bar with its stools and coffee machine), a reading and lecture space that featured the mezzanine library with carrels underneath in a slightly reduced form, and a gym and spa facility with the similar amenities of a swimming pool and massage chaise longue.[36] In the same year, Gropius also developed plans for a luxury high-rise apartment complex in a fashionable quarter of Nuremberg, which featured a gleaming white stone facade, marble-lined staircase walls, and amenities such as private large balconies and electric central heating.[37]

In many ways, the *German Section* was also the culmination of a series of avant-garde ideas, which can be read as equally, consistently elite. Bayer's installation of suspended large-scale photographs in Room 5, and the catalogue's illustration of an oversized, all-seeing eye placed on a man with a three-piece suit and tie, depicted how this radical exhibition design could alter the very act of seeing. In terms of light, space, and the subjectivity of the receiving audience, Moholy's Light Prop was an equally extreme proposal for the theater, as was Gropius's Total Theater and Oskar Schlemmer's Triadic Ballet, especially his avant-garde costuming and pared-down stage sets. Against the ideal of seriality and standardization, particularized examples of an as-of-yet unattainable mode of dwelling were put on show. Various strands of new materiality, along with new media—as evidenced in the exhibition's installation, lighting, use of photography, and its catalogue layout—were combined for an astonishing display not of what already existed, or was even possible, but of an avant-garde ideology significantly dependent on a knowledge of modernism's ideas. Although Sigfried Giedion claimed in his review that the exhibition was "ecstatically" received, period reviews were mostly hostile or lukewarm, illustrating the degree to which the viewing public and critics alike were estranged from this content.[38] Modernism was as theoretically luxurious as it was materially luxurious.

———

This examination has shown the modes by which luxury was embedded in the design, production, and promotion of modern objects and architecture in Germany in the period 1900–1933. It has argued that luxury was present in bold, literal form in modernism's creations—represented by luxurious materials, costly technology, objects, and buildings—and in more nuanced and subtle ways, present in discourses, economic structures, ways of living, and class constructions. Despite laudatory, egalitarian rhetoric, real access to modernism among a wider public was often stymied in this period.

The specific instances considered here are historically situated and object- and text-based, yet each of these cases can serve to open up broader, ongoing questions and issues in architecture and design. Through the tenure of Peter Behrens at the AEG, technological goods served as luxury objects, and the AEG stores functioned as architectural spaces of desire as well as sites of consumption. The allure of technology and the marketing of desire through architecture, especially in architect-designed, small-scale, elite brand interiors would continue throughout the twentieth century and beyond. Under the direction of Walter Gropius, the Bauhaus attempted to create practices by which to standardize architecture and its production without an attendant loss of material or aesthetic quality, and yet neither the base of producers nor consumers was readily available for the expensive buildings and elite object-types that emerged from the school's workshops. The inherent problems entailed in the coordination of design quality, production, and reproduction would be gradually resolved as modern design was more successfully promoted in the postwar period and accessibility to it was increased through advances in mass production and innovations in modes of selling. Concomitant issues of consumer desire, kitsch, and mass taste, raised here in connection to the Werkbund display window, continue to vex designers who seek to better design our world. Mies van der Rohe created interiors for a bourgeoisie in accordance with that group's desires and his own formulation of what spaces for the autonomous, privileged individual should mean. For the most part, he left these concerns behind in his move to America in 1937. Yet issues of surface, materiality, and interiority, particularly in relationship to the city, so key in Mies's Weimar era–work, endured in his design through the postwar period.

While objects, interiors, and architecture have been examined here as material constructions, in each case, they have also been used as the means by which to interrogate the conditions under which they came into being, specifically the cultural and social milieus in which they carried meaning—as modernism, as luxury. More broadly, by evaluating these canonical protagonists and examples from the modern movement, this study has sought to illustrate the role of social class in modernism, and how class-based consumption patterns affected the choices that were made available through modernism. It has considered what goods and interiors might say, either explicitly or implicitly, about members of different classes and backgrounds. By charting the bourgeoisie's social behaviors and patterns of living, for example, it has sought to discover what new modes of living this group adopted with modernism and which prior traditions modernism could absorb. The examination of real economic considerations, in terms of the costs of period goods and their materials, has illustrated which objects remained out of reach for which buyers. And it has investigated sites of consumption, pinpointing where modern objects could be bought and many methods by which they were sold to the public or, in some cases, not easily accessed by consumers.

Layering a consideration of the objects themselves with their wider cultural milieu, this study has utilized period thought to further understand these objects on the terms and in the context in which they were created. It has considered the role of modernism's rhetoric, whether by social and cultural critics and scholars, or by the architects and designers themselves. In effecting the social change to which modernism aspired, these expressions were often at odds with the practice that they inspired. The intellectual elite understood the underlying ideals of the objects of modernism but primarily sought to realize modernism aesthetically, further restricting modernism's influence to a consumer elite that could be sold on such luxurious innovation. Even among those who could afford a Mies chair, only a certain segment of the population understood it and desired to bring one home, to create an appropriate domestic setting for it. Larger issues in period theory have informed a broader understanding of nearly every object here, whether pertaining to materiality, consumption, production, and reproduction, or ideas of autonomy and interiority. Similarly, the crucial role that media played in the period, and for this study, cannot be overstated. Popular print journalism, fiction, and film, as well as architectural and design magazines and related trade journals, give an invaluable glimpse into the period's preoccupations, ambitions, and mood.

In light of the social, cultural, and economic formulations that modernism motivated, the idea of luxury was often posited in opposition to the canonical notions typically associated with the movement, and yet luxury played a powerful role in the design, dissemination, and consumption of modernism in its time. Part of modern architecture and design's historic and lasting allure was its connection to luxury, in its many manifestations.

ACKNOWLEDGMENTS

I can remember with absolute clarity the interior, the chair I sat upon, and the moment that the initial idea for what has become this book took form. It has since grown in scope, thanks to the kindness and assistance of so many individuals and institutions. My initial debt of gratitude belongs to K. Michael Hays and Antoine Picon at the Graduate School of Design and Alina Payne and Neil Levine in the Department of History of Art and Architecture at Harvard University. I am extremely grateful for the rigor of the time I had with them, and for their continued support and friendship since.

My subsequent three academic institutions provided intellectual conviviality and the resources that supported this work. I would like to thank all of my former colleagues at the University of Illinois at Chicago, especially Esra Akcan, Catherine Becker, Robert Bruegmann, Nina Dubin, Heather Grossman, Hannah Higgins and Martha Pollak. At the Humboldt University, Berlin, Horst Bredekamp, Susanne von Falkenhausen, Kai Kappel, and Charlotte Klonk warmly acclimated me to a new academic culture as well as a new country. I am extremely fortunate to be surrounded by wonderful colleagues at The Courtauld Institute of Art, and I would especially like to thank Jo Applin, Rebecca Arnold, Sussan Babaie, Alixe Bovey, Antony Eastmond, Klara Kemp-Welch, Maria Mileeva, Gavin Parkinson, Katie Scott, David Solkin, Deborah Swallow, Wenny Teo, Sarah Wilson, and Joanna Woodall.

For the longue durée that has constituted the research and writing of this book, I have been surrounded by talented mentors, colleagues, and friends, for whose expertise and intellectual exchange I am very thankful: Zeynep Celik Alexander, Erica Allen-Kim, Kristin Berry, Eve Blau, Annie Bourneuf, Magdalena Droste, Kristina van Dyke, Philipp Ekardt, Elisabeth Fertig, Clemens Finkelstein, Alanna Gedgaudas, Erik Ghenoiu, Sarah Goldhagen, Amy Hamlin, Markus Hardtmann, Charles W. Haxthausen, Jennifer Hock, Gordon Hughes, Timothy Hyde, David Young Kim, Jennifer King, Karen Koehler, Juliet Koss, Seng Kuan, Ewa Lajer-Burcharth, Matthew G. Lasner, Lisa Lee, Megan Luke, Cammie McAtee, Ana Miljacki, Wallis Miller, Thomas de Monchaux, Dietrich Neumann, Julia Ng, Elizabeth Otto, Julie Park, Ulla Prigge, Diana Ramirez-Jasso, Bill Rankin, Sasha Rossman, Jeffrey Saletnik, Frederic J. Schwartz, Beate Soentgen, Pepper Stetler, Martino Stierli, Despina Stratigakos, Adrian Sudhalter, Jan Tichy, Joyce Tsai, Sarah Whiting, David van Zanten and Claire Zimmerman. I am especially thankful for the careful reading of the manuscript and insight provided by Christopher Long,

Monica Penick, and Amy Ogata, and to Kathleen James-Chakraborty, for whose expertise, guidance, and friendship I am exceptionally grateful.

Curators, archivists, and librarians have shared their holdings and collections while giving generously of their time and expertise. At the Bauhaus Archiv, Berlin, I would like to especially thank Annemarie Jaeggi, Klaus Weber, Sabine Hartmann, Wencke Clausnitzer-Paschold, Nina Schönig, and Berthold Eberhard. The Busch-Reisinger Museum at Harvard University has always been a welcoming institution; I am grateful for the early support of Peter Nisbet and Laura Muir, and, more recently, Lynette Roth, while Amy Melissa Venator and Robert Wiesenberger assisted in numerous ways. At the Werkbundarchiv-Museum der Dinge I would like to thank Renate Flagmeier and Rita Wolters. I am indebted to Jörg Schmalfuss of the Historisches Archiv, Stiftung Deutsches Technikmuseum Berlin, who also arranged a memorable visit to the AEG Depot. I am very grateful to Barry Bergdoll for arranging access to the Mies van der Rohe Archive at the Museum of Modern Art. I would also like to thank Brenda Danilowitz of the Albers Foundation, Hattula Moholy-Nagy and Andreas Hug of the Moholy-Nagy Foundation, and Sylvia Martin of the Kunstmuseen Krefeld. I am also thankful to the reference staff at the Dessau Stadtarchiv, the Stiftung Bauhaus Dessau, the Bewag-Archiv, the Kunstbibliothek der Staatlichen Museen zu Berlin, and the Manuscripts Division at Library of Congress. For assistance with research and images, I would like to thank Kerstin Flasche, Kassandra Karabaich, Erica Morawski, and Julia Ryll. I am also very appreciative of discussions with my students, both in the seminar room and in front of the works themselves.

Publication of this book was assisted by an SAH/Mellon Author Award, Katja and Nicolai Tangen and the AKO Foundation, and The Courtauld Institute of Art, as well as, in earlier phases of travel, research, and writing, support from the Humboldt University, Berlin, the Graham Foundation for Advanced Studies in the Fine Arts, the Deutscher Akademischer Austausch Dienst, a Harvard University Sheldon Fellowship, and a Harvard Graduate Society Fellowship. For the invitation to present work in progress and for the discussion with the hosts and audience members that followed, I would like to thank the Bauhaus-Universität, Weimar; Radcliffe Institute for Advanced Study, Harvard University; ETH Zürich; Kunsthistorisches Institut, Universität Zurich; The School of the Art Institute of Chicago; School of Advanced Study, University of London; The University of Edinburgh, Dessau Institute of Architecture; and the Zentrum für interdisziplinäre Forschung, University of Bielefeld.

At Princeton University Press, I am very grateful for the expertise of Michelle Komie and the support of the editorial, production, and design team: Mark Bellis, Luke Bulman, Beth Gianfagna (copyediting), and Steven Sears.

My deepest gratitude goes to my family, extended as it is across continents, no less supportive than if we were in one time zone. I thank Eric Schuldenfrei and Marisa Yiu; Emily, Dylan and Lawrence Davey; Martha and Bruce Ackerman; Elaine Eskesen and John Neville. John Ackerman has traversed the ocean in connection with this book times too numerous to count, to be by my side as I researched and wrote it. And to Henry and Theo, I dedicate this book.

NOTES

INTRODUCTION: LUXURY IN MODERNISM

1. Walter Gropius, *Bauhausbauten Dessau*, Bauhausbücher series (Munich: A. Langen, 1930), 12:132.
2. Christopher Wilk, "Introduction: What Was Modernism?" in *Modernism: Designing a New World, 1914–1939* (New York: Harry N. Abrams, 2006), 14. Wilk further discusses the history and the use of the term "modernism," as well as related terms.
3. Rosemarie Haag Bletter offers a nuanced discussion of the use of *modern* versus *neu* in architectural writing of this period, arguing that *modern* was in common usage before 1923 (e.g., Behne's *Der moderne Zweckbau*, written in 1923 [published 1926]) but was soon overtaken by *neu* (Taut, *Die neue Wohnung*, 1924; Behne, *Neues Wohnen–Neues Bauen*, 1927; Hilberseimer, *Internationale neue Baukunst*, 1927), which for Bletter implies change and progressivism. She further posits that there was a political dimension to the terms in which *modern* may be understood as "of the present time" while *neue Zeit* and by association, *neu*, implies a rupture with the past period. She further points out that in translation into English these changes were not perceivable, since those titles originally containing *neu* were mostly translated as "modern." See Rosemarie Haag Bletter, introduction to Adolf Behne, *The Modern Functional Building* (Santa Monica, CA: Getty Research Institute for the History of Art and the Humanities, 1996), 2–3.
4. Karel Teige, *The Minimum Dwelling* (1932), trans. Eric Dluhosch (Cambridge, MA: MIT Press, 2002), 6–7.
5. See, for example, Frederic Schwartz, *The Werkbund: Design Theory and Mass Culture before the First World War* (New Haven, CT: Yale University Press, 1996).
6. This can also be charted with regard to ornament in modernism; the trajectory from individual design to mass-produced object is meticulously traced by Alina Payne with regard to the complex relationship between architecture and its ornament. With attendant consideration of the corresponding historiography, Payne argues that in modernism the discursiveness of architectural ornament did not disappear but rather was relocated in everyday objects, that is, mediating objects for—and which could be seen as—modern architecture. See Payne, *From Ornament to Object: Genealogies of Architectural Modernism* (New Haven, CT: Yale University Press, 2012).
7. Hermann Muthesius, *Style-Architecture and Building-Art: Transformations of Architecture in the Nineteenth Century and Its Present Condition* (1902), intro. and trans. Stanford Anderson (Santa Monica, CA: Getty Center for the History of Art, 1994), 79.
8. Ibid., 85.
9. For example, Walter Benjamin in reviewing Siegfried Kracauer's *The Salaried Masses* [*Die Angestellten*] points out that the left-radical wing "will never succeed in eliminating the fact that the proletarianization of the intellectual hardly ever turns him into a proletarian. Why? Because from childhood on, the middle class gave him a means of production in the form of an education—a privilege that establishes his solidarity with it and, perhaps even more, its solidarity with him. This solidarity may become blurred superficially, or even undermined, but it almost always remains powerful enough to exclude the intellectual from the constant state of alert, the sense of living your life at the front, which is characteristic of the true proletarian." Walter Benjamin, "An Outsider Makes His Mark" (1930), in *Walter Benjamin: Selected Writings; Volume 2, Part 1, 1927–1930*, ed. Michael W. Jennings, Howard Eiland, and Gary Smith (Cambridge, MA: Belknap Press of Harvard University Press, 1999), 309.
10. For more on the print culture surrounding modern architectural books, see Pepper Stetler and Julia Walker, eds., "Modern Architecture and the Book," special issue, *Journal of Architecture* 20, no. 4 (August 2015).
11. All translations, unless otherwise noted, are by the author.
12. On exhibitions and modern architecture in Germany, see Wallis Miller, "Cultures of Display: Exhibiting Architecture in Berlin, 1880–1931," in *Architecture and Authorship*, ed. Tim Anstey, Katja Grillner, and Rolf Hughes (London: Black Dog Press, 2007), 98–107; Miller, "Neues Bauen and the Exhibition of Modern German Identity," in *Nation, Style, Modernity*, ed. Wolf Tegethoff and Jacek Purchla (Munich: Zentralinstitut für Kunstgeschichte/International Cultural Centre, 2006), 223–36; Miller, "Mies and Exhibitions," in *Mies in Berlin*, ed. Terence Riley and Barry Bergdoll (New York: Museum of Modern Art, 2001), 338–49; and Miller's forthcoming book, *Architecture on Display: Exhibitions, Museums, and the Emergence of Modernism in Germany*.
13. For recent work on luxury, see, e.g., Jean-Noel Kapferer

and Vincent Bastien, *The Luxury Strategy: Break the Rules of Marketing to Build Luxury Brands* (Philadelphia: Kogan Page, 2012); Robin Lent and Geneviève Tour, *Selling Luxury: Connect with Affluent Customers, Create Unique Experiences through Impeccable Service, and Close the Sale* (Hoboken, NJ: Wiley, 2009); Pamela N. Danziger, *Putting the Luxe back in Luxury: How New Consumer Values Are Redefining the Way We Market Luxury* (Ithaca, NY: Paramount Market Publishing, 2011); María Eugenia Girón, *Inside Luxury: The Growth and Future of the Luxury Goods Industry; A View from the Top* (London: LID Publishing, 2011); and journals such as *Luxury: History, Culture, Consumption* and *Luxury Intelligence, an International Journal*.

14. Although there have not been any studies, to my knowledge, on the issue of luxury in terms of modern architecture and its objects, from the discipline of social history, a very important article by Warren Breckman, "Disciplining Consumption: The Debate about Luxury in Wilhelmine Germany, 1890–1914," *Journal of Social History* 24 (1991): 487–505, thoroughly examines the discussion of luxury in that period. Breckman argues that "luxury" was an important issue in the tension between a sense of continuity with intellectual and cultural traditions and the more destabilizing encounter with "modernity" in the late nineteenth century (487). For Breckman, the issue is significant because of what he sees as a "powerful ambivalence of the Wilhelmine bourgeoisie toward the novel developments associated with consumerism, and more generally, with modern industrial society" (487). In this prewar period, Breckman views bourgeois Germans not as pessimistic about modernity, as other intellectual and cultural historians have asserted, but ambivalent in terms of whether to renounce or enjoy modern life; owing to this ambivalence, bourgeois Germans were unable to formulate an adequate response to luxury (500). As Breckman observes, "The discourse on luxury illuminates a surprising range of acute concerns associated with the activity of consumption: the conditions and implications of bourgeois prosperity, the 'social question' and the related problem of social mobility, the decline of traditional forms of labor and commercial activity, and the changing status and roles of women, who were strongly associated with luxury and consumption" (486). These questions and issues either explicitly or implicitly concerned the architects and theorists under discussion in this study; it is precisely against this backdrop of shifting social concerns and new consumptive patterns that discussions of modern architecture and its objects should be considered. Though he does not directly tie specific products of modernity to a notion of "luxury," as this study does, Breckman convincingly links concerns regarding modernism to issues of luxury and consumption, and to social control.

15. Breckman, "Disciplining Consumption," 486.

16. Karl Marx, *Capital: A Critique of Political Economy* (1867), trans. Ben Fowkes (London: Pelican Books, 1976; repr., London: Penguin Classics, 1990), 1:727n2.

17. Marx, *Capital*, 1:1045–46.

18. Werner Sombart, *Luxury and Capitalism* (1913), trans. W. R. Dittmar (Ann Arbor: University of Michigan Press, 1967), 59–60.

19. Ibid., 117.

20. Ibid., 114. Sombart takes as his point of departure the merchants of eighteenth-century France to argue that luxury led the way for the development of capitalism. In all likelihood, the well-read Behrens would have known the work of Sombart, and he knew him personally as well; at least on one occasion Behrens joined Sombart for dinner, according to Walther Rathenau's diary for May 11, 1911. Hartmut Pogge von Strandmann, ed., *Walther Rathenau: Industrialist, Banker, Intellectual, and Politician: Notes and Diaries 1907–1922*, trans. Caroline Pinder-Cracraft (Oxford: Clarendon Press, 1985), 123.

21. Sombart, *Luxury and Capitalism*, 168.

22. Ibid., 169–70.

23. Hermann Obrist, "Luxuskunst oder Volkskunst?," *Dekorative Kunst* 9 (1902): 81–99; Alexander Elster, "Nützlicher und schädlicher Luxus," *Kunstwart* 23, no. 10 (February 1910): 279–83; "Die Luxusbesteuerung," *Mitteilungen DWB*, no. 2 (1918): 1–4; Adolf Behne, "Luxus oder Komfort?," *Das Neue Frankfurt* 2 (1928): 6–7.

24. See Bruno Taut, *Die neue Wohnung: Die Frau als Schöpferin* (Leipzig: Klinkhardt & Biermann, 1924). Albeit very different from the present study, for a nuanced and rich reading of Bruno Taut, Walter Benjamin, Georg Simmel, and others in terms of coldness versus *Gemütlichkeit* (or coziness) in modern dwelling, see Karina Van Herck, "'Only Where Comfort Ends, Does Humanity Begin': On the 'Coldness' of Avant-Garde Architecture in the Weimar Period," in *Negotiating Domesticity: Spatial Productions of Gender in Modern Architecture*, ed. Hilde Heynen and Gulsum Baydar (London: Routledge, 2005), 123–44.

25. Taut, *Die neue Wohnung*, 52.

26. Bruno Taut, *Ein Wohnhaus* (Stuttgart: Franck'sche Verlagshandlung W. Keller, 1927; repr., Berlin: Gebr. Mann Verlag, 1995), 34.

27. Adolf G. Schneck, "Über Typenmöbel" (1928), in *Innenräume: Räume und Inneneinrichtungsgegenstände aus der Werkbundausstellung "Die Wohnung," insbesondere aus den Bauten der städtischen Weissenhofsiedlung in Stuttgart*, ed. Werner Gräff (Stuttgart: Akad. Verlag Dr. Fr. Wedekind, 1928), 131.

28. Mart Stam, "Fort mit den Möbelkünstlern," in *Innenräume: Räume und Inneneinrichtungsgegenstände aus der Werkbundausstellung "Die Wohnung," insbesondere aus den Bauten der städtischen Weissenhofsiedlung in Stuttgart*, ed. Werner Gräff (Stuttgart: Akad. Verlag Dr. Fr. Wedekind, 1928), 128–29.

29. Werner Gräff, *Zweckmässiges Wohnen für jedes Einkommen* (Potsdam: Müller & I. Kiepenheuer, 1931), 16.

30. Ibid., 12. It is also useful to note that even as late as 1931, by which point the price of vacuum cleaners had substantially fallen, they were still considered an unattainable luxury.

31. Teige, *Minimum Dwelling*, 7.

32. Ibid., 182.

33. Christopher Isherwood, *Goodbye to Berlin* (London: Hogarth Press, 1939).

34. Christopher Isherwood, *Goodbye to Berlin*, in *The Berlin Stories* (New York: New Directions Books, 1945), 1–2.

35. For reproductions of Waldemar Titzenthaler interiors of this period, see Enno Kaufhold, *Berliner Interieurs 1910–1930: Photographien von Waldemar Titzenthaler* (Berlin: Nicolai, 1999).

36. Isherwood, *The Last of Mr. Norris*, in *The Berlin Stories*, 13. First published in England as *Mr. Norris Changes Trains*, the title was changed to *The Last of Mr. Norris* for its

37. Isherwood, *Goodbye to Berlin*, 14–15.

38. Originally published as Irmgard Keun, *Das kunstseidene Mädchen* (Berlin: Deutsche Verlags-Aktiengesellschaft Universitas, 1932). It was translated into English and several other languages one year later. The translation used here is *The Artificial Silk Girl*, trans. Kathie von Ankum, intro. Maria Tatar (New York: Other Press, 2002). See also Katharina von Ankum, "Gendered Urban Spaces in Irmgard Keun's *Das kunstseidene Mädchen*," in *Women in the Metropolis: Gender and Modernity in Weimar Culture*, ed. Katharina von Ankum (Berkeley: University of California Press, 1997), 162–84; von Ankum, "Material Girls: Consumer Culture and the 'New Woman' in Anita Loos' *Gentlemen Prefer Blondes* and Irmgard Keun's *Das kunstseidene Mädchen*," *Colloquia Germanica* 27, no. 2 (January 1994): 159–72.

39. Keun, *The Artificial Silk Girl*, 72–73. Translation slightly amended.

40. Ibid., 109.

41. Ibid., 136.

42. Weimar era reviews of the book alternate between designating her a member of the *kleinbürgerliches Proletariat* (petit bourgeois-proletariat) and a member of the *Angestellten*, the white-collar workers of Siegfried Kracauer's "little shop girls." For the *kleinbürgerliches Proletariat* designation, see Fritz Walter, "Zwei Bücher über die Liebe," *Berliner Börsen-Courier*, June 12, 1932, and for the *Angestellten* label, see Otto Hesse, "Eine Frau mit Humor," *B.Z. am Mittag*, June 17, 1932. Given her lack of skills and formal training, behavior, and her inability to perform the office tasks required of her, Doris seems to fall somewhere between the two classes.

43. For a discussion of living conditions in Berlin as gleaned from Weimar Republic fiction, see Carola Köhler, *Unterwegs zwischen Gründerzeit und Bauhaus: Wohnverhältnisse in Berlin in Romanen der Neuen Sachlichkeit* (Münster: Schüling, 2003). See also Sabina Becker und Christoph Weiss, eds., *Neue Sachlichkeit im Roman: Neue Interpretationen zum Roman der Weimarer Republik* (Stuttgart: Metzler, 1995). For the use of literary evidence by social historians and an evaluation of its reliability, see Alfred D. White, *The One-Eyed Man: Social Reality in the German Novel 1848–1968* (Oxford: Peter Lang, 2000).

44. *Die Grundstücks- und Wohnungsaufnahme sowie die Volks-, Berufs- und Betriebszahlung in Berlin im Jahre 1925*, 4, (Berlin, 1928), table 8, quoted in Nicholas Bullock, "First the Kitchen: Then the Façade," *Journal of Design History* 1, nos. 3–4 (1988): 188.

45. Examples of luxurious modern houses or renovations for an elite clientele in the leafy outskirts of Berlin include Mies's Perls House (1911–12), Werner House (1912–13), Eichstaedt House (1921–23); Walter Gropius's Dr. Fritz Otte House (1921–22) and Josef Lewin House (1928); Ludwig Hilberseimer's Dr. Blumenthal House (1932) and Dr. Alfred Fuchs House (1935); Marcel Breuer's Reidemeister Apartment (1931) and Dr. Kurt Lewin House (1928–29); Erich Mendelsohn's Dr. Kurt Heymann House (1921–22), Dr. Sternefeld Villa (1923–24), and Dr. Bejach House (1926–27); and the Villa am Ruperhorn (1928–29) and the Fritz Lang and Thea von Harbou Villa (1927), by Wassili and Hans Luckhardt, with Alfred Anker.

46. For example, Gropius, Mies, and Lilly Reich lived in traditional nineteenth-century apartments in central Berlin: Gropius at Potsdamer Str. 121a, Mies at Am Karlsbad 24, and Reich at Woyrschstrasse 9. Notable exceptions are the houses that Hans and Marlene Poelzig (1930, Grunewald) and Erich Mendelsohn (Villa Am Ruperhorn, 1929–30, Charlottenburg) designed for their families.

47. Research at the Bildarchiv Preussischer Kulturbesitz, a collection of thousands of photographs of Berlin, revealed hundreds of photographs of Berlin interiors in this period. Overwhelmingly, interiors belonging to lower-middle-class and working-class families were decorated in imitative "historical" or "traditional" styles. Even one-room dwellings occupied by many family members often featured an agglomeration of heavy wooden furniture and shelves decorated with lace doilies. These overcrowded apartments were the very types of interiors that modern designers railed against as unpractical. For elite interiors, see also Kaufhold, *Berliner Interieurs*.

48. For a discussion of types and location of housing owned by the wealthiest businessmen in Germany in the period 1890–1914, see chap. 5, "Residential Patterns, Villas, and Landed Estates," in Dolores L. Augustine, *Patricians and Parvenus: Wealth and High Society in Wilhelmine Germany* (Oxford: Berg, 1994), 160–88.

49. Augustine, *Patricians and Parvenus*, 1–2. For a thorough overview of German social categories, see Augustine, *Patricians and Parvenus*, 1–17; and Jürgen Kocka, ed., *Bürger und Bürgerlichkeit im 19. Jahrhundert* (Göttingen: Vandenhoeck & Ruprecht, 1987), 7–20. For a description of social identities and their relation to consumption, see Breckman, "Disciplining Consumption"; and Tim Coles, "Department Stores as Retail Innovation in Germany: A Historical-Geographical Perspective on the Period 1870–1914," in *Cathedrals of Consumption: The European Department Store 1850–1939*, ed. Geoffrey Crossick and Serge Jumain (Farnham: Ashgate, 1999), 78–79. For an investigation of the various social, cultural, and domestic milieus of the *Bürgertum*, see Werner Plumpe and Jörg Lesczenski, eds., *Bürgertum und Bürgerlichkeit: Zwischen Kaiserreich und Nationalsozialismus* (Mainz: P. Von Zabern, 2009).

50. See Jürgen Kocka, "Middle Class and Authoritarian State: Toward a History of the German 'Bürgertum' in the Nineteenth Century," in *Industrial Culture and Bourgeois Society: Business, Labor, and Bureaucracy in Modern Germany* (New York: Berghahn Books, 1999), 192–93. A third category, the propertied bourgeoisie, or *Besitzbürgertum*, was losing power in this period. For a thorough discussion of *Bürgerlichkeit* and the *Bürgertum* over time and in various political and cultural contexts, see Kocka, "Introduction" and "Bürgertum und Bürgerlichkeit als Probleme der deutschen Geschichte vom späten 18. zum frühen 20. Jahrhundert," in *Bürger und Bürgerlichkeit im 19. Jahrhundert*, 7–20 and 21–63. For an overview of historical scholarship on the *Bürgertum* and what the author poses as some problems and lacunae in the work, see Jonathan Sperber, "Bürger, Bürgertum, Bürgerlichkeit, Bürgerliche Gesellschaft: Studies of the German (Upper) Middle Class and Its Sociocultural World," *Journal of Modern History* 69, no. 2 (June 1997): 271–97. For more on the role of the bourgeois architects, writers, government officeholders, and other elite protagonists of this period, and the modernism they supported through their designs, activities, and urban

planning, see Maiken Umbach, *German Cities and Bourgeois Modernism, 1890–1924* (Oxford: Oxford University Press, 2009).

51. For modern interiors designed for prominent patrons who were Jewish or of Jewish descent, see the photographs of Marta Huth, a photographer who documented the interiors of prominent Berlin residents in the 1920s. See especially the interiors of Paul Boroschek, Richard Ginsberg, Gottfried Heinersdorff, Hilde Levi, Grete Ring (summer house), Adolf Sommerfeld, and Paul Zucker in *Berliner Lebenswelten der zwanziger Jahre: Bilder einer untergegangenen Kultur*, ed. Bauhaus-Archiv Berlin und der Landesbildstelle Berlin, photography by Marta Huth (Frankfurt: Gatza bei Eichborn, 1996).

CHAPTER 1: CONSUMPTION

1. The current understanding of Peter Behrens's work for the AEG is indebted to Frederic Schwartz, "Commodity Signs: Peter Behrens, the AEG, and the Trademark," *Journal of Design History* 9, no. 3 (1996): 153–84; and his groundbreaking book *The Werkbund: Design Theory and Mass Culture before the First World War* (New Haven, CT: Yale University Press, 1996), which situated Behrens's work culturally and theoretically by contextualizing it within active period discourse, thereby illustrating the meaning of both—design work and theoretical discourse—within commodity culture at large. The general standard work for Behrens has long been Stanford Anderson's 1968 dissertation, "Peter Behrens and the New Architecture of Germany, 1900–1917" (Ph.D. diss., Columbia University, 1968), and the subsequently revised book, *Peter Behrens and a New Architecture for the Twentieth Century* (Cambridge, MA: MIT Press, 2000), as well as a series of articles that emerged in the intervening period: see Anderson, "Modern Architecture and Industry: Peter Behrens and the Cultural Policy of Historical Determinism," *Oppositions* 11 (Winter 1977): 52–71; "Modern Architecture and Industry: Peter Behrens, the AEG, and Industrial Design," *Oppositions* 21 (Summer 1980): 78–93; "Modern Architecture and Industry: Peter Behrens and the AEG Factories," *Oppositions* 23 (Winter 1981): 52–83; "Peter Behrens's Highest Kultursymbol, the Theater," *Perspecta* 26 (1990): 103–34; "The Legacy of German Neoclassicism and Biedermeier: Behrens, Tessenow, Loos, and Mies," *Assemblage* 15 (August 1991): 62–87. Tilmann Buddensieg in collaboration with Henning Rogge added valuable writings by Behrens, scholarly essays, and an important catalog identifying the range of Behrens's work at the AEG with *Industriekultur: Peter Behrens and the AEG, 1907–1917*, trans. Iain Boyd Whyte (Cambridge, MA: MIT Press, 1984), originally published in German in 1979. Alan Windsor's *Peter Behrens: Architect and Designer* (London: Architectural Press, 1981) was an early comprehensive work in English. See also Peter Thomas Föhl and Claus Pese, eds., *Peter Behrens: Vom Jugendstil zum Industriedesign* (Weimar: Weimarer Verlagsgesellschaft, 2013), esp. Martina Fischer, "Vom Ornament ohne Form zur Form ohne Ornament? Peter Behrens und Industriedesign," 212–39.

2. Materials described by Kurt Pallmann, "Künstlerische Ladengestaltung als Aufgabe des Architekten," *Deutsche Bauhütte* 18, no. 9 (February 26, 1914): 110. Karl Ernst Osthaus, in his important article for the Werkbund on the topic of the shop window, calls attention to the necessity of a "frame" for bracketing wares from the busyness of the city streets, stating categorically that "the window needs a frame" and that what is often missing "is the frame" (62). Osthaus would have been very familiar with Behrens's facade and its "frame"; presumably, he would have been open to other less literal framing devices as solutions to the problem of storefront competition with—and differentiation from—the activities of the street. See Osthaus, "Das Schaufenster," in *Die Kunst in Industrie und Handel, Jahrbuch des Deutschen Werkbundes* (Berlin: Gebr. Mann Verlag, 1913), 59–69. For a discussion of Osthaus's essay and also the larger meaning of the frame in this period, see Schwartz, *The Werkbund*, 170–76.

3. In the same year that he executed the first AEG store, Behrens, in an important article on the stage, articulated ideas that might be read in the design of the stores, particularly their architectonic qualities, their display windows, and their carefully articulated, yet integrated, interiors. Behrens envisioned a theater that would be an "architecturally articulated whole whose center is likewise the architecturally emphasized stage," with a "relief stage," or shallow stage area in which the primary action takes place from side to side and a "space-articulating architectonic background." Additionally, Behrens called for simple theater props in direct relation to the architectonic order, similar to his "staging" of goods in the AEG stores. See Peter Behrens "Über die Kunst auf der Bühne," *Frankfurter Zeitung*, March 20, 1910, translated and reprinted as "On Art for the Stage" *Perspecta* 26 (1990): 141. Behrens, in the same article, calls for the theater to create a stage realm for the actor, a realm "which represents but does not reproduce the world," which also should be seen in relation to the realm he created in his stores and store windows (142). See also Anderson, "Peter Behrens's Highest Kultursymbol, the Theater." For Behrens's earlier thinking on the theater and his work at the Darmstadt Artists' Colony, see chap. 4, "The Nietzschean Festival," in Juliet Koss, *Modernism after Wagner* (Minneapolis: University of Minnesota Press, 2010), esp. 101–18.

4. The logo was designed by Behrens in 1908 and applied extensively to AEG surfaces. Although Behrens designed two famous typefaces at the beginning of his tenure at the AEG, Behrens-Kursiv (1907) and Behrens-Antiqua (1908), both used heavily in AEG-related advertising, as well as a later one, Behrens-Mediäval (1914), those used for the window lettering in both stores do not correspond with any published by Behrens. He may have designed the two different typefaces for the one-time use at each store, or it may have been designed by someone else. For more on Behrens's typography see chap. 4, "Behrens's Lettering and Typography," in Windsor, *Peter Behrens*, 38–49; Chris Burke, "Peter Behrens and the German Letter: Type Design and Architectural Lettering," *Journal of Design History* 5, no. 1 (1992): 19–37; and Gabriele Heidecker, "Peter Behrens's Publicity Material for the AEG," in Buddensieg, *Industriekultur*, 166–97.

5. Frederic Schwartz, in his pathbreaking analysis of the cultural and economic importance of the trademark in this period, analyzes its role as a "sign" of the new "bourgeois enterprising spirit" and as a "magical sign" (154), using the critical reception of Behrens's trademark for the AEG, among other evidence. See Schwartz, "Commodity Signs," 153–84; and chap. 3, "Magical Signs: Copyright, Trademarks, and 'Individuality'" in Schwartz, *The Werkbund*, 147–212.

6. Buddensieg, *Industriekultur*, 177.

7. Description of colors and materials for the store in Franz Mannheimer, "Arbeiten von Professor Behrens für die Allgemeine Elektrizitätsgesellschaft," *Der Industriebau* 2, no. 6 (June 15, 1911): 137.

8. Peter Jessen, "Der Werkbund und die Grossmächte der Deutschen Arbeit," in *Jahrbuch des Deutschen Werkbundes* (Berlin: Gebr. Mann Verlag, 1912), 5.

9. For an examination of how the ideas of luxury, control, and utility were related to lighting urban streets, see Mark J. Bouman, "Luxury and Control: The Urbanity of Street Lighting in Nineteenth-Century Cities," *Journal of Urban History* 14, no. 1 (November 1987): 7–37. For a typical article on the growth of electric illumination with accompanying images of electrically illuminated high-end restaurants, hotels, and specialty stores, see "Elektrische Glühlichtbeleuchtung einst und jetzt," *Mitteilungen der Berliner Elektricitäts-Werke* 8, no. 11 (November 1912): 162–64. This article concludes by noting that electric light was moving closer to the "long-desired" objective of becoming the "everyman's light," indicating that even as late as 1912, electricity was not widely available to the common citizen.

10. Ernst Bloch, "Berlin nach zwei Jahren," *Die Weltbühne* 24, no. 1 (January 3, 1928): 32, trans. and repr. as "Berlin after Two Years," trans. David Britt, in *Metropolis Berlin: 1880–1940*, ed. Iain Boyd Whyte and David Frisby (Berkeley: University of California Press, 2012), 380.

11. Berliner Elektricitäts-Werke, "Notiz Kalender," 1904, Bewag-Archiv, Vattenfall AG, Berlin. There was a minimum quota of 100 kilowatt-hours per year; if consumption fell under that level, a fee of 40 marks was levied.

12. Female casual help earned an average of 3–4 marks per day for a twelve-hour day (8:00 a.m.–8:00 p.m.), while men earned 5–6 marks per day, as noted in 1907 by Paul Göhre, *Das Warenhaus* (Frankfurt: Rütten & Loening, 1907), 74.

13. "Elektrizität im Haushalt," *Mitteilungen der Berliner Elektricitäts-Werke* 5, no. 1 (January 1909): 15.

14. "Elektrische Koch- und Heizapparate von geringem Stromverbrauch," *Mitteilungen der Berliner Elektricitäts-Werke* 5, no. 4 (April 1909): 60–61.

15. *Mitteilungen der Berliner Elektricitäts-Werke* 2, no. 8 (August 1906): 127.

16. Städtische Elektrizitätswerke Berlin, *Ratgeber für Besteller und Besitzer elektrischer Licht- und Kleinkraft-Anlagen* (Berlin: Otto Eisner A.-G., 1916), 51, Bewag-Archiv, Vattenfall AG, Berlin.

17. The meter rental rate was determined by actual kilowatt usage, beginning at 50 pfennig and capping off at 5 marks, measured between 0.75 and 20 kilowatts used. Berliner Elektricitäts-Werke, "Anmeldung zum Anschluss an die Leitungsnetze der Berliner Elektricitäts-Werke," 1912, [p. 3], Bewag-Archiv, Vattenfall AG, Berlin.

18. Berliner Elektricitäts-Werke, "Notiz Kalender," 1904, Bewag-Archiv, Vattenfall AG, Berlin.

19. These conversions were first calculated using R. L. Bidwell, *Currency Conversion Tables: A Hundred Years of Change* (London: Rex Collings, 1970), 22–24, for exchanging German marks to US dollars in 1915 (4.59 marks = $1) and then Samuel H. Williamson, "Seven Ways to Compute the Relative Value of a U.S. Dollar Amount, 1774 to Present," MeasuringWorth, http://www.measuringworth.com/uscompare, accessed April 10, 2017, to convert 1915 dollar amounts to 2015 dollar amounts

(the latest date for which data are available), adjusting for inflation.

In 2017, $3.92–$5.66 from 1915 is worth:

$95.40–$138.00 using the consumer price index
$67.90–$98.00 using the GDP deflator
$204–$294 using the value of consumer bundle
$400–$578 using the unskilled wage rate
$599–$865 using the production worker compensation
$567–$818 using the nominal GDP per capita
$1,810–$2,610 using the relative share of GDP

However, for an object such as a teakettle, the consumer price index (because it compares the costs of consumer items used in the home) and the unskilled wage rate (which determines relative costs in terms of the amount of work it would take to produce an object, or the relative time it would take to earn its cost) are the most useful indicators.

20. B. Monasch and Leopold Bloch, "Die gegenwärtigen elektrischen Lichtquellen. AEG-Vorträge," *Technische Mitteilungen aus der AEG-Zeitung* 8 (February 1908): 5, quoted in Buddensieg, *Formgestaltung für die Industrie*, 123.

21. Conrad Matschoss, E. Schultz, and Theodor A. Gross, eds., *50 Jahre Berliner Elektrizitätswerke 1884–1934* (Berlin: VDI Verlag, 1934), 56.

22. See Berliner Städtische Elektrizitätswerk Akt. Ges., *Jahrbuch der Verkehrsdirektion* (Berlin: Veröffentlichungen der BEWAG, 1928), 70.

23. "Stenographischer Bericht über die 17. ordentliche Generalversammlung der Vereinigung der Elektrizitätswerke in Brüssel. Vom 1. bis 4. Juni 1908," *Mitteilungen der Vereinigung der Elektrizitätswerke* 7, no. 8 (August 1908): 84.

24. Study by Stadtbaurat Lubszynski in which he measured electricity at 20 pfennig per kilowatt-hour, but using the Berlin Electricity Work's domestic pricing structure of 40 pfennig per hour, the 180 marks noted by Lubszynski would be doubled. "Stenographischer Bericht," 87. At the turn of the century, electric heat had been more prohibitively expensive; the 1896 AEG catalog noted that the electrical heating of a jewelry store salesroom was 760 marks for the autumn bill alone. See Allgemeine Elektricitäts-Gesellschaft, *50 Jahre AEG* (1933; Berlin: Allgemeine Elektricitäts-Gesellschaft, Abt. Presse, 1956), 381.

25. "Elektrizität im Haushalt," 120–22. For a lengthy article on domestic electricity, with many accompanying images of opulent, electrified interiors served by domestic staff, see "Die elektrische Beleuchtung unserer Wohnräume," *Mitteilungen der Berliner Elektricitäts-Werke* 7, no. 10 (October 1911): 147–54.

26. "Das moderne, elektrisch eingerichtete Wohnhaus," *Mitteilungen der Berliner Elektricitäts-Werke* 7, no. 5 (May 1911): 66.

27. "Die Technik im Leben des Kindes," *Mitteilungen der Berliner Elektricitäts-Werke* 7, no. 12 (December 1911): 188–90. Another article on electric toys for children notes that because of good insulation, the firm's toys were safe; see "Elektrisches Spielzeug," *Mitteilungen der Berliner Elektricitäts-Werke* 8, no. 12 (December 1912): 183–85.

28. Peter Behrens, "Zur Ästhetik des Fabrikbaus," *Gewerbefleiss* 108, nos. 7–9 (July–September 1929): 130 (translation in Buddensieg, *Industriekultur*, 227).

29. Advertisement for "Elektrische Plätteisen" bound in *Interne AEG-Zeitung* 15, no. 5 (November 1912).

30. "Elektrische Weihnachtsgeschenke," *Mitteilungen der Berliner Elektricitäts-Werke* 8, no. 12 (December 1912): 178.

31. Ibid., 180.

32. Particularly because AEG goods were an identifiable brand, as Frederic Schwartz has pointed out, the speculative gap between producers and consumers was closed through the subordination of the middleman to industry interests. Schwartz, "Commodity Signs," 158. In addition to the points Schwartz makes, including how Behrens seemed to offer, enticingly, "the relation of visual form to a modern economy" (153), it should be underscored here that the stores, which Schwartz does not mention in this context, were the literal sites at which the producer and consumer met, to the end profit of the AEG. By having its own sales outlets for its products, the AEG could circumnavigate the period critique on distribution and exchange that Schwartz notes (156).

33. Both stores were destroyed during World War II. The location and footprint of the stores, as well as adjacent urban amenities, can be found on maps from the period; for example, see Julius Straube, *Übersichtsplan von Berlin, aufgen. 1881–90 gezeichnet, berichtigt 1909, Städt. Vermessungs-Amt* (Berlin: Geographisches Institut und Landkarten-Verlag, Jul. Straube, 1910), 1:4000, Historic Map Collection (*Alte Karten Sammlung*), Staatsbibliothek, Berlin.

34. In the period, Königgrätzer Strasse was a major street connecting the Brandenburg Gate to Potsdamer Platz (today this section is Ebertstrasse) and the adjacent Leipziger Platz, then continuing to Hallesches Tor (today Stresemannstrasse). It also linked two important train stations—Potsdamer Bahnhof and Anhalter Bahnhof. Not only a main shopping street, Königgrätzer Strasse contained large hotels such as Hotel Saxonia, Palast Hotel, and Hotel Fürsten and also featured cultural sites such as architect Oskar Kaufmann's 1907–8 Jugendstil masterpiece the Hebbel Theater and two museums: the Ethnology Museum (Museum für Völkerkunde) and the Applied Arts Museum (Kunstgewerbe Museum) which was housed in a building by Martin Gropius. When the German Werkbund opened its administrative office (*Geschäftsstelle*) in 1927, it did so at Königgrätzer Strasse 28.

35. "Künstlerische Lichtreklame," *Mitteilungen der Berliner Elektricitäts-Werke* 8, no. 3 (March 1912): 34.

36. Pallmann, "Künstlerische Ladengestaltung," 110.

37. Franz Mannheimer, "A.E.G.-Bauten," *Jahrbuch des Deutschen Werkbundes* (Berlin: Gebr. Mann Verlag, 1913), 41.

38. Later the address was changed to 118 Potsdamer Strasse.

39. Franz Mannheimer, "Arbeiten von Professor Behrens," 136.

40. "Dauernde Ausstellung von A.E.G.-Fabrikaten," *Mitteilungen der Berliner Elektricitäts-Werke* 4, no. 7 (July 1908): 106. See also "Die Ausstellung der Apparatefabrik der AEG," *AEG-Zeitung* 8, no. 3 (September 1910): 7–9.

41. Allgemeine Elektricitäts-Gesellschaft, ed., *50 Jahre AEG*, 380–81.

42. Ibid.

43. Fritz von Meyer-Schönbrunn, ed., *Peter Behrens*, Monographien Deutscher Reklame-Künstler (Hagen: Verlag von Fr. Wilh. Ruhfus, 1912), 5:4.

44. "Die Ausstellung der AEG, Königgrätzerstrasse," *Mitteilungen der Berliner Elektricitäts-Werke* 7, no. 3 (March 1911): 34.

45. Fritz Hoeber, *Peter Behrens* (Munich: Georg Müller und Eugen Rentsch, 1913), 155.

46. *Sachlich* and *Sachlichkeit* are terms that are very difficult to translate precisely; they are generally translated as "objective" or "functional" and as "objectivity" and "functionalism," as well as "sober" and "sobriety." The terms refer to an interest in a cool examination of the present and the minimal necessities needed for life, which manifest themselves in stripped-down interiors and objects devoid of unnecessary elements and decoration. Recent scholars such as Rosemarie Bletter prefer to translate *Sachlichkeit* as "matter-of-factness," "objectivity," and "the simple, practical, straightforward solution to a problem." See Rosemarie Haag Bletter, "Introduction" to Adolf Behne, *The Modern Functional Building* (Santa Monica, CA: Getty Research Institute for the History of Art and the Humanities, 1996), 48–61.

47. Anton Jaumann, "Neues von Peter Behrens," *Deutsche Kunst und Dekoration* 23 (1908–9): 354.

48. Pallmann, "Künstlerische Ladengestaltung," 110.

49. Meyer-Schönbrunn, *Peter Behrens*, 4.

50. Thomas P. Hughes, *Networks of Power: Electrification in Western Society 1880–1930* (Baltimore, MD: Johns Hopkins University Press, 1983), 179.

51. For important philosophical and psychological discussions of perception vis-à-vis store window design of this period, particularly the impact of empathy theorists on the arrangement of structural and pattern ornament in displays, see Charlotte Klonk, "Patterns of Attention: From Shop Windows to Gallery Rooms in Early Twentieth-Century Berlin," *Art History* 28, no. 4 (September 2005): 468–96. For a discussion of Berlin display windows and class with regard to old, cluttered window designs associated with lower-class kitsch, versus new, modern *sachlich* displays of luxury stores aimed at the upper class, as well as changes in the meaning of the display window in this period, see Sherwin Simmons, "August Macke's Shoppers: Commodity Aesthetics, Modernist Autonomy and the Inexhaustible Will of Kitsch," *Zeitschrift für Kunstgeschichte* 63, no. 1 (2000): 47–88. Luxury was much discussed in this period in conjunction with store windows, generally in relation to women's fashion. Another interesting discussion by Simmons considers the rise of luxury as evidenced in display windows in the context of Ernst Ludwig Kirchner's Berlin street scenes, in "Ernst Kirchner's Streetwalkers: Art, Luxury, and Immorality in Berlin, 1913–16," *Art Bulletin* 82, no. 1 (March 2000): 117–48. Useful period discussions on techniques and theories of the display window include Erich Vogeler, "Schaufenster: Nach dem Berliner Wettbewerb," *Der Kunstwart* 23, no. 5 (December 1909): 358–59; August Endell, "Ladeneinrichtungen," *Jahrbuch des Deutschen Werkbundes* (Berlin: Gebr. Mann Verlag, 1913), 55–58; and Osthaus, "Das Schaufenster," 59–69.

52. "Elektrische Weihnachtsgeschenke," 178.

53. Robert Breuer, "Peter Behrens und die Elektrizität," *Deutsche Kunst und Dekoration*, 13, no. 10 (July 1910): 265.

54. Mannheimer, "Arbeiten von Professor Behrens," 124.

55. Werner Sombart, *Luxury and Capitalism* (1913), trans. W. R. Dittmar (Ann Arbor: University of Michigan Press, 1967), 59.

56. Ibid., 117.

57. Ibid., 114.

58. The store was located at 35 Elberfelderstrasse, Hagen, and destroyed during World War II. In 1913, Fritz Hoeber noted the Hagen precedence for Behrens's AEG stores in *Peter Behrens*, 155. The plans were completed by December 1905, and construction took place during 1906–7; see letters published in Herta Hesse-Frielinghaus, *Peter Behrens und Karl Ernst Osthaus: Eine Dokumentation nach den Beständen des Osthaus-Archivs* (Hagen: Karl-Ernst-Osthaus-Museum, 1966), 6. The store is just one of a number of notable buildings that Behrens designed in Hagen in this period, including the Eduard-Müller crematorium (1905–8) and three houses at "Villa Colony," an artists' colony above the city center (Cuno House: 1907–11; Schroeder House: 1907–9; and the Goedecke House 1910–12). Hagen was an important locus for modern architectural commissions in this period owing to the patronage and influence of banker and prominent member of the Werkbund, Karl Ernst Osthaus. Two Osthaus-sponsored commissions include the founding of the Deutsches Museum für Kunst in Handel und Gewerbe and the Museum Folkwang, with interiors designed by Henry van de Velde in 1901–2, for which Behrens designed the lecture hall in 1904–5. For Osthaus's involvement with the Deutsches Museum für Kunst in Handel und Gewerbe, as well as the role of the museum in promoting modern German architecture, see *Moderne Baukunst 1900–1914: Die Photosammlung des Deutschen Museums für Kunst in Handel und Gewerbe* (Oberhausen: Plitt Druck-und Verlag, 1993). See also Birgit Schulte, "Karl Ernst Osthaus, Folkwang and the 'Hagener Impuls': Transcending the Walls of the Museum," *Journal of the History of Collections* 21, no. 2 (2009): 213–20.

59. Hoeber, *Peter Behrens*, 69.

60. Osthaus, "Das Schaufenster," 66–67.

61. See Janet Ward, *Weimar Surfaces: Urban Visual Culture in 1920s Germany* (Berkeley: University of California Press, 2001).

62. As shown in the widely circulated photographs taken for the traveling exhibition *Moderne Baukunst* of modern German architecture organized by the Deutsches Museum für Kunst in Handel und Gewerbe. For photographs, see *Moderne Baukunst 1900–1914*, 106.

63. Modern architects rarely employed wallpaper in their own design work, but they were commissioned to design it for noted firms, as well on their own initiative in the case of the Bauhaus's (under the directorship of Hannes Meyer) very successful—remuneratively and in sheer quantity sold—series of wallpapers, manufactured by Rasch GmbH & Co. beginning in 1930, and Le Corbusier's wallpaper, manufactured by Salubra starting in 1931. Beginning around 1906 and continuing until at least 1912, thus spanning his tenure at the AEG, Behrens designed several wallpapers for the firm Ernst Schütz AG, which were produced by Anhalter Tapeten-Fabrik. See Sabine Röder and Gerhard Storck, eds., *Das Schöne und der Alltag: Deutsches Museum für Kunst in Handel und Gewerbe, Moderne Formgebung 1900–1914* (Hagen: Snoeck-Ducaju & Zoon, 1997), 267.

64. More widely known as "Anker-Marke," the official name of the company was Delmenhorster Linoleumfabrik AG, for which an anchor was the trademark. For more information on Behrens's work for Anker-Marke, especially the circumstances of his pavilion commission and the relationship between the linoleum company and the Werkbund, see Matthew Jefferies, "The Werkbund

in Delmenhorst: A Forgotten Episode in German Design History," *Journal of Design History* 7, no. 1 (1994): 13–27.

65. In an advertisement for the linoleum, Behrens is not noted as the designer—a situation similar to that at the AEG, in which the design, presumably, was to stand on its own merits and was not marketed using the famous designer's name. For reproductions of the linoleum patterns and advertisement, see Röder and Storck, *Das Schöne und der Alltag*, 84–85.

66. For an image of Peter Behrens's letterhead of 1905–6, see Röder and Storck, eds., *Das Schöne und der Alltag*, 226.

67. Jaumann, "Neues von Peter Behrens," 354.

68. See "Im Passagekaufhaus," *Mitteilungen der Berliner Elektricitäts-Werke* 4, no. 12 (December 1908): 185.

69. Although Behrens did not envision a similar solution for the AEG's retail needs, he, like other architects of his period, considered the Wertheim department store in Berlin by Alfred Messel to be an example of monumental modern building. See Peter Behrens, "Alfred Messel: Ein Nachruf," *Frankfurter Zeitung*, April 6, 1909, reproduced in Hoeber, *Peter Behrens*, 225. The period literature on German department stores is extensive; see esp. Göhre, *Das Warenhaus*; Leo Colze [pseud. Leo Cohn], *Berliner Warenhäuser* (1908; reprint, Berlin: Fannei & Walz Verlag, 1989); Hans Schliepmann, *Geschäfts- und Warenhäuser*, 2 vols. (Berlin: G. J. Göschen'sche Verlagshandlung, 1913); and *Wertheim Berlin*, Sonderdruck aus dem Archiv für Industrie und Handel (Berlin: Adolf Ecksteins Verlag, [1927]). For contemporary scholarship, see Peter Stürzebecher, *Das Berliner Warenhaus: Bautypus, Element der Stadtorganisation, Raumsphäre der Warenwelt* (Berlin: Archibook-Verlag, 1979); Helmut Frei, *Tempel der Kauflust: Eine Geschichte der Warenhauskultur* (Leipzig: Edition Leipzig, 1997); Geoffrey Crossick and Serge Jaumain, eds. *Cathedrals of Consumption: The European Department Store, 1850–1939* (Aldershot, UK: Ashgate, 1999); Detlef Briesen, *Warenhaus, Massenkonsum und Sozialmoral: Zur Geschichte der Konsumkritik im 20. Jahrhundert* (Frankfurt am Main: Campus Verlag, 2001); Alarich Rooch, *Zwischen Museum und Warenhaus: Ästhetisierungsprozesse und sozial-kommunikative Raumaneignungen des Bürgertums (1823–1920)* (Oberhausen: Athena Verlag, 2001); Helen Shiner, "Embodying the Spirit of the Metropolis: The Warenhaus Wertheim, Berlin, 1896–1904," in *Modernism and the Spirit of the City*, ed. Iain Boyd Whyte (London: Routledge, 2003), 97–118; and Robert Habel, *Alfred Messels Wertheimbauten in Berlin: Der Beginn der Modernen Architektur in Deutschland* (Berlin: Gebr. Mann Verlag, 2009).

70. Göhre, *Das Warenhaus*, 37. This slim book was vol. 12 of a widely printed series, Die Gesellschaft, which featured the work of many other leading period critics and academics, including *Der Architekt* by Karl Scheffler, *Das Proletariat* by Werner Sombart, and *Die Religion* by Georg Simmel. The title page and endpaper for the series were designed by Behrens.

71. Göhre, *Das Warenhaus*, 91.

72. Ibid.

73. Colze, *Berliner Warenhäuser*, 12.

74. Ibid., 11.

75. As noted in 1907 by Göhre, *Das Warenhaus*, 37. The sales techniques of Berlin department stores were similar to those employed by others throughout Europe, including the introduction of fixed prices, specific items not marked

up to lure consumers in, tempting displays of items to be bought on a whim, eye-catching displays, and multiple sales counters. See Meredith L. Clausen, "The Department Store: Development of the Type," *Journal of Architectural Education* 39, no. 1 (Autumn 1985): 20–29.

76. For an invaluable guide to designs by Behrens, see the "Catalog of Works" section in Buddensieg, *Industriekultur*.

77. The collection of advertisements in the AEG archives located at the Technical Museum, Berlin, demonstrate the immense number of anonymously designed objects produced at the AEG during Behrens's tenure.

78. "August 1906," *Mitteilungen der Berliner Elektricitäts-Werke* 2, no. 11 (August 1906): 162.

79. Hoeber, *Peter Behrens*, 103.

80. As reported in 1908–9; see Jaumann, "Neues von Peter Behrens," 353.

81. As revealed in a thorough search of the AEG archive, the *AEG Zeitung* and bound collections of previously loose materials (consisting of ephemera such as flyers, brochures, and advertisements) now at the Berlin Technical Museum. Secondary literature on Behrens has featured a single advertisement for teakettles that does feature Behrens's name, but this exemplar, often republished, is not representative of AEG advertising materials of this period.

82. "Die Ausstellung der AEG, Königgrätzerstrasse," 34.

83. Stanford Anderson established Behrens's role as one concerned with visual improvements, with engineers providing the technical expertise. For a thorough discussion on the design changes made by Behrens to AEG objects and an overall examination of Behrens's approach to industrial design, including his belief in a modern *Kunstwollen*, the use of *Tektonik* as a concept to establish a relationship between form and technical considerations, and *Stereotomie* and his opposition to Semper, see chap. 6, "Industrial Design, a Strategy for Uniting Technology and Art: Berlin II," in Anderson, *Peter Behrens and a New Architecture for the Twentieth Century*, 113–28.

84. Peter Behrens, text of lecture published in *AEG-Zeitung* 11, no. 12 (June 1909): 5–7 (translation in Buddensieg, *Industriekultur*, 208–9). Tombac is a brass alloy containing copper and zinc that results in a rich, coppery-colored metal.

85. "Neue Bogenlampen Ausstattungen," *Mitteilungen der Berliner Elektricitäts-Werke* 4, no. 3 (March 1908): 41.

86. Ibid., 44.

87. Mannheimer, "Arbeiten von Professor Behrens," 137.

88. Lecture by Behrens, cited in 1913 by Hoeber, *Peter Behrens*, 103.

89. Hoeber, *Peter Behrens*, 103.

90. "Die Ausstellung der AEG, Königgrätzerstrasse," 34.

91. For a discussion of the growth of the electrical industry and its cultural ramifications for Berlin, see Hughes, *Networks of Power*; and Andreas Killen, *Berlin Electropolis: Shock, Nerves, and German Modernity* (Berkeley: University of California Press, 2006).

92. Schwartz, *The Werkbund*.

93. See Ward, *Weimar Surfaces*.

CHAPTER 2: OBJECTIVITY

1. *Neue Sachlichkeit*, sometimes translated as "New Objectivity," was a term given to the new realism and purportedly factual observations represented in art and architecture in 1920s Germany. The term refers to an interest in a cool examination of the present and the minimal necessities needed for life, which manifest themselves in stripped-down interiors and objects devoid of unnecessary elements and decoration. Recent scholars such as Rosemarie Bletter prefer to translate *Sachlichkeit* as "matter-of-factness," "objectivity," and "the simple, practical, straightforward solution to a problem." See Rosemarie Haag Bletter, introduction to Adolf Behne, *The Modern Functional Building* (Santa Monica, CA: Getty Research Institute for the History of Art and the Humanities, 1996), 48–61. Scholarly discourse on *Neue Sachlichkeit* is extensive; for those examples most relevant to art, design, and architecture, see Stephanie Barron and Sabine Eckmann, eds., *New Objectivity: Modern German Art in the Weimar Republic 1919–1933* (Munich: Prestel, 2015); Janet Ward, *Weimar Surfaces: Urban Visual Culture in 1920s Germany* (Berkeley: University of California Press, 2001); Frederic J. Schwartz, "Form Follows Fetish: Adolf Behne and the Problem of *Sachlichkeit*," *Oxford Art Journal* 21, no. 2 (1998): 45–77; Sabine Hake, *Topographies of Class: Modern Architecture and Mass Society in Weimar Berlin* (Ann Arbor: University of Michigan Press, 2008); Helmut Lethen, *Neue Sachlichkeit, 1924–1932: Studien zur Literatur des "Weissen Sozialismus"* (Stuttgart: Metzler, 1970); Steve Plumb, *Neue Sachlichkeit 1918–33: Unity and Diversity of an Art Movement* (Amsterdam: Rodopi, 2006).

2. The foremost source on the German Werkbund is Frederic J. Schwartz, *The Werkbund* (New Haven, CT: Yale University Press, 1996); see also Winfried Nerdinger, ed., *100 Jahre Deutscher Werkbund 1907–2007* (Munich: Prestel, 2007); John V. Maciuika, *Before the Bauhaus: Architecture, Politics and the German State, 1890–1919* (New York: Cambridge University Press, 2005); Ot Hoffmann, ed., *Der Deutsche Werkbund, 1907, 1947, 1987* (Frankfurt: Deutscher Werkbund; Berlin: W. Ernst, 1987); Kurt Junghanns, *Der Deutsche Werkbund: Sein erstes Jahrzehnt* (Berlin: Henschelverlag: Vertrieb Elefanten Press, 1982); Joan Campbell, *The German Werkbund: The Politics of Reform in the Applied Arts* (Princeton, NJ: Princeton University Press, 1978); Landesgruppe Hessen, ed. *50 Jahre Deutscher Werkbund* (Frankfurt am Main: A. Metzner, 1958). For the Werkbund display window, see esp. Frederic Schwartz's *The Werkbund*, "Production and Visual Form," 96–105. See also Charlotte Klonk, "Patterns of Attention: From Shop Windows to Gallery Rooms in Early Twentieth-Century Berlin," *Art History* 28, no. 4 (September 2005): 468–96 and Klonk, chap. 3, "Exteriority and Exhibition Spaces in Weimar Germany," *Spaces of Experience: Art Gallery Interiors from 1800–2000* (New Haven, CT: Yale University Press, 2009), 87–133; Silke Strempel, "Karl Ernst Osthaus: Förderer der künstlerischen Schaufenstergestaltung" in *Deutsches Museum für Kunst in Handel und Gewerbe 1909–1919*, ed. Kaiser Wilhelm Museum Krefeld and Karl Ernst Osthaus-Museum der Stadt Hagen (Antwerp: Pandora, 1997), 390–399; Nina Schleif, *SchaufensterKunst: Berlin und New York* (Cologne: Böhlau Verlag, 2004); Lauren Kogod, "The Display Window as Educator: The German Werkbund and Cultural Economy," in *Architecture and Capitalism: 1845 to the Present*, ed. Peggy Deamer (New York: Routledge, 2014), 50–68; Sherwin Simmons, "August Macke's Shoppers: Commodity Aesthetics, Modernist Autonomy and the Inexhaustible Will of Kitsch," *Zeitschrift für Kunstgeschichte* 63, no. 1 (2000): 47–88.

3. See Karin Kirsch, *The Weissenhofsiedlung: Experimental Housing Built for the Deutscher Werkbund, Stuttgart, 1927* (New York: Rizzoli, 1989).

4. The eclectic interior that was struck through on the advertising poster was the living room of German composer Richard Strauss. "Ludwig Mies van der Rohe in Conversation with H T Cadbury-Brown," *AA Files*, no. 66 (2013): 72.

5. Schwartz, *The Werkbund.*

6. Ibid.

7. Along with their critique of inexpensive "sham ornament," many designers expressed concerns surrounding "truth to materials" following the industrial revolution's production of surrogate, imitative materials. The debate was particularly lively within the arts and crafts movement in England, led by William Morris, and similar issues were later reiterated by members of the Werkbund and modern architects in Germany. Hermann Muthesius, for example, railed against "irrational ornament and counterfeit material," "substitutes and simulations," calling for "inner truthfulness" and to let "every material appear in its own character." Muthesius, "The Significance of Applied Art" (1907), repr. in *The Theory of Decorative Art: An Anthology of European and American Writings, 1750–1940,* ed. Isabelle Frank (New Haven, CT: Yale University Press, 2000), 77.

8. Dürerbund-Werkbund Genossenschaft Dresden-Hellerau, ed. *Deutsches Warenbuch* (Leipzig: F. A. Brockhaus, 1915). See also Heide Rezepa-Zabel, *Deutsches Warenbuch—Reprint und Dokumentation: Gediegenes Gerät fürs Haus* (Berlin: Reimer, 2005); and Brigitte Kuntzsch, "'Steigerung der deutschen Qualitätsarbeit': Deutsches Warenbuch 1915," in *100 Jahre Deutscher Werkbund 1907–2007,* ed. Winfried Nerdinger (Munich: Prestel, 2007), 75–76.

9. Theodor Heuss, "Haus Werkbund," *Frankfurter Messe-Zeitung,* May 14, 1921; and Heuss, "Wertarbeit und Messe," *Die Hilfe,* October 15, 1921, 461–62. Cited by Campbell, *The German Werkbund,* 152.

10. Campbell, *The German Werkbund,* 152.

11. For an overview of the advertising program of the Bahlsen Company, which produced Leibniz Keks and other baked goods, see Reiner Meyer, "Die Reklamekunst der Keksfabrik Bahlsen in Hannover von 1889–1945" (Ph.D. diss., Georg-August-Universität zu Göttingen, 1999).

12. Erich Vogeler, "Schaufenster: Nach dem Berliner Wettbewerb," *Der Kunstwart* 23, no. 5 (December 1909): 359.

13. For an in-depth discussion of the Wertheim store, see Helen Shiner, "Embodying the Spirit of the Metropolis: The Warenhaus Wertheim, Berlin, 1896–1904" in *Modernism and the Spirit of the City,* ed. Iain Boyd Whyte (Abingdon: Routledge, 2003), 97–118.

14. On the architectural, urbanistic, and economic significance of the rise of the department store in Germany, see Kathleen James, *Erich Mendelsohn and the Architecture of German Modernism* (Cambridge: Cambridge University Press, 1997); and James, "From Messel to Mendelsohn: German Department Store Architecture in Defense of Urban and Economic Change," in *Cathedrals of Consumption: The European Department Store 1850–1939,* ed. Geoffrey Crossick and Serge Jumain (Farnham: Ashgate, 1999), 252–78. See also Tim Coles, "Department Stores as Retail Innovation in Germany: A Historical-Geographical Perspective on the Period 1870–1914," in *Cathedrals of Consumption,* 72–96; and Alarich Rooch, "Warenhäuser: Inszenierungsräume der Konsumkultur von der Jahrhundertwende bis 1930," in *Bürgertum und Bürgerlichkeit: Zwischen Kaiserreich und Nationalsozialismus,* ed. Werner Plumpe and Jörg Lesczenski (Mainz: P. Von Zabern, 2009), 17–30.

15. The Werkbund's ideas of display has been gleaned from many of its key sources from the period, for instance, from articles such as Karl Ernst Osthaus's 1913 essay "Das Schaufenster," accompanied by photographic reproductions of ideal windows in the Werkbund's own journal *Jahrbuch des Deutschen Werkbundes,* which often featured designs by Werkbund members, such as Lilly Reich's apothecary window. Other modes of promotion included pamphlets and guides on window display design written by Werkbund members who were also instructors on the topic, such as Else Oppler-Legband and Elisabeth von Stephani-Hahn. Ideal display windows were also featured at exhibitions mounted by the Werkbund, all to be discussed here.

16. Hans Bode, *Ein Schaufensterbilderbuch* (Hanover: S. Hein, 1926), 91.

17. Albert Walter, *Das Schaufenster und sein Schmuck: Ein kurzer Leitfaden für die Praxis* (Leipzig: G.A. Gloeckner, 1916), 43. The author then points out how misguided this type of display is, in that the public was not to buy an airship or the Eiffel tower, but rather the handkerchief.

18. Karl Ernst Osthaus, "Das Schaufenster," in *Die Kunst in Industrie und Handel, Jahrbuch des Deutschen Werkbundes* (Jena: Eugen Diederichs, 1913), 62. On Osthaus's shop window essay, see also Schwartz, *The Werkbund,* 168–73; Klonk, "Patterns of Attention," 473–74; Strempel, "Karl Ernst Osthaus" in *Deutsches Museum,* 390–99. For a translated excerpt, see Lauren Kogod, "The Display Window as Educator," in *Architecture and Capitalism,* ed. Peggy Deamer (London: Routledge, 2013), 62–67.

19. Osthaus, "Das Schaufenster," 63.

20. Alfred Wiener, "Das Warenhaus," *Jahrbuch des Deutschen Werkbundes* (Jena: Eugen Diederichs, 1913), 49.

21. Wiener, "Das Warenhaus," 50.

22. Letter, Mies to Adam firm, July 1928, quoted by Adrian Sudhalter, "S. Adam Department Store Project, Berlin-Mitte, 1928–29," in *Mies in Berlin,* ed. Terence Riley and Barry Bergdoll (New York: Museum of Modern Art, 2001), 230.

23. See esp. *Die Kunst in Industrie und Handel, Jahrbuch des Deutschen Werkbundes* (Jena: Eugen Diederichs, 1913), which featured important articles on various aspects of selling goods in different architectural contexts, and on various scales. Key texts include August Endell on "Ladeneinrichtungen" (55–58) and Karl Ernst Osthaus on "Das Schaufenster" (59–69), and many pages of images (93–108).

24. August Endell, "Ladeneinrichtungen," *Jahrbuch des Deutschen Werkbundes* (Jena: Eugen Diederichs, 1913): 55–58.

25. Ibid., 56.

26. Ibid.

27. For the five Berlin stores, see the photo section of *Jahrbuch des Deutschen Werkbundes* (Jena: Eugen Diederichs, 1913).

28. Prices cited by Simmons, "August Macke's Shoppers," 56.

29. For a period overview and reception of the 1914 Werkbund exhibition in Cologne, see Carl Rehorst, "Die Deutsche Werkbund-Ausstellung Köln 1914," *Die Kunst in Industrie und Handel, Jahrbuch des Deutschen Werkbundes* (Jena: Eugen Diederichs, 1913), 86–96; *Offizieller Katalog, Deutsche Werkbund Ausstellung Cöln 1914* (Cologne: Verlag von Rudolf Mosse, 1914); *Deutsche Form im Kriegsjahr: Die Ausstellung Köln 1914, Jahrbuch des Deutschen Werkbundes* (Munich: F. Bruckmann A.-G., 1915); Walter Curt Behrendt, "Die Deutsche Werkbund-Ausstellung in Köln," *Kunst und Künstler* 22 (1914): 615–26; C. H. Whitaker "Work-Pleasure:

The Remarkable Exhibition at Cologne," *American Institute of Architects Journal* 2 (1914): 420–32; Theodor Heuss, "Der Werkbund in Köln," *März* 8, no. 2 (1914): 907–13; Ernst Jäckh, "Deutsche Werkbundausstellung in Köln," parts 1 and 2, *Kunstwart und Kulturwart* 27, no. 18 (1914): 404–14 and no. 20 (1914): 137–40; Robert Breuer, "Die Kölner Werkbund-Ausstellung, Mai–Oktober 1914," *Deutsche Kunst und Dekoration* 34, no. 12 (September 1914): 417–36. More recently, see Wulf Herzogenrath, Dirk Teuber, and Angelika Thiekötter, eds., *Der Westdeutsche Impuls 1900–1914: Kunst und Umweltgestaltung im Industriegebiet, Die Deutsche Werkbund-Ausstellung, Cöln 1914* (Cologne: Kölnischer Kunstverein, 1984); Wulf Herzogenrath, ed. *Frühe Kölner Kunstausstellungen: Sonderbund 1912, Werkbund 1914, Pressa USSR 1928: Kommentarband zu den Nachdrucken der Ausstellungskataloge* (Cologne: Wienand, 1981), 37–67; Campbell, *The German Werkbund*, 57–81; and Maciuika, *Before the Bauhaus*, 248–82. On the relationship of the shop window to the theater, see Katherine M. Kuenzli, "Architecture, Individualism, and Nation: Henry van de Velde's 1914 Werkbund Theater Building," *Art Bulletin* 94, no. 2 (June 2012): 251–73, esp. 265–66.

30. On the role gender played in Werkbund discourse and design, see Despina Stratigakos, "Women and the Werkbund: Gender Politics and German Design Reform, 1907–14," *Journal of the Society of Architectural Historians* 62, no. 4 (December 2003): 490–511; Stratigakos, *A Women's Berlin: Building the Modern City* (Minneapolis: University of Minnesota Press, 2008). On the Werkbund and class, the desire to grow a stable and responsible bourgeoisie, and political aspects of the period's reforms and aesthetic turn leading up to—and around the time of—the Werkbund's formation, see Mark Jarzombek, "The Discourses of a Bourgeois Utopia, 1904–1908, and the Founding of the Werkbund," in Francoise Forster-Hahn, ed., *Imagining Modern German Culture: 1889–1910*, Studies in the History of Art, no. 53 (Washington, DC: National Gallery of Art, 1996): 126–45; and Jarzombek, "The Kunstgewerbe, the Werkbund, and the Aesthetics of Culture in the Wilhelmine Period," *Journal of the Society of Architectural Historians* 53, no. 1 (March 1994): 7–19.

31. See Heinrich Behr, "Deutsche Werkbund-Ausstellung in Cöln," *Baugewerks-Zeitung* 46 (1914): 429. See also Strempel, "Karl Ernst Osthaus," in *Deutsches Museum*, 396–99; Helga Kerp, "Die Ladenstrasse," in *Der Westdeutsche Impuls 1900–1914: Kunst und Umweltgestaltung im Industriegebiet, Die Deutsche Werkbund-Ausstellung, Cöln 1914*, ed. Wulf Herzogenrath, Dirk Teuber, and Angelika Thiekötter (Cologne: Kölnischer Kunstverein, 1984), 213–15.

32. Rehorst, "Die Deutsche Werkbund-Ausstellung Köln 1914," 91.

33. Ibid., 91–92.

34. Letter, Karl Ernst Osthaus to Oswin Hempel, July 18, 1913, Osthaus-Archiv, DWK/100, cited by Kerp, "Die Ladenstrasse," in *Der Westdeutsche Impuls 1900–1914*, 215.

35. Letter, Karl Ernst Osthaus to Carl Rehorst, January 13, 1914, Osthaus-Archiv, DWK/177, cited by Kerp, "Die Ladenstrasse," in *Der Westdeutsche Impuls 1900–1914*, 215.

36. Ibid.

37. *Offizieller Katalog, Deutsche Werkbund Ausstellung Cöln 1914*, 209–10.

38. Ibid., 208.

39. Heuss, "Der Werkbund in Köln," cited by Campbell, *The German Werkbund*, 73.

40. Georg Jacob Wolf, "Der Deutsche Werkbund und die Werkbund-Ausstellung in Köln," *Dekorative Kunst* 17, no. 12 (September 1914): 548.

41. Adolf Behne, *Wiederkehr der Kunst* (Leipzig: Kurt Wolff Verlag, 1919), 54.

42. Breuer, "Die Kölner Werkbund-Ausstellung, Mai–Oktober 1914," 427–30.

43. Wolf, "Der Deutsche Werkbund und die Werkbund-Ausstellung in Köln," 546.

44. Ibid., 546–47.

45. Peter Jessen, "Die Deutsche Werkbund-Ausstellung Köln 1914" in *Deutsche Form im Kriegsjahr: Die Ausstellung Köln 1914* (Berlin: Gebr. Mann Verlag, 1912), 32–33.

46. Lilly Reich's "Vitrinengang" formed an internal street of vitrines resembling shop windows along a central corridor of the Haus der Frau. See numbers 14 and 15 of the plan of the Haus der Frau in *Offizieller Katalog, Deutsche Werkbund Ausstellung Cöln 1914*, 198. For a thorough discussion of the Haus der Frau, see Stratigakos, "Women and the Werkbund," 490–511.

47. *Offizieller Katalog, Deutsche Werkbund Ausstellung Cöln 1914*, 199.

48. See Ludwig Hilberseimer, *Grosstadtarchitektur* (Stuttgart: J. Hoffmann, 1927); Richard Anderson, ed., *Metropolisarchitecture and Selected Essays* (New York: GSAPP Books, 2012); James, *Erich Mendelsohn and the Architecture of German Modernism*.

49. Ward, *Weimar Surfaces*, 201.

50. Schwartz, *The Werkbund*, esp. 192–212; and Schwartz, "Commodity Signs: Peter Behrens, the AEG, and the Trademark," *Journal of Design History* 9, no. 3 (1996): 153–84.

51. Peter Bruckmann, "Marke und Zwischenhandel," in *Die Kunst in Industrie und Handel, Jahrbuch des Deutschen Werkbundes* (Jena: Eugen Diederichs, 1913): 77–78.

52. Bruckmann, "Marke und Zwischenhandel," 77.

53. *H. Bahlsens Keks-Fabrik: Geschenk-Packungen und Schaufenster-Dekorationen* (Hanover: H. Bahlsens Keksfabrik, 1912), n.p.

54. Ibid.

55. Ibid. This was not an innovative idea. Albert Walter, author of the 1916 book *Das Schaufenster und sein Schmuck* [The display window and its decoration], 91, notes the predominance of manufacturers' loaning, selling at cost, or giving away display stands and other materials, as well as templates of display ideas, to retailers in order to best display their wares.

56. *Krauss Schaufensterbuch: Anregungen und Vorschläge* (Schwarzenberg: Verlag der Krausswerke, 1926), n.p.

57. Ibid.

58. Ibid.

59. Ibid.

60. Hans Meyer, "Grundsätze neuzeitlichen Ladenbaus," *Mitteilungen des Deutschen Werkbundes*, no. 2 (May 28, 1924): 6.

61. Gerta-Elisabeth Thiele, "Das Schaufenster," *Die Form* (1926): 146.

62. Osthaus, "Das Schaufenster," 69.

63. Else Oppler-Legband, "Die Höhere Fachschule für Dekorationskunst," in *Die Durchgeistigung der deutschen Arbeit: Ein Bericht vom Deutschen Werkbund*, ed. Deutscher Werkbund (Jena: Eugen Diederichs, 1911), 51.

64. Ibid.

65. Elisabeth von Stephani-Hahn, *Schaufensterkunst* (Berlin: Verlag L. Schottlaender, 1919 edition), 7. In the Wilhelmine period, the author published as "Hahn-Stephani," and later, in the Weimar period, reversed the order of her hyphenated last name to "Stephani-Hahn."

66. Ibid.

67. Ibid.

68. Marquitta Müller, "Dekoration des Schaufensters," *Zeit im Bild* 11 (September 3, 1913): 2432.

69. Stephani-Hahn, *Schaufensterkunst,* 1919 edition, 52.

70. Stephani-Hahn, *Schaufensterkunst*, 1926 edition, 126.

71. Marie Heller, "Die Frau in Beruf," *Die Deutsche Frau* 2, no. 14 (April 6, 1912): 2. Cited by Despina Stratigakos, "Skirts and Scaffolding: Women Architects, Gender, and Design in Wilhelmine Germany" (Ph.D. diss., Bryn Mawr College, 1999), 200n20.

72. Ernst Bloch, "Berlin nach zwei Jahren," *Die Weltbühne* 24, no. 1 (January 3, 1928): 32, trans. and repr. as "Berlin after Two Years," in *Metropolis Berlin: 1880–1940*, ed. Iain Boyd Whyte and David Frisby, trans. David Britt (Berkeley: University of California Press, 2012), 380.

73. Meyer, "Grundsätze neuzeitlichen Ladenbaus," 6.

74. P. Wagener, "Kunstgewerbler oder Berufsdekorateur," *Schaufensterkunst und -Technik* 2, no. 2 (November 1926): 14.

75. Peter Jessen, "Der Werkbund und die Grossmächte der Deutschen Arbeit," *Jahrbuch des Deutschen Werkbundes, 1912: Die Durchgeistung der deutschen Arbeit* (Jena: Eugen Diederichs, 1912), 7–8.

76. Ward, "The Display Window," in *Weimar Surfaces*, 200.

77. Deutscher Werkbund, "Bericht der Geschäftsstelle zur Vorstands- und Ausschusssitzung am 23. und 24. März 1910 in Berlin, Hotel Excelsior," March 23–24, 1910, 7 (Werkbund Archive D673, from Karl-Ernst-Osthaus Archiv, DWB1/43).

78. Ibid.

79. Jessen, "Der Werkbund und die Grossmächte der Deutschen Arbeit," 7.

80. Hermann Muthesius, "Die Notwendigkeit der Geschmacksbildung für den deutschen Kaufmann," *Jahresberichte DWB* (1909): 22–25.

81. Elisabeth von Hahn-Stephani, "Die Kunst der Schaufensterdekoration," in *Was die Frau von Berlin wissen muss* (Berlin: Herbert Loesdau, 1913), 273.

82. Naumann poses two general questions asserting the place of the Werkbund: "What does the Werkbund have to do with trade? Counterquestion: is there anything that doesn't have to do with trade?" Friedrich Naumann, "Werkbund und Handel," *Die Kunst in Industrie und Handel, Jahrbuch des Deutschen Werkbundes* (Jena: Eugen Diederichs, 1913): 5.

83. Ibid.

84. Ibid., 13.

85. Ibid.

86. Erich Vogeler, "Schaufenster: Nach dem Berliner Wettbewerb," *Der Kunstwart* 23, no. 5 (December 1909): 360–61.

87. Naumann, "Werkbund und Handel," 14. This idea of manifestly not displaying all the types of wares that the store had to offer, but rather reducing the number of articles in the window and changing that selection often, in order to entice shoppers from the street across the store's threshold would be repeated in later general guides of the decoration of windows. See, for example, Walter, *Das Schaufenster und sein Schmuck*, 42. On the other hand, Walter also warns against

too few articles in a large display window, what he termed an "artistic emptiness" (*künstlerische Leere*), which merely provokes yawns by the bored passerby (ibid.).

88. Naumann, "Werkbund und Handel," 14.

89. Ibid., 15.

90. Hermann Muthesius, "Wo stehen wir?" *Jahrbuch des Deutschen Werkbundes* (Jena: Eugen Diederichs, 1912): 19.

91. See also Leslie Topp, *Architecture and Truth in Fin-de-Siècle Vienna* (Cambridge: Cambridge University Press, 2004).

92. Osthaus, "Das Schaufenster," 61.

93. Stephani-Hahn, *Schaufensterkunst*, 1919 edition, 19.

94. See Lilly Reich, "Modefragen," *Die Form* 1, no. 5 (1922): 7–9; Robin Schuldenfrei, "Introduction" to the translation of Reich's essay, "Questions of Fashion," in *West 86th: A Journal of Decorative Arts, Design History and Material Culture* 21, no. 1 (Spring–Summer 2014): 102–20.

95. The Schule für Schaufensterdekoration or, as it was officially called, the Höhere Fachschule für Dekorationskunst, opened May 1, 1910, with the Werkbund supporting it with 300 marks, as announced in advance by the Deutscher Werkbund, "Bericht der Geschäftsstelle zur Vorstands- und Ausschusssitzung am 23. und 24. März 1910 in Berlin, Hotel Excelsior," 23–24 March 1910, 8–9 (Werkbund Archive D673, from Karl-Ernst-Osthaus Archiv, DWB1/43).

96. Stratigakos, *A Women's Berlin*, 107.

97. Ernst Jäckh, "6. Jahresbericht des Deutschen Werkbundes 1913/1914," *Jahrbuch des Deutschen Werkbundes* (Jena: Eugen Diederichs, 1914), 99.

98. Georg Fischer, "Höhere Fachschule für Dekorationskunst, Werkstatt für Praktisches Dekorieren," *Farbe und Form* 12, Sonderband (April 1, 1927), 137.

99. Jäckh, "6. Jahresbericht des Deutschen Werkbundes 1913/1914": 98.

100. Albert Reimann, "25 Jahre Schule Reimann, 1902–1927," special issue, *Farbe und Form* 12 (April 1, 1927): 16.

101. Albert Reimann, *Die Reimann-Schule in Berlin* (Berlin: Verlag Bruno Hessling, 1966), 59.

102. Bund der Schaufensterdekorateure Deutschlands, Staatliche Akademie für graphische Künste und Buchgewerbe Leipzig.

103. Olaf Thormann et al., eds. *125 Jahre Museum für Kunsthandwerk Leipzig / Grassimuseum: Die Museumschronik von den Anfängen bis zum Jahr 1929* (Leipzig: Passage-Verlag, 2003), 195.

104. *Leipziger Neueste Nachrichten*, October 14, 1928, quoted by Thormann et al., *125 Jahre Museum für Kunsthandwerk Leipzig / Grassimuseum*, 195.

105. Osthaus, "Das Schaufenster," 61.

106. Ibid., 64.

107. Ibid., 67.

108. Stephani-Hahn, *Schaufensterkunst*, 1919 edition, 19.

109. Osthaus, "Das Schaufenster," 64–65.

110. Stephani-Hahn, *Schaufensterkunst*, 1919 edition, 11–12.

111. Müller, "Dekoration des Schaufensters," 2430–32.

112. Oppler-Legband, "Die Höhere Fachschule für Dekorationskunst," 52.

113. Many examples of the *Stapelfenster* as a window display typology can be found in the period literature, see, for example, Werkbund member (whose book reproduces many of the Werkbund *Jahrbuch* images of ideal display windows) Stephani-Hahn, *Schaufensterkunst*, 1919 edition, 21–32; Hans Bode, *Das wirksame Schaufenster* (Hanover: S. Hein, 1925), 64–65, 74–75, 96–97; Bode,

Ein Schaufensterbilderbuch, 13–17; Bruno H. Jahn, *Reklame durch das Schaufenster* (Berlin: Verlag L. Schottlaender, 1926), 69; Fritz Ackermann, *Bessere Hausrat-Schaufenster—Steigende Umsätze* (Berlin: Hausrat-Verlags, 1930), 166.

114. Bode, *Ein Schaufensterbilderbuch*, 13–17; Bode, *Das wirksame Schaufenster*, 97.

115. For a discussion of the two versions of this photomontage, see Elizabeth Otto, *Tempo! Tempo! The Bauhaus Photomontages of Marianne Brandt* (Berlin: Jovis Verlag, 2005), 80–83; and Magdalena Droste and Jeannine Fiedler, eds., *Experiment Bauhaus: Das Bauhaus-Archiv, Berlin (West) zu Gast im Bauhaus Dessau* (Berlin: Kupfergraben, 1988), 226–27.

116. On the machine, nature, and *Sachlichkeit* in Weimar photography, see Pepper Stetler, "Man and Machine," in *New Objectivity: Modern German Art in the Weimar Republic 1919–1933*, ed. Stephanie Barron and Sabine Eckmann (Munich: Prestel, 2015), 203–27; and Stetler, "The Object, the Archive and the Origins of *Neue Sachlichkeit* Photography," *History of Photography* 35, no. 3 (August 2011): 281–95.

117. Kurt Wilhelm-Kästner, "Fotografie der Gegenwart: Grundsätzliches zur Ausstellung im Museum Folkwang Essen," *Photographische Rundschau und Mitteilungen* 66, no. 5 (1929): 93–94. Quoted and translated by Stetler, "Man and Machine," 208.

118. See, for example, his thoughts on *Neue Sachlichkeit* photography in Walter Benjamin, "Little History of Photography" (1931), in *Walter Benjamin: Selected Writings; Volume 2, Part 2, 1931–1934*, ed. Michael W. Jennings, Howard Eiland, and Gary Smith (Cambridge, MA: Belknap Press of Harvard University Press, 1999), 507–30. See also Stetler, "Man and Machine," 213.

119. Benjamin, "Little History of Photography," 519, 526.

120. Siegfried Kracauer, "Das Ornament der Masse," *Frankfurter Zeitung*, Feuilleton sec., June 9, 1927, parts 1–2, and *Frankfurter Zeitung*, Feuilleton sec., June 10, 1927, parts 3–6, translated as Kracauer, "The Mass Ornament," in *The Mass Ornament: Weimar Essays*, trans. and ed. Thomas Y. Levin (Cambridge, MA: Harvard University Press, 1995), 77, 81.

121. Ibid., 78.

122. Hannes Meyer, "Die neue Welt," *Das Werk* 13, no. 7 (July 1926): 216; trans. and repr. as "The New World" in *Architecture and Design: 1890–1939*, ed. Tim Benton and Charlotte Benton with Dennis Sharp (New York: Whitney Library of Design, 1975), 106–9. My reading of Meyer's *Co-op Vitrine* is significantly informed by K. Michael Hays, "*Co-op Vitrine* and the Representation of Mass Production," in *Modernism and the Posthumanist Subject: The Architecture of Hannes Meyer and Ludwig Hilberseimer* (Cambridge, MA: MIT Press, 1992), 24–53. See also Hannes Meyer, *Bauen und Gesellschaft: Schriften, Briefe, Projekte*, ed. Lena Meyer-Bergner (Dresden: Verlag der Kunst, 1980); *Hannes Meyer: Buildings, Projects and Writings*, ed. Claude Schnaidt (Stuttgart: Verlag Gerd Hatje, 1965); and Werner Möller and Tim Leik, eds., *The Co-op Principle: Hannes Meyer and the Concept of Collective Design*, trans. Rebecca Philipps Williams and Katrin Globke (Leipzig: Spector Books, 2015). The *Co-op Vitrine*, designed for an exhibition of Swiss cooperative products, was also part of a larger body of "cooperative" or "co-op" work by Meyer that included linocuts, prints, photographs, display cases, and architecture (Hays, 28, 25).

123. Möller and Leik, *The Co-op Principle*, 24–28.

124. Arieh Sharon, notes from the class "The Cooperative" with Hannes Meyer at the Bauhaus Dessau, 1927, p. 5, Bauhaus-Archiv, Berlin.

125. Ibid.

126. Meyer, "Die neue Welt," 222, trans. Benton, 108.

127. Meyer, "Die neue Welt," 221, trans. Benton, 107.

128. Möller and Leik, *The Co-op Principle*, 28–32.

129. Hays, *Modernism and the Posthumanist Subject*, 28–29, 32.

130. On production and reception, individuality versus subjectivity in Meyer, see ibid., 29–33.

131. Ibid., 45.

132. Ibid., 48–49; Georg Lukács, *History and Class Consciousness* (1923), trans. Rodney Livingstone (Cambridge, MA: MIT Press, 1971).

133. Erich Vogeler, "Schaufenster: Nach dem Berliner Wettbewerb," *Der Kunstwart* 23, no. 5 (December 1909): 360.

134. Naumann, "Werkbund und Handel," 5.

135. Osthaus, "Das Schaufenster," 69. On the related topic of women, shopping, and the modern city, esp. on themes of vision and control, see Charlotte Wildman, "'For Profit or Pleasure': New Cultures of Retail, Shopping and Consumer Culture," in *Urban Redevelopment and Modernity in Liverpool and Manchester, 1918–1939* (London: Bloomsbury, 2016); Anne Friedberg, "The Gender of the Observer: The Flâneuse," in *Window Shopping: Cinema and the Postmodern* (Berkeley: University of California Press, 1993), 32–38; and Jessica Sewell, "Errands," in *Women and the Everyday City: Public Space in San Francisco, 1890–1915* (Minneapolis: University of Minnesota Press, 2011), 25–65.

136. Curt Gravenkamp, "Mies van der Rohe: Glashaus in Berlin (Projekt Adam, 1928)," *Das Kunstblatt* (April 1930): 111–12, quoted and trans. in Franz Schulze and Edward Windhorst, *Mies van der Rohe: A Critical Biography* (Chicago: University of Chicago Press, 2012), 113.

137. On lighting and modern architecture, see Werner Oechslin, "Light Architecture: A New Term's Genesis," in *Architecture of the Night: The Illuminated Building*, ed. Dietrich Neumann (Munich: Prestel, 2002), 28–35; Dietrich Neumann, "*Lichtarchitektur* and the Avant-Garde," in ibid., 36–53; Marion Ackermann and Dietrich Neumann, eds., *Luminous Buildings: Night Architecture* (Ostfildern: Hatje Cantz, 2006); and Paul Monty Paret, "Berlin in Light: Wilhelmine Monuments and Weimar Mass Culture," in *Spectacle*, ed. Jennifer L. Creech and Thomas O. Haakenson, German Visual Culture, no. 2 (Bern: Peter Lang, 2015), 101–27.

138. Bloch, "Berlin nach zwei Jahren," 380.

139. Karl Scheffler, *Berlin: Wandlungen einer Stadt* (Berlin: Cassirer, 1931), 185–87, trans. Whyte, "Berlin: A City Transformed," in *Metropolis Berlin: 1880–1940*, 396.

140. Meyer, "Die neue Welt," 222, trans. Benton, 106, 108.

141. "Der Neue Baustil und die Reklame," *Schaufensterkunst und -Technik* 4, no. 3 (December 1928): 28.

142. Max Landsberg, "Lichtreklame im Stadtbild" *Der Städtebau* 22, no. 3 (1927): 35. Cited by Oechslin, "Light Architecture," in *Architecture of the Night*, 32.

143. Gerta-Elisabeth Thiele, "Der Einfluss Neuzeitlicher Architektur auf das Schaufenster," *Farbe und Form* 13, nos. 10–11 (October–November 1928): 184–85.

144. P. Martell, "Schaufenster und Werbekunst," *Schaufensterkunst und -Technik* 1, no. 11 (August 1926): 19–20. See also the section on "Die Beleuchtung des Firmenschildes" (The illumination of company signs) in Ackermann, *Bessere Hausrat-Schaufenster—Steigende Umsätze*, 208–12.

145. James, *Erich Mendelsohn and the Architecture of German Modernism*, 141.

146. Thiele, "Der Einfluss Neuzeitlicher Architektur auf das Schaufenster," 186.

147. James, *Erich Mendelsohn and the Architecture of German Modernism*, 142.

148. *Lichtreklame und Schaufensterbeleuchtung* (Basel: Gewerbe-Museum Basel, 1928). The period was awash in instruction, both technical and artistic in nature, on the effective night illumination of display windows; a sampling includes Walter, *Das Schaufenster und sein Schmuck*, 19–32; Bode, *Das wirksame Schaufenster*, 18–28; Jahn, *Reklame durch das Schaufenster*, 103–32; J. Guanter, "Lichtreklame: Grundsätzliche und die wichtigsten Arten," in *Lichtreklame und Schaufensterbeleuchtung* (Basel: Gewerbe-Museum Basel, 1928), 21–27; H. Sieber, "Moderne Lichtreklame," in ibid., 28–35; Ackermann, *Bessere Hausrat-Schaufenster—Steigende Umsätze*, 179–94; and Richard Müncheberg, *Wie mach ich's? Erprobte Tips für Schaufenster und Laden* (Berlin: Otto Elsner, 1933), 44–49. For lighting more generally in the period—from modern domestic lamps, to street lighting and advertising signage, to the illumination of display windows and buildings—see the Werkbund publication, Wilhelm Lotz et al., eds., *Licht und Beleuchtung: Lichttechnische Fragen unter Berücksichtigung der Bedürfnisse der Architektur* (Berlin: Verlag Hermann Reckendorf, 1928).

149. Martell, "Schaufenster und Werbekunst," 19–20.

150. Stephani-Hahn, *Schaufensterkunst*, 1919 edition, 121–25.

151. Walter, *Das Schaufenster und sein Schmuck*, 26.

152. Stephani-Hahn, *Schaufensterkunst*, 1919 edition, 121, 123.

153. Jahn, *Reklame durch das Schaufenster*, 108–9.

154. Wilhelm Theodor Schnarrenberger, "Reklame Architekturbildend," *Die Form*, vol. 3, no. 9 (September 1928): 268–72. See also general instruction on the placement of firms' names on storefronts, modern typefaces and layout of signage, and effective angles between the store's facade and the pedestrians on the street, in sources such as Müncheberg, *Wie mach ich's? Erprobte Tips für Schaufenster und Laden*, 18–23.

155. Schnarrenberger, "Reklame Architekturbildend," image on 269. For a separate, but typical, discussion of the renovation of shops, including the installation of modern signage to unify the street facade, see Bode, *Das wirksame Schaufenster*, 7–10.

156. Schnarrenberger, "Reklame Architekturbildend," 269–71.

157. *Moderne Ladenbauten: Aussen- und Innenarchitektur* (Berlin: Ernst Pollak Verlag, 1928), facing 106.

158. E. Wedepohl, "Ladenumbauten," *Schaufensterkunst und -Technik* 3, no. 9 (June 1928): 20–23.

159. For practical suggestions for improvements, see, for example, Walter, *Das Schaufenster und sein Schmuck*, 11–17; Jahn, *Reklame durch das Schaufenster*, 34–38; Ackermann, *Bessere Hausrat-Schaufenster—Steigende Umsätze*, 18–25;

Müncheberg, *Wie mach ich's? Erprobte Tips für Schaufenster und Laden*, 8–14.

160. Josef Albers, "Zum Entwurf für einen Ladenumbau," *Offset, Buch und Werbekunst* 7 (1926): 401. See also Ute Brüning, ed., *Das A und O des Bauhauses: Bauhauswerbung, Schriftbilder, Drucksachen, Ausstellungsdesign* (Berlin: Bauhaus-Archiv, 1995), 180, 309.

161. Albers, "Zum Entwurf für einen Ladenumbau," 401.

162. Ibid.

163. For an important discussion of Macke's subject matter with regard to the display window at the intersection of mass culture and modernism, see Simmons, "August Macke's Shoppers," 47–88. See also Sherwin Simmons, "Luxus, Mode, Unsittlichkeit," in *Der Potsdamer Platz: Ernst Ludwig Kirchner und der Untergang Preussens*, ed. Katharina Henkel and Roland März (Berlin: G+H Verlag; SMPK, Nationalgalerie Berlin, 2001), 129–36. For a full discussion of Kirchner's urban street scenes, see Deborah Wye, *Kirchner and the Berlin Street* (New York: Museum of Modern Art, 2008). Other key discussions of Kirchner's Berlin include Simmons, "Ernst Kirchner's Streetwalkers: Art, Luxury, and Immorality in Berlin, 1913–16," *Art Bulletin* 82, no. 1 (March 2000): 117–48; Charles W. Haxthausen, "'A New Beauty': Ernst Ludwig Kirchner's Images of Berlin," in *Berlin: Culture and Metropolis*, ed. Charles W. Haxthausen and Heidrun Suhr (Minneapolis: University of Minnesota Press, 1990), 58–94; Katarina Sykora, *Weiblichkeit, Grossstadt, Moderne: Ernst Ludwig Kirchners Berliner Strassenszenen, 1913–1915* (Berlin: Museumspädagogischer Dienst Berlin, 1996); and Magdalena M. Moeller, *Ernst Ludwig Kirchner: Die Strassenszenen, 1913–1915* (Munich: Hirmer, 1993).

164. Campbell, *The German Werkbund*, 40–41.

165. For a thorough discussion of theories of display, of commodities, and of (mass) consumer desire in relation to 1920s Berlin shop windows, see Ward, *Weimar Surfaces*, 191–240.

CHAPTER 3: CAPITAL

1. Gropius to Hildebrandt, undated (presumably September 1919), cited in Reginald Isaacs, *Gropius: An Illustrated Biography of the Creator of the Bauhaus* (Boston: Little, Brown, 1991), 83. Translation amended.

2. Oskar Schlemmer, "The Staatliche Bauhaus in Weimar" (1923), in Hans M. Wingler, *The Bauhaus: Weimar, Dessau, Berlin, Chicago*, trans. Wolfgang Jabs and Basil Gilbert (Cambridge, MA: MIT Press, 1969), 65–66.

3. For architecture at the Bauhaus, see esp. Kathleen James-Chakraborty, "Henry van de Velde and Walter Gropius: Between Avoidance and Imitation," in *Bauhaus Culture: From Weimar to the Cold War*, ed. Kathleen James-Chakraborty (Minneapolis: University of Minnesota Press, 2006), 26–42; Wallis Miller, "Architecture, Building, and the Bauhaus," in ibid., 63–89; Barry Bergdoll, "Bauhaus Multiplied: Paradoxes of Architecture and Design in and after the Bauhaus," in *Bauhaus 1919–1933: Workshops for Modernity*, ed. Barry Bergdoll and Leah Dickerman (New York: Museum of Modern Art, 2009), 40–61; Klaus-Jürgen Winkler, *Die Architektur am Bauhaus in Weimar* (Berlin: Verlag für Bauwesen, 1993); Winkler, "Das Staatliche Bauhaus und die Negation der klassischen Tradition in der Baukunst," in *Klassik und Avantgarde: Das Bauhaus in Weimar*

1919–1925, ed. Hellmut Th. Seemann and Thorsten Valk (Göttingen: Wallstein Verlag, 2009), 261–84. For the Haus am Horn, see in particular Adolf Meyer, ed., *Ein Versuchshaus des Bauhauses in Weimar* (Munich: Albert Langen Verlag, 1925); Winfried Nerdinger, "Project: Bauhaus Housing Development 'Am Horn,' Weimar," in *The Walter Gropius Archive: Volume 1*, ed. Winfried Nerdinger (New York: Garland Publishing, 1990), 53–55; Freundeskreis der Bauhaus-Universität Weimar e. V., ed., *Haus am Horn: Rekonstruktion einer Utopie* (Weimar: Verlag der Bauhaus-Universität Weimar, 2000); and Karin Wilhelm, "Typing and Standardization for a Modern Atrium House: The Haus am Horn in Weimar," in *Bauhaus: A Conceptual Model*, ed. Bauhaus-Archiv Berlin/Museum für Gestaltung, Stiftung Bauhaus Dessau, and Klassik Stiftung Weimar (Ostfildern: Hatje Cantz, 2009), 149–52.

4. Michael Siebenbrodt, ed., *Bauhaus Weimar: Designs for the Future* (Ostfildern-Ruit: Hatje Cantz Verlag, 2000), 9.

5. Gropius, "Recommendations for the Founding of an Educational Institution as an Artistic Counseling Service for Industry, the Trades, and the Crafts," January 25, 1916, in Wingler, *The Bauhaus*, 23.

6. Walter Gropius, "The Development of Modern Industrial Architecture" (1913), repr. in Tim Benton and Charlotte Benton with Dennis Sharp, eds., *Architecture and Design, 1890–1939* (New York: Whitney Library of Design, 1975), 53.

7. Peter Fritzsche, "Landscape of Danger, Landscape of Design," in *Dancing on the Volcano: Essays on the Culture of the Weimar Republic*, ed. Thomas W. Kniesche and Stephen Brockmann (Columbia, SC: Camden House, 1994), 38.

8. On changes in Gropius's architecture following his return from the war, and the early beginnings of the Bauhaus, see Wolfgang Pehnt, "Gropius the Romantic," *Art Bulletin* 53, no. 3 (September 1971): 379–92.

9. It should be noted that this is a later pronouncement; Gropius was remembering back to the formation of the Bauhaus in a letter to Tomás Maldonado, dated November 10, 1964, repr. in Jeannine Fiedler and Peter Feierabend, eds., *Bauhaus* (Cologne: Könemann, 1999), 22.

10. Walter Gropius to Karl Ernst Osthaus, December 23, 1918, Berlin, repr. in Frank Whitford, ed., *The Bauhaus: Masters and Students by Themselves* (London: Conran Octopus, 1992), 25. Gropius had conceived of the Bauhaus, yet not worked through the specific details, including the final choice of a name; here he still refers to a *Bauhütte*, or medieval guild. This letter also underscores the way in which Gropius was aware of the precarious economic situation and the care with which he needed to approach the authorities, given the uncertainty of the period.

11. Gropius, *Ausstellung für unbekannte Architekten* (1919), quoted in Iain Boyd Whyte, *Bruno Taut and the Architecture of Activism* (Cambridge: Cambridge University Press, 1982), 131.

12. Gropius, speech to students of the Bauhaus, spring 1919, repr. in Whitford, *The Bauhaus*, 49.

13. The merger was not entirely smooth. After a period of unrest and divisiveness among the former fine arts students who failed to embrace Gropius's ideal of artists working harmoniously with craftsmen, in September 1920, twenty-eight students left the Bauhaus to join the State School of Art under painting instructor Max Thedy, which opened in April 1921, taking away facilities and funding from the Bauhaus.

14. "Admittance as apprentice will be granted to any person regardless of age or sex, whose talent and previous education are deemed sufficient by the Council of Masters." Statutes of the Staatliche Bauhaus in Weimar, pamphlet, January 1921, in Wingler, *The Bauhaus*, 44.

15. See Celina Kress, *Adolf Sommerfeld / Andrew Sommerfield: Bauen für Berlin 1910–1970* (Berlin: Lukas Verlag, 2011); Bergdoll, "Bauhaus Multiplied," 43–45; Kathleen James-Chakraborty, "Expression and Experiment: The Sommerfeld House" in *Bauhaus: A Conceptual Model*, 51–54; Winfried Nerdinger, *Walter Gropius* (Berlin: Gebr. Mann Verlag, 1985), 44–45; Karin Wilhelm, "Adolf Sommerfeld," *Bauwelt* 77, no. 34 (1986): 1258–67; Wolfgang Pehnt, "Gropius the Romantic," *Art Bulletin* 53, no. 3 (September 1971): 379–92.

16. Gropius, "Neues Bauen," *Der Holzbau*, supplement to the *Deutsche Bauzeitung* (1920–21), quoted by Pehnt, "Gropius the Romantic," 384.

17. Gropius, "Wohnhaus-Industrie," in Meyer, *Ein Versuchshaus des Bauhauses in Weimar*, 8–9.

18. Winkler, "Das Staatliche Bauhaus," 270.

19. Fred Forbát, "Erinnerungen eines Architekten aus vier Ländern" (1969), Fred Forbát Nachlass, Bauhaus-Archiv, Berlin (hereafter BHA), 67–68, trans. in Nerdinger, *Walter Gropius*, 58.

20. Gropius, "Wohnhaus-Industrie," in Meyer, *Ein Versuchshaus des Bauhauses in Weimar*, 8.

21. Gropius, "Wer hat Recht? Traditionelle Baukunst oder Bauen in neuen Formen," *Uhu* 7 (April 1926): 30–40, trans. in *The Weimar Republic Sourcebook*, ed. Anton Kaes, Martin Jay, and Edward Dimendberg (Berkeley: University of California Press, 1994), 441.

22. The Bauhaus Siedlung GmbH is alternatively listed in archival documents as "Bauhaussiedlung GmbH" and "Bauhaus-Siedlungsgenossenschaft" and appears as "Bauhaus-Siedlung" on the company stamp. See "Vorbereitung und Durchführung von Arbeiten am Siedlungsgelände am Horn," July 20, 1923, Thüringisches Hauptstaatsarchiv Weimar (hereafter ThHStAW). The Bauhaus GmbH was formed in 1924 for the development of Bauhaus products, while the Bauhaus-Verlag GmbH was conceived and registered as a publishing venture, also in 1924.

23. See "Gründung und Hauptversammlungen sowie Aufsichtsrats- und Vorstandssitzungen der Bauhaus-Siedlung e. GmbH," ThHStAW; Satzungen der Bauhaus Siedlung GmbH, April 13, 1921, p. 1, BHA.

24. Umlauf an die Meister, October 1 and November 11, 1920, ThHStAW.

25. Gropius to Finanzministerium, Staatsrat Palm, June 29, 1921, ThHStAW.

26. Bauhaus to Thüringische Finanzministerium Weimar, June 29, 1922, ThHStAW.

27. Forbát, "Erinnerungen," 67–68, trans. in Nerdinger, *Walter Gropius*, 58.

28. Ibid. They encountered difficulties, however, with the building authorities because of the flat roof designs.

29. Landtag von Thüringen, 1922, p. 841, ThHStAW, trans. in Klaus-Jürgen Winkler, ed., *Bauhaus-Alben 4: Bauhausausstellung, Haus am Horn, Architektur, Bühne, Druckerei* (Weimar: Verlag der Bauhaus-Universität Weimar, 2009), 20. The sum was 2 million marks given on August 23, 1922, and intended for the "Produktivbetrieb"

of the Bauhaus workshops. See letter, Thüringisches Ministerium für Volksbildung to Bauhaus, June 29, 1922, ThHStAW.

30. Winkler, *Bauhaus-Alben 4*, 20.

31. Kaes et al., *Weimar Republic Sourcebook*, 60–61.

32. Gropius, "Proposed Budget for the Art Academy and the School of Arts and Crafts in Weimar 1919–1920," February 28, 1919, in Wingler, *The Bauhaus*, 26.

33. Schlemmer to Otto Meyer, December 19, 1922, *The Letters and Diaries of Oskar Schlemmer*, ed. Tut Schlemmer, trans. Krishna Winston (Evanston, IL: Northwestern University Press, 1990), 136.

34. "Planung einer Bauhausausstellung für 1922 und Vorbereitung der Bauhausausstellung im Sommer 1923," November 23, 1922, ThHStAW.

35. Correspondence in the ThHStAW reveals that the Bauhaus paid the Reichsbahn for posters to be mounted on trains and in stations.

36. Sitzung des Meisterrates, March 24, 1922, ThHStAW, in Volker Wahl, ed., *Die Meisterratsprotokolle des Staatlichen Bauhauses Weimar 1919–1925* (Weimar: Böhlaus Nachfolger, 2001), 158.

37. Meeting minutes, September 15, 1922, ThHStAW, in Wahl, *Meisterratsprotokolle*, 235, 283.

38. All quotes in bold in original. Advertising leaflet announcing exhibition, Bauhaus Ausstellung Weimar, 1923, BHA.

39. "Protokoll der Sitzung—Entwurf," October 18, 1923, ThHStAW, in Wahl, *Meisterratsprotokolle*, 313.

40. Meeting minutes and supporting documents, September 15, 1922, ThHStAW, in Wahl, *Meisterratsprotokolle*, 235.

41. Information sheet with statement (verso), perspective drawing, plan, and Bauhaus seal, for the Haus am Horn exhibition house, 1923, BHA.

42. On the dressing table, see also Lutz Schöbe, "'Liberated Combing' at Modernism's Vanity Table: The Lady's Dressing Table by Marcel Breuer," in *Bauhaus: A Conceptual Model*, 162–64.

43. See Barbara Happe, "Farbigkeit," in *Haus am Horn: Rekonstruktion einer Utopie*, 36–46.

44. "Preise der Einrichtungs-Gegenstände im Wohnhaus am Horn," BHA. Following the show, efforts to swiftly sell the house and its contents failed, and by default they became the property of Adolf Sommerfeld, who had the contents shipped to Berlin. Their whereabouts have since then been unknown. See Winkler, *Bauhaus-Alben 4*, 90.

45. Meyer, *Ein Versuchshaus des Bauhauses in Weimar*, 49.

46. Ibid., 63.

47. "Waschanlage im Keller des Hauses am Horn," BHA.

48. "Einrichtungsgegenstände des Hauses am Horn," BHA.

49. "Haus-Telefonanlage im Hause am Horn," BHA.

50. Westheim, "Bemerkungen: Zur Quadratur des Bauhauses" *Das Kunstblatt* 7, no. 10 (October 1923): 320.

51. One exception to this pattern was the exterior wall construction, which utilized insulation between cinder blocks that were then uniformly plastered over, and the roof, which was made of hollow ceramic bricks in reinforced concrete; about these genuinely practical material and construction innovations, the Bauhaus announced that the 25 cm–thick wall boasted as much insulation against heat and cold as a 75 cm–thick brick wall and that the central heating system accordingly saved the equivalent of 4,200 kilos of coke annually. Josef

Albers, "Werkstatt-Arbeiten des Staatlichen Bauhauses zu Weimar," *Neue Frauenkleidung und Frauenkultur* 21 (1925): 1–2. A pamphlet for Torfoleum, the insulation material used, in a nod to the times noted "an urgent imperative in this time of economic need" (Leaflet for Torfoleum, firm of Eduard Dyckerhoff, 1924; repr. in *Haus am Horn: Rekonstruktion einer Utopie*, 34).

52. For costs and correspondence with the firms supplying materials and products to the Haus am Horn, see "Vorbereitung und Bau des Musterwohnhauses am Horn für die Bauhausausstellung im Sommer 1923," ThHStAW.

53. It is important to note that the goods were not donated to the Haus am Horn; letters in the BHA document various firms' attempts in trying to recuperate costs and collect payment from the Bauhaus, and in some cases, in a last desperate attempt, items were repossessed.

54. See "Technische Ausführung" and "Bauhaus Werkstätten" in Meyer, *Ein Versuchshaus des Bauhauses in Weimar*, 25–78. Although the presentation of the wares from the Bauhaus's own workshops was in the same straightforward format as the corporate goods, the Bauhaus objects, which were mostly of wood, appear very craft-orientated and individualistic (such as Marcel Breuer's women's dressing table, 75–76) in comparison with the very industrial-looking outside products.

55. Bauhaus secretary Weidler to the exhibition committee, "Planung einer Bauhausausstellung für 1922 und Vorbereitung der Bauhausausstellung im Sommer 1923," May 17, 1923, ThHStAW.

56. Kaes et al., *Weimar Republic Sourcebook*, 60.

57. For further discussion, see Nele Heise, "Das Bauhaus in allen Taschen," *Bauhaus-kommunikation: Innovative Strategien im Umgang mit Medien, Interner und Externer Öffentlichkeit*, ed. Patrick Rössler (Berlin: Gebr. Mann Verlag, 2009), 265–80.

58. See "Bauhausausstellung, Musterwohnhaus und andere Ausstellungen," ThHStAW.

59. "Aktennotiz," March 19, 1923, BHA. Benscheidt first committed 500,000 marks, then gave another million. Benscheidt to Gropius, January 19 and April 6, 1923, ThHStAW.

60. "Finanzierung der Bauhausausstellung im Sommer 1923 und des Baues des Musterwohnhauses," April 6, 1923, ThHStAW. Sommerfeld would continue to financially support the house.

61. Emil Lange to Hermann Lange, August 4, 1923, ThHStAW.

62. Cited by Winkler, *Architektur am Bauhaus*, 98.

63. Emil Lange to Sommerfeld, September 4, 1923, p. 4, BHA.

64. Emil Lange, "Sachlage auf das Schreiben Sommerfelds vom 8. Mai 1923," May 15, 1923, BHA.

65. Gropius to Baer (lawyer), March 6, 1923, pp. 1–2, BHA.

66. Gropius to Baer, March 10, 1923, pp. 3–4, BHA.

67. These were the terms for most firms; see, for example, Bauhaus to Firma B. Harrass GmbH, June 26, 1923, BHA.

68. "Verkaufsbedingungen für die ausgestellten Werkstättenerzeugnisse und Bilder der Ausstellung," 1923, BHA.

69. Gropius cites a letter from the Verein Deutscher Spiegelglasfabriken in Cologne to lawyer Baer, March 10, 1923, pp. 2–3, BHA.

70. See, for example, letters from the purveyor of the house's boiler and the radiators to Gropius: J. Lastin and M. Külzow to Gropius, May 18, 1923, BHA.

71. Postcard notice, Ruberoidwerke Aktien Gesellschaft to Sommerfeld, November 10, 1923, BHA.

72. Schlemmer to Otto Meyer, December 7, 1921, *Letters and Diaries*, 114.

73. Schlemmer, diary entry, November 1922, *Letters and Diaries*, 135.

74. Muche, "Das Versuchshaus des Bauhauses," in Meyer, *Ein Versuchshaus des Bauhauses in Weimar*, 17.

75. Gropius, "Wer hat Recht?," trans. in Kaes et al., *Weimar Republic Sourcebook*, 441.

76. Although it was not published until 1935, the manuscript dates from 1925. Walter Gropius, *The New Architecture and the Bauhaus*, trans. P. Morton Shand (1935; repr., Cambridge, MA: MIT Press, 1965), 89–90.

77. Meyer, "Schön, neu und zweckmässig: Zur Bauhausausstellung in Weimar im August 1923," *Fachblatt für Holzarbeiten* (1923): 165.

78. B.A., *Das Volk*, September 27, 1923.

79. Adolf Behne, "Das Musterhaus der Bauhausausstellung," *Die Bauwelt* 14, no. 41 (October 11, 1923): 591–92.

80. Adolf Behne, "Das Bauhaus Weimar," *Die Weltbühne* 19, no. 38 (September 20, 1923): 291, trans. in Rosemarie Haag Bletter, "Introduction," in Adolf Behne, *The Modern Functional Building*, trans. Michael Robinson (Santa Monica, CA: Getty Research Center for the History of Art and the Humanities, 1996), 31. Translation amended.

81. M. [Ernst May], "Bauhaus-Ausstellung in Weimar," *Schlesisches Heim* 4, nos. 8–9 (1923): 195.

82. Wilhelm Limper, *Kölnische Volkszeitung*, August 30, 1923.

83. Sommerfeld to Gropius, May 8, 1923, p. 2, BHA.

84. Sommerfeld to Gropius, September 17, 1923, BHA.

85. Fritz Wichert, "Ein Haus, das Sehnsucht weckt," *Frankfurter Zeitung*, October 10, 1923.

86. G. Fischer, "Streife nach dem Positiven, Epilog zur Weimarer Bauhauswoche," *Berliner Börsen-Courier*, August 26, 1923.

CHAPTER 4: PRODUCTION

1. For related discussion of these concerns, see esp. Frederic J. Schwartz, "Utopia for Sale: The Bauhaus and Weimar Germany's Consumer Culture," in *Bauhaus Culture: From Weimar to the Cold War*, ed. Kathleen James-Chakraborty (Minneapolis: University of Minnesota Press, 2006),115–38; and Anna Rowland, "Business Management at the Weimar Bauhaus," *Journal of Design History* 1, nos. 3–4 (1988): 153–75. See also Regina Bittner, "The Bauhaus on the Market: On the Difficult Relationship between the Bauhaus and Consumer Culture," in *Bauhaus: A Conceptual Model*, ed. Bauhaus-Archiv Berlin/Museum für Gestaltung, Stiftung Bauhaus Dessau, and Klassik Stiftung Weimar (Ostfildern: Hatje Cantz, 2009), 331–36.

2. When Benjamin makes his famous proclamation, "What withers in the age of the technological reproducibility of the work of art is the latter's aura," he immediately follows it with: "This process is symptomatic; its significance *extends far beyond the realm of art*." Walter Benjamin, "The Work of Art in the Age of Its Technological Reproducibility," in *Walter Benjamin: Selected Writings; Volume 3, 1935–1938*, ed. Howard Eiland and Michael W. Jennings (Cambridge, MA: Belknap Press of Harvard University Press, 2002), 104, emphasis added. Benjamin composed this essay in the autumn of 1935; the version used here is the 1936 second version, which the

editors note represents the form in which Benjamin originally wished to see the work published. A third, revised version remained unfinished at Benjamin's death and was published posthumously. See also Benjamin, *The Work of Art in the Age of Its Technological Reproducibility, and Other Writings on Media*, ed. Michael W. Jennings, Brigid Doherty, and Thomas Y. Levin (Cambridge, MA: Belknap Press of Harvard University Press, 2008). He begins his essay, in a similar vein, with Marx, noting that it "has taken more than half a century for the change in the *conditions of production* to be manifested in *all areas of culture*" (101, emphasis added). Therein, Benjamin largely discusses this process as it manifests itself in images and film. However, it is clear throughout that the significance of the phenomena he explicates is not limited to these areas of culture alone; Benjamin also specifically addresses architecture, literature, medicine, music, and coins. Moreover, he uses a number of different terms to refer to his subject, not only "artwork" (*Kunstwerk*) but also "object of art" (*Gegenstand der Kunst*), "object" (*Objekt*), and "thing" (*Sache*)—all of which have been predominantly translated as "artwork," perhaps contributing to a common perception that Benjamin is only talking about the visual arts.

The distinct importance of architecture at a late stage in Benjamin's discussion—which brings it into particular proximity with film and makes "the laws of its reception … the most instructive" in relation to new forms of mass participation in art—lies in the fact that buildings are received in a twofold manner: by perception and by use (120). The significance of Benjamin's essay for understanding the problem of the reproducibility of Bauhaus objects hangs precisely on the potential for technologically reproducible objects to make themselves available for mass use.

On reproduction and reproduction in architecture and art, see Beatriz Colomina, ed., *Architectureproduction* (New York: Princeton Architectural Press, 1988), esp. K. Michael Hays, "Reproduction and Negation: The Cognitive Project of the Avant-Garde," 153–79; Charles W. Haxthausen, "Reproduction/Repetition: Walter Benjamin/Carl Einstein," *October* 107, no. 47 (Winter 2004): 47–74; and Esther Leslie, "Walter Benjamin: Traces of Craft," *Journal of Design History* 11, no. 1 (1998): 5–13. For contacts between—and influence on—Walter Benjamin by Moholy-Nagy during his years at the Bauhaus, see "Walter Benjamin and the Avant-Garde," in Frederic J. Schwartz, *Blind Spots: Critical Theory and the History of Art in Twentieth-Century Germany* (New Haven, CT: Yale University Press, 2005), esp. 42–50.

In other writings, Benjamin devotes sustained attention to domestic objects as part of the same constellation of themes also found in the "Work of Art" essay. See, for example, "Louis-Philippe, or the Interior," sec. 4, "Paris, Capital of the Nineteenth Century," in *Walter Benjamin: Selected Writings; Volume 3, 1935–1938*, ed. Eiland and Jennings, 38–39; and June 8 entry in "May–June 1931," in *Walter Benjamin: Selected Writings; Volume 2, Part 2, 1931–1934*, ed. Michael W. Jennings, Howard Eiland, and Gary Smith (Cambridge, MA: Belknap Press of Harvard University Press, 1999), 479–80.

3. Again, *Sachlichkeit* presents difficulties in translation; it could be translated as "factualness" or "objectiveness." As Rosemarie Bletter has pointed out, the term simultaneously suggests the "world of real objects" and that of "conceptual rationalism." See Bletter, introduction to Adolf Behne, *The Modern Functional Building* (Santa Monica, CA: Getty

Research Institute for the History of Art and the Humanities, 1996), 48.

4. A version of MT 49 was later available from the Bauhaus in brass or red brass with a silver-plated interior and a silver strainer, but it was not among the chosen objects featured in the *Katalog der Muster*. Klaus Weber, curator at the Bauhaus-Archiv / Museum für Gestaltung, notes that there are presently only seven known period examples of this teapot (correspondence with author, March 9, 2009).

5. This was also the case for the other objects featured in the Bauhaus catalog, as well as for the overwhelming majority of the products of the Bauhaus in this period.

6. Walter Gropius, "Bauhaus Produktion," *Qualität* 4, nos. 7–8 (July–August 1925): 130. Translation from a nearly identical version of the essay in Hans Maria Wingler, *The Bauhaus: Weimar, Dessau, Berlin, Chicago*, trans. Wolfgang Jabs and Basil Gilbert, ed. Joseph Stein (Cambridge, MA: MIT Press, 1976), 110. Gropius continued to recall this purpose long after leaving: "The creation of standard types for the articles of daily use was their main concern. These workshops were essentially laboratories in which the models for such products were carefully evolved and constantly improved." Walter Gropius, "Education toward Creative Design," *American Architect and Architecture* (May 1937): 28.

7. For invaluable research on the entire span of production in the Bauhaus's metal workshops and their main artisans, see Klaus Weber, ed., *Die Metallwerkstatt am Bauhaus* (Berlin: Kupfergraben Verlagsgesellschaft, 1992).

8. The 1915 Werkbund *Warenbuch* [Book of wares] was a selection of domestic German goods that met the Werkbund's design standards. See Heide Rezepa-Zabel, *Deutsches Warenbuch Reprint und Dokumentation: Gediegenes Gerät fürs Haus* (Berlin: Dietrich Reimer, 2005).

9. Benjamin, "The Work of Art," 104–6.

10. *Die Lebenshaltung von 2,000 Arbeiter-, Angestellten-, und Beamten-Haushaltungen: Erhebungen von Wirtschaftsrechnungen im Deutschen Reich vom Jahre 1927–1928*, Einzelschriften zur Statistik des deutschen Reichs, no. 22 (Berlin: R. Hobbing, 1932). Specific industries paid significantly less; for example, a male spinner in the textile industry earned 44 marks per week in 1927, while a female spinner earned 28 marks per week, and unskilled workers earned even less. Statistischen Reichsamt, *Statistisches Jahrbuch für das Deutsche Reich* (Berlin: Verlag von Reimar Hobbing, 1930). For the day-to-day struggle to live on this wage, see Deutscher Textilarbeiterverband, ed., *Mein Arbeitstag, Mein Wochenende: 150 Berichte von Textilarbeiterinnen* (Berlin: Textilpraxis Verlag, 1930), 187–89; and "Die Misere des 'neuen Mittelstands,'" *Die Weltbühne* 24, no. 4 (January 22, 1929): 130–34.

11. Standard-Möbel catalog, 1927, n.p., BHA.

12. Otto Rittweger, *Vivos Voco* 5, nos. 8–9 (1926): 293–94; translated in Bruno Pedretti, ed., *Posthumous Works Designed while Living: Metallwerkstatt Bauhaus 20's/90's* (Milan: Electa, 1995), 34–35.

13. *Die Grundstücks- und Wohnungsaufnahme sowie die Volks-, Berufs- und Betriebszahlung in Berlin im Jahre 1925* (Berlin, 1928), table 8; quoted in Nicholas Bullock, "First the Kitchen: Then the Façade," *Journal of Design History* 1, nos. 3–4 (1988): 188.

14. For example, see Dr. Necker and Walter Gropius, "Bericht über die wirtschaftlichen Aussichten des Bauhauses," October 19, 1924, typed manuscript, pp. 1–2, BHA.

15. Anne Bobzin and Klaus Weber, *Das Bauhaus-Schachspiel von Josef Hartwig* (BHA, 2006), 17–21.

16. Ausstellung "Die Form," 1924, exhibition checklist with prices, BHA.

17. Chess table with armchair, Bauhaus Archive object file, inv. no. 2002/55–56, BHA.

18. For example, the Czech architect and critic Karel Teige chastised the Bauhaus early on for its emphasis on the crafts: "Today, the crafts are nothing but a luxury, supported by the bourgeoisie with their individualism and snobbery and their purely decorative point of view." Karel Teige, *Stavba* (1924); translated in Herbert Bayer, Walter Gropius, and Ise Gropius, eds., *Bauhaus, 1919–1928* (New York: Museum of Modern Art, 1938; repr., Boston: Charles T. Branford Co., 1952), 91.

19. Walter Gropius, Weimar, to Staatsminister Greil, November 11, 1922, p. 2, BHA.

20. László Moholy-Nagy (presumed), "Dialogue between a Well-Meaning Critic and a Representative of the Bauhaus, Weimar-Dessau" (c. 1928), trans. in Krisztina Passuth, *Moholy-Nagy* (London: Thames and Hudson, 1985), 400. The identity of the author of this document has not been conclusively established; the document is in the possession of Moholy-Nagy's daughter, Hattula Moholy-Nagy and presumed to be written by Moholy-Nagy.

21. Ibid., 401.

22. Benjamin, "The Work of Art," 104.

23. Ibid., 102.

24. Ibid., 106.

25. See Ise Gropius, *Diary*, esp. December 1926 and early 1927, BHA.

26. Lyonel Feininger, Dessau, to Julia Feininger, October 2, 1927, Houghton Library, Harvard University, Cambridge, MA, trans. in Lyonel Feininger, *Lyonel Feininger*, ed. June L. Ness (New York: Praeger, 1974), 158.

27. Fritz Hesse, *Von der Residenz zur Bauhausstadt* (Hanover: Schmorl & von Seefeld, 1963), 238.

28. Lyonel Feininger, Dessau, to Julia Feininger, August 6, 1926, Houghton Library; trans. in Feininger, *Feininger*, 152.

29. Walter Gropius, *Bauhausbauten Dessau* (Munich: A. Langen, 1930), 112.

30. Protokoll, Sitzung der Meister und Werkstättenleiter des Staatlichen Bauhauses, April 7, 1922, Weimar, BHA; Protokoll des Bauhausrates, October 22, 1923, in Volker Wahl, ed., *Die Meisterratsprotokolle des Staatlichen Bauhauses Weimar 1919 bis 1925* (Weimar: Verlag Hermann Böhlaus Nachfolger, 2001), 319. *Produktiv-Betrieb* can also be translated as "productive company," but it is not clear from the original context if a company is specifically meant at this early date.

31. Gropius, "Bauhaus Produktion," 135; trans. in Wingler, *The Bauhaus*, 110.

32. Walter Gropius, "Education toward Creative Design," *American Architect and Architecture* 150 (May 1937): 28. Although this was written years later, it succinctly captures the direction of this period: "The aim of this training was to produce designers who were able, by their intimate knowledge of material and working processes to influence the industrial production of our time."

33. Word of mouth and personal recommendations between customers accounted for much of this small-scale work, such as a request for a silver tea caddy from Herr Architekt Bernard in December 1924 and an order from Herr

Regierungsrat Döpel in January 1925 for a silver pin "like the one the metal workshop had made for the kindergarten teachers." Rowland, "Business Management at the Weimar Bauhaus," 154.

34. The archives of the Stiftung Bauhaus Dessau hold original records, including letters, bills of sale, and drawings of commissions. Notable Dessau commissions include Erich Dieckmann's work for Hinnerk and Lou Scheper in 1925, which included chairs, stools, tables, desks, cupboards, and bookshelves; Dieckmann's designs for the home of Pauline Schwickert; and Breuer's furniture and kitchen cabinetry for the Ludwig Grote apartment at the Palais Reina in Dessau of 1927. For a full range of rare photographs of interiors, see Christian Wolsdorff, *Bauhaus-Möbel: Eine Legende wird besichtigt / Bauhaus Furniture: A Legend Reviewed* (Berlin: Bauhaus-Archiv, 2002).

35. Emil Lange to Gropius, Weimar, February 16, 1924, typescript, BHA.

36. Protokoll, Formenmeister-Besprechung, October 18, 1923, in Wahl, *Die Meisterratsprotokolle*, 319. Originally the minutes were written with "GmbH," which was then struck out and replaced with "AG," possibly indicating some question of what designation the company should have. AG, for *Aktiengesellschaft*, is a public limited company, while GmbH, or *Gesellschaft mit beschränkter Haftung*, represents a limited liability company.

37. Wahl, *Die Meisterratsprotokolle*, 520–21.

38. Protokoll der Sitzung des Bauhausrates, February 18 and 20, 1924, in Wahl, *Die Meisterratsprotokolle*, 323–24. The meeting lasted three and a half hours.

39. "Vertrag zwischen dem Bauhaus und Bauhausangehörigen," n.d., typescript, p. 1 verso, BHA. Several designers, when they left the Bauhaus, continued to fill orders for their designs personally, notably Josef Hartwig, who continued to produce his famous chess set. This document was designed to prevent this practice in the future.

40. Protokoll der Sitzung des Bauhausrates, February 18 and 20, 1924, Thüringisches Hauptstaatsarchiv Weimar. The "Work Plan of the Metal Workshop" (c. 1925–26) also codifies payment, noting that either a single-payment compensation or royalties would be paid for models used in series production (trans. in Wingler, *The Bauhaus*, 111).

41. This small catalog lacks a formal name in the literature, and even the Bauhaus Archive has not reached a consensus on what to call it. In the Bauhaus exhibition and accompanying catalog, *Das A und O des Bauhauses: Bauhauswerbung: Schriftbilder, Drucksachen, Ausstellungsdesign*, Ute Brüning refers to it as the "Katalog der Muster," while Klaus Weber in *Die Metallwerkstatt am Bauhaus* refers to it as the "Musterkatalog der Bauhausprodukte." In the period, the journal *Bauhaus* referred to a page from it as a "Prospektseite" of the Bauhaus GmbH (*Bauhaus* 1 [1926]: 6). Because the title page of the loose-leaf sheets that make up the catalog says "Katalog der Muster," that title will be used here. In English it has been translated as "Catalog of Designs" (Schwartz, "Utopia for Sale," 124) and "Bauhaus Sample Catalog" (collection accession file, Harvard Art Museum / Busch-Reisinger Museum).

42. On Lucia Moholy's Bauhaus photographs, see Robin Schuldenfrei, "Images in Exile: Lucia Moholy's Bauhaus Negatives and the Construction of the Bauhaus Legacy," *History of Photography* 37, no. 2 (May 2013): 182–203; and

Rolf Sachsse, *Lucia Moholy: Bauhaus Fotografin* (Berlin: Bauhaus-Archiv Berlin, 1995).

43. Reproduced in Wingler, *The Bauhaus*, 98–101.

44. For more on the role of trade shows in the display and sale of Bauhaus objects in the Weimar period, as well as efforts by the Bauhaus to bring early goods to market, see Rowland, "Business Management at the Weimar Bauhaus," esp. 163–67.

45. The basic plan of the Bauhaus to produce machine prototypes rather than the standard fare of a regular school of applied art was also reported in countless newspaper articles. For a typical example, see Dr. Grote, "Das Weimarer Bauhaus und seine Aufgaben in Dessau," *Anhaltische Rundschau*, March 11, 1925, 1.

46. László Moholy-Nagy, "Eine bedeutsame Aussprache: Konferenz der Vertreter des Bauhauses Dessau und des Edelmetallgewerbes am 9. März 1928 in Leipzig," *Deutsche Goldschmiede-Zeitung* 13 (1928): 123.

47. Rudolf Arnheim, "Das Bauhaus in Dessau," *Die Weltbühne* 23, no. 22 (May 31, 1927): 921, trans. in Anton Kaes, Martin Jay, and Edward Dimendberg, eds., *The Weimar Republic Sourcebook* (Berkeley: University of California Press, 1994), 451.

48. *Bauhaus* 4 (1927): 5. It was also reported that a related catalog was in production. However, this relationship appears to have been short-lived, as the lamp division folded, causing the Bauhaus to begin anew in the search for a manufacturer. See Ise Gropius, *Diary*, November 30, 1927, pp. 205–6.

49. A new contract for lighting came through in February 1928, as noted in Ise Gropius's diary (February 10, 1928, p. 224). In the July 1928 issue, *Bauhaus* announced that both lighting companies, Körting & Mathiesen and Schwintzer & Gräff, were producing Bauhaus designs. See "Industrie und Bauhaus," *Bauhaus* 2–3 (1928): 33. For a full account of the Bauhaus's relationship with Körting & Mathiesen and the line of modern lighting produced by the company from Bauhaus prototypes, see Justus Binroth et al., *Bauhausleuchten? Kandemlicht! Die Zusammenarbeit des Bauhauses mit der Leipziger Firma Kandem / Bauhaus Lighting? Kandem Light! The Collaboration of the Bauhaus with the Leipzig Company Kandem* (Leipzig: Grassi Museum, Museum für Kunsthandwerk Leipzig; Stuttgart: Arnoldsche Art Publishers, 2002). This arrangement, while fulfilling Gropius's aims for the school, did so in an anonymous manner, because except for one mention in 1931, Körting & Mathiesen did not acknowledge the association of its Kandem line with the Bauhaus until its seventy-fifth anniversary, in 1964; see Ulrich Krüger, "Leutzsch Lighting: On the Collaboration of Körting & Mathiesen AG in Leipzig-Leutzsch with the Bauhaus in Dessau," in Binroth et al., 11.

50. Christian Wolsdorff, "Bauhaus-Produkte: Zusammenarbeit mit der Industrie," in *Bauhaus Berlin: Auflösung Dessau 1932, Schliessung Berlin 1933, Bauhäusler und Drittes Reich*, ed. Peter Hahn (Weingarten: Kunstverlag Weingarten, 1985), 183. The pottery workshop also began to make contacts with—and supply models to—industry (porcelain and stoneware) but did not accompany the Bauhaus to Dessau and ceased to exist.

51. Gropius, "Bauhaus Produktion," 130, trans. in Wingler, *The Bauhaus*, 110.

52. Like *Sachlichkeit*, the term *Intellektuell-Sachliches* presents difficulties in translation; it could be translated as "intellectual factualness" or "intellectual objectiveness."

53. *Bauhaus* 1 (1926): 3.

54. Among the hundreds of photographs of Berlin interiors, both known and anonymous dwellings, at the Bildarchiv Preussischer Kulturbesitz in Berlin, there are relatively few modern interiors, and in these interiors, Bauhaus domestic objects are in scant evidence, while Breuer's tubular steel chairs and Bauhaus furniture are fairly common. For example, the Breuer-designed apartment interior for Edwin Piscator, 1927, featured Bauhaus furniture and lighting fixtures but not its other products.

55. Grete Lihotzky, "Rationalisierung im Haushalt," *Das neue Frankfurt* 5 (1926–27): 120, trans. in Kaes et al., *The Weimar Republic Sourcebook*, 463.

56. Fritz Wichert, "Ein Haus, das Sehnsucht weckt," *Frankfurter Zeitung*, October 10, 1923.

57. Benjamin, "The Work of Art," 104.

58. Gropius, "Bauhaus Produktion," 135–36, trans. in Wingler, *The Bauhaus*, 110.

59. Ibid., 136.

60. Benjamin was a member of artistic and architectural circles in Berlin and was certainly conversant with key concepts of the day. He was part of a group that met often at Hans Richter's house, which included Raoul Hausmann, Tristan Tzara, Frederick Kiesler, and Hans (Jean) Arp, which would launch the magazine *G* in 1923, led by Richter, Lissitzky, Van Doesburg, and Mies.

61. Arnd Bohm, "Artful Reproduction: Benjamin's Appropriation of Adolf Behne's 'Das reproduktive Zeitalter' in the *Kunstwerk*-Essay," *Germanic Review* 68, no. 4 (1993): 149. Cf. Adolf Behne, "Das reproduktive Zeitalter," *Marsyas* (1917): 219–25.

62. Moholy-Nagy, "Production-Reproduction," *De Stijl* 7 (1922): 97–101, trans. in Passuth, *Moholy-Nagy*, 289.

63. The slippage in this essay between the terms "mass production" and (mass) "reproduction" reflects this problem: to speak of mass production is really to speak of mass *reproduction*—as Benjamin's essay illuminates—but the standard usage of the former term highlights the tendency to conceive it in the terms of production alone.

64. Hays, "Reproduction and Negation," 163, emphasis in the original.

65. Moholy-Nagy, "Dialogue," trans. in Passuth, *Moholy-Nagy*, 400.

66. Benjamin, "The Work of Art," 106.

67. Josef Albers, "Thirteen Years at the Bauhaus," in *Bauhaus and Bauhaus People*, ed. Eckhard Neumann (New York: Van Nostrand Reinhold, 1970), 171.

CHAPTER 5: SUBJECTIVITY

1. Walter Curt Behrendt, *The Victory of the New Building Style*, trans. Harry Francis Mallgrave (Los Angeles: Getty, 2000), 129. Originally published as *Sieg des neuen Baustils* (Stuttgart: Akademischer Verlag Wedekind, 1927).

2. My thinking on Mies's materials has been very much influenced by the sustained discussions of glass, transparency, and other key period concepts in Detlef Mertins's body of work on Mies. See esp. Mertins, *Mies* (London: Phaidon, 2014); Mertins, ed., *The Presence of Mies* (New York: Princeton Architectural Press, 1994); and the collection of Mertins's essays, *Modernity Unbound: Other Histories of Architectural Modernity* (London: Architectural Association, 2011). In the vast literature on Mies, in-depth and sustained discussions of Mies's materiality are less prevalent than would be expected, and mainly directly connected to discussions of individual buildings; see Terence Riley and Barry Bergdoll, eds., *Mies in Berlin* (New York: Museum of Modern Art, 2001); Wolf Tegethoff, *Mies van der Rohe: The Villas and Country Houses*, trans. Russell M. Stockman (Cambridge, MA: MIT Press, 1985). Ignasi de Solá-Morales Rubió argues convincingly, albeit too briefly, that "Mies's work is developed, not out of images, but out of materials—materials in the strongest sense of the word, that is naturally, the matter from which objects are constructed. This matter is abstract, general, geometrically cut, smooth and polished, but it is also material that is substantial, tangible, and solid. … [T]he perceptual conditions established by the materiality of the building are at the very origins of its spiritual signification" (Solá-Morales Rubió, "Mies van der Rohe and Minimalism," in Mertins, ed., *The Presence of Mies*, 151). For particularly germane discussions of the meaning and signification of Mies's materials, see also Desley Luscombe, "Drawing the Barcelona Pavilion: Mies van der Rohe and the Implications of Perspectival Space," *Journal of Architecture* 21, no. 2 (March 2016): 210–43. From the perspective of the conservation of the Tugendhat House, see Ivo Hammer, "Materiality: History of the Tugendhat House 1997–2012, Conservation-Science Study and Restoration," in *Tugendhat House: Ludwig Mies van der Rohe*, ed. Daniela Hammer-Tugendhat, Ivo Hammer, and Wolf Tegethoff (Basel: Birkhäuser, 2015), 162–223.

3. For discussions of Reich's work, see Sonja Günther, *Lilly Reich 1885–1947: Innenarchitektin, Designerin, Austellungsgestalterin* (Stuttgart: Deutsche Verlags-Anstalt, 1988); essays by Matilda McQuaid and Magdalena Droste in McQuaid, *Lilly Reich: Designer and Architect* (New York: Museum of Modern Art, 1996); Christiane Lange, *Ludwig Mies van der Rohe & Lilly Reich: Furniture and Interiors*, trans. Allison Plath-Moseley (Ostfildern: Hatje Cantz, 2006); Robin Schuldenfrei, "Introduction to 'Lilly Reich: Questions of Fashion' (1922)," *West 86th: A Journal of Decorative Arts, Design History and Material Culture* 21, no. 1 (Spring–Summer 2014): 102–20; Kathleen James-Chakraborty, "Ausstellungen erleben: Lilly Reichs Produktdisplays 1927–31," in *Sowohl als auch dazwischen: Erfahrungsräume der Kunst*, ed. Jörn Schafaff and Benjamin Wihstutz (Paderborn: Fink, 2015), 57–76.

4. Neil Levine has noted Mies's interest in surface, through, for example, his collage technique, which dramatically foregrounded the surface qualities inherent in Mies's work. See Levine, " 'The Significance of Facts': Mies's Collages up Close and Personal," *Assemblage* 37 (December 1998): 72; and more generally, Levine, "The Reemergence of Representation out of Abstraction in Mies van der Rohe," in *Modern Architecture: Representation and Reality* (New Haven, CT: Yale University Press, 2009), 213–42.

5. Mies employed some of the visual language of industry—which had resulted in the period's expansion of genuine and pseudo-luxury goods through its rationalized production methods—to create his own version of luxury goods, namely, interior finishings and furnishings. For a concise discussion of the industrialization of artistic tradition and the ways in which the middle class produced and consumed luxury, see chap. 2, "The Industry of Tradition," esp. 125–26, in Mitchell Schwarzer, *German Architectural*

Theory and the Search for Modern Identity (Cambridge: Cambridge University Press, 1995), 88–127.

6. Oswald Spengler, a period philosopher who influenced Mies's thinking, connected the development of culture to the elitism implied by the few members of society who could afford luxury objects, as a means to develop art. Spengler asked the question, "What is luxury but Culture in its most exacting form?" See Spengler, *Der Mensch und die Technik* (Munich: C. H. Beck'sche Verlagsbuchhandlung, 1931), trans. as *Man and Technics: A Contribution to a Philosophy of Life* (New York: Knopf, 1932), 76. Mies likely would have agreed with Spengler's assessment. Looking back on past cultures, from Greek to rococo, Spengler noted that "without an economic wealth that is concentrated in a few hands, there can be no 'wealth' of art, of thought, of elegance, not to speak of the luxury of possessing a world-outlook, of thinking theoretically instead of practically" (77). For more on Mies's reading of Spengler, see Fritz Neumeyer, *The Artless Word: Mies van der Rohe on the Building Art*, trans. Mark Jarzombek (Cambridge, MA: MIT Press, 1991). See also Detlef Mertins, "Living in a Jungle: Mies, Organic Architecture, and the Art of City Building," in *Mies in America*, ed. Phyllis Lambert (New York: Harry N. Abrams, 2001), 590–641.

7. The Palais Stoclet (1905–11) in Brussels by Josef Hoffmann, in collaboration with the Wiener Werkstätte, is a notable forerunner to Mies's interior use of stone for walls. While the interior of the Palais Stoclet is overall much more elaborately decorated and furnished than Mies's interiors, and thus a true art nouveau *Gesamtkunstwerk*, a prominent feature are the walls clad in flat, richly veined marble and other stone specimens, most strikingly in the entry vestibule, living room, dining room, and music room. Also notable is the flat marble-cladding of the entry vestibule of Horta House (1898) by Victor Horta in Brussels.

8. As Stanford Anderson and Kenneth Frampton have argued, Mies was aware that his architecture was uneasily suspended between the radical avant-garde and the restraint of tradition, which can be viewed as a response to perceived conditions, esp. common in the context of the rapid change and confusion of the 1920s. See Anderson, "The Legacy of German Neoclassicism and Biedermeier: Behrens, Tessenow, Loos, and Mies," *Assemblage* 15 (August 1991): 83; and Kenneth Frampton, "Notes on Classical and Modern Themes in the Architecture of Mies van der Rohe and Auguste Perret," in *Classical Tradition and the Modern Movement*, ed. Asko Salokorpi (Helsinki: Museum of Finnish Architecture, 1985), 23. See also Detlef Mertins, "Architectures of Becoming: Mies van der Rohe and the Avant-Garde," in Riley and Bergdoll, eds., *Mies in Berlin*, 106–33.

9. Karel Teige, *The Minimum Dwelling* (1932), trans. Eric Dluhosch (Cambridge, MA: MIT Press, 2002), 181.

10. Although it is outside the scope to be discussed here, his use of luxury materials extends into his American period after 1938.

11. Irene Nierhaus has written compellingly about the encounter between the social and the subject in the Tugendhat's interior, in which she views the interior as one of "screens" or "displays," grouped in constellations of objects having a relationship to each other and to the perceiving spectator ("The Modern Interior as a Geography of Images, Spaces and Subjects: Mies van der Rohe's and Lilly Reich's Villa Tugendhat, 1928–1931," in *Designing the Modern Interior: From the Victorians to Today*, ed. Penny Sparke et al. [Oxford:

Berg, 2009], 107–8). In contradistinction to my reading, she argues for the visual rather than the material, and, dependent on understanding spaces in terms of images, contends that the smooth and gleaming surfaces found within the Tugendhat House are "less about the haptic mediation of the material than about its visual presence and variety" (110).

12. Grete Tugendhat, transcript of speech given in Brno, 1969, Ludwig Mies van der Rohe Archive, Museum of Modern Art, New York (hereafter Mies Archive, MoMA). The lecture was originally presented in Czech. A slightly different translation is published as Tugendhat, "On the Construction of the Tugendhat House," in Hammer-Tugendhat et al., eds., *Tugendhat House: Ludwig Mies van der Rohe*, 20; and in German: "Zum Bau des Hauses Tugendhat," *Die Bauwelt* 60, no. 36 (September 1969): 1246–47.

13. For the stone grains, see Tugendhat, "On the Construction of the Tugendhat House," 20. Drawings in the Mies Archive, MoMA, illustrate the direction the wood grain was meant to be orientated, as wall paneling and as veneering on furniture. See, for example, Mies's drawing for the children's playroom in the Esters House or his design for Mr. Tugendhat's desk in Arthur Drexler, ed. *The Mies van der Rohe Archive*, vol. 1 (New York: Garland Publishing, 1986), 73, 452.

14. He did design at least two unbuilt house projects for himself—the first in 1914 for a piece of property near Potsdam and again in 1923 for the project known as the Concrete Country House. See "House for the Architect Project" (174) and "Concrete Country House Project" (190), in Riley and Bergdoll, eds., *Mies in Berlin*.

15. Franz Schulze and Edward Windhorst, *Mies van der Rohe: A Critical Biography* (Chicago: University of Chicago Press, 2012), 43–55. With regard to Mies's manipulation of both photography and publicity to construct his public persona, see Beatriz Colomina, "Mies Not," in Mertins, ed., *The Presence of Mies*, 193–221. Detlef Mertins examines the unheroic and unmonumental in Mies's self-fashioning, finding the modern subject at odds with his role as architect in "Goodness Greatness: The Images of Mies Once Again," *Perspecta* 37 (2005): 112–21.

16. Scholars have noted Mies's conveyance of luxury, particularly with regard to the Tugendhat Villa. This study is an attempt to more deeply investigate what many critics and scholars, both in Mies's period and today, have noted in passing—the aspect of luxury in Mies's work. For example, about the Tugendhat Villa, Kenneth Frampton has stated, "That Mies intended a transcendental Baudelairean sense of *luxus* is borne out by Walter Riezler's contemporary appraisal of the house" (Frampton, *Studies in Tectonic Culture: The Poetics of Construction in Nineteenth and Twentieth Century Architecture* [Cambridge, MA: MIT Press, 1995], 179–80).

17. For authoritative studies of the villas, see also Kent Kleinman and Leslie Van Duzer, *Mies van der Rohe: The Krefeld Villas* (New York: Princeton Architectural Press, 1995); and Christiane Lange, *Ludwig Mies van der Rohe: Architecture for the Silk Industry*, trans. Michael Wolfson (Berlin: Nicolai, 2011).

18. Lange, *Ludwig Mies van der Rohe: Architecture for the Silk Industry*, 104.

19. Kleinman and Van Duzer, *Mies van der Rohe*, 116.

20. Ibid., 69–70.

21. Mies Archive, MoMA, cited by Kleinman and Van Duzer, *Mies van der Rohe*, 90.

22. Kleinman and Van Duzer, *Mies van der Rohe*, 90.

23. Mies developed these hinged casement windows together with the firm Fenestra Crittall AG. Lange, *Ludwig Mies van der Rohe: Architecture for the Silk Industry*, 104.

24. Letter, Esters to Lange, October 15, 1928, Krefeld, Mies Archive, MoMA.

25. Lange, *Ludwig Mies van der Rohe & Lilly Reich*, 61.

26. Lange, *Ludwig Mies van der Rohe: Architecture for the Silk Industry*, 109.

27. Lange, *Ludwig Mies van der Rohe & Lilly Reich*, 78.

28. Alfred Flechtheim, "Die Einbahnstrasse," *Omnibus: Eine Zeitschrift, Almanach für das Jahr* 1 (1931): 13. Located in Potsdam, just outside of Berlin, Sans Souci, also known as "Sanssouci," was the former summer palace of Frederick the Great, king of Prussia, and is roughly the German equivalent of Versailles.

29. Letter, Lange to Mies, October 10, 1928, Mies Archive, MoMA.

30. Lange, *Ludwig Mies van der Rohe: Architecture for the Silk Industry*, 105.

31. For rare images of the Lange and Esters interiors with the antique furnishings, see Kleinman and Van Duzer, *Mies van der Rohe*, 43, 45. For photographic reproductions of the images commissioned by Mies, taken by the Berliner Bildbericht photo agency, see Lange, *Ludwig Mies van der Rohe & Lilly Reich*, 33–48.

32. This set of entrance hall furniture was brought by the Langes from their previous home. Mies suggested a design that included a grouping of furniture set in a rectilinear formation, composed of two Barcelona chairs, a Tugendhat armchair, and several small, square tables.

33. For a significant discussion of Mies's early Berlin villas, see Riley and Bergdoll, eds., *Mies in Berlin*. Claire Zimmerman's meticulous work on the visual implications of the architectural photograph for modernism, esp. in the work of Mies van der Rohe, is particularly helpful in light of the images under discussion here. See Zimmerman, *Photographic Architecture in the Twentieth Century* (Minneapolis: University of Minnesota Press, 2014), esp. chap. 3, "Architectural Abstraction: The Tugendhat Photographs," 85–124; Zimmerman, "Photographic Modern Architecture: Inside 'the New Deep,'" *Journal of Architecture*, 9, no. 3 (Autumn 2004): 331–54; Zimmerman, "Tugendhat Frames," *Harvard Design Magazine* 15 (Fall 2001): 24–31; Zimmerman, "Modernism, Media, Abstraction: Mies van der Rohe's Photographic Architecture in Barcelona and Brno (1927–1931)" (Ph.D. diss., City University of New York, 2005). On the Tugendhat House, see Ivan Wahla and Petr Pelčák, *Mies van der Rohe: Villa Tugendhat in Brno* (Brno: Brno City Museum, 2016); Hammer-Tugendhat, et al., eds. *Tugendhat House: Ludwig Mies van der Rohe*; Iveta Černá and Dagmar Černoušková, eds. *Mies in Brno: The Tugendhat House* (Brno: Brno City Museum, 2013); Tegethoff, *Mies van der Rohe: The Villas and Country Houses*; Dietrich Neumann, "Can One Live in the Tugendhat House? A Sketch," *Wolkenkuckucksheim* 17, no. 30 (2012): 87–99.

34. Wolf Tegethoff, "The Tugendhat 'Villa': A Modern Residence in Turbulent Times," in Hammer-Tugendhat et al., eds., *Tugendhat House: Ludwig Mies van der Rohe*, 102.

35. Daniela Hammer-Tugendhat, "Living in the Tugendhat House," in Hammer-Tugendhat et al., eds., *Tugendhat House: Ludwig Mies van der Rohe*, 50.

36. As told by the Tugendhat's former nursemaid to Ivo Hammer, see Hammer, "Materiality: History of the Tugendhat House 1997–2012," 186.

37. P[eter] M[eyer], "Haus Tugendhat, Brünn (Tschechoslowakei)," *Das Werk* 20, no. 2 (January 1933): 42.

38. After the introduction of the chromed cruciform column at the Barcelona Pavilion, Mies employed them or suggested them in the following projects over the next seven years: Tugendhat Villa (1928–1930), Nolde House project (1929), Golf Club Project in Krefeld (1930), Ernst Henke House addition (1930), *German Building Exhibition* (1931, for Mies's Exhibition House but not his Apartment for a Bachelor), Gericke House Project (1932), Lemke House (1932–33, suggested in early sketches but not executed, most likely because of cost), German Pavilion of the International Exposition in Brussels project (1934), Hubbe House project in Magdeburg (1934–35), and the Ulrich Lange House project in Krefeld (1935).

39. Sergius Ruegenberg noted that it was during the construction of the Tugendhat Villa, whose surfaces had been intended to be nickel-plated as with previous Mies work, that they learned about the process of chroming metal and thus the decision was made to chrome-plate the relevant surfaces at the Tugendhat, rather than nickel-plate them. Ruegenberg, interview by Ludwig Glaeser, Berlin, September 8, 1972, corrected typescript in German, p. 29, Mies Archive, MoMA.

40. Nolde House and Henke House, Kostenanschlag (price quote), Berliner Metall-Gewerbe Josef Müller to Mies van der Rohe, May 10, 1929, and July 22, 1930, Berlin, Mies Archive, MoMA. It was because of the high cost of the design that Emil Nolde decided against building the Mies-designed house, which, after all of the bids were returned, was cost estimated at 99,833 marks. Nolde House files, Mies Archive, MoMA.

41. For an important related discussion, see, for example, Antoine Picon, "The Freestanding Column in Eighteenth-Century Religious Architecture," in *Things That Talk: Object Lessons from Art and Science*, ed. Lorraine Daston (New York: Zone Books, 2008), 67–99.

42. The cruciform column, as Neil Levine has observed, can be seen as a negative, inward-turning form—chromed, it is perceived as a linear abstraction of a point support, different from the strong figural presence of the solid vertical I-beam. Levine, "'The Significance of Facts,'" 88. Wolf Tegethoff argues that the chromed cruciform column's structural function is almost negated by their dematerializing effect. Tegethoff, "The Tugendhat 'Villa': A Modern Residence in Turbulent Times," 105. See also Roberto Gargiani, ed., *La colonne: Nouvelle histoire de la construction* (Lausanne: Presses polytechniques universitaires romandes, 2008), therein see especially Bruno Reichlin, "Conjectures à propos des colonnes réfléchissantes de Mies van der Rohe," 455–66; Kenneth Frampton, "Modernism and Tradition in the Work of Mies van der Rohe, 1920–1968," in *Mies Reconsidered: His Career, Legacy, and Disciples*, ed. John Zukowsky et al. (Chicago: Art Institute of Chicago/Rizzoli, 1986), 35–53.

43. Mies's "skin and bones" architecture is a widely discussed trope in his work; see, for example, Neumeyer, *Artless Word*, 116–19.

44. Along with their critique of inexpensive "sham ornament," many designers expressed concerns surrounding "truth to materials" following the Industrial Revolution's production of surrogate, imitative materials. The debate was particularly lively within the arts and crafts movement in England, led by William Morris, and similar issues were later reiterated by members of the Werkbund and modern architects in Germany. Hermann Muthesius, for example, railed against "irrational ornament and counterfeit material," "substitutes and simulations," calling for "inner truthfulness" and to let "every material appear in its own character." Muthesius, "The Significance of Applied Art" (1907), repr. in *The Theory of Decorative Art*, ed. Isabelle Frank (New Haven, CT: Yale University Press, 2000), 77.

45. The apartment was located at Duisburger Strasse 3. The Hess correspondence has not survived. For what little is known, see Jan Thomas Köhler and Jan Maruhn, "Less Is More," *Berliner Lebenswelten der zwanziger Jahre: Bilder einer untergegangenen Kultur*, ed. Bauhaus-Archiv Berlin und der Landesbildstelle Berlin, photographs by Marta Huth (Frankfurt: Gatza bei Eichborn, 1996), 80–81. The authors note that the building was designed by the Berlin architect Wilhelm Gutzeit.

46. *The Bauhaus Interior: Idea, Reality, Utopia*, ex. cat. (Qatar: Virginia Commonwealth University of the Arts in Qatar, VCUQ Gallery, 2007), 97.

47. Although a modest commission, Mies's drawings for this apartment were deemed important enough for Lilly Reich to box them and store them safely with the rest of Mies's office materials after he had left Berlin, unlike the drawings for many of his other small commissions. The Hess drawings include detailed plans for the wall cupboard, heater encasements for the living room and dressing room, designs for the round dining table and sideboard, a table (presumably the desk in the study), a linen and shoe cupboard, a wardrobe, a small tea table, the wall lighting, and a bed and two designs, in wood and in metal, for the windowsill intended for plants. See "Planverzeichnis betr. Wohnung Hess, Berlin," Mies Archive, MoMA. See also the Hess Apartment catalog of drawings in Drexler, *The Mies van der Rohe Archive*, 3:119–120.

48. The sofa is attributed to Mies, rather than to Reich, whose work is also depicted in the book. Werner Gräff, *Jetzt wird Ihre Wohnung eingerichtet: Das Warenbuch für den neuen Wohnbedarf* (Potsdam: Müller & I. Kiepenheuer, 1933), n.p. (cat. entry 9). To calculate the value of RM 1,050 in 1933 into today's dollars, the consumer price index was used, adjusting for inflation. First, the price of German marks was converted to US dollars for 1933 (4.2 marks = $1), using R. L. Bidwell, *Currency Conversion Tables: A Hundred Years of Change* (London: Rex Collings, 1970), 22–24. Then Samuel H. Williamson, "Seven Ways to Compute the Relative Value of a U.S. Dollar Amount, 1774 to Present," *MeasuringWorth*, http://www.measuringworth.com/uscompare, accessed April 10, 2017, was used to convert 1933 dollar amounts to 2015 dollar amounts (the latest date for which data is available), adjusting for inflation.

The average blue-/white-collar salary ranged between 40 to 45 RM per week in 1930. See Sandra Karina Löschke, "Communication Material: Experiments with German Culture in the 1930 Werkbund Exhibition," in *The Material Imagination: Reveries on Architecture and Matter*, ed. Matthew Mindrup (Farnham: Ashgate, 2015), 233n34.

49. Georgia van der Rohe, *La donna è mobile: Mein bedingungsloses Leben* (Berlin: Aufbau-Verlag, 2001), 53–54. Mies and his family moved into the apartment in central Berlin (Am Karlsbad 24) in 1915, just before he was drafted into World War I. He lived there until his departure for the United States in 1938. After Mies left for America, his wife, Ada, inherited his furniture, which was then passed down to Georgia. They repurposed the dark blue Chinese silk curtains and Mies's silk shirts into desperately needed items of clothing for the family during the war (82).

50. Ibid., 53–54.

51. According to Ludwig Glaeser, the rosewood veneer chairs in Mies's own apartment were originally intended for the Tugendhat Villa. Glaeser, *Ludwig Mies van der Rohe: Furniture and Furniture Drawings from the Design Collection and the Mies van der Rohe Archive* (New York: MoMA, 1977), 13.

52. George Nelson, "Architects of Europe Today: Van der Rohe, Germany," *Pencil Points* 16, no. 9 (September 1935): 453.

53. James Johnson Sweeney, tribute to Mies van der Rohe, delivered October 25, 1969, repr. in Peter Carter, *Mies van der Rohe at Work* (London: Pall Mall Press, 1974), 183–84.

54. Jan Maruhn, "Building for Art: Mies van der Rohe as architect for Art Collectors," in Riley and Bergdoll, eds., *Mies in Berlin*, 332. The Henke House was located at Virchowstrasse 124, in Essen, but destroyed in World War II. This commission was important in that it featured many of the by-then standard elements of Mies's architecture of this period.

55. Letter, Mies to Henke, November 18, 1930, Berlin, Mies Archive, MoMA.

56. Letter, Mies to Henke, July 21, 1930, Berlin, Mies Archive, MoMA.

57. Kostenanschlag (price quote), Alex Herman GmbH to Mies, May 31, 1930, Berlin, Mies Archive, MoMA. Mies also obtained a price quote for the sinkable window from the Berliner Metallgewerbe, which came to RM 5,200. Berliner Metallgewerbe to Mies, June 18, 1930, Mies Archive, MoMA. The Berliner Metallgewerbe was selected to supply the window, working with Siemen-Schukert-Werke in Essen, who provided the electrical mechanism.

58. Kostenanschlag (price quote), Berliner Metallgewerbe to Mies, June 18, 1930, Mies Archive, MoMA.

59. Rechnung (bill), Berliner Metallgewerbe to Mies for Henke House, September 4, 1930, Mies Archive, MoMA.

60. Angebot (bid), Fenestra-Crittall to Mies, July 30, 1930, Düsseldorf, Mies Archive, MoMA.

61. Johnson commissioned Mies to design the interior of his New York apartment in a contract dated September 12, 1930; see letter, Philip Johnson to Mies van der Rohe, September 12, 1930, Berlin, Mies Archive, MoMA. The document cites RM 2,000 as the architectural honorarium for Mies.

62. Johnson specifically mentions that he sought out Mies's apartments in Berlin, indicating that he probably saw Mies's most recent work, most likely the newly completed Hess and Crous apartments. Johnson notes that he tried to convince Hitchcock of Mies's talent by showing him an apartment with a "canary yellow" Barcelona chair (probably in the Crous Apartment), but Hitchcock remained unmoved. Philip Johnson, "Epilogue," *Mies van der Rohe* (New York: Museum of Modern Art, 1947; 1978 edition), 205. See also Johnson, *The Philip Johnson Tapes: Interviews by Robert A. M.*

Stern, ed. Kazys Varnelis (New York: Monacelli Press, 2008), 44–45.

63. Letter, Philip Johnson to J.J.P. Oud, September 17, 1930, Berlin, Mies Archive, MoMA, quoted by Franz Schulze, *Philip Johnson: Life and Work* (New York: Alfred A. Knopf, 1994), 425n67.

64. Genereller Kostenanschlag für die Einrichtung der Wohnung des Herrn Johnson, Atelier Mies van der Rohe, September 12, 1930, Berlin, Mies Archive, MoMA.

65. Johnson account and packing list, Atelier Mies van der Rohe, December 16, 1930, Berlin, Mies Archive, MoMA. An exact count of the number of furniture pieces sent is difficult to determine, as the packing list enumerates the furniture in parts, for example: "5 seat stands," "5 parchment cushions," two lengths of "7 wood plates" finished in palissander wood (presumably to be constructed on site as two bookshelves).

66. Ibid.

67. Atelier Mies van der Rohe to Fa. Günther & Co., November 5, 1930, Berlin, Mies Archive, MoMA. In a letter to Mies dated October 16, 1930, Johnson's unnamed agent requests that the matting be shipped as soon as possible in order for it to be installed prior to the arrival of the furniture, Mies Archive, MoMA. From period photographs, this appears identical to the matting Mies laid in his renovated director's house in Dessau.

68. Purchase order, Atelier Mies van der Rohe to Berliner Metallgewerbe Josef Müller, October 22, 1930, Berlin, Mies Archive, MoMA.

69. Terms for the Johnson Apartment furniture, three letters (to the firms Berliner-Metallgewerbe, Richard Fahnkow, and Günther & Co.), dated September 23, 1930, Berlin, Mies Archive, MoMA.

70. Genereller Kostenanschlag für die Einrichtung der Wohnung des Herrn Johnson, New York, durch das Atelier Mies van der Rohe, Berlin, September 12, 1930, Berlin, Mies Archive, MoMA. This document lists the entire commission, organized by room, with measurements, materials, and prices.

71. Johnson, *Mies van der Rohe* (1978), 206. Without attribution, Sandra Honey notes that Lilly Reich designed the interior of the Johnson Apartment, not Mies, although the true genesis of its design is impossible to substantiate. See Sandra Honey, "Mies in Germany," in *Mies van der Rohe: European Works* (London: Academy Editions, 1986), 19. First settling in his 52nd Street apartment in late December 1929 or early January 1930, Johnson moved in 1933 to 230 East 49th Street, followed by a move to 241 East 49th Street in 1934. He took most of his Mies furniture with him when he moved.

72. Mies's lack of responsiveness in providing plans for promised work sometimes resulted in commissions withering away, perhaps to some degree on purpose, as was the case of a potential house commission for Walter Dexel and the installation design for the 1932 *Modern Architecture* exhibition at the Museum of Modern Art. See Schulze and Windhorst, *Mies van der Rohe: A Critical Biography*, 82–83, 142.

73. Nelson, 454.

74. Emphasis added. Brochure, Werkbundausstellung, "Die Wohnung," Stuttgart, 1927, n.p.

75. Paul Westheim, "Die Wohnung zur Stuttgarter Ausstellung," *Das Kunstblatt* 11 (Sept. 1927): 335. Westheim also notes that the majority of the masses could not afford

the type of dwelling on display, a problem not addressed in the exhibition.

76. On Mies and Lilly Reich's exhibition designs, see especially McQuaid, "Lilly Reich and the Art of Exhibition Design," in *Lilly Reich*, 9–45 and Wallis Miller, "Mies and Exhibitions," in Riley and Bergdoll, eds., *Mies in Berlin*, 338–349.

77. The most cogent source on the exhibition is Wallis Miller, "Tangible Ideas: Architecture and the Public at the 1931 German Building Exhibition in Berlin" (Ph.D. diss., Princeton University, 1999). Among the official publications produced for the exhibition, see especially *Programm der Deutschen Bauausstellung*, Berlin, 9. Mai–9. August, 1931 (Berlin: Rudolf Mosse, 1931) and Ausstellungs-, Messe- und Fremdenverkehrs-Amt der Stadt Berlin, *Deutsche Bauausstellung, Amtlicher Katalog und Führer* (Berlin: Bauwelt-Verlag, 1931). See also "Mies van der Rohe: Casas/Houses," *2G*, n. 48–49 (2008–2009), 148–155; Ludwig Mies van der Rohe, "Programm zur Berliner Bauausstellung," *Die Form* 6, no. 7 (June 1931): 242.

78. McQuaid, *Lilly Reich*, 26.

79. Mies fielded at least one inquiry about the potential cost of building the "House for a Childless Couple" for a prospective client, estimating costs to be about 50,000 Marks, not inclusive of site costs and any additions to the floor plan. Mies to Herrn Dr. med. Georg Volk, 22 Sept. 1932, Offenbach, Mies Archive, MoMA.

80. Schulze and Windhorst, *Mies van der Rohe: A Critical Biography*, 143.

81. "Rundschau in Baupolitik und Bauwirtschaft," *Die Form* 6, no. 7 (July 15, 1931): 279.

82. Philip Johnson, "The Berlin Building Exposition of 1931," *T-Square* (January 1932); repr. in *Oppositions* (January 1974): 88. For the German architectural response to the exhibition, see Wilhelm Lotz, "Die Halle II auf der Bauausstellung," *Die Form* 6, no. 7 (July 15, 1931): 241–49; Lotz, "Die Wohnung unserer Zeit," *Innen-Dekoration* 42 (July 1931): 250–81; Lotz, "'Die Wohnung unserer Zeit' auf der Deutschen Bauausstellung Berlin 1931," *Moderne Bauformen* 30, no. 7 (July 1931): 329–47.

83. Philip Johnson, "In Berlin: Comment on Building Exposition," *New York Times*, August 9, 1931.

84. Winfried Nerdinger, *Walter Gropius* (Berlin: Gebr. Mann Verlag, 1985), 158.

85. Philip Johnson, "In Berlin."

86. Johnson, "The Berlin Building Exposition of 1931," 88.

87. Teige, *The Minimum Dwelling*, 195–97.

88. Lotz, "Die Halle II," 247.

89. F. Czeminski, "Berlin," in *Wohnen und Bauen*, Kongress Publikation I, vol. 3, nos. 1–2 (1931): 12.

90. Johnson, *Mies van der Rohe* (1947), 60. This was in reference to the Tugendhat House.

91. Howard Dearstyne, "Miesian Space Concept in Domestic Architecture," in *Four Great Makers of Modern Architecture: Gropius, Le Corbusier, Mies van der Rohe, Wright*, published proceedings of symposium, School of Architecture, Columbia University, March–May 1961 (1963), 138.

92. Mies was not only concerned about how his furniture would form the interior space, but he also addressed other needs, such as the placement of a grand piano—a provision included on the floor plan of every significant commission in this period. Though he made studies through the 1940s, Mies never again successfully designed any other item of furniture to the point of manufacture. In the postwar period, when

he was no longer in partnership with Lilly Reich, he ceased designing furniture, utilizing his designs from the Weimar period throughout the rest of his career. This gives the furniture a universalizing legacy, whereas in the time frame under discussion here, Mies and Reich were in a flourishing creative period that resulted in an astonishing number of furniture pieces being designed for specific interiors. Although on some price lists Reich's initials clearly indicate her designs, it remains unknown whether she should be credited outright for some that have been subsequently credited to Mies, but Reich certainly inspired his design process and improved on many of his ideas, particularly the coverings and cushions. For example, according to Ludwig Glaeser, Reich was responsible for the continuous caning of the cantilevered chair and the chaise longue's one-piece roll and pleat cushion supported by straps attached to the frame. Glaeser, *Ludwig Mies van der Rohe: Furniture*, 13. Mies also relied heavily on Reich's expertise concerning fabric selections for the chairs, curtains, and materials for rugs, acquired through her earlier work in fashion and clothing design.

93. Glaeser, *Ludwig Mies van der Rohe: Furniture*, 9.

94. Lange, *Ludwig Mies van der Rohe & Lilly Reich*, 151.

95. Bamberg Metallwerkstätten, Berlin-Neukölln, illustrated products price list, furniture designs by Ludwig Mies van der Rohe and Lilly Reich, October 11, 1931, visual materials from Howard Dearstyne Papers, Prints and Photographs Division, Library of Congress (hereafter Dearstyne Archive, Prints and Photographs Division, LoC), Washington, DC.

96. Berliner Metallgewerbe, price list, n.d., n.p., Mies Archive, MoMA; Bamberg Metallwerkstätten, Berlin-Neukölln, illustrated products price list, furniture designs by Ludwig Mies van der Rohe and Lilly Reich, October 11, 1931, Dearstyne Archive, Prints and Photographs Division, LoC.

97. Ibid.

98. See, for example, furniture orders for the Tugendhat, Johnson, or Lemke commissions. Mies Archive, MoMA.

99. Contract between Mies van der Rohe and Thonet-Mundus AG Zuerich, November 9, 1931, Patent Materials, folder 8.1, Mies Archive, MoMA. The royalties from furniture kept Mies afloat financially, esp. during the 1930s when he had little income-generating work. Howard Dearstyne, in response to an inquiry from Elaine Hochman concerning how Mies managed to remain in Berlin for so long before emigrating, notes, "I have always heard that he was able to support himself in Berlin until 1938, when he left for the United States, on royalties paid him on the sale of his furniture." Howard Dearstyne, Alexandria, Virginia to Elaine Hochman, New York, New York, November 10, 1972, Dearstyne Archive, Manuscript Division, LoC. John Barney Rodgers, who studied with Mies at the Bauhaus, similarly noted, "He was not as badly off because he had these patents on his furniture, on which he got enough income to keep going in spite of not having any architectural work" (Rodgers, to unknown interviewer, January 26 and 28, 1976, corrected typescript, Hillsborough, pp. 12–13, Mies Archive, MoMA). Following his emigration, Lilly Reich's letters to Mies in the United States seem to be answering a series of questions and concerns on his part regarding the patents. These are heartbreaking missives in which she regularly sent him news of his family and the situation in Germany leading up to and during the war, and entreats him to continue sending CARE packages, esp. those containing

dairy products to be given to relatives expecting children, and coffee for herself, but only if it "wouldn't cause any trouble or cost too much." In the letters, Mies seems to have underlined only the passages concerning the patents, such as "wallpaper patents," and "Swiss patents" (letter, July 7, 1939) but sends little in the way of personal messages for Reich and his family. Reich writes wistfully for a greeting or reply from him (letter, September 22, 1939), and in a letter on December 2, 1939, notes that she has not heard from him since October 30 (in this letter "Swedish" patent application is underlined). The letters chart the years that she spent working tirelessly with a series of lawyers to protect Mies's patents, as well as managing his contracts from Thonet and his bank account. See General Office File, Patents, Lorenz and Reich, 1937–1940, boxes 47 and 48, Mies Archive, LoC.

100. Otakar Mácel, "From Mass Production to Design Classic: Mies van der Rohe's Metal Furniture," in *Mies van der Rohe: Architecture and Design in Stuttgart, Barcelona, Brno*, ed. Alexander von Vegesack and Matthias Kries (Vienna: Vitra Design Museum; Geneva: Skira Editore, 1998), 44.

101. Tugendhat, "On the Construction of the Tugendhat House," 21.

102. For reproductions of the photographs taken by Fritz Tugendhat, see Robin Schuldenfrei, "Contra the Grossstadt: Mies van der Rohe's Autonomy and Interiority," in *Interiors and Interiority*, ed. Ewa Lajer-Burcharth and Beate Soentgen (Berlin: De Gruyter, 2015), 279–94; Ilsebill Barta, *Wohnen in Mies van der Rohes Villa Tugendhat: Fotografiert von Fritz Tugendhat 1930–1938* (Vienna: Eigenverlag der Museen des Mobiliendepots Wien, 2002); and Hammer-Tugendhat, "Living in the Tugendhat House" (24–55) and "Fritz Tugendhat as a Photographer" (56–67) in Hammer-Tugendhat et al., eds., *Tugendhat House: Ludwig Mies van der Rohe*.

103. Ritter to Lilly Reich, September 10, 1929, Barcelona, Mies Archive, MoMA.

104. For a more in-depth discussion of modern architecture and ornament, including the work of Peter Behrens, the Bauhaus under Walter Gropius, and Mies, see Robin Schuldenfrei, "Sober Ornament: Materiality and Luxury in German Modern Architecture and Design," in *Histories of Ornament: From Global to Local*, ed. Alina Payne and Gülru Necipo lu (Princeton, NJ: Princeton University Press, 2016), 334–47. For a nuanced analysis of surface and materiality in film, media, and the arts, see esp. Giuliana Bruno, *Surface: Matters of Aesthetics, Materiality, and Media* (Chicago: University of Chicago Press, 2014).

105. Sergius Ruegenberg, interview by Ludwig Glaeser, Berlin, September 8, 1972, corrected typescript in German, p. 20, Mies Archive, MoMA.

106. Hans Eckstein, introduction to *Neue Wohnbauten: Ein Querschnitt durch die Wohnarchitektur in Deutschland* (Munich: Bruckmann, 1932). Cited by Janet Ward, *Weimar Surfaces: Urban Visual Culture in 1920s Germany* (Berkeley: University of California Press, 2001), 70.

107. Hans Poelzig, "The Architect," speech to the Bund Deutscher Architekten, June 4, 1931, then published in *Bauwelt* 24 (1931), trans. in *Architecture and Design 1890–1939: An International Anthology of Original Articles*, ed. Tim Benton and Charlotte Benton (New York: Whitney Library of Design, 1975), 57.

108. Hammer-Tugendhat, "Living in the Tugendhat House," 41.

109. Schuldenfrei, "Introduction to 'Lilly Reich: Questions of Fashion' (1922)," 104.

110. Tugendhat, "On the Construction of the Tugendhat House," 21.

111. Johnson, *Mies* (1947), 60.

112. For more on this design, see Marianne Eggler, "Divide and Conquer: Ludwig Mies van der Rohe and Lilly Reich's Fabric Partitions at the Tugendhat House," *Studies in the Decorative Arts* 16, no. 2 (Spring–Summer 2009): 66–90. On the café, see Enrique Colomés and Gonzalo Moure, *Mies van der Rohe Café de Terciopelo y Seda Berlín, 1920–27* (Madrid: Ed. Rueda, 2004).

113. Elsa Herzog, "Die Berlinerin ist Mode," *Berliner Nachtausgabe*, September 21, 1927, Mies Archive, MoMA.

114. On the Barcelona Pavilion, see Tegethoff, *Mies van der Rohe: The Villas and Country Houses*, 66–89; Josep Quetglas, *Fear of Glass: Mies's Pavilion in Barcelona* (Basel: Birkhäuser, 2001); George Dodds, *Building Desire: On the Barcelona Pavilion* (London: Routledge, 2005); Dietrich Neumann, "The Barcelona Pavilion," in *Barcelona and Modernity: Picasso, Gaudí, Miró, Dalí*, ed. William R. Robinson, Jordi Falgàs, and Carmen Belen Lord (New Haven, CT: Yale University Press, 2006), 390–99; Claire Zimmerman, "German Pavilion," in Riley and Bergdoll, eds., *Mies in Berlin*, 236–41; Dietrich Neumann, "Der Barcelona Pavillon," in *Mythos Bauhaus*, ed. Anja Baumhoff and Magdalena Droste (Berlin: Reimer, 2009), 232–43; and Mertins, *Mies*, 138–67.

115. Justus Bier, "Mies van der Rohes Reichspavillon Barcelona," *Die Form* 4, no. 16 (August 1929): 424.

116. Additionally, he requested an explanation of the overall meaning of the pavilion, asking that Mies write a short explanation to give out to inquiring visitors, Ministerialdirektor Ritter to Mies, July 15, 1929, Barcelona, Mies Archive, MoMA.

117. The structure alone, before the costs of the furniture and of the interior, should have cost about 35,000 RM (Reichsmark) but actually cost 338,422 RM (roughly $1.4 million today), which included 175,000 RM worth of stone. This sum did not include Mies and Reich's fee of 125,000 RM. See letters: Der deutsche Generalkommissar, expenses incurred to date for the Internationale Ausstellung Barcelona, July 9, 1929; Anlagen for the Reichspavillion, sent to Dr. Georg von Schnitzler, September 28, 1929; Kettler to Lilly Reich, December 16, 1929, Barcelona, all located in the Mies Archive, MoMA. The metalwork and furniture from Berliner Metallgewerbe totaled 28,759 RM; see letter, Mies Atelier to Dr. Georg von Schnitzler, September 28, 1929, Mies Archive, MoMA. The materials for the Barcelona Pavilion were so costly that the marble, travertine, and chromed columns were shipped back to Germany to be resold. In October 1929, the authorities wrote to Mies and Reich, asking if they could assist with the possible resale of the materials, and by March 1930, as a letter to Mies indicates, they planned to send the marble back to Hamburg; the travertine was to follow two weeks later, and eventually the chromed columns, also intended for resale. The iron construction was to be sold in Barcelona, with the proceeds to be used to pay for the costs for dismantling the pavilion. Letters, Dr. von Kettler to Lilly Reich, October 29, 1929, Barcelona, Mies Archive, MoMA; unknown author [on stationary headed:

Internationale Ausstellung Barcelona 1929, Der deutsche Generalkommissar] to Mies, March 5, 1930, Barcelona, Mies Archive, MoMA.

118. Mies, interview, February 13, 1952, "6 Students Talk with Mies," *Master Builder: Student Publication of the School of Design, North Carolina State College* 2, no. 3 (Spring 1952): n.p., offprint in Mies van der Rohe Papers, Manuscript Division, LoC. A student followed up this statement with the question: "When you say you got a shock it is obvious that such an experience is extremely emotional …" Mies: "Certainly. The shock is emotional but the projection into reality is by the intellect."

119. K. Michael Hays, "Critical Architecture: Between Culture and Form," *Perspecta* 21 (1984): 24.

120. Although now known only through black-and-white photography, the installation was colorful. The floors were of white, gray, and red linoleum, sponsored by the Deutsche Linoleum Werke, which had an adjacent showroom accessible from the Glass Room. Werner Gräff, ed., *Innenräume* (Stuttgart: Wedekind, 1928), 163.

121. In the same article he mentions, again, "the play of the desired light reflection." Mies, "Skyscrapers," *Frühlicht* 1, no. 4 (1922), trans. in Neumeyer, *Artless Word*, 240. See also Mertins, *Mies*, 58–86.

122. Siegfried Kracauer, *Frankfurter Zeitung*, July 1927, cited and trans. in Jeannine Fiedler and Peter Feierabend, eds., *Bauhaus* (Potsdam: H. F. Ullman, 2006), 224.

123. Nicholas M. Rubio Tuduri, "Le pavillon de l'Allemagne à l'exposition de Barcelone" [The German Pavilion at the Barcelona Exposition], *Cahiers d'art* 4 (1929): 408–12. Typescript translation, Barcelona research and photo files, Mies Archive, MoMA, p. 2.

124. Hammer, "Materiality: History of the Tugendhat House 1997–2012," 186.

125. The lamp had been created by repurposing a clear glass vase that the family already owned. Hammer-Tugendhat, "Living in the Tugendhat House," 41.

126. Mies, diary entry, p. 62, 1928, reproduced in Neumeyer, *Artless Word*, 289. Here Mies is reading and taking notes from Romano Guardini's *Von heiligen Zeichen*. A slightly different translation of Mies's quote is cited by Fritz Neumeyer in "Barcelona Pavilion and Tugendhat House: Spaces of the Century," *Global Architecture* 75 (1995), n.p. [6]. Neumeyer points out in *The Artless Word* that when Mies states, "One has lost the meaning of this language," it is in reference to the symbolic experience of space. Neumeyer, *Artless Word*, 289n62.

127. The underlining of the Guardini passage is reproduced by Neumeyer, *Artless Word*, 289n61. Mies's underlining includes the passage "… language with its names is no longer a numinous communication with the essence of things, no longer an encounter between object and soul." See Mies's personal copy of Guardini, *Von heiligen Zeichen*, 3rd ed. (Würzburg: Deutsches Quickbornhaus, 1925), Mies van der Rohe Collection, Special Collections, Daley Library, University of Illinois at Chicago, Chicago. See also English translation, *Sacred Signs*, trans. G.C.H. Pollen (London: Sheed & Ward, 1930).

128. Mies, foreword, *Official Catalogue of the Stuttgart Werkbund Exhibition "Die Wohnung"* (Stuttgart: Deutscher Werkbund, 1927), trans. in Neumeyer, *Artless Word*, 259.

129. Mies, "On the Theme: Exhibitions," *Die Form* 3, no. 4 (1928): 121, trans. in Neumeyer, *Artless Word*, 304.

130. Mies, "We Stand at the Turning Point of Time:
Building Art as the Expression of Spiritual Decisions,"
Innendekoration 29, no. 6 (1928): 262, trans. in Neumeyer,
Artless Word, 304, emphasis in the original.

131. Mies continues, "Is it not one of the most important tasks
of the Werkbund [he is writing in its own journal] to
illuminate the spiritual and concrete situation in which
we find ourselves, make it visible, order its currents, and
thereby direct it?" Mies, "On Form in Architecture," *Die
Form* 2, no. 2 (1927): 59, trans. in Neumeyer, *Artless Word*,
257. This letter followed up on an initial letter that Mies
had written suggesting that the name of the Werkbund
journal *Die Form* be changed. For a discussion of Mies's
rejection of formalism, see Werner Oechslin, " 'Not from an
Aestheticizing, but from a General Cultural Point of View':
Mies's Steady Resistance to Formalism and Determinism;
A Plea for Value-Criteria in Architecture," in Lambert, ed.,
Mies in America, 22–89.

132. Mies, diary entry, p. 20, 1928, reproduced in Neumeyer,
Artless Word, 274.

133. Hans Richter, "Der neue Baumeister," *Qualität* 4, nos. 1–2
(1925), quoted by Neumeyer, *Artless Word*, 140.

134. Mies, "On the Meaning and Task of Criticism," as part
of a series of reports on art criticism held on the occasion
of a meeting of the Association of Art Critics, April 1930,
minutes published in *Das Kunstblatt* 14, no 6 (1930): 178,
trans. in Neumeyer, *Artless Word*, 308.

135. Ibid., 308–9.

136. Bier, "Mies van der Rohes Reichspavillon Barcelona,"
423–24.

137. Tuduri, "Le pavillon de l'Allemagne," 408–12. Typescript
translation, Barcelona research and photo files, Mies
Archive, MoMA, p. 3.

138. Tugendhat, "On the Construction of the Tugendhat
House," 20.

139. Mies, "On Form in Architecture," 59, trans. in Neumeyer,
Artless Word, 257.

140. Mies, diary entry, p. 62, 1928, reproduced in Fritz
Neumeyer, *Artless Word*, 289.

141. Mies, "Build Beautifully and Practically! Stop This Cold
Functionality," *Duisburger Generalanzeiger* 49 (January 26,
1930): 2, trans. in Neumeyer, *Artless Word*, 307.

142. Fritz Neumeyer, "A World in Itself: Architecture and
Technology," in Mertins, ed., *The Presence of Mies*, 76.

143. Ibid., 78. Neumeyer continues, "The frame is the
instrument of perception that creates isolation and
connection at the same time. It frees objects and subjects
from their context, puts them into a poetic dialogue that
creates new relations and insights into the whole" (81).

144. Mies, "What Would Concrete, What Would Steel Be
without Mirror Glass?" prospectus, Verein Deutscher
Spiegelglas-Fabriken (Association of German Mirrorglass
Factories), March 13, 1933, not printed; manuscript in
Library of Congress, trans. in Neumeyer, *Artless Word*, 314.

145. "Ein Moderner Klassiker, Interview von Katherine Kuh
mit Mies van der Rohe in Chicago, 1964," in Mies van der
Rohe, *Die neue Zeit ist eine Tatsache* (Berlin: Archibook-
Verlag Düttmann, 1986), 9. Translated in Katherine Kuh,
"Mies van der Rohe: Modern Classicist," *Saturday Review*
48 (January 23, 1965): 22–23, 61.

146. K. Michael Hays, "Odysseus and the Oarsmen, or, Mies's
Abstraction Once Again," in Mertins, ed., *The Presence of
Mies*, 237.

CHAPTER 6: INTERIORITY

1. Two notable exceptions are Mies's Afrikanische Strasse
Apartments and the Weissenhof Housing Settlement, both
1927. Mies was as qualified as his fellow modern architects
to participate in this type of mass building. According to
Barbara Miller Lane, between 1926 and 1932, 150,000 new
buildings were built in Berlin generally, while in the period
1924–33, more than 14,000 units in Berlin were built by
modern architects, more than 70 percent of them under
the aegis of the Gehag Building Society (Gemeinnützige
Heimstätten-Aktiengesellschaft), see Lane, *Architecture and
Politics in Germany, 1918–1933* (Cambridge, MA: Harvard
University Press, 1968), 103–4 and n. 32.

2. Scholars cite Mies's tenure with both Peter Behrens and
Bruno Paul, followed by his association with Lilly Reich,
as an explanation for his minute attention to the interior.
Certainly Mies gained valuable experience with all three;
however, this chapter seeks to argue that it was his own
belief in creating a space for the autonomous individual in
modern society that led him to carefully design his interiors.
Throughout, his working relationship with Lilly Reich
must be considered an essential aspect of the commissions
executed in this period; though it is impossible to know for
certain many of her specific contributions to these projects,
her influence must be generally understood as an integral
and largely inseparable part of Mies's oeuvre in this period
and key to the development of his ideas of modernism's
domestication generally.

3. Christine McCarthy, "Toward a Definition of Interiority,"
Space and Culture 8, no. 2 (May 2005): 112–13. My
understanding of interiority is very much indebted to
McCarthy's important article.

4. Siegfried Kracauer, *Die Angestellten: Aus dem neuesten
Deutschland* (Frankfurt a.M.: Societäts-Verlag, 1930), trans.
Quintin Hoare as *The Salaried Masses: Duty and Distraction
in Weimar Germany* (London: Verso, 1998).

5. Daniela Hammer-Tugendhat (daughter of Grete and
Fritz Tugendhat) describes a close-knit family and social
group, which Fritz Tugendhat's photographs of family
life underscore. Although Grete Tugendhat worked with
refugees at the Human Rights League, Hammer-Tugendhat
notes that they lived a secluded life in which only members
of the family and a few close friends came to visit and that
big celebrations were rare. See Daniela Hammer-Tugendhat,
"Living in the Tugendhat House," in *Tugendhat House:
Ludwig Mies van der Rohe*, ed. Daniela Hammer-Tugendhat,
Ivo Hammer, Wolf Tegethoff (Basel: Birkhäuser, 2015),
44–45.

6. The house was extraordinarily expensive to build. The
majority of the Tugendhat House correspondence and
documents had been stored in Lilly Reich's office and were
destroyed, along with much of her own archive, during
World War II. However, Philip Johnson noted in a letter that
it cost a million marks, more than the Barcelona Pavilion
and an extraordinary expense for the period. Letter, Philip
Johnson to Louise Johnson, undated, probably late August
1930, Berlin, MoMA Archive, quoted by Franz Schulze,
Philip Johnson: Life and Work (New York: Alfred A. Knopf,
1994), 425n67.

7. On the complexity of Mies and Reich's curtain partitions, see
Marianne Eggler, "Divide and Conquer: Ludwig Mies van
der Rohe and Lilly Reich's Fabric Partitions at the Tugendhat

House," *Studies in the Decorative Arts* 16, no. 2 (Spring–Summer 2009): 66–90.

8. Grete and Fritz Tugendhat, "Die Bewohner des Hauses Tugendhat äussern sich," *Die Form* 6, no. 11 (November 15, 1931): 437–38, trans. in Wolf Tegethoff, *Mies van der Rohe: The Villas and Country Houses* (New York: MoMA, 1985), 98. The unexpected success of the heating system was remarked upon by visitors, too. For example, an American couple, after visiting the house in March 1933, wrote to Mies, "The house is beyond anything that I had imagined from the photographs I had seen in America. It is a masterpiece of modern work and contrary to popular fear at home, warmer than the average house of ordinary construction." Henry M. Shrady to Ludwig Mies van der Rohe, March 7, 1933, Brno, Correspondence, Private, Papers of Mies van der Rohe, Manuscript Division, Library of Congress (henceforth Mies Archive, LoC), Washington, DC.

9. Unlike many of his colleagues, Mies said and wrote very little on the topic of how modern lives should be lived and how his spaces should be most beneficially used, by either gender. Compared with his peers, such as Bruno Taut, he did not express a desire to see daily life greatly altered or envision a future different from the present in which he found himself.

10. For a thorough discussion of the period literature surrounding the new role modern designers envisioned for women as the modern organizers and consumers, for the new home esp. as it relates to surfaces and domestic hygiene, see Janet Ward, *Weimar Surfaces: Urban Visual Culture in 1920s Germany* (Berkeley: University of California Press, 2001), 76–81.

11. Ise Gropius notes, "From July to October 1926 I was so busy trying to equip our new house with fitting household utensils, with deciding on what to order from the Bauhaus workshops, with discussing with my husband and the wallpainting workshop what colors to use on the outside and the interior, etc. etc., that I had to give up making entries in my diary. Since my husband had sold all our former furnishings to start with a clean slate and since I had spent untold hours with the designing of a modern kitchen and pantry which did not exist yet in the Germany of that time, I now ran myself ragged trying to find the right gadgets for it. Practically nothing existed in the normal market that would fit not only our new, practical demands but also our aesthetic preferences. It was then that I began, on my husband's advice, to haunt technical and scientific production places where I often found well designed items that had never been meant to grace private households." Ise Gropius, Diary/Tagebuch Fassung [additional letters and commentary to diary], comment for p. 157 related to diary pp. 102–3, Bauhaus Archive, Berlin.

12. Mies, Notebook, 1927–1928, p. 64, Mies Archive, MoMA, trans. in Fritz Neumeyer, *The Artless Word: Mies van der Rohe on the Building Art*, trans. Mark Jarzombek (Cambridge, MA: MIT Press, 1991), 290.

13. See Mark Peach, "'Der Architekt Denkt, Die Hausfrau Lenkt': German Modern Architecture and the Modern Woman," *German Studies Review* 18, no. 3, (October 1995): 441–63; Nicholas Bullock, "First the Kitchen: Then the Façade," *Journal of Design History* 1, nos. 3–4 (1988): 177–92; Leif Jerram, "Kitchen Sink Dramas: Women, Modernity and Space in Weimar Germany," *Cultural Geographies* 13, no. 4 (October 2006): 538–56.

14. See Volker M. Welter. "The Limits of Community—The Possibilities of Society: On Modern Architecture in Weimar Germany," *Oxford Art Journal* 33, no. 1 (2010): 63–80.

15. Karel Teige, *Nejmensi byt* [*The Minimum Dwelling*] (Prague: Ceskoslovensky Kompas, 1932), 182, quoted in Richard Pommer, "Mies van der Rohe and the Political Ideology of the Modern Movement in Architecture," in *Mies van der Rohe: Critical Essays*, ed. Franz Schulze (Cambridge, MA: MIT Press, 1989), 141n124.

16. The full debate and controversy surrounding whether the Tugendhat House was habitable took place via a series of articles and responses over the course of three issues of *Die Form*. See Walter Riezler, "Das Haus Tugendhat in Brünn," *Die Form* 6, no. 9 (September 15, 1931): 321–32; Justus Bier, "Kann man im Haus Tugendhat wohnen?" *Die Form* 6, no. 10 (October 15, 1931): 392–93; Walter Riezler, "Kommentar zum Artikel von Justus Bier," *Die Form* 6, no. 10 (October 15, 1931): 393–94; Roger Ginsburger and Walter Riezler, "Zweckhaftigkeit und geistige Haltung: Eine Diskussion zwischen Roger Ginsburger und Walter Riezler," *Die Form* 6, no. 11 (November 15, 1931): 431–37; Tugendhat, "Die Bewohner," 437–38; Ludwig Hilberseimer, "Nachwort zur Diskusion um das Haus Tugendhat," *Die Form* 6, no. 11 (November 15, 1931): 438–39. The debate has also been covered extensively by architectural historians; see for example, Dietrich Neumann, "'Can One Live in the Tugendhat House?' A Sketch," *Cloud-Cuckoo-Land—International Journal of Architectural Theory* 17, no. 32 (2012): 87–99; Daniela Hammer-Tugendhat, "Is the Tugendhat House Habitable?" in Hammer-Tugendhat et al., eds., *Tugendhat House: Ludwig Mies van der Rohe*, 68–73; Barry Bergdoll, "The Nature of Mies's Space," in *Mies in Berlin*, ed. Terence Riley and Barry Bergdoll (New York: Museum of Modern Art, 2001), 98–99.

17. Bier, "Kann man im Haus Tugendhat wohnen?," 392–93.

18. Tugendhat, "Die Bewohner," 437–8, trans. in Tegethoff, *Mies van der Rohe: The Villas and Country Houses*, 98.

19. Ibid., 97, emphasis added.

20. Paul Westheim, "Mies van der Rohe: Entwicklung eines Architekten," *Das Kunstblatt* 11 (February 1927): 58, emphasis added.

21. Mies van der Rohe, interview by Graeme Shankland for the BBC, 1959, repr. in Peter Carter, *Mies van der Rohe at Work* (New York: Praeger, 1974), 181.

22. Ginsburger and Riezler, "Zweckhaftigkeit und geistige Haltung," 433. An excerpt is translated in Hammer-Tugendhat, "Is the Tugendhat House Habitable?," 71.

23. Riezler, "Das Haus Tugendhat in Brünn," 324, 326.

24. Grete Tugendhat, "Architekt und Bauherr," in *Was gibt Ihnen der Architekt?* (Brno: Architekten-Interessengemeinschaft, 1934), trans. in Tegethoff, *Mies van der Rohe: The Villas and Country Houses*, 38.

25. Mies van der Rohe, "The Preconditions of Architectural Work" (1928), in Neumeyer, *Artless Word*, 301.

26. Mies van der Rohe, "Speech on the Occasion of the Anniversary Meeting of the Deutsche Werkbund," October 1932, repr. and trans. in Neumeyer, *Artless Word*, 311.

27. J. E. Hammann, "Weiss, alles Weiss: Von der Werkstellung der Farbe 'Weiss' in unserer Zeit," *Die Form* 5, no. 5 (1930): 122. Although she is arguing the opposite, this passage is cited by Klonk, *Spaces of Experience*, 105.

28. Grete Tugendhat, "Architekt und Bauherr," trans. in Tegethoff, *Mies van der Rohe: The Villas and Country Houses*, 38.

29. Tugendhat, "Die Bewohner," trans. in Tegethoff, *Mies van der Rohe: The Villas and Country Houses*, 97, 98.

30. Georg Simmel, *Philosophie des Geldes* (Leipzig, 1900), published in English as *The Philosophy of Money*, trans. Tom Bottomore and David Frisby (London: Routledge & Kegan Paul, 1978), 460. Cited by K. Michael Hays, *Modernism and the Posthumanist Subject: The Architecture of Hannes Meyer and Ludwig Hilberseimer* (Cambridge, MA: MIT Press, 1995), 56.

31. Leora Auslander, "Beyond Words," *American Historical Review* 110, no. 4 (October 2005): 1022–23. Germane to the period and modern objects under discussion, Auslander offers this useful summary: "Transformations in the nature of capital, as well as of the organization of the relations of production, distribution, and consumption, necessarily alter people's relations to things and how things mediate relations among people. Here the work of Marx and Marxian theorists, as well as some of their critics, is invaluable. These theorists argue persuasively for the decreased meaning of labor and a distanciation of workers from the product of that labor in a moment of its division and mechanization, as well as for a more systemic change in how people relate to others and to things under capitalism" (1022).

32. Walter Benjamin, *Berliner Kindheit um neunzehnhundert*, various versions written over the period 1933–38, and published posthumously in German in 1950; published in English as *Berlin Childhood around 1900*, trans. Howard Eiland (Cambridge, MA: Harvard University Press, 2006).

33. Simmel, *Philosophie des Geldes*, trans. Bottomore and Frisby, *The Philosophy of Money*, 2nd ed (London: Routledge, 1990), 459–62. As cited by Walter Benjamin, *The Arcades Project*, ed. Rolf Tiedemann, trans. Howard Eiland and Kevin McLaughlin (Cambridge, MA: Harvard University Press, 1999), 226. Benjamin's own writing and thought was very much influenced by Simmel's thinking, and he had attended Simmel's seminars. See Ralph M. Leck, *Georg Simmel and Avant-Garde Sociology: The Birth of Modernity, 1880–1920* (Amherst, NY: Humanity Books, 2000), 17, cited by Karina Van Herck, "'Only Where Comfort Ends, Does Humanity Begin': On the 'Coldness' of Avant-Garde Architecture," in *Negotiating Domesticity: Spatial Productions of Gender in Modern Architecture*, ed. Hilde Heynen and Gulsum Baydar (London: Routledge, 2005), 137.

34. Simmel, *Philosophie des Geldes*, trans. Bottomore and Frisby, *The Philosophy of Money*, 2nd ed., 459–62. As cited by Walter Benjamin, *The Arcades Project*, trans. Eiland and McLaughlin, 226–27.

35. Walter Benjamin, diary entry, June 8, 1931, in *Walter Benjamin: Selected Writings; Volume 2, Part 2, 1931–1934*, ed. Michael W. Jennings, Howard Eiland, and Gary Smith (Cambridge, MA: Belknap Press of Harvard University Press, 1999), 479–80.

36. Also, according to one of his earliest references to what would become his notion of the "aura," Benjamin related the aura to a setting and an object—he described it as the ornamental surrounding [*Umzirkung*] in which a thing lies embedded [*eingesenkt*], as in a case [*Futteral*]. Samuel Weber, *Mass Mediauras: Form, Technics, Media* (Stanford, CA: Stanford University Press, 1996), 85.

37. Friedrich Dessauer, *Philosophie der Technik* (Bonn: F. Cohen, 1927), 142, trans. in Neumeyer, *Artless Word*, 275n11, emphasis added.

38. Mies, Notebook, 1927–1928, p. 6, Mies Archive, MoMA, trans. in Neumeyer, *Artless Word*, 269. Translation amended.

39. Benjamin's ideas found early support amongst his peers; for example, in August 1935, he received a letter from Theodor Adorno praising this work as "full of important ideas. Amongst these I would particularly like to emphasize the magnificent passage about living as a leaving of traces, the definitive remarks about the collector, the liberation of things from the curse of utility." Letter, Teddie Wiesengrund to Walter Benjamin, August 2–4,1935, in *Theodor W. Adorno and Walter Benjamin: The Complete Correspondence 1928–1940*, ed. Henri Lonitz, trans. Nicholas Walker (Cambridge, MA: Harvard University Press, 1999), 104. Adorno signed the letter "Teddie Wiesengrund." Benjamin and Adorno begin using each others' first names after Adorno visited him in Paris in October 1936.

40. Walter Benjamin, diary entry, May 5, 1931 in *Selected Writings; Volume 2, Part 2, 1931–1934*, 472–73. Translation slightly amended.

41. See Rosemarie Haag Bletter, "Mies and Dark Transparency," (350–57) and Detlef Mertins, "Architectures of Becoming: Mies van der Rohe and the Avant-Garde," (109–10, 117–22) in Riley and Bergdoll, eds., *Mies in Berlin*.

42. Adolf Behne, *Wiederkehr der Kunst* (Leipzig: Kurt Wolff Verlag, 1919), 67, trans. in *Architecture and Design 1890–1939: An International Anthology of Original Articles*, ed. Tim Benton and Charlotte Benton (New York: Whitney Library of Design, 1975), 77. Translation amended.

43. Ibid., 67–68, trans. in Benton and Benton, *Architecture and Design 1890–1939*, 77. Translation amended. For "bourgeois comfort" and the architectural ramifications of "coziness" in this period, see Van Herck, "'Only Where Comfort Ends, Does Humanity Begin,'" in Heynen and Baydar, eds., *Negotiating Domesticity*, 123–44.

44. Behne, *Wiederkehr der Kunst*, 69, trans. in Benton and Benton, *Architecture and Design 1890–1939*, 78. Translation amended.

45. Arthur Korn, *Glas im Bau und als Gebrauchsgegenstand* (Berlin: Pollack, 1929), published as *Glass in Modern Architecture*, trans. Design Yearbook Limited (London: Barrie and Rockliff, 1967), 6. Although the book's title has been translated into English as "Glass in Modern Architecture," a more accurate translation of the full title from the German would be "Glass in Building and as a Use Object."

46. On Benjamin, modern architecture, and glass, see Detlef Mertins, "Walter Benjamin and the Tectonic Unconscious: Using Architecture as an Optical Instrument," in *The Optic of Walter Benjamin*, vol. 3: *de-, dis, ex-*, ed. Alex Coles (London: Black Dog Publishing, 1999), 196–221; and Mertins, "The Enticing and Threatening Face of Prehistory: Walter Benjamin and the Utopia of Glass," *Assemblage* 29 (April 1996): 6–23. For an important discussion of Benjamin and interiors, in light of period thinking, see Hilde Heynen, "'Leaving Traces': Anonymity in the Modernist House," in *Designing the Modern Interior: From the Victorians to Today*, ed. Penny Sparke et al. (Oxford: Berg, 2009), 119–29; and Heynen, "Modernity and Domesticity: Tensions and Contradictions," in *Negotiating Domesticity: Spatial Productions of Gender in Modern Architecture*, ed. Hilde

Heynen and Gulsum Baydar (London: Routledge, 2005), 1–29, esp. 20–21. For an in-depth discussion situating the complex set of ideas surrounding the architectural image in Walter Benjamin's historical materialism—as influenced by his study of Sigfried Giedion and Carl Linfert—as read through Mies's 1920s drawings and collages, see Lutz Robbers, "Without Pictorial Detour: Benjamin, Mies and the Architectural Image," *Footprint: Delft Architecture Theory Journal* 18 (Spring/Summer 2016): 27–50.

47. Walter Benjamin, "4. Louis-Philippe, or the Interior," in *Paris, Capital of the Nineteenth Century* (1935), in *Walter Benjamin: Selected Writings; Volume 3, 1935–1938*, ed. Howard Eiland and Michael W. Jennings (Cambridge, MA: Harvard University Press, 2002), 39.

48. Walter Benjamin, *The Arcades Project*, trans. Eiland and McLaughlin, 226.

49. Walter Benjamin, "Exposé of 1939," in ibid., 20.

50. Walter Benjamin, "Experience and Poverty" (1933), in *Walter Benjamin: Selected Writings; Volume 2, Part 2, 1931–1934*, 733–34. The concept that the dweller can no longer leave traces is one he borrows from Bertolt Brecht. Benjamin himself notes that he takes the rejoinder, "erase the traces!" from his friend Brecht, while stating, "this has now been achieved by Scheerbart, with his glass, and the Bauhaus, with its steel. They have created rooms in which it is hard to leave traces" (734).

51. Benjamin, "Experience and Poverty," 734. See also Mertins, "Enticing and Threatening Face of Prehistory."

52. As Benjamin clarifies in a letter to Adorno, "The concept of the trace finds its philosophical determination in opposition to the concept of aura." Walter Benjamin to Theodor Adorno, Paris, December 9, 1938, trans. in *Aesthetics and Politics: Theodor Adorno, Walter Benjamin, Ernst Bloch, Bertolt Brecht, Georg Lukács* (London: Verso, 2007), 135.

53. Benjamin, "Experience and Poverty," 734.

54. Walter Benjamin, "One-Way Street" (published 1928, written 1923–26), in *Walter Benjamin: Selected Writings; Volume 1, 1913–1926*, ed. Marcus Bullock (Cambridge, MA: Harvard University Press, 2004), 453–54.

55. Benjamin, "Experience and Poverty," 732, 735, 733.

56. For sources on the importance of Bloch's writing for art and architecture of the 1920s and 1930s, see esp. Hilde Heynen, "Building on Hollow Space: Ernst Bloch's Criticism of Modern Architecture," in *Architecture and Modernity: A Critique* (Cambridge, MA: MIT Press, 1999), 118–28; Frederic J. Schwartz, "Nonsimultaneity: Ernst Bloch and Wilhelm Pinder," in *Blind Spots: Critical Theory and the History of Art in Twentieth-Century Germany* (New Haven, CT: Yale University Press, 2005), 103–36; and Hays, *Modernism and the Posthumanist Subject*. On the relevance of Bloch's thought for early post–World War II Germany, see Frederic J. Schwartz, "The Disappearing Bauhaus: Architecture and Its Public in the Early Federal Republic," in *Bauhaus Construct: Fashioning Identity, Discourse, and Modernism*, ed. Jeffrey Saletnik and Robin Schuldenfrei (London: Routledge, 2009), esp. 61–65. Schwartz argues that by 1959, Bloch's topic was no longer relevant. Germane to, but outside the scope of this present chapter, is Schwartz's useful discussion of the distinction between ornament and function made by Theodor W. Adorno in his "Functionalism Today" lecture of 1965 (published in 1967); see ibid., 64–65.

57. "Chronology, 1935–1938," in *Walter Benjamin: Selected Writings; Volume 3, 1935–1934*, 422.

58. Ernst Bloch, "Building in Empty Spaces" ["Die Bebauung des Hohlraums"] (1938–47), in *The Utopian Function of Art and Literature: Selected Essays*, trans. Jack Zipes and Frank Mecklenburg (Cambridge, MA: MIT Press, 1988), 186–87.

59. Ernst Bloch, *Heritage of Our Times* (1935), trans. Neville Plaice and Stephen Plaice (Berkeley: University of California Press, 1991), 201.

60. Bloch, "Building in Empty Spaces," 189.

61. Bloch, *Heritage of Our Times*, 198, 202.

62. Ibid., 198, 197.

63. Bloch, "Building in Empty Spaces," 188.

64. Bloch, *Heritage of Our Times*, 199. Translation slightly amended.

65. Bloch, "Building in Empty Spaces," 188. Translation slightly amended.

66. Bloch, "The Creation of the Ornament," repr. in *The Utopian Function of Art and Literature: Selected Essays*, trans. Jack Zipes and Frank Mecklenburg (Cambridge, MA: MIT Press, 1988), 78. Hilde Heynen, however, makes an important distinction between Bloch and Benjamin's assessments of modernism, in which Benjamin "had much more faith in qualities such as sobriety, transparency, and functionalism," and points out that Benjamin believed in the "possibility that stylistic coldness and rationality could lead to revolutionary change, and that it could contribute to building a genuinely humane society. For a radical thinker such as Benjamin, the modernist aesthetics of montage, which is concerned with exteriority and with surfaces, was intended less to 'redeem' elements of the old order than to make room for a radically new form of living." Heynen reads Bloch, among other differences, as viewing warmth and seclusion as positive values. Heynen, *Architecture and Modernity*, 127.

67. Bloch, "Building in Empty Spaces," 196.

68. Ibid., 189–90, 198.

69. Benjamin, "Little History of Photography" (1931), in *Walter Benjamin: Selected Writings; Volume 2, Part 2, 1931–1934*, 518.

70. Benjamin, "The Work of Art in the Age of Its Technological Reproducibility," in *Walter Benjamin: Selected Writings; Volume 3, 1935–1938*, 104–5.

71. Mies, diary entry, p. 62, 1928, reproduced in Neumeyer, *Artless Word*, 289.

72. Benjamin, "Work of Art," 101–36.

73. Ibid., 105.

74. As Franz Schulze and Fritz Neumeyer have demonstrated, Oswald Spengler's popular book, *The Decline of the West*, was carefully read by Mies and influenced his thinking in the late 1920s. In a later book, trans. as *Man and Technics: A Contribution to a Philosophy of Life* [*Der Mensch und die Technik*] (1931) (New York: Knopf, 1932), Spengler considered the issue of luxury and bourgeoisie in light of technical developments. He traces the rise of technology over time, and in this case, he ties the growth of an urban bourgeoisie to the rise of the machine (86). Spengler continues, "The number of necessary hands grows with the number of machines, since technical luxury surpasses every other sort of luxury, and our artificial life becomes more and more artificial" (88). Spengler also notes, concerning luxury and the machine, "[T]he luxury of the machine is the consequence of a necessity of thought. In last analysis, the machine is a *symbol*, like its secret ideal, perpetual motion—a spiritual and intellectual, but no vital necessity (88, emphasis in the original). Spengler, resolved to his fate, begins his final chapter by saying, "[I]t is out of the power

either of heads or of hands to alter in any way the destiny of machine-technics, for this has developed out of inward spiritual necessities and is now correspondingly maturing towards its fulfillment and end. … The last decisions are taking place, the tragedy is closing" (90). See Franz Schulze and Edward Windhorst, *Mies van der Rohe: A Critical Biography* (Chicago: University of Chicago Press, 2012), 91–93; Mies, Notebook, 1927–1928, p. 14, Mies Archive, MoMA, trans. in Neumeyer, *Artless Word*, 272; Spengler, *Der Mensch und die Technik* (1931).

75. Francesco Dal Co, *Figures of Architecture and Thought: German Architecture Culture, 1880–1920* (New York: Rizzoli, 1990), 28. See Spengler, *Der Untergang des Abendlandes: Umrisse einer Morphologie der Weltgeschichte*, vol. 2 (Munich: C. H. Beck, 1922).

76. Dal Co, *Figures of Architecture and Thought*, 31–32, emphasis in the original. Dal Co is citing chap. 48 of Sombart, *Der moderne Kapitalismus*, vol. 2 (Munich: Duncker & Humblot, 1916). See also Sombart, *Luxus und Kapitalismus* (Munich: Duncker & Humblot, 1913).

77. Harry Liebersohn, *Fate and Utopia in German Sociology, 1870–1923* (Cambridge, MA: MIT Press, 1988), 126–27. For a careful reading of Georg Simmel's thought, contextualized with German philosophy and sociology, see chap. 5, "Georg Simmel: From Society to Utopia," in Liebersohn, 126–58. For writing by Simmel on the "individual," see the following essays: "Vom Wesen der Kultur" ["Subjective Culture"] of 1908, "Der platonische und der moderne Eros" ["Eros, Platonic and Modern"] of 1921, and "Das Individuum und die Freiheit" ["Freedom and the Individual"], published posthumously, as well as sections from his full-length book *Soziologie* (1908), such as "Die Erweiterung der Gruppe und die Ausbildung der Individualität" ["Group Expansion and the Development of Individuality"]. See esp. Donald N. Levine, ed., *Georg Simmel on Individuality and Social Forms* (Chicago: University of Chicago Press, 1971).

78. Simmel, "The Metropolis and Mental Life" (1903), repr. in Richard Sennett, ed., *Classic Essays on the Culture of Cities* (Englewood Cliffs, NJ: Prentice-Hall, 1969), 47.

79. Ibid., 49.

80. Ibid., 53.

81. Ibid., 59.

82. Simmel, "Das Individuum und die Freiheit" ("Freedom and the Individual"), trans. in Levine, *Georg Simmel on Individuality and Social Forms*, 223.

83. This characterization is presented by Liebersohn, *Fate and Utopia in German Sociology*, 127.

84. For an important reading of Mies's contextualizing of the architectural object to the specific situation of the city, as a critical response to the problem of the debilitating effects of the metropolis, see K. Michael Hays, "Critical Architecture: Between Culture and Form," *Perspecta* 21 (1984): 14–29. Hays argues that in evaluating architecture as an instrument of culture rather than reading it as autonomous form, Mies's architecture serves to demonstrate a crucial, central premise that his work "cannot be reduced either to a conciliatory representation of external forces or to a dogmatic, reproducible formal system" (17).

85. Mies, "Preconditions," 301. With regard to the masses, however, Mies does not approach the question of *die Wohnung* (the dwelling), an issue that the majority of avant-garde and modern architects of the period attempted to address. *Wohnungsnot*, the acute housing shortage following

World War I and continuing through the 1920s, was an area of intense consideration by architects who strove to find the ideal dwelling type for the urban lower-middle and working classes, who were largely confined to substandard living conditions as a result of continuing financial crises. These included shared toilets, large families crammed into a very few rooms, sometimes with extra boarders, even located below ground level in the basement. For a detailed account of Mies's extreme depoliticization of architecture and his rejection of the socially oriented modern architectural movement in Berlin during its peak years and subsequent joining of important associations of architects once they lost their radical, visionary, or social impetus, see Pommer, "Mies van der Rohe and the Political Ideology of the Modern Movement in Architecture," 97–145.

86. Other Weimar critics and authors took a similar approach, for example, Alfred Döblin, who warned against the conformity and subordination of the masses, arguing that it led the single person astray from an obligation to his being, the individual away from his responsibility for his life. Döblin, "Dass der Einzelne unter dem Einfluss der Masse nicht verkrüppelt" ["May the Individual Not Be Stunted by the Masses"], *Uhu* 8, no. 6 (1932): 7–8 repr. in *The Weimar Republic Sourcebook* , ed. Anton Kaes, Martin Jay, and Edward Dimendberg (Berkeley: University of California Press, 1994), 386–87.

87. See Hays, "Critical Architecture," 20–21. Hays argues that meaning derives not from the placement of these forms, or from formal operations or representational devices, but precisely from these impersonal productive systems (21). As Donald Kuspit has noted, "Mies's skyscrapers assume the routine conformity of a mass society, just as his private structures assume the exciting nonconformity of the privileged individuals who inhabit them." Kuspit, "Report from New York: Mies van der Rohe's Divided Consciousness," *Art New England* 22, no. 6 (October–November 2001): 13. Projects by Mies that fit this description include the skyscraper projects of 1919 and 1922, the Concrete Office Building project of 1922, the Stuttgart Bank project of 1928, and the Alexanderplatz project of 1928.

88. See Ludwig Hilberseimer, *Groszstadt Architektur* (Stuttgart: Verlag Julius Hoffmann, 1927), trans. in *Metropolisarchitecture and Selected Essays*, ed. Richard Anderson (New York: GSAPP Books, 2012).

89. See K. Michael Hays's discussion of Hilberseimer and the city in "Reproduction and Negation: The Cognitive Project of the Avant-Garde," in *Architectureproduction*, ed. Beatriz Colomina (New York: Princeton Architectural Press, 1988), 153–79; and Hays, "Ludwig Hilberseimer and the Inscription of the Paranoid Subject," in *Modernism and the Posthumanist Subject*, 185–278.

90. George Grosz, "Unter anderem ein Wort für die deutsche Tradition," *Das Kunstblatt* 15, no. 3 (1931): 80, repr. in Kaes, Jay, and Dimendberg, eds., *The Weimar Republic Sourcebook*, 499–502.

91. Westheim, "Mies van der Rohe: Entwicklung eines Architekten," 57–58.

92. Through his involvement with the Werkbund, and from the rapid changes to commercial spaces that had taken place in Berlin more generally, Mies would have been very aware of new developments related to the urban store window. See chapter 2, above. On the importance of the display window in the Weimar city, see Ward, *Weimar Surfaces*.

93. For earlier, straightforward, technocratic-style writing by Mies, see examples such as "Bürohaus" ["Office Building"], *G* 1 (July 1923): 3, or "Industrielles Bauen" ["Industrial Building"], *G* 3 (June 1924): 8–13; trans. in *G: An Avant-Garde Journal of Art, Architecture, Design, and Film, 1923–1926*, ed. Detlef Mertins and Michael W. Jennings, trans. Steven Lindberg with Margareta Ingrid Christian (Los Angeles: Getty Research Institute, 2010), 103, 120–25. Mies's divergence from other architects in terms of an interest in rationalization and standardization is perhaps best exemplified in his "Foreword to the Official Catalog of the Stuttgart Werkbund Exhibition 'Die Wohnung,'" in which Mies forcefully rejected the purely technical solution, asserting, "The problem of rationalization and typification is only part of the problem. Rationalization and typification are only the means, they must never be the goal. The problem of the new housing is basically a spiritual problem, and the struggle for new housing is only an element of the larger struggle for new forms of living." "Vorwort," *Amtlicher Katalog der Stuttgarter Werkbund-Ausstellung "Die Wohnung"* (Stuttgart: Deutscher Werkbund, 1927), trans. in Neumeyer, *Artless Word*, 258. Period accounts suggest the breadth of Mies's reading and knowledge. Howard Dearstyne, while a student at the Bauhaus under Mies, wrote of his interactions with Mies to his mother: "We discuss everything, architecture, art, philosophy, politics, etc. These discussions don't, therefore, always have a direct bearing upon our work but are tremendously interesting and valuable because Mies van der Rohe is a man of profundity and richness of experience. It would be worth my while being here just for these discussions if I did no designing whatsoever." Letter, Howard Dearstyne to his mother, June 12, 1932, Dessau, repr. in Dearstyne, *Inside the Bauhaus*, ed. David Spaeth (New York: Rizzoi, 1986), 233. For a thorough discussion and contextualization of Mies's thinking and writing of this period, see esp. Pommer, "Mies van der Rohe and the Political Ideology of the Modern Movement in Architecture," 110 and n. 77; Fritz Neumeyer, "Nexus of the Modern: The New Architecture in Berlin," in *Berlin 1900–1933: Architecture and Design*, ed. Tilmann Buddensieg, trans. John Gabriel (New York: Cooper-Hewitt Museum, Smithsonian Institution's National Museum of Design, 1987), 71; and Neumeyer, *Artless Word*, 156–61. Franz Schulze notes that Mies began reading philosophy in earnest before World War I, influenced by his first patron, the philosophy professor Alois Riehl, but that his library increased significantly after returning from the war (Schulze and Windhorst, *Mies van der Rohe: A Critical Biography*, 91). See also Detlef Mertins, "Living in a Jungle: Mies, Organic Architecture, and the Art of City Building," in *Mies in America*, ed. Phyllis Lambert (New York: Harry N. Abrams, 2001), 590–641.

94. Only a few years earlier, in the midst of his most functionalist period, Mies had cited the diminished importance of the individual, a position he relinquished around 1927. See, for example his statement of 1924: "The demands of the time for realism and functionality have to be filled. … Questions of a general nature are of central interest. The individual becomes less and less important; his fate no longer interests us." Mies, "Baukunst und Zeitwille!" ["Building Art and the Will of the Epoch!"], *Der Querschnitt* 4, no. 1 (1924), trans. in Neumeyer, *Artless Word*, 246. As Philip Johnson observed in a letter to J.J.P. Oud in 1930, in

reference to Mies, "It was so refreshing for me to meet a German architect who has no illusions about *Sachlichkeit* or *Technic* [*sic*] or *Material*. … He tells amusing stories about Gropius' *Acht vor der Technic* [respect for technology]. He worships it because he knows so little about it. Especially Mies hates this *Zweckmässigkeit* [functionalism] carried to extremes." Letter, Philip Johnson to J.J.P. Oud, September 17, 1930, Berlin, MoMA, New York, quoted by Schulze, *Philip Johnson*, 425n67.

95. See Mies van der Rohe, "Schön und praktisch bauen! Schluss mit der kalten Zweckmässigkeit" ["Build Beautifully and Practically! Stop This Cold Functionality"], *Duisburger General Anzeigers* 49 (January 26, 1930), 2, trans. in Neumeyer, *Artless Word*, 307.

96. The meaning of autonomy in Mies's architecture and the role of the individual has been discussed in various contexts by scholars. For a nuanced assessment of Mies and individuality, in relationship to modernity, the masses, and period literature, see Detlef Mertins, "Goodness Greatness: The Images of Mies Once Again," *Perspecta* 37 (2005): 112–21. Mertins does not, however, distinguish between Mies's earliest writings and later thinking, presenting a cumulative mission for Mies that, he asserts, was ultimately a failed "battle of spirit" at the end of Mies's life. Stanford Anderson has argued that architecture remained for Mies a strict and lofty discipline, that Mies held to an architectural autonomy to serve in idealization of a culture. Anderson, "The Legacy of German Neoclassicism and Biedermeier: Behrens, Tessenow, Loos, and Mies," *Assemblage* 15 (August 1991): 83. See also Hays, "Critical Architecture," 14–29. Donald Kuspit notes, "When Mies speaks of 'the organizing principle of order as a means of achieving the successful relationship of the parts to each other and the whole,' he is speaking of social as well as architectural management—of a society in which each individual is coordinated with every other individual in a whole that subordinates them all, that is, a collective grid from which there is no personal escape" (Kuspit, "Report from New York: Mies van der Rohe's Divided Consciousness," 13). As Fritz Neumeyer has shown through his demonstration of Mies's reading of Dietrich Heinrich Kerler, *Weltwille und Wertwille: Linien des Systems der Philosophie* [*World Will and Will to Value: Outline of a System of Philosophy*] (Leipzig: Alfred Kröner, 1925), Mies described a position nearly analogous to that of Kerler, in which the "world will" (Mies's "will of the epoch") turns to "will to value" (Mies's "spiritual will"). As Neumeyer points out, Mies's underlined passages are important in the examination of his position vis-à-vis the individual, in which the "source of value in the world, the culture, the spiritual" must stem from the "combined effect of purpose-orientated individuals" (*Artless Word*, 159–60). More generally, as Mitchell Schwarzer has pointed out, middle-class social identity revolved around the notion of individuality—a process of differentiation expressed through education, the acquisition of wealth and possessions, cultural expression through lifestyle, and a rejection of imitation—and middle-class architectural identity as an intrinsically differentiating process. Schwarzer, *German Architectural Theory and the Search for Modern Identity* (Cambridge: Cambridge University Press, 1995), 7.

97. Mies, "Preconditions," 299. As Fritz Neumeyer has noted, Mies is using many of the ideas about technology found in Friedrich Dessauer's 1927 book, *Philosophie der Technik:*

Das Problem der Realisierung, as a basis for his own thinking about technology as it applies to architecture. Neumeyer, *Artless Word*, 290–94nn64–85. Mies brought his original 1927 copy with him to the United States; it is included in his personal library that was given to the University of Illinois at Chicago.

98. Mies, "Preconditions," 299–300. Francesco Dal Co has noted Mies's very specific differentiation between the terms *Architektur* and *Baukunst*, in which *Baukunst*, usually translated as "building art," was used by Mies to communicate a practice and spiritual expression distinct from need and necessity, whereas *Architektur* connoted function and the mechanical conjoining of forms imposed by necessity. See Francesco Dal Co, "Excellence: The Culture of Mies as Seen in His Notes and Books," in *Mies Reconsidered: His Career, Legacy, and Disciples*, comp. John Zukowsky (New York: Rizzoli, 1986), 72.

99. Mies, "Preconditions," 301. *Geistlich* has been translated into "spiritual," but a more fitting translation for Mies's thought might be, in this context and elsewhere, "human," as in the *Geisteswissenschaften* (i.e., human sciences, or humanities) and sometimes "mindful." *Geist* and *geistlich* have many meanings and nuances in German, so approaching a single translation is difficult; even a stable translation in a single text proves challenging in the case of Mies because his emphasis shifts among its different resonances. Mies's nuanced attitude toward technology in light of human needs in this period has been discussed in depth by scholars; see, for example, Richard Pommer, who notes that "Mies believed that there was no choice except to affirm one's own time. The answer, he concluded, was not less but more technology and knowledge; more control of nature, but also more freedom; and greater power over their lives for the masses as well as for the individual through a more human and spiritual technology based on 'life'" (Pommer, "Mies van der Rohe and the Political Ideology of the Modern Movement in Architecture," 111).

100. Mies's close reading of Romano Guardini is in evidence here. In his *Briefe vom Comer See* [*Letters from Lake Como*] of 1927 (the letters were individually published between 1923 and 1925 in the journal *Die Schildgenossen*) Guardini sounds the ominous warning, "The objects of consumption are slowly being reduced to a few very practical types, whether it be casks, automobiles, houses, clothes, words, schools, or, finally, people. … When the Taylor system is perfected, manufacturing will be able to throw unlimited quantities on the market, and everything that has a personal soul, all individually developed creativity, will basically end." Guardini, *Letters from Lake Como* (Grand Rapids, MI: Wm. B. Eerdmans, 1994), 58.

101. Review of the lecture, given as part of the "Neues Bauen," lecture series at the Staatliche Kunstbibliothek in Berlin. See "Neues Bauen," *Berliner Tageblatt*, March 2, 1928, repr. in Neumeyer, *Artless Word*, 302.

102. Mies, illustrated lecture, manuscript dated March 17, 1926 (place, date, and occasion of lecture unknown), repr. in Neumeyer, *Artless Word*, 252, 255. That there are three manuscript versions of the lecture in the collection of Dirk Lohan indicates that Mies in fact gave the lecture at least once, and possibly on several occasions.

103. Ibid., 253.

104. The first sentence Mies has condensed from Friedrich Dessauer's *Philosophie der Technik* (1927). Mies, Notebook,

1927–1928, p. 65, Mies Archive, MoMA. Quoted by Neumeyer, *Artless Word*, 290.

105. Mies, illustrated lecture, manuscript dated March 17, 1926, repr. in Neumeyer, *Artless Word*, 256.

106. Detlef Mertins, "Mies's Skyscraper 'Project': Towards the Redemption of Technical Structure," in *The Presence of Mies*, ed. Detlef Mertins (New York: Princeton Architectural Press, 1994), 52.

107. Mies, "Preconditions," 299.

108. This has been noted by scholars, for example, in Franz Schulze's assessment of the Barcelona Pavilion: "Thus movement was a factor central to the concept of form and space in the Barcelona Pavilion. All that Mies had postulated in the Brick Country House about the dynamic interaction of inner and outer space was now fulfilled, moreover in a built work. His debts to both Frank Lloyd Wright and Theo van Doesburg were manifest in his union of the American's concept of free-flowing interior space with the de Stijl precedent of sliding geometric planes" (Schulze and Windhorst, *Mies van der Rohe: A Critical Biography*, 157). For Mies's description of the impact of the 1910 exhibition of Wright's work on Europe, see Mies, "A Tribute to Frank Lloyd Wright," *College Art Journal* 6, no. 1 (1946): 41–42.

109. Mies, illustrated lecture, manuscript dated March 17, 1926, repr. in Neumeyer, *Artless Word*, 252.

110. Beatriz Colomina, *Privacy and Publicity: Modern Architecture as Mass Media* (Cambridge, MA: MIT Press, 1994), 9.

111. Detlef Mertins offers an important analysis of the "folding" in Mies's 1922 skyscraper project, related to what has been described as "skin and bones" architecture. Mertins argues that Mies, as read through Alois Riegl, is following a period concern with Hegel's teleology of the spirit, demonstrated through the moving from the originary solid and tactile masses of the Egyptian pyramids to optical, modern spatial sensibility. He presents an appraisal of Mies's evolution that eventually leads to the curtain wall, arguing that the building has been transformed from "mass" into "spatial volume." Mertins suggests that after the open spatiality of De Stijl and the free plan, Mies returned to "an architecture of integral objects" with a reiteration of the elemental block accompanied by research into the dematerialized skin. Mertins, "Mies's Skyscraper 'Project,'" in *The Presence of Mies*, 58–59.

112. Hammer-Tugendhat, "Living in the Tugendhat House," 41.

113. Barry Bergdoll, "The Nature of Mies's Space," in Riley and Bergdoll, eds., *Mies in Berlin*, 84.

114. Tugendhat, "Die Bewohner," trans. in Tegethoff, *Mies van der Rohe: The Villas and Country Houses*, 98.

115. McCarthy, "Toward a Definition of Interiority," 113.

116. Ibid., 115.

117. Mies, diary entry, p. 62, 1928, reproduced in Neumeyer, *Artless Word*, 289.

118. Tugendhat, "Die Bewohner," trans. in Tegethoff, *Mies van der Rohe: The Villas and Country Houses*, 98.

119. For example, Mies read Spengler's *The Decline of the West* very carefully, in which Spengler posited the importance of seeing one's present position in culture and society, and one's destiny, clearly. As Franz Schulze has pointed out, Mies abandoned the *Kunstwollen*—the overarching cultural will of an era—for the scientism of Berlage and

Spengler's specific "facts" of modern history. See Schulze and Windhorst, *Mies van der Rohe: A Critical Biography*, 93.

CONCLUSION: LUXURY'S LAST MANIFESTATIONS

1. The exhibition was held at the Grand Palais from May 14 to July 13, 1930. The most authoritative period reports on the Paris Werkbund exhibition are the following: the official exhibition catalogue, *Section allemande: Exposition de la Société des artistes décorateurs* (Berlin: Verlag Hermann Reckendorf, 1930), unpaginated; Marcel Breuer, "Die Werkbundausstellung in Paris 1930," *Zentralblatt der Bauverwaltung* 50, no. 27 (July 9, 1930): 477–81; Wilhelm Lotz, "Ausstellung des Deutschen Werkbundes in Paris," *Die Form* 5, nos. 11–12 (June 7, 1930): 281–96; Sigfried Giedion, "Der Deutsche Werkbund in Paris," *Der Cicerone* 22, nos. 15–16 (August 1930): 429–34 (identical article published in the *Neue Zürcher Zeitung*, June 17, 1930); Durand-Dupont (pseudonym for Roger Ginsburger), "Der Deutsche Werkbund im Salon der 'Artistes-Décorateurs' Paris," *Das Werk* 27, no. 7 (1930): 197–204; Julius Posener, "Die Deutsche Abteilung in der Ausstellung der Sociéte des artistes décoratifs français [sic]," *Die Baugilde* 12, no. 11 (1930): 968–81. For recent scholarship, see esp. two meticulously researched essays: Paul Overy, "Visions of the Future and the Immediate Past: The Werkbund Exhibition, Paris 1930," *Journal of Design History* 17, no. 4 (2004): 337–57; and Sandra Karina Löschke, "Communication Material: Experiments with German Culture in the 1930 Werkbund Exhibition," in *The Material Imagination: Reveries on Architecture and Matter*, ed. Matthew Mindrup (Farnham: Ashgate, 2015), 215–35. See also Isabelle Ewig, Thomas W. Gaehtgens, and Matthias Noell, eds., *Das Bauhaus und Frankreich 1919–1940 / Le Bauhaus et la France 1919–1940* (Berlin: Akademie Verlag, 2002), 255–363; Yvonne Brunhammer and Suzanne Tise, *The Decorative Arts in France, 1900–1942: La Société des Artistes Décorateurs* (New York: Rizzoli, 1990), 157–83; Winfried Nerdinger, *Walter Gropius* (Berlin: Gebr. Mann, 1985), 142–45; Annemarie Jaeggi, *Werkbundausstellung Paris 1930: Leben im Hochhaus* (Berlin: Bauhaus-Archiv, 2007); Jaeggi, "Werkbundausstellung Paris 1930," in *100 Jahre Deutscher Werkbund 1907–2007*, ed. Winfried Nerdinger (Munich: Prestel, 2007), 149–50; Christopher Wilk, *Marcel Breuer: Furniture and Interiors* (New York: Museum of Modern Art, 1981), 94–98; and Markus Eisen, "Der hotelartige 'Grosshaushalt' in 'modernster Formgebung'—Die Ausstellung des Deutschen Werkbundes 1930 in Paris," in *Vom Ledigenheim zum Boardinghouse: Bautypologie und Gesellschaftstheorie bis zum Ende der Weimarer Republik* (Berlin: Gebr. Mann Verlag, 2012), 245–65.

2. See register of participants, *Section allemande*, n.p. (46–48). Because the exhibition catalogue was prepared in time for the opening, it does not include images of the show, as installed. However, comprehensive installation photographs of the exhibition are held at the Bauhaus-Archiv, Berlin. See also Wallis Miller, "Points of View: Herbert Bayer's Exhibition Catalogue for the 1930 *Section allemande*," *Architectural Histories* 5, no. 1 (2017): 1–22. Especially key is Miller's insight into the catalogue, like the exhibition itself, as a spatial experience, and the modes by which both catalogue and installation constructed the way in which visitors encountered, and thus understood, the new interiors and objects on display.

3. *Section allemande*, n.p. (3).

4. Archival documents relating to the Trolit panels note the range of colors used in the installation, which would have greatly enlivened the exhibition. Gropius's Room 1 included Trolit in black, white, red, gray, beige, light yellow, citron, blue-gray, vermilion, and pink; Moholy-Nagy's Room 2 had Trolit specified in black, red, gray, yellow, and white; Breuer's Room 3 used vermilion and white; and Bayer's Room 4 included white, black, red, blue, and gray panels. "Trolitauszug," March 3, 1930, Marcel Breuer Papers, Syracuse University Library, Syracuse, NY (hereafter Breuer Papers).

5. Moholy's exhibition design and its contents fed into his subsequent plans for the unrealized Room of Our Time (*Raum der Gegenwart*) developed for museum director Alexander Dorner's Hanover Provincial Museum. See Jennifer King, "Back to the Present: Moholy-Nagy's Exhibition Designs," in *Moholy-Nagy: Future Present*, ed. Matthew S. Witkovsky, Carol S. Eliel, and Karole P. B. Vail (Chicago: Art Institute of Chicago, 2016), 139–50; and Noam M. Elcott, "Rooms of Our Time: László Moholy-Nagy and the Stillbirth of Multi-media Museums," in *Screen/Space: The Projected Image in Contemporary Art*, ed. Tamara Trodd (Manchester: Manchester University Press, 2011), 25–52.

6. Breuer, "Werkbundausstellung," 477–81.

7. Nerdinger, *Walter Gropius*, 303.

8. These installation details were expensive, as per Gropius's accounting documents. The fish aquarium was priced at 2,000 marks. Gropius spent 3,975 marks on the Trolit in his section of the exhibition. Trolit's relative expense can be understood when compared with similar materials. For example, for the Paris exhibition, it was more than five times as much as the linoleum used in the installations, which cost 4.70 marks per square meter, while the Trolit was priced at 26.50 marks per square meter. See Gropius, "Kostenzusammenstellung für den Raum I Ausstellung Deutscher Werkbund Paris," typescript, 1930, BHA. I would like to thank Sandra Löschke for providing a copy of this document during a period in which the Bauhaus-Archiv was closed to researchers.

9. See *Section allemande*, n.p. (19–21); and Overy, "Visions of the Future," 341.

10. *Section allemande*, n.p. (16).

11. For the exhibition, forty pieces of nickel-plated tubular steel furniture, including ten folding theater seats for Moholy-Nagy's room, were ordered from the Berlin branch of Thonet for a total cost of 1,969 marks. "Rechnung," April 17, 1930, Paris Werkbund Exhibition, Breuer Papers. Paul Overy notes that Thonet had only begun to produce Breuer's designs the year before (1929); though perceived as mass-produced, the process would more accurately be described as small-scale, workshop-based, serial production. See Overy, "Visions of the Future," 339; *Section allemande*, n.p. (32); and Otakar Mácel, "Avantgarde Design and the Law: Litigation of the Cantilever Chair," *Journal of Design History* 1, nos. 2–3 (1990): 125–44.

12. Breuer, "Werkbundausstellung," 479.

13. Ibid.

14. Ibid., 477.

15. The complete materials, furnishings, and objects for Breuer's rooms are detailed in "Appartements eines Wohnhotels," March 31, 1930, Breuer Papers.

16. *Section allemande*, n.p. (16, 30).

17. Nerdinger, *Walter Gropius*, 116. This design is often referred to as the Haselhorst project, which was the name of the area in Berlin's Spandau district where it was slated to be developed.

18. Nerdinger, *Walter Gropius*, 136.

19. The exhibition catalogue, *Section allemande*, listed the materials and the firms that produced them. See also Gropius, "Kostenzusammenstellung," cited by Löschke, "Communication Material," 223; and "Rechnung," March 15, 1930, Breuer Papers.

20. Lotz, "Ausstellung des Deutschen Werkbundes," 293.

21. Löschke, "Communication Material," 220.

22. Durand-Dupont, "Der Deutsche Werkbund," 197, 198.

23. Gropius, "Kostenzusammenstellung," cited by Löschke, "Communication Material," 222. Löschke points out that average blue- and white-collar salaries ranged between 40 and 45 RM per week in 1930. To calculate the value of RM 24,000 in 1930 into today's dollars, the consumer price index was used, adjusting for inflation. First, the price of German marks was converted to US dollars for 1933 (4.2 marks = $1), using R. L. Bidwell, *Currency Conversion Tables: A Hundred Years of Change* (London: Rex Collings, 1970), 22–24. Then, Samuel H. Williamson, "Seven Ways to Compute the Relative Value of a U.S. Dollar Amount, 1774 to Present," *MeasuringWorth*, http://www.measuringworth.com/uscompare, accessed April 10, 2017, was used to convert 1933 dollar amounts to 2015 dollar amounts (the latest date for which data are available), adjusting for inflation.

24. Wilhelm Hausenstein, "Französisches und deutsches Kunstgewerbe in Paris," *Münchner Neueste Nachrichten*, July 7, 1930, cited by Nerdinger, *Walter Gropius*, 142.

25. For a nuanced discussion of the controversial critical reception of the *Section allemande*, in the period and subsequently, esp. its role as a "Bauhaus exhibition," see Overy, "Visions of the Future," 339–45.

26. "Geldverteilungsplan für die Ausstellung Pairs 1930," March 7, 1930, Breuer Papers.

27. Breuer, "Werkbundausstellung," 477.

28. *Section allemande*, n.p. (34–41).

29. Löschke, "Communication Material," 219.

30. See, for example, Walter Gropius, "Wie Bauen wir gute, schöne, billige Wohnungen?" *Offset* 7 (1926): 367–70, trans. as "How Do We Build Decent, Beautiful, and Inexpensive Housing?" *West 86th* 23, no. 1 (Spring–Summer 2016): 121–24.

31. *Section allemande*, n.p. (3–16); Lotz, "Ausstellung des Deutschen Werkbundes," 284.

32. Lotz, "Ausstellung des Deutschen Werkbundes," 281, English trans. on 293.

33. *Section allemande*, n.p. (18). The coffee machine cost 900 marks. Gropius, "Kostenzusammenstellung."

34. Gropius, "Reise nach Paris vom Sonnabend d.14.12—Donnerstag d. 19.12 mit den Herren Prof. Moholy und Herbert Bayer," December 14–19, 1929, p. 1, Breuer Papers. See also Gropius's list of related questions compiled in preparation for his Paris visit, "Fragebogen für Reise Paris," November 27, 1929, Breuer Papers.

35. Overy, "Visions of the Future," 342.

36. See Eisen, *Vom Ledigenheim zum Boardinghouse*, 280–81; and Nerdinger, *Walter Gropius*, 158–59.

37. Nerdinger, *Walter Gropius*, 168. See also Walter Gropius, Nagel Apartment Complex prospectus, BHA.

38. Overy, "Visions of the Future," 343. Overy also notes that recent historians of the Paris 1930 exhibition have uncritically repeated Sigfried Giedion's positive assessment of the critics' reaction to it.

INDEX

IMAGE CREDITS

I.1 left, 2.31, 4.9, 6.2, 6.12. Bauhaus-Archiv, Berlin. © 2017 Artists Rights Society (ARS), New York / VG Bild-Kunst, Bonn.

I.1 right. Walter Gropius, *Bauhausbauten Dessau*, (München: A. Langen 1930), 132. Photograph: Lucia Moholy, retouched. © 2017 Artists Rights Society (ARS), New York / VG Bild-Kunst, Bonn.

I.2, 6.1 right. Ullstein Bild.

I.3 left. Daimler-Benz-Archiv, Stuttgart.

I.3 right (photograph: Dr. Lossen & Co / Lichtbildgesellschaft), I.4 (photograph: Cami Stone), 1.28 (photograph: Dr. Lossen & Co / Lichtbildgesellschaft), 3.2 (photograph: Staatliche Bildstelle, Berlin), 3.4, 3.9 (photographs: Staatliche Bildstelle, Berlin), 4.14, 5.30, 7.2 (photographs: Berliner Bildbericht), 7.4 left (photograph: Photo L' Illustration Paris), 7.4 right (photograph: Berliner Bild-Bericht), 7.10 top (photograph: André Kertész). Bauhaus-Archiv, Berlin.

I.5, 5.28. Photograph: Marta Huth, Landesarchiv Berlin/Marta Huth.

1.1, 1.5, 1.6, 1.23, 2.3, 2.9, 5.26. Bildarchiv Foto Marburg.

1.2 (photograph: Bernd Kuhnert), 5.5 left (photograph: Volke Döhne), 5.11 (photograph: Volke Döhne), 5.13 (photograph: Volke Döhne). Kunstmuseen Krefeld.

1.3, 2.7, 4.6 right. Photographs: Armin Hermann, Sammlung Werkbundarchiv—Museum der Dinge.

1.4, 1.8, 1.9, 1.10, 1.11, 1.12, 1.13, 1.14, 1.16, 1.17, 1.18. Stiftung Deutsches Technikmuseum Berlin, Historisches Archiv.

1.7. Franz Stoedtner photo service.

1.15. © bpk—Bildagentur für Kunst, Kultur und Geschichte.

1.19, 1.21, 1.22. Fritz von Meyer-Schönbrunn, ed., *Peter Behrens*, Monographien Deutscher Reklame-Künstler, vol. 5 (Hagen: Ruhfus, 1912).

1.20. Franz Mannheimer, "Arbeiten von Professor Behrens für die Allgemeine Elektrizitätsgesellschaft," *Der Industriebau*, Jg. 2, Heft 6 (15 Juni 1911): 139.

1.24. Ludwig Pietsch, "Das Hohenzollern-Kunstgewerbehaus—Berlin," *Deutsche Kunst und Dekoration* 15 (October 1904-March 1905): 169.

1.25. Universität der Künste Berlin, Universitätsarchiv, Bestand 330, Nr. 207.

1.26. Werkbundarchiv—Museum der Dinge.

1.27. Warenhaus A. Wertheim Berlin, *Mode-Katalog*, 1903–1904.

2.1, 2.2, 2.8. Bahlsen GmbH & Co. KG.

2.4, 5.31, 5.33, 5.34, 5.35 right. Digital image © The Museum of Modern Art/Licensed by SCALA / Art Resource, NY.

2.5. Werkbundarchiv—Museum der Dinge, © 2017 Artists Rights Society (ARS), New York / VG Bild-Kunst, Bonn.

2.6. Staatliche Museen zu Berlin—Preußischer Kulturbesitz, Kunstbibliothek.

2.10, 2.12, 2.13, 2.17, 2.18, 2.25. *Jahrbuch des Deutschen Werkbundes* (Jena: Eugen Diederichs, 1913).

2.11. Erich-Mendelsohn-Sammlung, Baukunstarchiv, Akademie der Künste, Photograph: Arthur Köster.

2.14. *Jahrbuch des Deutschen Werkbundes* (Jena: Eugen Diederichs, 1913). © 2017 Artists Rights Society (ARS), New York / SABAM, Brussels.

2.16 (photograph of photomontage: Curt Rehbein), 2.29 right (photograph of photomontage: Wilhelm Niemann, Berliner Bild-Bericht), 5.8, 5.29 left, 5.42, 5.45. Digital image © The Museum of Modern Art/Licensed by SCALA / Art Resource, NY, © 2017 Artists Rights Society (ARS), New York / VG Bild-Kunst, Bonn.

2.19 top. Dr. E. Schlieter, Köln.

2.19 bottom, 2.21. *Jahrbuch des Deutschen Werkbundes* (Munich: F. Bruckmann A.-G., 1915). © 2017 Artists Rights Society (ARS), New York / VG Bild-Kunst, Bonn.

2.20. Robert Breuer, "Die Kölner Werkbund-Ausstellung," *Deutsche Kunst und Dekoration* 34, no. 12 (September 1914): 419.

2.23 top. *Der Schaufensterdekorateur: Illustrierte Anleitung zum Erlernen des Dekorierens der Schaufenster* (Berlin: Verlag L. Schottlaender & Co., 1906).

2.23 bottom. "Vorschlag zu einer wirkungsvollen Herrenhemdendekoration," *Architektur und Schaufenster* 115 (August 1913).

2.24 top. "Zwei Dekorationen, ausgeführt von Mitgliedern des Verbandes der Schaufenster-Dekorateure Deutschlands e.V. in Berlin," *Architektur und Schaufenster* (October 1919).

2.24 bottom. "Dekorationen zur 'Weißen Woche,'" *Architektur und Schaufenster* (January 1913).

2.26. "25 Jahre Schule Reimann, 1902–1927," *Farbe und Form* 12, Sonderband (1 April 1927).

2.27, 4.5. © Grassi Museum für Angewandte Kunst Leipzig.

2.29 left. Elisabeth von Stephani-Hahn, *Schaufensterkunst* (Berlin: Verlag L. Schottlaender, 1919).

2.30. Hans Bode, *Ein Schaufensterbilderbuch* (Hannover: S. Hein, 1926).

2.32. The J. Paul Getty Museum, Los Angeles © Albert Renger-Patzsch Archiv / Ann u. Jürgen Wilde, Zülpich, 2017 Artists Rights Society (ARS), New York.

2.33. Wilhelm Lotz, "Das Massenerzeugnis," *Die Form,* vol. 4, no. 18 (15 September, 1929): 500.

2.34 Photograph: Th. Hoffmann, Hannes Meyer, "Die neue Welt," *Das Werk* (July 1926): 216.

2.36. Wilhelm Theodor Schnarrenberger, "Reklame Architekturbildend," *Die Form* 3, no. 9 (September 1928): 269.

2.38. *Offset: Buch und Werbekunst*, vol. 7, 1926. © 2017 The Josef and Anni Albers Foundation / Artists Rights Society (ARS), New York.

2.39. © Rheinisches Bildarchiv, Museum Ludwig, Cologne.

2.40. Westfälisches Landesmuseum für Kunst und Kulturgeschichte, Münster.

2.41. © bpk, Kupferstichkabinett, Staatliche Museen zu Berlin Art © Estate of George Grosz/Licensed by VAGA, New York, NY.

3.1, 3.8, 3.10, 3.13 bottom. Bauhaus-Universität Weimar, Archiv der Moderne.

3.3, 4.11, 4.16, 7.1, 7.3, 7.5, 7.6, 7.7, 7.8, 7.9, 7.10 bottom. Harvard Art Museums/Busch-Reisinger Museum, Gift of Walter Gropius. Photograph: Imaging Department © President and Fellows of Harvard College.

3.5. Klassik Stiftung Weimar, L 2108 A, on loan from the Bauaktenarchiv Weimar © 2017 Artists Rights Society (ARS), New York / VG Bild-Kunst, Bonn.

3.6, 3.11, 3.12, 3.13 top. Adolf Meyer, Ed., *Ein Versuchshaus des Bauhauses in Weimar* (München: Albert Langen Verlag, 1925). © 2017 Artists Rights Society (ARS), New York / VG Bild-Kunst, Bonn.

3.7, 4.2, 4.3, 4.4, 4.6 left, 4.7, 4.8, 4.10, 4.12, 4.13, 4.15. Harvard Art Museums/Busch-Reisinger Museum. Photographs: Imaging Department © President and Fellows of Harvard College, © 2017 Artists Rights Society (ARS), New York / VG Bild-Kunst, Bonn.

3.14. Fotolibra.

4.1. Courtesy Sotheby's © 2017 Artists Rights Society (ARS), New York / VG Bild-Kunst, Bonn.

5.1 left, 5.20, 5.21, 5.25, 5.37. Photograph: David Židlický.

5.1 right, 5.23. Photographs: Tom Wilkinson.

5.2, 5.3, 5.15, 5.16, 5.18, 5.19, 5.35 left (photographs: Curt Rehbein), 5.38 top (photograph: Globophot), 5.40, 5.41. Berliner Bild-Bericht.

5.12. Photographs: Christian Richters.

5.14. Reymann Architekten, Krefeld, Germany. Photograph: Patrick Hoefer.

5.22, 5.24, 5.27, 6.3, 6.4, 6.6., 6.7. Atelier de Sandalo, courtesy of Brno City Museum.

5.29 right. Private collection.

5.36. Architecture, Design & Engineering Drawings Collection, Prints & Photographs Division, Library of Congress.

5.38 bottom. Enrique Colomés and Gonzalo Moure, *Mies van der Rohe Café de Terciopelo y Seda Berlín, 1920–27* (Madrid: Ed. Rueda, 2004), 39.

5.39 top. © Pepo Segura—Fundació Mies van der Rohe.

5.39 bottom. Gili Merin.

5.43. Photographer: Walter Lutkat. Arthur Korn, *Glas: im Bau und als Gebrauchsgegenstand* (Berlin-Charlottenburg: Ernst Pollak Verlag, 1929).

5.44. The Art Institute of Chicago / Art Resource, NY.

6.5, 6.8, 6.9, 6.10, 6.11, 6.13. © Fritz Tugendhat, Archiv Daniela Hammer-Tugendhat.

Published by Princeton University Press
41 William Street, Princeton, New Jersey 08540

In the United Kingdom:
Princeton University Press, 6 Oxford Street,
Woodstock, Oxfordshire OX20 1TR

press.princeton.edu

Pages iv–v: Mies, German Pavilion, interior (reconstructed). Photograph: Gili Merin

Library of Congress Cataloging-in-Publication Data
Names: Schuldenfrei, Robin, author.
Title: Luxury and modernism : architecture and the object in Germany 1900–1933 / Robin
Schuldenfrei.
Description: Princeton : Princeton University Press, 2018. | Includes bibliographical refer-
ences and index.
Identifiers: LCCN 2017031657 | ISBN 9780691175126 (hardback : alk. paper)
Subjects: LCSH: Modern movement (Architecture)—Germany. | Modernism
    (Aesthetics)—Germany—History—20th century. | Design—Germany—History—20th
    century. | Technology—Social aspects—Germany—History—20th century. | Luxury.
Classification: LCC NA1068.5.M63 S38 2018 | DDC 724/.6—dc23 LC record available at
https://lccn.loc.gov/2017031657

British Library Cataloging-in-Publication Data is available

Illustrations in this book were funded by a grant from the SAH/Mellon Author Awards of
the Society of Architectural Historians.

Ludwig Mies van der Rohe, excerpt of passages totaling approximately 1000 words,
translated by Mark Jarzombek, from Fritz Neumeyer, *The Artless Word: Mies van der Rohe
on the Building Art* © 1991 Massachusetts Institute of Technology, by permission of
The MIT Press.

Design: Luke Bulman—Office
This book has been composed in Atlas Grotesk and Granjon

Printed on acid-free paper. ∞
Printed in China

10 9 8 7 6 5 4 3 2 1

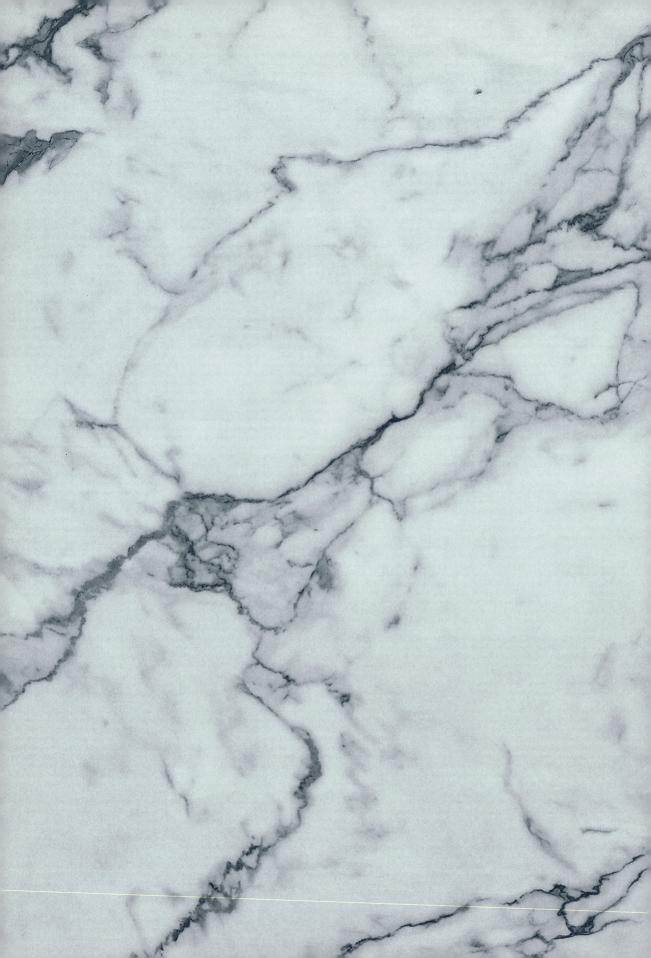